ENGLAND IS HERE

in active preparation

SPIRIT OF AMERICA

a selection from the Speeches and Writings of

THE PRESIDENTS OF THE UNITED STATES OF AMERICA

from *George Washington* to *Franklin D. Roosevelt*

edited and with an Introduction by W. L. Hanchant

uniform with this volume

THE BODLEY HEAD

PRIME MINISTER AND PRESIDENT

The Prime Minister of Britain and the President of the United
States on board the cruiser *Augusta*, *somewhere in the
Atlantic*, at the time of their joint declaration of the Atlantic
Charter, August 1941

ENGLAND IS HERE

a selection
from the Speeches and Writings of
THE PRIME MINISTERS OF ENGLAND
from *Sir Robert Walpole* to
the *Rt. Hon. Winston Spencer Churchill*

edited and with an Introduction by W. L. HANCHANT

> . . . *great-hearted men*
> *That take up England's cause—England is here.*
> ROBERT BROWNING : Strafford

> *We are of the same humours and inclinations*
> *as our predecessors were : you shall find us all*
> *alike, much at one, we and our sons.*
> ROBERT BURTON : The Anatomy of Melancholy

ILLUSTRATED

LONDON   John Lane The Bodley Head   MDCCCCXLIII

First published 1943

R. A. B.

d.d.

W. L. H.

This book is produced in
complete conformity with the
Authorised Economy Standards

Printed in Great Britain by
WILLIAM CLOWES AND SONS, LIMITED, LONDON AND BECCLES
for JOHN LANE THE BODLEY HEAD LIMITED
8 Bury Place, London, W.C.1

CONTENTS

WINSTON SPENCER CHURCHILL

ILLUSTRATIONS

The Prime Minister of Britain and the President of the United States on board the cruiser *Augusta, somewhere in the Atlantic*, at the time of their joint declaration of the Atlantic Charter, August 1941.

From an official photograph by courtesy of the Ministry of Information. Crown copyright reserved.

A detail from the wax effigy, now in Westminster Abbey, by Mrs. Mehetabel Wright, an American artist, to whom Chatham sat in 1774.

By courtesy of the Dean and Chapter of Westminster.

A detail from the painting by Karl Anton Hickel. Speaker Addington, Pitt's successor as Prime Minister, is in the Chair.

By courtesy of the Trustees of the National Portrait Gallery.

CALENDAR OF LIBERTY

The dates given below are intended to suggest, in briefest outline only, the progress of English liberties, religious, political and civil, and thus to indicate a background for the book.

1215   *Magna Carta:* the *bold and broad foundation* of English liberties, making the law supreme above all else; the rule of England passes from the monarchy to the aristocracy.

1265   Simon de Montfort's Parliament: the beginning of a representative House of Commons.

1295   The Model Parliament: *what touches all should be approved by all.*

1360   Justices of the Peace first appointed.

1476   Caxton sets up the first printing press in England.

1533   The beginning of the English Reformation.

1552   The Second Prayer Book of Edward VI appointed to be used in all English churches *that the people . . . might continually profit more and more in the knowledge of God.*

1588   The defeat of the Spanish Armada secures the freedom of the seas. *Flavit Deus et dissipati sunt.*

1601   Poor Law passed: the basis of all poor law legislation until 1834.

1611   The Authorised Version issued that the Scripture *may . . . be understood even of the very vulgar:* the English become a Bible-reading people.

1620   The Pilgrim Fathers sail from Plymouth in the *Mayflower.*

1621   The Petition of Right insists on the financial prerogative of Parliament and the liberty of the subject.

1642–52   The Civil War: the overthrow of attempted despotism.

1679   *Habeas Corpus* Act *for the better securing the Liberty of the Subject,* safeguarding his right not to be imprisoned without a firm charge being preferred and a speedy trial arranged for.

1689   The Bill of Rights: a reaffirmation of English liberties in the last of the great charters.
The Toleration Act provides greater freedom of worship.

1695   The refusal of Parliament to renew the Licensing Act, thus depriving government of the power of censorship, establishes the liberty of the Press.

1707   The Union of England with Scotland.

1719   Rejection of the Peerage Bill.

1739   Wesley's Apostolate begins: the rise of Methodism.

1768   The Middlesex Election: the cause of Wilkes begins agitation for constitutional reform.

1772   Chief Justice Mansfield rules that a slave once landed on English soil is free.

1775–82   The War of the American Revolution.

1776   American Declaration of Independence.

1780   Raikes establishes the first Sunday School.

1782   Britain recognises the Independence of the United States.

1787   The Society for the Abolition of the Slave Trade is formed.

1789   The outbreak of the French Revolution.

1793   France declares war against Great Britain.

1801   The Union of Great Britain with Ireland.

1802   The first Factory Act.

1805   Victory at Trafalgar gives Britain command of the seas.

1807   Abolition of the Slave Trade.

1808–14   The Peninsular War: England frees a despot-ridden Europe.

1815   Waterloo: the final overthrow of Napoleonic Cæsarism.

1826   Peel reforms the penal code and abolishes the death penalty for more than a hundred felonies.

1828   Repeal of the Test and Corporation Acts: Nonconformist emancipation from civil disabilities.

1829   The Catholic Emancipation Act: the Catholics freed from civil disabilities.

1832   The first Reform Bill carried; the balance of political power passes from the landed aristocracy to the middle classes.

1833   Abolition of Slavery.

1835   The Municipal Corporations Act: the reform of local follows that of central government: the beginnings of modern local government.

1846   Repeal of the Corn Laws: the people get cheap bread.

1848   The Public Health Act: the foundation of modern sanitary legislation.

1858   Members of the Jewish faith admitted to sit in Parliament.
The India Act: the East India Company abolished, the Indian Empire coming under the direct control of the British government.

1860   Abolition of Paper Duties encourages a cheap Press.

1867   The second Reform Bill passed: a great step towards democracy taken with the enfranchisement of the artisan class.
Canada becomes a Dominion.

1869   The Irish Church Act disestablishes the Church in Ireland.

1870   The Education Act: the State becomes responsible for the elementary education of the people.

1871   The Universities of Oxford and Cambridge fully thrown open to Nonconformists and Catholics by the abolition of religious tests.
The Trade Union Act legalises trade unions.

1876   New Zealand Constitution: New Zealand becomes a united colony.

1882   The Married Women's Property Act: the beginning of equal rights for women.

1884   The third Reform Act: England becomes a democracy with the extension of franchise to agricultural workers and every male head of a household.

1887   The first Colonial Conference: the statesmen of the Empire take counsel together.

1888   The Local Government Act provides for the democratic administration of county affairs by elected County Councils in place of nominated Justices of the Peace.

1900   The Commonwealth of Australia Act: Australia becomes a Federal Commonwealth, 1 January 1901.

1902   The Education Act extends secondary education to the mass of the people.

1908   Old-Age Pensions instituted: the power of taxation used for the redistribution of income.

1909   The Housing and Town Planning Act cedes the people the
        right to healthy homes.
        Trade Boards and Labour Exchanges set up in an attempt to
        organise the labour market and to check unemployment.
        The South Africa Act; South Africa becomes a federation,
        1910.

1911   The Parliament Act determines the relations of the two
        Chambers.
        The National Insurance Act provides health and unemploy-
        ment schemes in an attempt to banish insecurity from the lives
        of the working classes.

1914–18 The Great War: the first outbreak of German aggrandize-
        ment.

1918   The Education Act extends public provision for higher educa-
        tion.
        The fourth Reform Act; the Representation of the People Act
        gives the vote to all women over thirty.

1920   The first meeting of the League of Nations.
        Establishment of the Irish Free State with Dominion status.
        Disestablishment of the Church in Wales.

1922   The Independence of Egypt recognised.

1928   The fifth Reform Act: the Equal Franchise Act extends the
        franchise equally to men and women and completes the
        structure of political democracy.

1931   The Statute of Westminster cedes equality in independence to
        all self-governing members of the British Commonwealth of
        Nations.

1939   The World War: the second outbreak of German aggrandize-
        ment. *We are fighting to save the whole world from the pesti-
        lence of Nazi tyranny and in defence of all that is most sacred to
        man.*

1941   The Lease-Lend Bill signed by President Roosevelt, 11 March.
        *The Government and people of the United States have in fact
        written a new Magna Carta.*
        The joint signing of the Atlantic Charter by Mr. Churchill and
        President Roosevelt made known, 14 August.

1942   Publication of the Beveridge Report on Social Insurance and
        Allied Services, 20 November: a plan to secure freedom from
        want.

PREFACE

THIS is an anthology for the times. It has been England's fortune at her moments of gravest crisis seldom to lack in her prime ministers leaders whose words have inspired her utmost efforts. As during the long years of the wars with France, sometime under the menace of invasion, we went forward together inspired by the patriotic fervour of the younger Pitt; as in 1914 we went to our task stirred by the eloquence of Asquith and of Lloyd George; so in the dark days of 1940, when England stood desperately alone against the dread forces of Nazi despotism, we were heartened in our endeavours by the high heroic words of Mr. Churchill. All that we are as a nation is owed in great measure to such words as these. It thus seemed fitting to collect from the speeches and writings, political and non-political, of our prime ministers those passages which, showing forth the Spirit of England in the past, best serve our present recollection.

Such the main purpose of the book: in its development I have tried to show England's zeal for freedom, at home and abroad, in times of peace as well as those of war; her transition from a rule of aristocracy to a more democratic ideal; the enlargement of her religious, political, and civil liberties; the progress of her domestic, imperial, and foreign policies; and, not least, when for a second time in the short space of a quarter-century, American allies stand forth with us in the cause of freedom, the constant growth, despite occasional differences, of Anglo-American friendship and common understanding. Limitations of space necessarily preclude full illustration of all these themes; thus, extracts from the speeches of Peel and Palmerston on the second reading of the Catholic Emancipation Bill must stand exemplar for all the measures which secured freedom to worship at the dictates of conscience rather than at the bidding of the State, and the words of Grey and Russell in the cause of Parliamentary Reform and the first Reform Bill presage the unrepresented successive stages in the extension of the suffrage which culminated in the passing of the Equal Franchise Act of 1928. Such extracts in the book as fall outside the scope of history have been chosen either for their concern with national life and character or in recollection of these words of Bishop Berkeley: *Whatever the world thinks, he who hath not much*

18

meditated upon God, the human mind and the summum bonum, *may possibly make a thriving earthworm, but will most indubitably make a sorry patriot and a sorry statesman.*

The first part of the book suffers from the deficiencies of eighteenth-century Parliamentary reporting. The *Journals of the House of Commons,* for the private use of members, began to appear in 1742, and separate speeches had always been printed by their authors or others as occasion prompted, but records are not only incomplete but further, as shown by varying versions of the same speech, inaccurate. Until 1771 unauthorised publication of Parliamentary debates was punished as a breach of privilege; and though, in spite of this, disguised reports—prodigious efforts of memory, surreptitious notetaking, and invention—appeared regularly in the magazines, their eloquence is too often recognisably that of reporter rather than putative orator; as, for example, in those debates of the Senate of Lilliputia reported for *The Gentleman's Magazine* by Doctor Johnson who, as a staunch Tory, owned he *took care the Whig dogs did not have the best of it.* The attitude of eighteenth-century Parliamentary speakers towards publication of debates varied between the favouring of strict suppression in the interest of privilege and the casualness of Pelham remarking, *Let them alone; they make better speeches for us than we can make for ourselves.* The surrender of privilege and the introduction in 1802 of shorthand writing for Parliamentary reporting made for more accurate and complete reports towards which the general attitude changed until, in contrast, we have a glimpse of the dying Disraeli correcting a proof of his last Parliamentary speech for *Hansard* and protesting, *I will not go down to posterity talking bad grammar.*

Three of the eighteenth-century prime ministers are represented here by no more than their names and a record of their various offices, left standing that the rota might be complete. Inadequacy of material, however, only provides a partial explanation: the nebulous Wilmington, Cartaret's puppet, was indeed briefly reported but, save as examples of the art of sinking, his fatuous speeches do not deserve quotation;* Devonshire, eclipsed by the brilliancy of his colleague, Chatham, remains unreported; Portland's name, though *he possessed in an eminent degree the talent of dead silence,* occurs frequently enough in the reports but his tedious brief speeches have long since lost their savour.

* One example may suffice the curious. In returning thanks to the House for his election as Speaker, Wilmington thus apostrophized the members: *You have stopped the cries of orphans and dried up the tears of the widow; even those who must ever be insensible of the benefits they receive, idiots and lunatics (and such only can be insensible of them) will be partakers of the fruits of your labours.*

Generally throughout the book the space allotted to each prime
minister is intended to bear an approximate relation to his historical
importance, with some advantage of space to those of more recent
date. I have attempted to show as many characteristic aspects of their
thought as possible, not restricting myself to their periods of office,
but this aim has been modified by historical events ; Pitt, for
instance, is shown almost wholly concerned with the wars with
France, Wellington is mainly seen engaged in freeing Europe from
Napoleonic despotism, and Mr. Churchill is represented almost
entirely by his utterances since May 1940. If war and rumours of
war seem to provide an unduly frequent subject it should be remembered that for more than a third of the period covered by the
book England has been engaged in greater or lesser conflicts.

The various sections of the book occur in order of the respective
prime minister's first taking office. The arrangement within the sections is chronological. The exigencies of wartime publication have
kept explanatory notes to a scanty minimum.

My grateful acknowledgements for the use of copyright material are
due:

To His Majesty the King for gracious permission to quote the
extract on pages 42–3 from a letter by Bute in the Royal Archives at
Windsor.

To the Rt. Hon. Winston Churchill and Messrs. Macmillan & Co.
Ltd. for the extract from *The River War*, and to Messrs. Cassell & Co.
Ltd. for the extract on pages 246–7 from the collection of Mr.
Churchill's speeches, *Into Battle*: to the Editor of *The Daily Telegraph*
for the account of a blackbird in Downing Street by Neville
Chamberlain: to Messrs. Cassell & Co. Ltd. for material from Ramsay
Macdonald's preface to *The Life of Keir Hardie* by W. Stewart, and
to Messrs. Jonathan Cape Ltd. and the author's representatives for
the two extracts from Macdonald's collection of *American Speeches*:
to Earl Baldwin and Messrs. Hodder and Stoughton for the passages
here entitled *The Abbey* and *Service of Democracy*, both from *Our
Inheritance*, and to the Secretary of the Royal Society of St. George
for the extract on page 227: to Lord Beaverbrook for the quotation
from the preface by Bonar Law to his *Canada in Flanders*: to the
Rt. Hon. D. Lloyd George for extracts from his collection of speeches,
Slings and Arrows, published by Messrs. Methuen & Co. Ltd., and
for the extract on Jew-baiting from his volume, *Is it Peace?* published
by Messrs. Hodder and Stoughton: to the executors of the late Earl
Balfour and to Messrs. Longmans Green & Co. Ltd., for two extracts
from *Foundations of Belief*, to the Cambridge University Press for the

extract from Balfour's Sedgwick Memorial Lecture, and to Messrs. Blanche C. Dugdale and to Messrs. Hutchinson & Co. (Publishers) Ltd. for the letter to Lady Desborough quoted from *Arthur James Balfour*: to the Marquess of Crewe for the extracts here entitled *The Commonwealth of Nations* and *Hymn* by Lord Rosebery, both quoted from his life of *Lord Rosebery* published by Messrs. John Murray: to the Editor of *The Scotsman* for extracts from reports of speeches by Rosebery on pages 188–9 and 193–4, to the Homeland Association Ltd. for the quotation from Rosebery's preface to *Epsom* by Gordon Home, and to Messrs. John Lane The Bodley Head Ltd. for the extract on page 191 quoted from a volume of Rosebery's *Appreciations and Addresses* edited by C. Geake: to Messrs. John Murray for excerpts from contributions by the Marquis of Salisbury to *The Quarterly Review*: to the Gladstone Owners Trust for the quotations on page 173 from Gladstone's Diary and on page 181 from a letter to Sir John Cowan, both taken from Lord Morley's *Life of Gladstone* published by Messrs. Macmillan & Co. Ltd.: and to the Earl of Derby for two extracts from the privately printed *Diary of a Tour in America, 1824–5*.

A generous permission to include extracts from reports of speeches has been accorded by *The Times* and to this source are due passages on pages 144, 146–8, 159, 186–7, 192–3, 199–200, 201–2, 204–8, 210–11, 212–15, 225, 230–2, 238–40, 247 and 254–5. Extracts from the *Official Reports of the Parliamentary Debates* are reprinted by courteous permission of the Controller of His Majesty's Stationery Office.

I also wish to thank my publishers for an exemplary patience: for their appreciation I include a final quotation from the philosophic Balfour: *The only rule I have found invariable in this world of change is that everything, from shaving to literary composition, takes longer than one expects.*

INTRODUCTION

How the power of prime minister grew up into its present form, wrote Lord Melbourne, himself just out of office, to his pupil in politics, the young Queen, in 1841, *it is difficult to trace precisely, as well as how it became attached, as it were, to the office of First Commissioner of the Treasury. But Lord Melbourne apprehends that Sir Robert Walpole was the first man in whose person this union of powers was decidedly established.* His lordship's apprehension confirms the statements of more professional historians who generally allow Sir Robert Walpole to have been the first English prime minister as we have come to understand that title.

The accident of a Hanoverian king whose lazy ignorance of the language of his English subjects allowed his absence from the Cabinet Councils, while an enthusiasm for Hanover, inherited with like result by the second George, occasioned his frequent absence from their country altogether, permitted the executive power, which the theory of the constitution still gave to the king, to pass into the hands of the Cabinet under the chairmanship of a first minister. From Elizabethan times the first minister had nearly always been the Treasurer, perhaps almost necessarily so when the management of the House depended largely on bribery disbursed from the secret service monies. By the Restoration the office had become so powerful that it was usually placed in commission, as it was on the accession of George I, and has since continued, generally with the First Commissioner or First Lord of the Treasury, as he came to be styled, as the king's chief adviser and prime minister.*

Walpole, thus prime minister in fact, nevertheless repudiated a title (all the more dangerous because then constitutionally unrecognised) which his political enemies attempted to fasten on him. *I equivocally deny that I am sole and prime minister,* he retorted, and set a precedent for his near successors. Grenville declared that *Prime minister is an odious title,* and North, even in his own family, would never allow himself to be so called: their diffidence may perhaps be

* The exceptions to this are Chatham who was Lord Privy Seal, 1766–68, and Salisbury who was Secretary of State for Foreign Affairs and Lord Privy Seal respectively in his second and third administrations, 1885–92 and 1900–2. Macdonald in his first brief tenure of office, 1924, was, with equal distinction, both First Lord of the Treasury and Secretary of State for Foreign Affairs.

understood in an age when the case against a fallen minister could still uncomfortably conclude on the sharp argument of the headsman's axe.

George III, a patriot king who gloried in the name of Briton, attempted to recover for the monarchy the power which his predecessors had allowed to fall from them. He wished arbitrarily to dictate the policy of England and was in constant conflict with his ministers who claimed a collective responsibility under the leadership of one of them. The struggle ended with the accession of the younger Pitt to office and in face of common danger in the wars with France. Pitt, as the pilot that weathered the storm, successfully contended, out of that experience, *the absolute necessity there is in the conduct of the affairs of this country, that there should be an avowed and real minister, possessing the chief weight in the Council, and the principal place in the confidence of the king.* He easily assumed a title over which there has been little, though some, disputation since, but it was not until 1907 that the official position of the prime minister was formally recognised, and his precedence determined as second layman in the kingdom, ranking next after the Lord Chancellor.

The prime minister, whose office thus casually evolved in the progression of history, is the king's chief adviser; he is necessarily the leader of the most powerful political party in the country and is almost certainly the leader of the House of Commons;* he is chairman of the Cabinet and, usually, the First Lord of the Treasury—and more may be added unto him.

Not all the holders of so exigent an office have been comparably worthy; not all have been *men renowned for their power, giving counsel by their understanding, and declaring prophecies; leaders of the people by their counsels, and by their knowledge of learning meet for the people, wise and eloquent in their instructions.* Spoils of place and highest office fall sometimes to God-circumventing politicians rather than to statesmen

> *Who know the seasons, when to take*
> *Occasion by the hand, and make*
> *The bounds of Freedom wider yet.*

There is a Wilmington on the roll as well as a Walpole; Grafton succeeds to Chatham's place; Pitt makes way for Addington, *London*

* In 1923, when a successor to Bonar Law came to be appointed, in spite of, or perhaps because of, precedents of administrations being led from the Lords, the comparatively obscure Mr. Baldwin was chosen from the Commons, rather than that very superior person, Lord Curzon, who had had far greater ministerial experience. Curzon wept.

is to Paddington as Pitt is to Addington; the jingle belongs to Canning, himself overtopping his predecessors, Perceval and Liverpool, as he did his successor, Goderich; and so until we come to the sorry record of our own times in the years between.

Action, however, is not our present measure. The forty-one prime ministers of England, from Sir Robert Walpole to Mr. Churchill, are not here ostensibly arraigned before the bar of history. Words, not deeds, are our immediate concern. And yet? *I am not fond of making speeches . . . I never cultivated the talent but as an instrument of action.* Thus Chatham, the speeches of whose son in turn Carlyle declared to be *not Parliamentary Eloquences, but things which with his whole soul he means, and is intent to* do. Given the man who with his own greatness of spirit can meet the challenge of events, words are no longer mere vocables falling on the empty air but, transcending rhetoric, may themselves attain the measure of great deeds. Such words shape history. Such were the words of Chatham thundering forth in the cause of the American colonies; such were the words of Pitt pleading for the abolition of the slave trade and, again, throwing down the gage to Napoleonic Cæsarism; such were the words of Canning calling the New World into existence to redress the balance of the Old; such were the words of Russell when languid Johnny glowed to glorious John; such on occasion were the words of Grey, Palmerston, Disraeli, Gladstone, Asquith, Lloyd George; such, variously at our present juncture, have been the words of Mr. Churchill; *Come then; let us to the task . . . I have nothing to offer but blood, toil, tears, and sweat. . . . We shall defend our Island . . . men will say*, This was their finest hour . . . *never was so much owed by so many to so few . . . it just keeps rolling along . . .* these phrases in their context, not least of the weapons with which the menace of Nazism is being met, have even now become part of the English heritage; they

> *Will spread with ageing, lodge, and crystallize,*
> *And stand embedded in the English tongue*
> *Till it grow thin, outworn, and cease to be.*

But, nevertheless, the power of oratory is greatest at the moment of its utterance, when the spirit of a great leader, matched with the hour, charges his words and raises, for a while, his sympathetic hearers to the level of his own passion. For those who come after there may be some record which however full yet cannot be all; the tones of the living voice, the inspiration of a presence, the gestures of the orator, audience and occasion, all integral, these are gone, and the words alone lie coldly on the printed page to point the difference between the spoken and the written word. A speech, effective in its utterance, may seem clumsy in the constraints of print; emphasis is changed, a spoken iteration becomes a printed awkwardness, and all too surely *verba volent*.

But *scripta manent* completes the tag; and if a minister, whose sole survival is in the record of his speeches, lives, as Hazlitt suggested, only in the shadow of a name, there are others whose more secure claim to recollection lies in the record of their writings. Many of our statesmen, and most of our prime ministers, have not been bred to politics; they have served their various apprenticeships to law, to letters, to philosophy, to arms, or, as the background of politics became less aristocratic and more democratic, they have been men of business, and thus brought a wider experience and a more general intelligence to a particular task.

Few prime ministers, it must be admitted, find more than brief mention in the histories of English literature; Canning and Disraeli by right of genius, Gladstone perhaps and possibly Rosebery and Balfour on the exercise of talents, and, in the histories of the future, to hazard a modest prophecy, Mr. Churchill; on that the tale of names is done. Yet many more contrived an unpretentious place in letters, even though only as dilettanti; and some were more than competent journalists.

Bute and Shelburne were types of the eighteenth-century aristocratic amateur; both, with a slender performance, affected an enthusiasm for literature, the reality of which on his part the former proved when he secured a pension to Dr. Johnson. Neither Pitt finds place in the list of literary prime ministers although the Great Commoner showed in a rhymed invitation to Garrick that he could turn a couplet on provocation, and the younger Pitt, at a precocious thirteen, composed a tragedy, *Laurentius, King of Clarinium*, which Macaulay, after a perusal of the manuscript, reassures us contains no hint of love. A political pamphlet first brought Perceval to the notice of Pitt much as Canning first came forward on his *Anti-Jacobin* parodies and satires. Also about the turn of the century the elderly Grafton, unexpectedly after the ardours of his youth, turned to the study of theology and the composition of his *Serious Reflections* and the memoirs which might be so much more entertaining had he chosen to remember the whores and the horse-racing rather than less lively political business.

The eighteenth-century tradition continued for a while into the nineteenth as when the younger Grenville eased his retirement by

reviving an early talent for versifying, in editing a series of Chatham's
letters, in Latin verse translations, and in annotating Homer, an
author whom Derby, later in the century, was to translate into blank
verse to such purpose that five editions were clamoured for within
seven months. Aberdeen, whose *Essay on the Principles of Grecian
Architecture* enjoyed a slighter success, was an early contributor to
the *Edinburgh Review* as Canning was to the *Quarterly*, for which both
Gladstone and Salisbury were to write later. Salisbury over a period
of six years contributed a series of brilliant political essays to the
Quarterly; Gladstone's contributions, as his books and other essays,
were mainly on the questions of theology and classical scholarship
over which he pondered so much and almost deeply.

The prolific writings of Russell—verses, tragedies, translations,
polite essays and political pamphlets, histories, memoirs and bi-
ographies—now lie mostly with the dusty unread, although they yield
such passages as that here quoted, *When I am asked whether such or
such a nation is fit to be free,** which Gladstone placed among those
by Russell about which he declared, *Burke never wrote anything
better.* The width of Russell's range was only equalled and perhaps
excelled among literary prime ministers by Disraeli, greatest of them
all; yet, though his political writings and the rest, a Golconda to the
epigrammatist, may still find a few readers, it is the rococo broidery
of the novels that mainly attracts us now.

Rosebery, who had more enthusiasm for letters than for politics,
with his studies of Chatham, Pitt, and Napoleon almost attained first
rank as an historian, as did Balfour (deflected from philosophy to
politics by the influence of his uncle, Salisbury) as a philosopher,
although his later work never moved far beyond the standpoint of his
early *Defence of Philosophic Doubt.* The cool classicism of Asquith's
style, like the contrasted vehemence of Mr. Lloyd George, showed
more to advantage in his oratory than in his general writing. The
latter statesman, like most of his colleagues of 1914–18, has left an
apologia to posterity in his *War Memoirs* and his *Truth about the
Peace Treaties.* Both Asquith and Mr. Lloyd George, though in less
degree than Ramsay Macdonald, depended to some extent on
journalism in their early careers; and here they are joined by Mr.
Churchill, a brilliant war correspondent, a less brilliant novelist, and
a biographer in the grand style, whose lives of his father, Lord
Randolph, of his ancestor, the famous Duke of Marlborough, and of
his early self take high rank indeed. He, too, has given us a voluminous
account of *The World Crisis* which provoked Balfour to the description of *brilliant autobiography, disguised as a history of the universe.*

* See pages 133–5.

Such, summarily, is the literary achievement of the prime ministers. And, though so many men, such various opinions, so many talents, such various expressions, one common quality, beneath the divergences and the differences in all their writings and the records of their spoken words, may be discerned. That quality is love of England. The roll of our prime ministers is a roll of patriots. Each in his kind loved England, her laws, her liberties, her people, and her landscape. Each served her as best he might. Not all succeeded in their high endeavours. History is a record of failure as well as of success; yet

> *Such vast integrity can well afford*
> *Some stains in working,*

and all might claim, as the dying Russell, who had written of England as *the country whose freedom I have worshipped,* uttered to his wife, *I have made many mistakes, but in all I did my object was the public good.*

Public good is a generous term capable of infinite interpretation; it may be narrowed here to Russell's own conception of personal, political, and civil liberty. Every movement for freedom, at home or abroad, had his support. He championed every cause that would seem to increase the happiness of the people or widen their liberties. And so his zeal for freedom inevitably informs his words, as the words of our prime ministers in general of necessity reflect the enlargements of our liberties when so often they were the instruments by which those liberties were gradually gained.

It is well that such words, the struggles which inspired them, and the liberties they established as our national heritage, should be remembered in this present time of war. The lamps are out, not only over Europe, but over the greater part of the world as once again England, leagued with the British commonwealth of nations, is ranged with the great democracies in bloody conflict against the forces of tyranny, despotism, and aggression. Never before has war been waged on such titanic scale; never has so much been demanded from so many. To the great cause of world freedom lesser liberties have had to be surrendered. In all past times of war our civil liberties have been relinquished to the greater service of the State. As then, so now, and when on the morning of 3 September 1939 Mr. Chamberlain announced to the Commons that we were at war with Germany, Mr. Churchill spoke of a *thankfulness that . . . there is a generation of Britons here now ready to prove itself not unworthy of the days of yore and not unworthy of those great men, the fathers of our land, who* laid the foundations of our laws and shaped the greatness of our country. . . .

We are fighting to save the whole world from the pestilence of Nazi tyranny and in defence of all that is most sacred to man. This is no war for domination or imperial aggrandisement or material gain; no war to shut any country out of its sunlight and means of progress. It is a war, viewed in its inherent quality, to establish, on impregnable rocks, the rights of the individual, and it is a war to revive the stature of man. Perhaps it might seem a paradox that a war undertaken in the name of liberty and right should require, as a necessary part of its processes, the surrender for the time being of so many liberties and rights. In these last few days the House of Commons has been voting dozens of Bills which hand over to the executive our most dearly valued traditional liberties. We are sure that these liberties will be in hands which will not abuse them, which will use them for no class or party interests, which will cherish and guard them, and we look forward, surely and confidently, to the day when our liberties and rights will be restored to us, and when we shall be able to share them with the peoples to whom such blessings are unknown.

Liberties and rights have been surrendered in that spirit which brought them into being; in that spirit, when the day of victory comes, we shall again resume them, made more precious by their temporary surrender, part of a cherished heritage of freedom to be handed on to our children and our children's children, who themselves shall march forward on the inspiration of their past, our present, as we ourselves are doing on the great example of generations gone. We are of the same humours and inclinations as our predecessors were; you shall find us all alike, much at one, we and our sons.

> It is not to be thought of that the Flood
> Of British freedom, which, to the open sea
> Of the world's praise, from dark antiquity
> Hath flowed, with pomp of waters, unwithstood . . .
> That this most famous Stream in bogs and sands
> Should perish.

ROBERT WALPOLE

later Sir Robert Walpole

and, afterwards, Earl of Orford

1676 – 1745

Whig M.P., 1701–42; Secretary for War, 1708–10; Leader of the Opposition, 1711–14 and 1717–20; Paymaster-General of the Forces, 1714 and 1720; First Lord of the Treasury and Chancellor of the Exchequer, 1715–17 and 1721–42

THE TEMPLE OF FAME

The Peerage Bill of 1719 was a Whig measure ostensibly intended to limit the numbers of the House of Lords and so provide against a risk of the King's successor creating a preponderating number of Tory peers. If passed, it would have destroyed the balance between Crown, Lords, Commons, and People, and would have surrendered the government of the country to a closed oligarchy. Walpole's speech in the cause of political freedom and against the Bill resulted in its being thrown out in the Commons after it had easily passed the Lords.

AMONG the Romans, the Temple of Fame was placed behind the Temple of Virtue, to denote that there was no coming to the Temple of Fame but through that of Virtue. But if this Bill is passed into law, one of the most powerful incentives to virtue would be taken away, since there would be no arriving at honour but through the winding-sheet of an old decrepit lord or the grave of an extinct noble family: a policy very different from that glorious and enlightened nation, who made it their pride to hold out to the world illustrious examples of merited elevation,

> *Patere honoris scirent ut cuncti viam.*

It is very far from my thoughts to depreciate the advantages or detract from the respect due to illustrious birth; for though the philosopher may say with the poet,

> *Et genus et proavos, et quae non fecimus ipsi,*
> *Vix ea nostra voco;*

yet the claim derived from that advantage, though fortuitous, is so generally and so justly conceded that every endeavour to subvert the principle would merit contempt and abhorrence. But though illustrious birth forms one undisputed title to pre-eminence and superior consideration, yet surely it ought not to be the only one. The origin of high titles was derived from the will of the sovereign to reward signal services or conspicuous merit by a recompense which, surviving to posterity, should display in all ages the virtues of the receiver and the gratitude of the donor. Is merit then so rarely discernible, or is gratitude so small a virtue in our days, that the one must be supposed to be its own reward, and the other limited to a barren display of impotent goodwill?

But the strongest argument against the Bill is that it will not only be a discouragement to virtue and merit, but would endanger our excellent Constitution; for, as there is a due balance between the three branches of the Legislature, it will destroy that balance, and consequently subvert the whole Constitution, by causing one of the three powers, which are now dependent on each other, to preponderate in the scale. The Crown is dependent upon the Commons by the power of granting money; the Commons are dependent on the Crown by the power of dissolution: the Lords will now be made independent of both.

The present view of the Bill is dangerous; the view to posterity, personal and unpardonable; it will make the Lords masters of the king, according to their own confession, when they admit that a change of administration renders a new creation of peers necessary; for by precluding the king from making peers in future, it at the same time precludes him from changing the present administration, who will naturally fill the vacancies with their own creatures.

How can the Lords expect the Commons to give their concurrence to a Bill by which they and their posterity are to be for ever excluded from the peerage? How would they themselves receive a Bill which should prevent a baron from being made a viscount, a viscount an earl, an earl a marquis, and a marquis a duke? Would they consent to limit the number of any rank of peerage? Certainly none; unless, perhaps, the dukes. If the pretence for this measure is that it will tend to secure the freedom of Parliament, I say that there are many other steps more important and less equivocal, such as the discontinuance of bribes and pensions.

That this Bill will secure the liberty of Parliament I totally deny; it will secure a great preponderance to the peers; it will form them into a compact impenetrable phalanx, by giving them the power to exclude, in all cases of extinction and creation, all such persons from their body

who may be obnoxious to them. In the instances we have seen of their
judgment in some late cases sufficient marks of partiality may be
found to put us on our guard against committing to them the power
they would derive from this Bill, of judging the right of latent or
dormant titles, when their verdict would be of such immense importance. If gentlemen will not be convinced by argument, at least let
them not shut their ears to the dreadful example of former times; let
them recollect that the overweening disposition of the great barons
to aggrandize their own dignity, occasioned them to exclude the lesser
barons, and to that circumstance may be fairly attributed the
sanguinary wars which so long desolated the country.

House of Commons: 18 December 1714

SI PACEM DESIDERAT . . .

When the world shall see that you will not suffer the British Crown
and nation to be menaced and insulted, those who most envy the
present happiness and tranquillity of this kingdom, and who are
endeavouring to make us subservient to their ambition, will consider
their own interest and circumstances before they make any attempt on
so brave a people, strengthened and supported by prudent and powerful alliances; and, though desirous to preserve the peace, able and
ready to defend themselves against the efforts of all aggressors. Such
resolutions and such measures, timely taken, I am satisfied are the
most effectual means of preventing a war and continuing to us the
blessings of peace and prosperity.

Speech from the Throne, drafted by Walpole:
20 January 1726

THE DEMOCRATICAL FORM OF GOVERNMENT

*In 1716, fearing to risk a general election so soon after the disturbance of
the 1715 rebellion, the government repealed the Triennial Act of 1694, in
favour of a Septennial Act increasing the duration of Parliament from
three to seven years. There was a constant Tory clamour for the repeal of
this latter and in 1734 a motion to that effect was made excuse for an
attack on the Walpole administration. Walpole's mistrust of mob-
opinion, in its influence on individual members rather than directly
affecting the Ministry, was a reflection of his anxiety for peace, at home
and abroad, in which to secure the Hannoverian succession and to extend
the commerce of the country.*

*The Septennial Act remained in force until the Parliament Act of 1911
reduced the maximum duration of a parliament to five years.*

It is certain that ours is a mixed Government, and the perfection of our Constitution consists in this, that the monarchical, aristocratical, and democratical forms of government are mixed and interwoven so as to give us all the advantage of each without subjecting us to the dangers and inconveniences of either. The democratical form of government, which is the only one I have now occasion to take notice of, is liable to these inconveniences, that they are generally too tedious in their coming to any resolution and seldom brisk and expeditious enough in carrying their resolutions into execution; that they are always wavering in their resolutions and never steady in any of the measures they resolve to pursue; and that they are often involved in factions, seditions and insurrections, which exposes them to be made the tools, if not the prey of their neighbours. Therefore, in all the regulations we make with respect to our Constitution, we are to guard against running too much into that form of government which is properly called democratical: this was, in my opinion, the effect of the Triennial Law, and will again be the effect if ever it should be restored.

That triennial elections would make our Government too tedious in all their resolves is evident; because in such case, no prudent administration would ever resolve upon any measure of consequence till they had felt not only the pulse of the Parliament, but the pulse of the people; and the ministers of State would always labour under this disadvantage, that, as secrets of State must not be immediately divulged, their enemies (and enemies they will always have) would have a handle for exposing their measures and rendering them disagreeable to the people, and perhaps thereby carrying a new election against them before they could have an opportunity of justifying their measures by divulging those facts and circumstances whence the justice and the wisdom of their measures would clearly appear.

Then, it is by experience well known that what is called the populace of every country are apt to be too much elated with success and too much dejected with every misfortune. This makes them wavering in their opinions about affairs of the State and never long of the same mind; and, as this House is chosen by the free and unbiased voice of the people in general, if this choice were so often renewed, we might expect that this House would be as wavering and as unsteady as the people usually are; and it being impossible to carry on the public affairs of the nation without the concurrence of this House, the ministers would always be obliged to comply, and consequently would be obliged to change their measures as often as the people changed their minds.

With septennial Parliaments we are not exposed to either of these misfortunes, because, if the ministers, after having felt the pulse of the Parliament, which they can always soon do, resolve upon any measures, they have generally time enough before the new election comes on to give the people a proper information, in order to show them the justice and the wisdom of the measures they have pursued; and, if the people should be at any time too much elated, or too much dejected, or should without a cause change their minds, those at the helm of affairs have time to set them right before a new election comes on.

As to faction and sedition, I will grant, that in monarchical and aristocratical governments, it generally arises from violence and oppression; but, in democratical governments, it always arises from the people's having too great share in the government. For, in all countries, and in all governments, there always will be many factions and unquiet spirits, who can never be at rest, either in power or out of power. When in power they are never easy, unless every man submits entirely to their direction; and, when out of power, they are always working and intriguing against those that are in, without any regard to justice or to the interest of their country. In popular governments such men have too much game, they have too many opportunities for working upon and corrupting the minds of the people in order to give them a bad impression of, and to raise discontents against, those that have the management of the public affairs for the time; and those discontents often break out into seditions and insurrections.

This would, in my opinion, be our misfortune, if our Parliament were either annual or triennial: by such frequent elections, there would be so much power thrown into the hands of the people as would destroy that equal mixture, which is the beauty of our Constitution. In short, our Government would really become a democratical government, and might from thence very probably diverge into a tyrannical. Therefore, in order to preserve our Constitution, in order to prevent our falling under tyranny and arbitrary power, we ought to preserve that law which I really think has brought our Constitution to a more equal mixture, and consequently to a greater perfection than it was ever in before that law took place.

House of Commons: 13 March 1734

COOLNESS AND CAUTION

Amid constant temptations to war, Walpole tenaciously strove for the peace he held necessary to the country's interests. Madam, *he had said to the queen in 1734*, there are fifty thousand men slain this year in Europe, and not one Englishman. *But in 1739 a divided Cabinet, a hostile Opposition, and mob-passion were to jockey him into an unhappy war with Spain, against which he made his utmost protest:* They may ring the bells now; before long they will be wringing their hands.

It is, without doubt, a very popular way of arguing, to talk highly of the honour, the courage, and the superior power of this nation; and, I believe, I have as good an opinion of the honour, courage, and power of this nation as any man can, or ought to, have; but other nations must be supposed to have honour as well as we, and all nations generally have a great opinion of their courage and power. If we should come to an open rupture with Spain, we might in all probability have the advantage; but victory and success do not always attend upon that side which seems to be the most powerful. Therefore, an open rupture, or declared war, between two potent nations must always be allowed to be an affair of the utmost importance to both; and as this may be the consequence of our present deliberations, we ought to proceed with great coolness and with the utmost caution.

House of Commons: 12 May 1738

THE LAST REFUGE OF A SCOUNDREL

Walpole here turns on his political enemies and their cant of patriotism with an effectiveness that recalls Dr. Johnson's famous apophthegm.

Gentlemen have talked a great deal of patriotism. A venerable word, when duly practised. But I am sorry to say that of late it has been so much hackneyed about that it is in danger of falling into disgrace: the very idea of true patriotism is lost, and the term has been prostituted to the very worst of purposes. A patriot, sir? Why! patriots spring up like mushrooms. I could raise fifty of them within the four-and-twenty hours. I have raised many of them in one night. It is but refusing to gratify an unreasonable or an insolent demand, and up starts a patriot.

House of Commons: 13 February 1740

MINISTER IN ARCADY

After his resignation in 1742, Walpole divided a busy retirement between town and Houghton, whence, 24 June 1743, to an unidentified correspondent, he dates this charming invitation:

This place affords no news, no subject of entertainment, or amusement; for fine men of wit and pleasure about town understand not the language, and taste not the pleasures of the inanimate world. My flatterers here are all mutes. The oaks, the beeches, the chestnuts, seem to contend which best shall please the lord of the manor. They cannot deceive, they will not lie. I in sincerity admire them, and have as many beauties about me as fill up all my hours of dangling, and no disgrace attends me from sixty-seven years of age. Within doors we come a little nearer to real life, and admire, upon the almost speaking canvas, all the airs and graces which the proudest ladies can boast. With these I am satisfied, as they gratify me with all I wish, and all I want, and expect nothing in return which I cannot give.

If these, dear Charles, are any temptations, I heartily invite you to come and partake of them. Shifting the scene has sometimes its recommendation, and from country fare you may possibly return with a better appetite to the more delicate entertainments of a court life.

Spencer Compton, later Baron Wilmington

and, afterwards,

EARL OF WILMINGTON

1673 – 1743

Whig M.P., 1698–1710 and 1713–27; Speaker of the House of Commons, 1715–27; Paymaster-General, 1722–30; Lord Privy Seal, 1730; Lord President of the Council, 1730–41; First Lord of the Treasury, 1741–43

HENRY PELHAM
1695–1754

Whig M.P., 1717–54; Secretary at War, 1724–30; Paymaster-General of the Forces, 1730–43; First Lord of the Treasury and Chancellor of the Exchequer, 1743–54

BACK'D WITH GOD AND WITH THE SEAS

WHILE Great Britain retains her invincible navy, she will possess an argument more cogent than any pledge, and will never have to make a sacrifice for any compliance which she can reasonably demand. But we ought never to employ that invincible navy to enforce an unjust claim, lest it should incur the only peril which it has to apprehend, the vengeance of the Almighty.

House of Commons: 7 February 1749

THE TRUE WHIG PRINCIPLE

In a debate on the army estimates, the opposition had suggested that a reduction in the standing army was only consistent with the Whig doctrine of resistance.

When the noble lord spoke of resistance as being the Whig principle, and the principle on which the Revolution and our present happy establishment are founded, he should have distinguished between a constitutional and a factious resistance. A constitutional resistance is that made against an administration which advises the sovereign to encroach upon the liberties of the people or the privileges of Parliament and to pursue measures evidently subversive of the constitution. A factious resistance is that which is offered to a just and wise government and a sovereign who has ever made the law of the land the rule of his conduct. This first resistance is the true Whig principle, and in this respect, I am still, and shall always be, as much a Whig as ever; and shall constantly hold myself bound, in duty to my country and to posterity, to join with those who unite, even in forcible measures, when such become absolutely necessary, for removing evil counsellors from our sovereign and for punishing those who have given him wicked advice. But while a government pursues right measures, and attempts

36

nothing that can be deemed inconsistent with our Constitution, it shall always be my principle so to strengthen the hands of that government as to render any factious or seditious resistance not only ridiculous but mad.

The measures of government, therefore, form the only criterion by which we can determine whether resistance be constitutional or factious, just or unjust; and in this case the decision must be left to the public voice. Legislators in either House of Parliament may differ in opinion on this or that particular plan; and they ought to vote accordingly. But when a measure is adopted by the king, and approved by a majority in each House, surely I am not to resist the execution of that measure because I am of a contrary opinion. On that principle no government could be conducted; no society could subsist for twelve months. Therefore, I conclude that while we have a Parliament, regularly and duly assembled, there can be no such thing as a constitutional resistance; because if, during the interval of parliament, the government should pursue any scheme which some persons might deem hostile to the Constitution, those who disapprove it may wait and apply for redress the ensuing session; and if Parliament should differ from them, they ought in modesty to consider their judgment erroneous, or at least they ought to submit.

But when the king seems resolved to govern without a Parliament, or manifestly employs illegal means for the choice of such a Parliament as shall be devoted to him, the case becomes very different. The people have no resource but in arms, and resistance becomes constitutional. In this light, let us consider our regular army, and we shall find that in such a case it would be a safeguard for our liberties. Both officer and soldier would then be free from every sort of legal restraint, and would certainly act like the military in the time of King James. They would either join the people, or refuse to fight against their countrymen to support a tyrannical government.

House of Commons: 26 January 1753

HAD WE BUT CHARITY

Pelham showed more tolerance than his times when, in 1753, he introduced a Bill permitting the naturalisation of Jews which, though carried, had to be repealed the next year in deference to popular clamour: No Jews, long beards, nor whiskers!

The objection that, as Christianity is part of our establishment, we ought not to allow its professed enemies to live among us, any more than we should grant the same favour to the enemies of our civil establishment, is an argument that extends too far. Christianity, as professed and practised by the Church of England, is a part of our establishment; but will any gentleman say that we ought not to allow any person to live among us who will not in every particular conform to the profession and practice of the Church of England? Surely I am not to deem every man my enemy who differs from me on a point of religion. This would be a most unchristian principle. Considering Jews, then, much in the same light as other dissenters, we ought to regard them, not as enemies of our ecclesiastical establishment, but as men whose consciences will not allow them to conform to it. Therefore we may, and in charity should, indulge them to an extent not inconsistent with its security.

House of Commons: 7 May 1753

Thomas Pelham, later Pelham-Holles and second Lord Pelham and, afterwards, first

DUKE OF NEWCASTLE

1693-1768

Whig; Secretary of State for the Southern Department, 1724-46, and for the Northern Department, 1748-54; First Lord of the Treasury, 1754-56 and 1757-62; Lord Privy Seal, 1765-66

A MINISTER'S CONVICTION

Walpole's political enemies, not satisfied at contriving his resignation and fomenting mob-prejudice against the fallen minister, further secured a secret committee of the Commons to inquire into his administration. The papers they examined disclosed nothing; whereupon they further brought in an odious Bill to indemnify persons who shall make discoveries concerning the Earl of Orford's conduct which, after the debate in which Newcastle spoke, was rejected by the Lords.

BUT whether the nation is really exasperated to such a degree as is represented, whether it is the general opinion of mankind that the public affairs have been unfaithfully administered, and whether this Bill has been dictated by a desire of public justice or of private revenge, I have not thought it necessary to inquire; having long learned to act in consequence of my own conviction, not of the opinions of others, at least not of those who determine upon questions which they cannot understand and judge without having ever obtained an opportunity of examining.

Such must be the opinions of the people upon questions of policy, opinions not formed by reflection but adopted from those whom they, sometimes with very little reason, imagine nearer spectators of the government than themselves, and in whom they place an implicit confidence on account of some casual act of popularity.

I shall not, therefore, think the demands of the people a rule of conduct, nor shall ever fear to incur their resentment in the prosecution of their interest. I shall never flatter their passions to obtain their favour or gratify their revenge for fear of their contempt.

The inconstancy of public applause, all of us have observed, and many of us have experienced; and we know that it is very far from being always the reward of merit. We know that the brightest character may be easily darkened by calumny; that those who are labouring for the welfare of the public may be easily represented as traitors and oppressors, and that the people may quickly be persuaded to join in the accusation.

That the people, however deceived, have a right to accuse whomsoever they suspect, and that their accusation ought to be heard, I do not deny; but surely the opinion of the people is not such a proof of guilt as will justify a method of prosecution never known before, or give us a right to throw down the barriers of liberty, and punish by power those whom we cannot convict by law.

Let any of your lordships suppose himself by some accident exposed to the temporary malice of the populace, let him imagine his enemies inflaming them to a demand of a prosecution and then proposing that he should be deprived of the common methods of defence, and that evidence should be hired against him, lest the public should be disappointed, and he will quickly discover the unreasonableness of this Bill.

I suppose no man will deny that methods of prosecution introduced on one occasion may be practised on another and that, in the natural rotation of power, the same means may be used for very different ends. Nothing is more probable, if a Bill of this kind should be ever passed, in compliance with the clamours of the people to punish ministers and to awe the court, than that it may in time, if a wicked minister should arise, be made a precedent for measures by which the Court may intimidate the champions of the people; by which those may be pursued to destruction who have been guilty of no other crime than

that of serving their country in a manner which those who are ignorant
of the circumstances of affairs happen to disapprove.

The measures now proposed, my lords, are therefore to be rejected.

House of Lords: 25 May 1742

THE POPULAR GOOD

That every government ought to endeavour to gain the esteem and
confidence of the people, I suppose we are all equally convinced; but
I am very far from thinking that measures ought only to be pursued or
rejected as they are immediately favoured or disliked by the populace.
For as they cannot know either the causes or the end of public
transactions, they can judge only from fallacious appearances, or the
information of those whose interest it may perhaps be to lead them
away from the truth. That monarch will be certainly and most
permanently popular who steadily pursues the good of his people, even
in opposition to their own prejudices and clamours; who disregards
calumnies which, though they may prevail for a day, time will sufficiently confute, and who slights objections which he knows may be
answered, and answered beyond reply.

House of Lords: 21 December 1742

THE BOUNDS OF LIBERTY

I am jealous of liberty as any man can be in reason, but some people
pretend to be so jealous of liberty that they will not admit even of those
regulations that are necessary for the support of government; and this
I think of much more dangerous consequence to liberty, because it
must introduce anarchy, of which the certain consequence has always
been found to be tyranny.

House of Lords: 15 March 1749

William Cavendish, later Marquis of Hartington

and, afterwards, fourth

DUKE   OF   DEVONSHIRE

1720 – 1764

---

*Whig M.P., 1741–51; Lord-Lieutenant of Ireland,
1755–56; First Lord of the Treasury, 1756–57*

EARL OF BUTE

1713–1792

Scottish representative peer, Tory, 1737–41 and 1761–80; Secretary of State for the Northern Department, 1761–62; First Lord of the Treasury, 1762–63

GENESIS OF GOVERNMENT

Bute, acting as finishing-tutor to the Prince of Wales, afterwards George III, in June 1756, provided his pupil with a short abstract of the history of the world of which this is the commencement:

IN the first ages of the world, while parental fondness, filial piety and brotherly affection engrossed the mind, government subsisted only in the father's management of his family; to whom the eldest son succeeding became at once the prince and parent of his brethren. But mankind grew numerous, vice crept in, love, ambition, cruelty, with envy, malice and the like produced unnatural parents, disobedient children, diffidence and hatred between the nearest relations; this broke every tender tie and bid defiance to the mild parental authority; this forced men together for their mutual safety, and society became the securest as well as the most agreeable choice. Hence villages, towns, cities, with laws suited to the peculiar wants of the inhabitants; these were generally speaking founded by men of superior parts, to whom the rest paid a willing obedience, so that in these early days the peopled part of the globe probably consisted of as many little monarchies as towns. Some of these grew of course more powerful than the rest, the weaker neighbours becoming first tributaries, then slaves, to bold and enterprising spirits; such were the beginnings of those mighty empires that history has transmitted to us, Egyptian, Babylonian, Persian, Greek and Roman, besides innumerable other lesser states, some of whom shook off the royal yoke and formed new systems as aristocracies where the nobility governed, democracies where the whole people shared the power, while some again combined these various forms and raised mixed fabrics different from them all.

THE DUTY OF A PRINCE

On 4 September 1759 Princess Elizabeth died of appendicitis. The twenty-one years' old Prince of Wales keenly felt the loss of his sister and wrote to Bute: I have attempted this morning to read but find it impossible as yet to do anything except think of that dear sister I have lost:

I am not at all surprised to find by my Prince's letter that serious study proves irksome. Where the heart has met with a violent convulsion, 'tis long before reason entirely resumes its empire. You have had a great loss, a companion, sister, friend; but you have advantages to bear it that few of your age, still fewer of your rank, enjoy. Accustomed from your childhood to look up to Heaven, you can in the day of affliction put full confidence in Him who gives and resumes at pleasure; who being infinitely good, as well as omniscient and omnipotent, cannot take delight in poor mortal sufferings. He who can read that book of fate He Himself dictates, is frequently most compassionate when we, smarting under grinding sorrow, think him most severe. 'Tis infinite consolation to be able to take fast hold on our great Creator, our best Preserver, in all the good or bad that happens to us; to have our souls so pure, our consciences so free, that opprest with misery we may at once fly to Him, our best and surest friend, open all our griefs unto Him, implore His assistance, deprecate His wrath and finally submit entirely to His high will, fully convinced that as nothing can befall us, without His almighty fiat, or sufferance, neither can anything finally hurt us, if we serve Him faithfully. Poor short-sighted creatures, we are for ever reasoning on single events; could we perceive at one view, the whole plan of Omnipotence; the reasons consequently of this or that event; we should, I make no doubt, feel a double passion, and in the midst of human sufferings, be adoring the tender hand inflicting them. Thoughts like this turn evil into blessings; and render us after every trial of this kind, better men, warmer friends, nobler and more exalted creatures.

But I must not tire you; though it were easy to write whole sheets on this subject let me finish with inculcating one great truth. You are the second person in a most extensive polished empire; you will, please God, be the first. To act so supreme a part well is perhaps the height of human wisdom; and yet virtue, religion, joined to nobility of sentiment, will support a prince better and make a people happier, than all the abilities of an Augustus with the heart of a Tiberius. The inference I draw from this is that a prince ought to endeavour in all his thoughts and actions to excel his people in virtue, piety, generosity, nobility of sentiment; that when they have occasion to approach him, they may do it with love and veneration; and feel he merits, by his own virtue, and not the fickle die of fortune, the vast superiority he enjoys above them.

Letter to the Prince of Wales: 7 September 1759

GEORGE   GRENVILLE

1712–1770

Whig M.P., 1741–70; Junior Lord of the Admiralty, 1744–47; Junior Lord of the Treasury, 1747–54; Treasurer of the Navy, 1754–56 and 1757–62; Leader of the House of Commons, 1761–70; Secretary of State for the Northern Department, 1762; First Lord of the Admiralty, 1762–63; First Lord of the Treasury and Chancellor of the Exchequer, 1763–65

. . . *PRAEPARET BELLUM*

England, already engaged with France in the distant struggle for India and North America, was yet unprepared for the outbreak of the Seven Years' War in Europe.

WHAT strange, what unmanly fears, have been thrown out upon this occasion! We must not prepare for war for fear of rendering a peace impracticable! We must not prepare for war for fear of offending the allies of France! We must not prepare for war for fear of raising the resentment of the people of France! I am really ashamed to hear such arguments made use of in a British parliament. Sorry I am to hear such a suggestion from the mouth of any Englishman. If such a suggestion should have any weight with the people of this country, how justly may it be said, *Quantum mutatus ab illo!*

If we are suing, if we are begging for a peace upon any terms, I grant that our preparations may offend our enemies; if we are resolved to accept such a peace as French allies may dictate to us, I shall grant that our preparations may offend them. But if we are resolved to command an honourable peace, the more we are prepared, the more able we shall be to command; the less will every nation in Europe be inclined to risk joining with France against us. For nations are pretty much like old gamesters; they compare the chance they have of gaining with the chance they have of losing, and they never venture when they plainly see that the odds are against them.

House of Commons: 2 December 1755

LIBERTY AND LICENCE

Grenville here refers to a libel on that faction in Parliament which had refused to acknowledge the imminence of war; it had been insinuated that their opposition was induced by French bribery.

But I am so far from being angry at this freedom, though it may justly be called licentious, that I am glad to see the press so free. It makes me recollect what I have somewhere read of one of the greatest generals of the Athenian commonwealth, who was accused by a most low and abject citizen; though the accusation was false, he was so far from resenting it, that he rejoiced at it, and said he was glad to find he had so well established the liberties of his country that an accusation might be brought by the meanest citizen against the greatest man in the republic. I hope this will always be the case in this country; for though it may be sometimes necessary to punish licentiousness, yet even licentiousness itself ought not, I think, to be ever so severely punished as may encroach upon the liberty of the press.

Ibid

BE BOLD

I love a bold Minister when he keeps in the true sphere. In times of distress or danger, boldness is a jewel: and with joy have I seen bold, even wild enterprises succeed, though hardly within the die when undertaken.

A Speech against the Suspending and Dispensing
Prerogative, etc., 1767

AN HONOURABLE AND NOBLE OFFICE

In 1763 Grenville prosecuted John Wilkes for an attack on the King's Speech in his scurrilous North Briton. *The arrest, on a general warrant, was, however, declared illegal and Wilkes secured damages against the Government. Faced with a new charge of blasphemy and libel, he fled to France but returned, although meanwhile outlawed, to imprisonment, to popular acclamation on a confused cry of* Wilkes *and* liberty! *and to election as member for Middlesex. As often as Government led the*

*Commons to annul the election, so often did the Middlesex electors
return their dubious hero.*

*In 1769 a motion to expel Wilkes from the House posed Grenville the
dilemma he describes:*

I am thoroughly sensible that whatever my opinion shall be, it will
be liable to great misconstructions and great misrepresentations, both
within these walls and without doors. If I give my vote for the motion
as it was made to you, it will be said that I do it from a cruel unrelenting disposition, to gratify a private and personal resentment for
the abuse Mr. Wilkes has so liberally thrown upon me, and under the
mask of zeal for the cause of God and of the king, to persevere in
loading an unhappy man, who, it has been frequently said in this
House, has been already too severely oppressed by my means or at
least with my concurrence; or it would perhaps be attributed, especially after the temperate conduct which I have endeavoured to hold
during this session, to an abject flattery to power, with the mean paltry
view of obtaining court favour. On the other hand, if I give my vote
against the expulsion of Mr. Wilkes, I shall be charged with levity and
inconsistency, with changing my opinions as it may best suit my
situation either in or out of office; with adopting new principles from
new habitudes and connections, and with a factious design of courting
popularity, and distressing all legal government by supporting and
protecting a man whose behaviour I had so repeatedly and so heavily
censured. If I know my own failings, revenge and cruelty are among the
vices to which I am least inclined; and if I may trust to the reproaches
thrown out against me by my enemies, I have often been accused of
obstinacy and inflexibility of temper, but seldom or never I think with
being too much disposed to alter my opinions according to the will of
others, or to sail along the tide of popular prejudice. I should flatter
myself, therefore, that the charge of applying principles to court
favour or popular applause could not with justice be applied to me,
notwithstanding which I will again freely own that I should have
wished for many reasons not to have been under the necessity of
deciding upon this question either one way or the other. But as it has
been proposed to you, I think it would be a base and unworthy
conduct meanly to hide my head or to run away from the difficulty. It
is the duty of every honest man, if he is convinced that the judgment
he has formed is a right one, to declare it publicly in his place, to abide
by it, and boldly to face any difficulties which may encounter it. I am
under no restraint either from this or that side of the House; I know
and feel my own independence on both; and while I continue here, I
will exert it; and upon this occasion exercise an office greater than any

which the wildest applause of the multitude can give, or than the king himself can bestow, greater than the office of First Commissioner of the Treasury, or either of the Secretaries of State: the honourable and noble office of speaking the truth, and of doing impartial justice. I will not palliate this man's offences, or try to move your compassion: for that would be to appeal to your weakness against your judgment: much less will I inveigh against him in bitter terms, and strive to excite your indignation; for, instead of your weakness, I should then apply to your wicked passions. With these sentiments I shall proceed to the immediate examination of the question before you.

House of Commons: 3 February 1769

Charles Watson-Wentworth, Viscount Higham
and Earl of Malton, afterwards second

MARQUIS OF ROCKINGHAM
1730–1782

---

*Whig; took seat in House of Lords, 1751; First
Lord of the Treasury, 1765–66 and 1782*

A DEFENCE OF AMERICA

An awakening sense of nationality impelled the American colonists to allow a smouldering conflict between constitutional and legal rights to develop into the American Revolution which at last flared up in 1775. Rockingham, as Chatham and the Whigs generally, was strongly in favour of a policy of conciliation and staunchly supported the cause of the colonists.

IT is universally allowed, however we may censure the conduct of the Americans, that the first exercise of a power to tax them in the parliament of this country was at least extremely injudicious, if it was not actually illegal, since much more was to be got from their affection than their fear, from the extension of their commerce than the increase of their public burdens. While they submitted, therefore, to regulate their commerce by our discretion, they thought it hard that their property should also be at our disposal, and that we should not only restrain them in the acquisition of this property, but apply it when acquired to answer our own exigencies. To obtain their little wealth, they contentedly pursued those paths which we judged most conducive to our interest, but they denied our right of taking away that wealth when obtained, and of trusting to the discretion of any authority what they naturally enough considered to appertain wholly to themselves. It was of course no way wonderful that, in opposing what they deemed a palpable invasion of everything dear, they should fly to some excesses. The mother country herself upon particular occasions is not able to restrain the spirit of her own populace, even when they have apparently less foundations for complaint. She should, consequently, learn to make the same excuses for the Americans which she requires for herself, and recollect that few popular insurrections have ever taken place in an English government without having a strong appearance of justice, if they were not originally justified by the error of the governors.

There is the greater necessity for treating the colonies mildly on this occasion because we ourselves are exceedingly divided with regard to the necessary measures of effecting a reconciliation between them and the mother country. Many of the ablest members in both Houses think that we have no right whatever to tax them. Others contend for the right, but exclaim against the exercise; and all are satisfied that the happiness of the British Empire immediately depends upon the termination of our unfortunate dissensions. Thus situated, therefore, I am not surprised that the Americans should think themselves oppressively treated when numbers on this side of the Atlantic are heartily of the same opinion; nor am I surprised at the excesses they run to in defence of privileges which so many, even of their British fellow-subjects, pronounce to be their birthright and exhort them to assert with their blood.

I candidly confess that Government has a very delicate part to act in so critical a conjuncture; to maintain the due authority of the mother country and yet to satisfy the demands of the Americans is no easy circumstance. But still, as the first cause of complaint seems to be given by us; as we shall always have the power of enforcing a just authority over the colonies if they should at any time mistake an act of indulgence for an instance of timidity; and as it is for our own interest to bring them as speedily back to their duty as possible, I hope we shall not insist too rigidly upon the punctilios of pre-eminence; nor set an inconsiderable tax by any means in competition with the trade and the affection of America.

House of Lords: 18 May 1770

William Pitt, afterwards

EARL OF CHATHAM

1708-1778

Whig M.P., 1735-66; Vice-Treasurer of Ireland, 1746; Paymaster-General of the Forces, 1746-54; Secretary of State for the Southern Department, 1756-57 and 1757-61; Prime Minister and Lord Privy Seal, 1766-68

NO FREE MAN

Chatham despised Wilkes as man and agitator but, in the Commons rejection of the representative of the Middlesex electors, he saw an illegal and unconstitutional attack on the rights of every free elector in the country.

I THOUGHT the slavish doctrine of passive obedience had long since been exploded: and, when our kings were obliged to confess that their title to the Crown, and the rule of their Government, had no other foundation than the known laws of the land, I never expected to hear a divine right, or a divine infallibility, attributed to any other branch of the Legislature. I beg to be understood; no man respects the House of Commons more than I do, or would contend more strenuously than I to preserve them their just and legal authority. Within the bounds prescribed by the Constitution, that authority is necessary to the well-being of the people: beyond that line, every exertion of power is arbitrary, is illegal; it threatens tyranny to the people and destruction to the State. Power without right is the most odious and detestable object that can be offered to the human imagination: it is not only pernicious to those who are subject to it, but tends to its own destruction. It is what my noble friend has truly described it, *Res detestabilis et caduca*. I acknowledge the just power and reverence the constitution of the House of Commons. It is for their own sake that I would prevent their assuming a power which the Constitution has denied them, lest, by grasping an authority they have no right to, they should forfeit that which they legally possess. I affirm that they have betrayed their constituents and violated the Constitution. Under pretence of declaring the law, they have made a law, and united in the same persons the offices of legislator and judge.

WILLIAM PITT, EARL OF CHATHAM

A detail from the wax effigy, now in Westminster Abbey, by
Mrs. Mehetabel Wright, an American artist, to whom Chatham
sat in 1774

THE YOUNGER PITT ADDRESSING THE HOUSE OF
COMMONS, 1793

A detail from the painting by Karl Anton Hickel. Speaker
Addington, Pitt's successor as Prime Minister, is in the Chair

I am a plain man, and have been brought up in a religious reverence for the original simplicity of the laws of England. By what sophistry they have been perverted, by what artifices they have been involved in obscurity, is not for me to explain; the principles, however, of the English laws are still sufficiently clear: they are founded in reason, and are the masterpiece of the human understanding; but it is in the text that I would look for a direction to my judgment, not in the commentaries of modern professors. The noble lord assures us that he knows not in what Code the law of Parliament is to be found; that the House of Commons, when they act as judges, have no law to direct them but their own wisdom; that their decision is law; and that if they determine wrong, the subject has no appeal but to Heaven. What, then, are all the generous efforts of our ancestors, are all those glorious contentions, by which they meant to secure themselves, and to transmit to their posterity, a known law, a certain rule of living; reduced to this conclusion, that instead of the arbitrary power of a king, we must submit to the arbitrary power of a House of Commons? If this be true, what benefit do we derive from the exchange? Tyranny is detestable in every shape; but in none so formidable as when it is assumed and exercised by a number of tyrants. But, this is not the fact, this is not the constitution; we have a law of Parliament, we have a code in which every honest man may find it. We have a Magna Carta, we have the Statute Book, we have the Bill of Rights.

If a case should arise unknown to these great authorities, we have still that plain English reason left, which is the foundation of all our English jurisprudence. That reason tells us that every judicial court, and every political society, must be vested with those powers and privileges which are necessary for performing the office to which they are appointed. It tells us also that no court of justice can have a power inconsistent with, or paramount to, the known laws of the land; that the people when they choose their representatives never mean to convey to them a power of invading their rights, or trampling upon the liberties of those whom they represent. What security would they have for their rights if once they admitted that a court of judicature might determine every question that came before it, not by any known positive law but by the vague indeterminate arbitrary rule of what the noble lord is pleased to call the wisdom of the court? With respect to the decisions of the courts of justice, I am far from denying them their due weight and authority; yet, placing them in the most respectable view, I still consider them not as law, but as an evidence of the law; and before they can arrive even at that degree of authority, it must appear that they are founded in, and confirmed by, reason; that they

4

are supported by precedents taken from good and moderate times; that they do not contradict any positive law; that they are submitted to, without reluctance, by the people; that they are unquestioned by the legislature (which is equivalent to a tacit confirmation); and what, in my judgment, is by far the most important, that they do not violate the spirit of the Constitution. This last is not a vague or loose expression: we all know what the Constitution is; we all know that the first principle of it is that the subject shall not be governed by the arbitrium of any one man, or body of men (less than the whole legislature), but by certain laws, to which he has virtually given his consent, which are open to him to examine and not beyond his ability to understand.

Now, I affirm, and am ready to maintain, that the late decision of the House of Commons upon the Middlesex election is destitute of every one of those properties and conditions which I hold to be essential to the legality of such a decision. It is not founded in reason; for it carries with it a contradiction that the representative should perform the office of the constituent body. It contradicts Magna Carta and the Bill of Rights, by which it is provided that no subject shall be deprived of his freehold, unless by the judgment of his peers or the law of the land; and that elections of members to serve in Parliament shall be free. And so far is this decision from being submitted to by the people, that they have taken the strongest measures and adopted the most positive language to express their discontent. Whether it will be questioned by the legislature will depend upon your lordships' resolution; but that it violates the spirit of the Constitution will, I think, be disputed by no man who has heard this day's debate and who wishes well to the freedom of his country. Yet, if we are to believe the noble lord, this great grievance, this manifest violation of the principles of the Constitution, will not admit of a remedy; it is not even capable of redress unless we appeal at once to Heaven. I have better hopes of the Constitution, and a firmer confidence in the wisdom and constitutional authority of this House. It is your ancestors, my lords—it is to the English barons that we are indebted for the laws and Constitution we possess. Their virtues were rude and uncultivated, but they were great and sincere. Their understandings were as little polished as their manners, but they had hearts to distinguish right from wrong; they had heads to distinguish truth from falsehood; they understood the rights of humanity, and they had spirit to maintain them.

I think that history has not done justice to their conduct when they obtained from their sovereign that great acknowledgement of national rights contained in Magna Carta. They did not confine it to themselves alone, but delivered it as a common blessing to the whole people. They did not say: *These are the rights of the great barons, or these are the rights of the great prelates.* No, my lords; they said, in the simple Latin of the times: *Nullus liber homo,* and provided as carefully for the meanest subject as for the greatest. These are uncouth words, and sound but poorly in the ears of scholars; neither are they addressed to the criticisms of scholars, but to the hearts of free men. These three words, *nullus liber homo,* have a meaning which interests us all; they deserve to be remembered—they deserve to be inculcated in our minds—they are worth all the classics. Let us not, then, degenerate from the glorious example of our ancestors. These iron barons (for so I may call them when compared with the silken barons of modern days) were the guardians of the people; yet their virtues were never engaged in a question of such importance as the present. A breach has been made in the Constitution, the battlements are dismantled, the citadel is open to the first invader, the walls totter, the Constitution is untenable. What remains then but for us to stand foremost in the breach, to repair it or perish in it?

Great pains have been taken to alarm us with the consequences of a difference between the two Houses of Parliament; that the House of Commons will resent our presuming to take notice of their proceedings; that they will resent our daring to advise the Crown, and will never forgive us for attempting to save the State. I am sensible of the importance and the difficulty of this great crisis; at a moment such as this we are called upon to our duty, without dreading the resentment of any man. But if apprehensions of this kind are to affect us, let us consider which we ought to respect most—the representative or the collective body of the people. Five hundred gentlemen are not ten millions; and if we must have a contention, let us take care to have the English nation on our side. If this question be given up, the freeholders of England are reduced to a condition baser than the peasantry of Poland. If they desert their own cause, they deserve to be slaves! This is not merely the cold opinion of my understanding, but the glowing expression of what I feel: it is my heart that speaks. I know I speak warmly; but this warmth shall neither betray my argument nor my temper. The kingdom is in a flame: as mediators between the king and his people, it is our duty to represent to him the true condition and temper of his subjects. It is a duty which no particular respects should hinder us from performing; and whenever his Majesty shall demand our advice, it will then be our duty to enquire more minutely into the causes of the present discontents. Whenever that inquiry shall come on, I pledge myself to the House to prove that since the first institution of the House of Commons not a single precedent can be produced to justify their late proceedings.

The character and circumstances of Mr. Wilkes have been very improperly introduced into this question, not only here, but in that court of judicature where his cause was tried; I mean the House of Commons. With one party he was a patriot of the first magnitude; with the other the vilest incendiary. For my own part I consider him merely and indifferently as an English subject, possessed of certain rights which the laws have given him, and which the laws alone can take from him. I am neither moved by his private vices, nor by his public merits. In his person, though he were the worst of men, I contend for the safety and security of the best; and, God forbid, that there should be a power in this country of measuring the civil rights of the subject by his moral character, or by any other rule than the fixed laws of the land. I believe I shall not be suspected of any personal partiality to this unhappy man: I am not very conversant in pamphlets or newspapers; but, from what I have heard and from the little I have read, I may venture to affirm that I have had my share in the compliments which have come from that quarter; and, as for motives of ambition, if I am now suspected of coming forward in the decline of life in the anxious pursuit of wealth and power, which it is impossible for me to enjoy, be it so; there is one ambition at least which I ever will acknowledge, which I will not renounce but with my life. It is the ambition of delivering to my posterity those rights of freedom which I have received from my ancestors. I am not now pleading the cause of an individual, but of every freeholder in England.

House of Lords: 9 January 1770

COMMON CAUSE

My lords, I myself am one of the people. I esteem that security and independence which is the original birthright of an Englishman, far beyond the privileges, however splendid, which are annexed to the peerage. I myself am by birth an English elector, and join with the freeholders of England as in a common cause. Believe me, my lords, we mistake our real interest as much as our duty, when we separate ourselves from the mass of the people.

House of Lords: 22 November 1770

TOLERANCE

I am for this bill, because I am for toleration, that sacred right of nature and bulwark of truth and most interesting of all objects to fallible man.

House of Lords: 19 May 1772

JUSTICE TO AMERICA

Chatham spent himself in striving to stem an oppressive policy towards America and in pleading for satisfaction of her just claims. He inveighed, with horror and with a magnificence of language which has grown to be a part of English literature, against the perverse folly of prolonging a hopeless and disastrous civil war, and against the inhuman barbarities that too often disgraced it.

I contend not for indulgence, but justice to America; a brave, generous, and united people, with arms in their hands, and courage in their hearts; three millions of people, the genuine descendants of a valiant and pious ancestry, driven to those deserts by the narrow maxims of a superstitious tyranny.

Their resistance to your arbitrary system of taxation might have been foreseen; it was obvious from the nature of things, and of mankind; and above all, from the Whiggish spirit flourishing in that country. The spirit which now resists your taxation in America is the same which formerly opposed loans, benevolences, and ship-money in England; the same spirit which called all England on its legs, and by the Bill of Rights vindicated the English Constitution; the same spirit which established the great fundamental, essential maxim of your liberties—that no subject of England shall be taxed but by his own consent.

This glorious spirit of Whiggism animates three millions in America, who prefer poverty with liberty to gilded chains and sordid affluence; and who will die in defence of their rights as men, as freemen. What shall oppose this spirit, aided by the congenial flame glowing in the breast of every Whig in England, to the amount, I hope, of double the American numbers? Ireland they have to a man. In that country, joined as it is with the cause of colonies, and placed at their head, the distinction I contend for is and must be observed. This country superintends and controls their trade and navigation; but they tax themselves. And this distinction between external and internal control is sacred and insurmountable; it is involved in the abstract nature of things. Property is private, individual, absolute. Trade is an extended and complicated consideration; it reaches as far as ships can sail or winds can blow; it is a great and various machine. To regulate the numberless movements of its several parts, and combine them with effect, for the good of the whole, requires the superintending wisdom and energy of the supreme power in the Empire. But this supreme power has no effect towards internal taxation, for it does not exist in that relation; there is no such thing, no such idea in this constitution, as a supreme power operating upon property. Let this distinction remain for ever ascertained; taxation is theirs, commercial regulation is ours. As an American, I would recognise to England her supreme right of regulating commerce and navigation; as an Englishman by birth and principle, I recognise to the Americans their supreme unalienable right to their property—a right which they are justified in defending to the last extremity. To maintain this principle is the common cause of the Whigs on the other side of the Atlantic, and on this. *'Tis liberty to liberty engaged*, that they will defend themselves, their families, and their country. In this great cause they are immovably allied; it is the alliance of God and nature—immutable, eternal, fixed as the firmament of heaven.

To such united force, what force shall be opposed? What, my lords? A few regiments in America, and seventeen or eighteen thousand men at home! The idea is too ridiculous to take up a moment of your lordships' time. Nor can such a rational and principled union be resisted by the tricks of office or ministerial manœuvre. Laying of papers on your table, or counting numbers on a division, will not avert or postpone the hour of danger; it must arrive unless these fatal Acts are done away; it must arrive in all its horrors, and then these boastful ministers, in spite of all their confidence, and all their manœuvres, shall be forced to hide their heads. They shall be forced to a disgraceful abandonment of their present measures and principles, which they avow but cannot defend—measures which they presume to attempt but cannot hope to effectuate. They cannot, my lords, they cannot stir a step; they have not a move left; they are checkmated.

But it is not repealing this Act of Parliament, it is not repealing a piece of parchment, that can restore America to our bosom; you must repel her fears and her resentments; and you may then hope for her love and for her gratitude. But now, insulted with an armed force posted at Boston, irritated with an hostile array before her eyes, her concessions, if you could force them, would be suspicious and insecure; they would be *irato animo*; they would not be the sound honourable passions of freemen, they would be dictates of fear, and extortions of force. But it is more than evident that you cannot force them, united as they are, to your unworthy terms of submission—it is impossible.

When your lordships look at the papers transmitted us from America, when you consider their decency, firmness, and wisdom, you cannot but respect their cause, and wish to make it your own. For myself, I must declare and avow, that in all my reading and observation—and it has been my favourite study: I have read Thucydides, and have studied and admired the master-states of the world—that for solidity of reasoning, force of sagacity, and wisdom of conclusion, under such a complication of difficult circumstances, no nation or body of men can stand in preference to the General Congress at Philadelphia. I trust it is obvious to your lordships, that all attempts to impose servitude upon such men, to establish despotism over such a mighty continental nation, must be vain, must be fatal. We shall be forced ultimately to retract; let us restrain while we can, not when we must. I say we must necessarily undo these violent oppressive Acts; they must be repealed—you will repeal them; I pledge myself for it, that you will in the end repeal them. Avoid, then, this humiliating, disgraceful necessity. With a dignity becoming your exalted situation, make the first advances to concord, to peace, and happiness; for that is your true dignity, to act with prudence and justice. That you should first concede is obvious, from sound and rational policy. Concession comes with better grace and more salutary effect from superior power; it reconciles superiority of power with the feelings of men, and establishes solid confidence on the foundations of affection and gratitude.

House of Lords: 20 January 1775

IF I WERE AN AMERICAN, AS I AM AN ENGLISHMAN

The desperate state of our arms abroad is in part known. I love and honour the English troops: no man thinks more highly of them than I do: I know their virtues and their valour: I know they can achieve anything except impossibilities; and I know that the conquest of English America is an impossibility. You cannot, I venture to say it, you cannot conquer America. Your armies last war effected everything that could be effected; and what was it? It cost a numerous army, under the command of a most able general, a long and laborious campaign, to expel five thousand Frenchmen from French America. My lords, you cannot conquer America. What is your present situation there? We do not know the worst; but we know that in three campaigns we have done nothing, and suffered much. Besides the sufferings, perhaps total loss, of the Northern force; the best appointed army that ever took the field, commanded by Sir William Howe, has retired from the American lines; he was obliged to relinquish his attempt, and, with great delay and danger, to adopt a new and distant plan of operations. We shall soon know, and in any event have reason to lament, what may have happened since. As to conquest, therefore, my lords, I repeat, it is impossible. You may swell every expense, and every effort, still more extravagantly; pile and accumulate every assistance you can buy or borrow; traffic and barter with every little pitiful German prince, that sells and sends his subjects to the shambles of a foreign prince; your efforts are for ever vain and impotent—doubly so from this mercenary aid on which you rely; for it irritates, to an incurable resentment, the minds of your enemies—to overrun them with the mercenary sons of rapine and plunder, devoting them and their possessions to the rapacity of hireling cruelty! If I were an American, as I am an Englishman, while a foreign troop was landed in my country, I would never lay down my arms—never—never—never!

House of Lords: 20 November 1777

THESE ABOMINABLE PRINCIPLES

The Earl of Suffolk, in the course of debate, had defended the employment of Indians against the Colonists, saying that it was perfectly justifiable to use all the means that God and nature put into our hands.

I am astonished! I am shocked to hear such principles confessed, to hear them avowed in this House, or in this country: principles equally unconstitutional, inhuman and unchristian!

My lords, I did not intend to have encroached again upon your attention: but I cannot repress my indignation; I feel myself impelled by every duty. We are called upon as members of this House, as men, as Christian men, to protest against such notions standing near the throne, polluting the ear of Majesty. *That God and nature put into our hands!* I know not what ideas that lord may entertain of God and nature; but I know that such abominable principles are equally abhorrent to religion and humanity. What! to attribute the sacred sanction of God and nature to the massacres of the Indian scalping knife, to the cannibal savage torturing, murdering, roasting and eating, literally, my lords, eating the mangled victims of his barbarous battles! Such horrible notions shock every precept of religion, divine or natural, and every generous feeling of humanity. They shock every sentiment of honour. They shock me as a lover of honourable war and a detester of murderous barbarity.

These abominable principles, and this more abominable avowal of them, demand the most decisive indignation. I call upon that right reverend bench, those holy ministers of the gospel and pious pastors of our Church, I conjure them to join in the holy work, and vindicate the religion of their God; I appeal to the wisdom and law of this learned bench to defend and support the justice of their country. I call upon the bishops to interpose the unsullied sanctity of their lawn; upon the learned judges to interpose the purity of their ermine to save us from this pollution. I call upon the honour of your lordships to reverence the dignity of your ancestors and to maintain your own. I call upon the spirit and humanity of my country to vindicate the national character. I invoke the genius of the Constitution.

From the tapestry that adorns these walls, the immortal ancestor of this noble lord frowns with indignation at the disgrace of his country. In vain he led your victorious fleets against the boasted Armada of Spain; in vain he defended and established the honour, the liberties, the religion, the Protestant religion, of this country, against the arbitrary cruelties of Popery and the Inquisition, if these more than popish cruelties and inquisatorial practices are let loose among us; to turn forth into our settlements, among our ancient connections, friends and relations, the merciless cannibal, thirsting for the blood of man, woman and child; to send forth the infidel savage—against whom?—against your Protestant brethren, to lay waste their country, to desolate their dwellings, and extirpate their race and name, with these horrible hell-hounds of savage war. Spain armed herself with blood-hounds to extirpate the wretched natives of America; and we improve on the inhuman example even of Spanish cruelty: we turn loose these savage hell-hounds against our brethren and countrymen in America, of the same language, laws, liberties and religion; endeared to us by every tie that should sanctify humanity.

This awful subject, so important to our honour, our Constitution, and our religion, demands the most solemn and effectual inquiry. And I again call upon your lordships, and the united powers of the State, to examine it thoroughly and decisively, and to stamp upon it an indelible stigma of the public abhorrence. And I again implore those holy prelates of our religion, to do away with these iniquities from among us. Let them perform a lustration; let them purify this House, and this country, from this sin.

House of Lords: 20 November 1777

LET US FALL LIKE MEN!

On 7 April 1778 Chatham, feeble and racked with pain, was led into the House by his son, William, the future statesman, and his son-in-law, Lord Mahon. With their help, dauntless in spirit, he rose to protest against the imminent severance from America now aided by her alliance with France.

Struggling to rise a second time, Chatham collapsed; he was carried from the House, to linger for a few weeks before, on 11 May, he died.

I thank God that I have been enabled to come here this day. I am old and infirm, have one foot, more than one foot in the grave. I am risen from my bed, to stand up in the cause of my country, perhaps never again to speak in this House.

I rejoice that the grave has not closed upon me; that I am still alive to lift up my voice against the dismemberment of this ancient and most noble monarchy. Pressed down as I am by the hand of infirmity, I am little able to assist my country in this most perilous conjuncture; but, while I have sense and memory, I will never consent to deprive the royal offspring of the House of Brunswick, the heirs of the Princess Sophia, of their fairest inheritance. Where is the man that will dare to advise such a measure? His Majesty succeeded to an Empire as great in extent as its reputation was unsullied. Shall we tarnish the lustre of this nation by an ignominious surrender of its rights and fairest possessions? Shall this great kingdom, that has survived whole and entire the Danish depredations, the Scottish inroads, and the Norman Conquest; that has withstood the threatened invasion of the Spanish Armada, now fall prostrate before the House of Bourbon? Surely this nation is no longer what it was! Shall a people that fifteen years ago was the terror of the world now stoop so low as to tell its ancient inveterate enemy: *Take all we have, only give us peace.* It is impossible!

In God's name, if it is absolutely necessary to declare either for peace or war, and the former cannot be preserved with honour, why is not the latter commenced straightway? I am not, I confess, well informed of the resources of the kingdom; but I trust it has still sufficient to maintain its just rights, though I know them not. But, my lords, any state is better than despair. Let us at least make one effort; and if we must fall, let us fall like men!

Augustus Henry Fitzroy,

Earl of Euston and, afterwards, third

DUKE OF GRAFTON

1735–1811

Whig M.P., 1756–57; Secretary of State for the Northern Department, 1765–66; First Lord of the Treasury, 1766–70; Lord Privy Seal, 1771–75 and 1782–83

THE BILL OF RIGHTS

I AM astonished that any lord in this House, any real friend to his country, any man who loved the Constitution under which he was born, could employ his time in commenting on the letter and explaining away the spirit of that great bulwark of the Constitution, the Bill of Rights; that law which, as it were, circumscribes within it the laws and liberties of the people of England. I will not enter into the quibbles or distinctions of Westminster Hall, or weigh each word and sentence to see what its distinct legal or grammatical import. No! I shall appeal to the spirit, the intention, of that new Magna Carta, that claim of old rights newly ascertained, the manifest purpose for which it was framed, and the coexisting purposes that gave it being on the part of an oppressed people. I shall look upon it in the light of a solemn contract entered into between the people and their newly elected sovereign, a compact meant to be binding on their respective posterity and their successors. Whenever that sacred palladium is taken away, at that instant, I will be bold to affirm, the laws, Constitution, and liberties of England will be annihilated.

House of Lords: 1 November 1775

SERIOUS REFLECTIONS

On the truth of the Christian dispensation and religion I confidently rest my only hopes of immortality; and, with thankfulness for so great a boon, I trust to the mercy of God towards me who stand so much in need of it.

Creeds we all know are matters of human composition and, as such,

59

fallible; and we have a fair right to consider these as Christian or otherwise in proportion as they approach to, or depart from, the plain language of Scripture: but it behoveth us in so doing, to show all moderation and goodwill towards those whose opinions are even most opposite to our own. No individual, or body of individuals, can possibly have a right to interfere between God and a man's conscience, except by the most friendly admonition and interposition; much less can any man have a right to doom his neighbour to everlasting punishment merely because he cannot bend his mind to adopt what the other believeth.

Serious Reflections of a Rational Christian: 1797

Frederick North, later

L O R D   N O R T H

and, afterwards, second Earl of Guilford

Whig M.P., 1754–90; Junior Lord of the Treasury, 1759–65; Joint Paymaster-General of the Forces, 1766–67; Chancellor of the Exchequer, 1768–82; First Lord of the Treasury, 1770–82; Secretary of State for Home Affairs, 1783

NATURAL AND CIVIL LIBERTY

TO restrain liberty is the very essence and end of all government, which became necessary when a state of nature was improved into civil society, merely because it became necessary that natural liberty should be restrained. It is by the restraint of natural liberty that the weak are protected against the strong, that property is secured against the thief, and life against the assassin. There is, however, such a thing as civil liberty, which, I believe, our bellowers against the powers of government are neither willing nor able to define; let me then acquaint them that civil liberty subsists wherever natural liberty is no further restrained than is absolutely necessary to secure the advantages of civil society. Whatever restraint is necessary for this purpose is compatible with the most perfect civil liberty, and the liberty which is compatible

with these restraints is that alone for which honesty and common sense
can be advocates. As these restraints are more necessary in one
country, and at one time than another, natural liberty may, and must
be circumscribed within narrower bounds in one country, and at one
time than another; yet civil liberty may be kept equally sacred and
uninfringed. Thus it has happened that all attempts to recover natural
liberty from the restraints which are necessary to secure the advantages
of civil society, have either ended in the dissolution of all government,
or in a more rigorous and extensive application of its powers. Liberty,
carried beyond the bounds within which the interest of civil society
requires it to ·be confined, is licentiousness, and the natural and
necessary consequences of prevailing licentiousness in the members of
any state or community, must be either anarchy or a government less
lenient and gentle. If no power of government which restrains liberty
can be defended, government itself is indefensible; if any power of
government restraining liberty for the common advantage of a civil
community can be defended, every power, the exertion of which is
absolutely necessary for this purpose, may be defended, and the only
inquiry concerning the powers of government should be, whether the
exertion of them is necessary for this great purpose, or not.

House of Commons: 27 November 1770

THE BATTLE OF THE PEOPLE

*John Horne, afterwards Horne Tooke, accused of libelling the
Speaker, had been taken into the custody of the Serjeant-at-Arms for
refusing to attend the House. He was, however, discharged for lack of
evidence with which to connect him with the offending libel.*

Whose battle are we fighting upon this occasion? Is it not the battle
of the people? We have no privileges but what we derive from them:
we have no authority but that with which they have invested us. Can
it be supposed then that the people will be angry with us for maintaining their rights, for defending their political omnipotence, and preserving that reverence for their authority, which gives them so happy
an equipoise in the great scale of the constitution? We are only the
meteors of a moment and when we are in the dust, it will little signify
to us whether there is a single privilege of this House remaining: but
the people will continue to the latest hour of time I trust, and if we
suffer an invasion of their powers, the precedent may wound them to
the last line of posterity. The right honourable gentleman has often
accused us of destroying the people's liberties, and now he is angry

with us for standing forth in their defence; fault, however, must be found, and so the wicked minister is blamed, no matter what is the ground of accusation. Various gentlemen in the course of the debate have introduced a very whimsical doctrine, and insisted that the House must be overwhelmed with disgrace if Mr. Horne is not convicted. And why so? Is a court of law ever disgraced because a prisoner may be acquitted on his trial? If the position of these gentlemen holds good, the judges, in defence of their own honour, must labour to condemn every culprit. The more they hang upon this principle, the more they will raise themselves into estimation. But I am weary of refuting such puerilities. While we do justice, we need never be apprehensive of disgrace; and it will be a greater glory to let a man escape with impunity, whom we all believe in our consciences to be guilty, because there is not a sufficiency of legal evidence against him, than to decline an inquiry which may have an eventual tendency to maintain the legislative authority of the people.

House of Commons: 7 February 1774

AN ENGLISHMAN'S DEMEANOUR

North's demeanour at a time of grave national anxiety had been challenged by a member of the House.

I did not know that I had worn any particular smile at entering the House, yet if I did, a grave or melancholy brow is not a look best suited to times of danger. Englishmen must feel like Englishmen, and are not to be easily sunk down.

House of Commons: 18 June 1779

William Petty FitzMaurice, later second

EARL OF SHELBURNE

and, afterwards, first Marquess of Lansdowne

1737 – 1805

Whig M.P., 1760–61; President of the Board of Trade, 1762–63; Secretary of State for the Southern Department, 1766–68; Secretary of State for Home Affairs, 1782; First Lord of the Treasury, in Coalition Ministry, 1782–83

A NOBLE ARDOUR

Shelburne, though in sympathy with the American colonists, strove hard for reconciliation and strongly resisted the idea of independence. But when that independence was an accomplished fact Shelburne, with vision to foresee America's future, strove, in his own phrase, for an eternal amity between England and America.

THE idea I have ever entertained of the connection between both countries was that they should have one friend, one enemy, one purse, and one sword; that both countries should have but one will, though the means of expressing that will may be different, distinct, and varied. All this might have been procured not long since; and I still retain strong hopes that it can be effected, and that, too, without measures of blood. It was once optional and is still possible.

House of Lords: 5 March 1778

The American War is the native offspring of ministerial ignorance, obstinacy, and want of political principle. It has for its immediate object the increasing the influence of the Crown and the power of the sovereign. It was conceived in ambition, it was nurtured by folly and rashness, it was founded in ideas totally subversive of the British Constitution. It is unjust and wicked in the extreme, it is carried on with violence and want of prudence, and prosecuted in all its parts with the most unrelenting and unheard of cruelties.

I confess in respect to the recovery of North America I have been a very Quixote, and have expected, because I most anxiously wished,

63

that our colonies might be prevailed upon to return to their former state of connection with this country, but my hopes have long since vanished. I have waked from those dreams of British dominion, and every important consequence which I flattered myself might be derived from them. But as, in the course of what I might have urged in favour of those delusive hopes and vain and idle expectations, some expressions of a loose, general, and indeterminate nature might have fallen from me, I wish to be perfectly understood. Much as I value America, necessary as the possession of the colonies might be to the power, glory, dignity, and independence of Great Britain, fatal as her final separation would prove, whenever that event might take place, as a friend to liberty, as a reverer of the English Constitution, as a lover of natural and political justice, I would be much better pleased to see America for ever severed from Great Britain, than restored to our possession by force of arms, or conquest. I love my country, I admire its political institutions, but if her future greatness, power, and extent of dominion are only to be established and maintained on the ruins of the constitution, I would be infinitely better pleased to see this country a free one, though curtailed in power and wealth, than possessing everything the most sanguine expectation could picture to itself if her greatness were to be purchased at the expense of her Constitution and liberties.

House of Lords: 25 January 1781

I have never made a secret of the deep concern I feel in the separation of countries united by blood, by principles, habits, and every tie short of territorial proximity. But you very well know that I have long since given it up, decidedly though reluctantly, and the same motives which made me perhaps the last to give up all hope of reunion make me most anxious if it is given up that it shall be done decidedly, so as to avoid all future risk of enmity and lay the foundation of a new connection better adapted to the present temper and interests of both countries. In this view I go farther with Dr. Franklin perhaps than he is aware of, and farther perhaps than the professed advocates of independence are prepared to admit. My private opinion would lead me to go a great way for Federal Union; but is either country ripe for it? If not, means must be left to advance it.

Letter to Richard Oswald: 27 July 1782

A FAIR EQUALITY

Monopolies, some way or other, are ever justly punished. They forbid rivalry, and rivalry is of the very essence of the well-being of trade. This seems to be the era of protestantism in trade. All Europe appears enlightened and eager to throw off the vile shackles of oppressive ignorant monopoly, that unmanly and illiberal principle which is at once ungenerous and deceitful. A few interested merchants might complain, for merchants would always love monopoly without taking a moment's time to think whether it was for their interest or not. I avow that monopoly is always unwise; but if there is any nation under heaven who ought to be the first to reject monopoly it is the English. Situated as we are between the old world and the new, and between the southern and northern Europe, all that we ought to covet upon earth is free trade and fair equality. With more industry, with more enterprise, with more capital than any trading nation upon earth, it ought to be our constant cry, let every market be open, let us meet our rivals fairly, and we ask no more.

House of Lords: 17 February 1783

William Henry Cavendish Bentinck,

Marquis of Titchfield, afterwards third

DUKE OF PORTLAND

1738–1809

Whig M.P., 1760–62; Lord-Lieutenant of Ireland, 1782; First Lord of the Treasury, 1783, in Coalition Ministry, and 1807–9; Secretary of State for the Northern Department, 1794–1801; Lord President of the Council, 1801–4

WILLIAM PITT

1759-1806

Tory M.P., 1781–1806; Chancellor of the Exche-
quer, 1782; First Lord of the Treasury and Chan-
cellor of the Exchequer, 1783–1801 and 1804–6

PROUD PATRIOT

The preliminary articles of peace with the United States and with
France, Spain, and Holland, concluded by the Shelburne ministry,
though confirmed in consideration of the public faith, were violently
attacked by the Opposition. Fox led the Opposition attack and the
twenty-three years' old Chancellor of the Exchequer replied for the
Government.

THE triumphs of party, with which this self-appointed minister seems
so highly elated, shall never seduce me to any inconsistency which the
busiest suspicion shall presume to glance at. I will never engage in
political enmities without a public cause. I will never forego such
enmities without the public approbation; nor will I be questioned and
cast off in the face of this House by one virtuous and dissatisfied
friend. These, the sober and durable triumphs of reason, over the weak
and profligate inconsistencies of party-violence; these, the steady
triumphs of virtue over success itself shall be mine, not only in my
present situation, but through every future condition of my life:
triumphs which no length of time shall diminish; which no change of
principles shall ever sully.

I have ever been most anxious to do my utmost for the interest of
my country; it has been my sole concern to act an honest and upright
part, and I am disposed to think every instance of my official deport-
ment will bear a fair and honourable construction. With these intentions, I ventured forward on the public attention; and can appeal with
some degree of confidence to both sides of the House, for the consistency of my political conduct. My earliest impressions were in
favour of the noblest and most disinterested modes of serving the
public: these impressions are still dear, and will, I hope, remain for
ever dear to my heart; I will cherish them as a legacy infinitely more
valuable than the greatest inheritance. On these principles alone I
came into Parliament and into place; and I now take the whole House

to witness, that I have not been under the necessity of contradicting one public declaration I have ever made.

I am, notwithstanding, at the disposal of this House, and with their decision, whatever it shall be, I will cheerfully comply. It is impossible to deprive me of those feelings which must always result from the sincerity of my best endeavours to fulfil with integrity every official engagement. You may take from me the privileges and emoluments of place, but you cannot, and you shall not, take from me those habitual and warm regards for the prosperity of Great Britain which constitute the honour, the happiness, the pride of my life, and which, I trust, death alone can extinguish.

House of Commons: 21 February 1783

NECESSITY

Necessity is the plea for every infringement of human freedom. It is the argument of tyrants; it is the creed of slaves.

House of Commons: 18 November 1783

LIBERTY AND LAW

It should perhaps be emphasised that Pitt's reverence for the Constitution did not blind him to the necessity for Parliamentary Reform, though the early excesses of the French Revolution caused him to modify his first enthusiasms for more democratic government. It is the irony of his great career that the causes he early had at heart—peace, economy, and reform—were all swept aside, never to be resumed by him, in the urgencies of the conduct of the war with France.

It is this union of liberty with law, which, by raising a barrier equally firm against the encroachments of power and the violence of popular commotion, affords to property its just security, produces the exertion of genius and labour, the extent and solidity of credit, the circulation and increase of capital; which forms and upholds the national character, and sets in motion all the springs which actuate the great mass of the community through all its various descriptions.

The laborious industry of those useful and extensive classes (who will, I trust, be in a peculiar degree this day the object of the consideration of the House) the peasantry and yeomanry of the country; the skill and ingenuity of the artificer; the experiments and improvements of the wealthy proprietor of land; the bold speculations and successful adventures of the opulent merchant and enterprising manufacturer; these are all to be traced to the same source, and all derive from hence both their encouragement and their reward. On this point, therefore, let us principally fix our attention. Let us preserve this first and most essential object, and every other is in our power. Let us remember that the love of the Constitution, though it acts as a sort of natural instinct in the hearts of Englishmen, is strengthened by reason and reflection, and every day confirmed by experience; that it is a Constitution which we do not merely admire from traditional reverence, which we do not flatter from prejudice or habit, but which we cherish and value, because we know that it practically secures the tranquillity and welfare both of individuals and of the public, and provides, beyond any other frame of government which has ever existed, for the real and useful ends which form at once the only true foundation and only rational object of all political societies.

House of Commons: 17 February 1792

BEREAV'D OF LIGHT

The eighteenth-century conscience was slow in waking to the horrors of the slave traffic. Mainly Quaker protests led to the founding in 1787 of the Society for the Abolition of the Slave Trade, a leading member of which was Pitt's friend, Wilberforce. Wilberforce, with Pitt's support, moved for abolition in 1788 and again in 1792 when the motion was carried but with an amendment introducing the word gradually.

It was not until 1807 that the House was entirely pledged to abolition and the final Emancipation Act was not carried until 1833.

We have long since emerged from barbarism. We have almost forgotten that we were once barbarians. We are now raised to a situation which exhibits a striking contrast to every circumstance by which a Roman might have characterised us, and by which we now characterise Africa. There is, indeed, one thing wanting to complete the contrast and to clear us altogether from the imputation of acting even to this hour as barbarians; for we continue to this hour a barbarous traffic in slaves; we continue it even yet in spite of all our great and undeniable pretensions to civilisation. We were once as obscure among the nations of the earth, as savage in our manners, as debased in our morals, as degraded in our understandings, as these unhappy Africans are at present. But in the lapse of a long series of years, by a progression slow and for a time almost imperceptible, we have become rich in a variety of acquirements, favoured above measure in the gifts of Providence, unrivalled in commerce, pre-eminent in arts, foremost in the pursuits of philosophy and science, and established in all the blessings of civil society. We are in the possession of peace, of happi-

ness and of liberty. We are under the guidance of a mild and beneficent religion; and we are protected by impartial laws and the purest
administration of justice. We are living under a system of government
which our own happy experience leads us to pronounce the best and
wisest which has ever yet been framed; a system which has become the
admiration of the world. From all these blessings we must for ever
have been shut out had there been any truth in those principles which
some gentlemen have not hesitated to lay down as applicable to the
case of Africa. Had those principles been true, we ourselves had
languished to this hour in that miserable state of ignorance, brutality
and degradation in which history proves our ancestors to have been
immersed. Had other nations adopted these principles in their conduct
towards us, had other nations applied to Great Britain the reasoning
which some of the senators of this very island now apply to Africa,
ages might have passed without our emerging from barbarism; and
we who are enjoying the blessings of British civilisation, of British
laws, and British liberty, might at this hour have been little superior,
either in morals, in knowledge, or refinement, to the rude inhabitants
of the Coast of Guinea.

If then we feel that this perpetual confinement in the fetters of
brutal ignorance would have been the greatest calamity which could
have befallen us; if we view with gratitude and exultation the contrast
between the peculiar blessings we enjoy and the wretchedness of the
ancient inhabitants of Britain; if we shudder to think of the misery
which would still have overwhelmed us had Great Britain continued
to the present times to be the mart for slaves to the more civilised
nations of the world, through some cruel policy of theirs, God forbid
that we should any longer subject Africa to the same dreadful scourge,
and preclude the light of knowledge, which has reached every other
quarter of the globe, from having access to her coasts.

I trust we shall no longer continue this commerce, to the destruction of every improvement on that wide continent; and shall not
consider ourselves as conferring too great a boon in restoring its
inhabitants to the rank of human beings. I trust we shall not think
ourselves too liberal if, by abolishing the slave trade, we give them the
same common chance of civilisation with other parts of the world, and
that we shall now allow to Africa the opportunity, the hope, the
prospect of attaining to the same blessings which we ourselves,
through the favourable dispensations of Divine Providence, have been
permitted, at a much more early period, to enjoy. If we listen to the
voice of reason and duty, and pursue this night the line of conduct
which they prescribe, some of us may live to see a reverse of that

picture from which we now turn our eyes with shame and regret. We may live to behold the natives of Africa engaged in the calm occupations of industry, in the pursuit of a just and legitimate commerce. We may behold the beams of science and philosophy breaking in upon their land, which, at some happy period in still later times, may blaze with full lustre; and joining their influence to that of pure religion, may illuminate and invigorate the most distant extremities of that immense continent. Then may we hope that even Africa, though last of all the quarters of the globe, shall enjoy at length, in the evening of her days, those blessings which have descended so plentifully upon us in a much earlier period of the world. Then, also, will Europe, participating in her improvement and prosperity, receive an ample recompense for the tardy kindness (if kindness it can be called) of no longer hindering that continent from extricating herself out of the darkness which, in other more fortunate regions, has been so much more speedily dispelled.

> *Nos primus equis oriens afflavit anhelis;*
> *Illic sera rubens accendit lumina Vesper.*

House of Commons: 3 April 1792

THE GAGE FLUNG DOWN

Although France, by the execution of Louis XIV, had thrown down the gage, there still remained some hope of an improbable peace. War, however, was declared 12 February 1793.

If France is really desirous of maintaining friendship and peace with England, she must show herself disposed to renounce her views of aggression and aggrandizement, and to confine herself within her own territory, without insulting other governments, without disturbing their tranquillity, without violating their rights. And unless she consent to these terms, whatever may be our wishes for peace, the final issue must be war. As to the time, as to the moment when war is to commence, if there is yet any possibility of satisfactory explanation and security for the future, it is not to the last moment precluded. But I should disguise my sentiments to the House if I stated that I thought it in any degree probable. This country has always been desirous of peace. We desire it still, but such as may be real and solid, and consistent with the interests and dignity of Britain, and with the general security of Europe. War, whenever it comes, will be preferable to peace without honour, without security, and which is incompatible either with the external safety or the internal happiness of this country.

House of Commons: 1 February 1793

OUTRAGED HUMANITY

We are called in the present age to witness the political and moral phenomenon of a mighty and civilised people, formed into an artificial horde of banditti, throwing off all the restraints which have influenced men in social life, displaying a savage valour directed by a sanguinary spirit, forming rapine and destruction into a system, and perverting to their detestable purposes all the talents and ingenuity which they derived from their advanced stage of civilisation, all the refinements of art, and the discoveries of science. We behold them uniting the utmost savageness and ferocity of design with consummate contrivance and skill in execution, and seemingly engaged in no less than a conspiracy to exterminate from the face of the earth all honour, humanity, justice, and religion. In this state, can there be any question but to resist, where resistance alone can be effectual, till such time as, by the blessing of Providence upon our endeavours, we shall have secured the independence of this country and the general interests of Europe?

House of Commons: 21 January 1794

LET US GO FORWARD TOGETHER

The failure of negotiations for peace, naval mutiny at the Nore, Irish rebellion, a financial crisis and the Republican threats of invasion, left the spirit of Pitt undaunted. Unfaltering, he embodied the spirit of the nation.

I wish for such a unanimity as will lay a just foundation for future prosperity, for one on which I place the most favourable augury, the unanimity of the nation at large—a unanimity not in support of the administration, but in support of the Constitution itself, and of all those laws by which it is guarded. The country is called upon to be unanimous in a contest which embraces everything that is most valuable to its dearest interests. Whatever difference of opinion may prevail in the minds of gentlemen on former points, there cannot exist a shadow of doubt with respect to the present question. It is now indispensably necessary for us to unite in one common cause; it is incumbent on us to consolidate our efforts, to reconcile our different views, to concentrate our individual exertions, and to give energy and vigour to the laws, without which it is impossible there can be any solid happiness. It is not merely by declarations that we are bound to proceed, but by a spirit and promptitude of action, and a firm resolution and readiness to support the execution of the laws by military subordination and legal obedience. It becomes our duty to give a resistless efficacy to this conduct through every corner of the metropolis and through every part of the kingdom. By such measures we can alone disappoint the dark and malignant efforts of the enemy; and I am proud to say that to so glorious a unanimity there is nothing that I would not cheerfully sacrifice.

House of Commons: 2 June 1797

THE ISSUE

You have it stated in the subsequent declaration of France itself, that it is not against your commerce, it is not against your wealth, it is not against your possessions in the East or colonies in the West, it is not against even the source of your maritime greatness, it is not against any of the appendages of your Empire, but against the very essence of your liberty, against the foundation of your independence, against the citadel of your happiness, against your Constitution itself, that their hostilities are directed. They have themselves announced and proclaimed the proposition, that what they mean to bring with their invading army is the genius of *their* liberty—I desire no other word to express the subversion of the British Constitution, and the substitution of the most malignant and fatal contrast—and the annihilation of British liberty, and the obliteration of everything that has rendered you a great, a flourishing, and a happy people.

This is what is at issue; for this are we to declare ourselves in a manner that deprecates the rage which our enemy will not dissemble and which will be little moved by our entreaty. Under such circumstances, are we ashamed or afraid to declare, in a firm and manly tone, our resolution to defend ourselves, or to speak the language of truth with the energy that belongs to Englishmen united in such a cause? I do not scruple to say, if I knew nothing by which I could state to myself a probability of the contest terminating in our favour, I would maintain, that the contest with its worst chances is preferable to an acquiescence in such demands.

If I could look at this as a dry question of prudence, if I could calculate it upon the mere grounds of interest, I would say, if we love that degree of national power which is necessary for the independence of the country and its safety; if we regard domestic tranquillity, if we look at individual enjoyment, from the highest to the meanest among us, there is not a man whose stake is so great in the country that he ought to hesitate a moment in sacrificing any portion of it to oppose the violence of the enemy; nor is there, I trust, a man in this happy and free nation whose stake is so small that would not be ready to sacrifice his life in the same cause. If we look at it with a view to safety, this would be our conduct; but if we look at it upon the principle of true honour, of the character which we have to support, of the example which we have to set to the other nations of Europe, if we view rightly the lot in which Providence has placed us, and the contrast between ourselves and all the other countries in Europe, gratitude to that Providence should inspire us to make every effort in such a cause. There may be danger; but on the one side there is danger accompanied with honour, on the other side there is danger with indelible shame and disgrace. Upon such an alternative Englishmen will not hesitate.

I wish to disguise no part of my sentiments upon the grounds on which I put the issue of the contest. I ask whether, up to the principles I have stated, we are prepared to act. Having done so, my opinion is not altered; my hopes, however, are animated from the reflection that the means of our safety are in our own hands. For there never was a period when we had more to encourage us; in spite of heavy burdens, the radical strength of the nation never showed itself more conspicuous; its revenue never exhibited greater proofs of the wealth of the country. The same objects, which constitute the blessings we have to fight for, furnish us with the means of continuing them. But it is not upon that point I rest it. There is one great resource which I trust will never abandon us. It has shone forth in the English character, by which we have preserved our existence and fame as a nation, which I trust we shall be determined never to abandon under any extremity, but shall join hands and heart in the solemn pledge that is proposed to us, and declare to his Majesty that we know great exertions are wanting, that we are prepared to make them, and at all events determined to stand or fall by the laws, liberties, and religion of our country.

House of Commons: 10 November 1797

THE ONLY PEACE

I am as impatient for the hour of peace as that honourable gentleman, or as any man in this House, or in this country. I have as much reason as any man in this country can have for wishing to see peace return, when it is accompanied by security. But when I say I do not wish to see a nominal and delusive peace, it is because I value peace. I do not wish to have peace proclaimed for a moment in order to unnerve your strength, to slacken your efforts, to disband your force, to expose you to sudden and violent hostility, without your present means of defence or any effectual resistance. Should peace be proclaimed without security, you may indeed have a peace that is nominal and delusive.

I wish, for the benefit of Europe—I wish, for the benefit of the world at large, and for the honour of mankind as well as for the happiness of the people of France, although now your enemies, but who are objects of compassion—I wish, I say, that the present spirit of their rulers, and the principles they cherish, may be extinguished and that other principles may prevail there. But whether they do so or not is more immediately their concern than ours. It is not to any alteration in that country, but to the means of security in this, that I look with anxiety and care. I wish for peace, whether their principles be good or bad; but not to trust to their forbearance. Our defence should be in our own hands. In that we shall find the bulwark of our safety against France, whatever may be the pride, ambition, or animosity of that Power against us, and which it has manifested in almost all the periods of its history; and I agree with what has been lately said, that its tone was never higher than it is at present.

Certainly much depends upon the posture in which you converse of peace. What is the real foundation of the strength of a nation? Spirit, security, and conscious pride, that cannot stoop to dishonour. It comprehends a character that will neither offer nor receive an insult. Give me peace consistently with that principle, and I will not call it a peace nominal or delusive; and there is no man who will go farther than I will to obtain it. To anything dishonourable I will never submit; nor will this country ever submit to it, I trust. There can be no man who has an English heart within his bosom who can wish it; or can wish that you may, by an untimely diminution of your strength, expose yourselves to the renewal, with aggravated insults, of those evils which we have already had too much reason to deplore.

House of Commons: 5 December 1797

AT WAR WITH ARMED OPINIONS

We are not in arms against the opinions of the closet nor the speculations of the school. We are at war with armed opinions. We are at war with those opinions which the sword of audacious, unprincipled, and impious innovation seeks to propagate amidst the ruins of empires, the demolition of the altars of all religion, the destruction of every venerable and good and liberal institution, under whatever form of polity it has been raised: and this, in spite of the dissenting reason of men, in contempt of that lawful authority which, in the settled order, superior talents and superior virtues attain, crying out to them not to enter on holy ground, nor to pollute the stream of eternal justice, admonishing them of their danger, whilst like the genius of evil they mimic their voice, and, having succeeded in drawing upon them the ridicule of the vulgar, close their day of wickedness and savage triumph with the massacre and waste of whatever is amiable, learned, and pious in the districts they have overrun.

House of Commons: 7 June 1799

YOU ASK WHAT IS OUR AIM

In the course of debate, Tierney challenged Pitt to define the real object of the war: It is not the destruction of Jacobin principles; it may be the restoration of the House of Bourbon; but I would wish the right honourable gentleman in one sentence to state, if he can, without his *ifs* and *buts* and special pleading ambiguity, what this object is.

The observation with which the honourable gentleman concluded his speech, appears to me one of the strangest I ever heard advanced, and first challenges my attention. He defies me to state, in one sentence, what is the object of the war. I know not whether I can do it in one sentence; but in one word I can tell him that it is *security*: security against a danger, the greatest that ever threatened the world. It is security against a danger which never existed in any past period of society. It is security against a danger which in degree and extent was never equalled; against a danger which threatened all the nations of the earth; against a danger which has been resisted by all the nations of Europe, and resisted by none with so much success as by this nation, because by none has it been resisted so uniformly and with so much energy.

The honourable gentleman took another ground of argument, to which I shall now follow him. He said that the war could not be just, because it was carried on for the restoration of the House of Bourbon; and, secondly, that it could not be necessary, because we had refused to negotiate for peace when an opportunity for negotiation was offered us. As to the first proposition, that it cannot be just, because it is carried on for the restoration of the House of Bourbon, he has assumed the foundation of the argument, and has left no ground for controverting it, or for explanation, because he says that any attempt at explanation upon this subject is the mere ambiguous unintelligible language of *ifs* and *buts*, and of special pleading. Now I never had much liking to special pleading; and if ever I had any, it is by this time almost entirely gone. He has besides so abridged me in the use of particles, that though I am not particularly attached to the sound of an *if* or a *but*, I would be much obliged to the honourable gentleman if he would give me some others to supply their places. Is this, however, a light matter, that it should be treated in so light a manner? The restoration of the French monarchy, I will still tell the honourable gentleman, I consider as a most desirable object, because I think that it would afford the strongest and best security to this country and to Europe. *But* this object may not be attainable; and *if* it be not attainable, we must be satisfied with the best security which we can find independent of it. Peace is most desirable to this country; *but* negotiation may be attended with greater evils than could be counterbalanced by any benefits which would result from it. And *if* this be found to be the case; *if* it afford no prospect of security; *if* it threaten all the evils which we have been struggling to avert; *if* the prosecution of the war afford the prospect of attaining complete security; and *if* it may be prosecuted with increasing commerce, with increasing means, and with increasing prosperity, except what may result from the visitations of the seasons; then I say that it is prudent in us not to negotiate at the present moment. These are my *buts* and my *ifs*. This is my plea, and of no other do I wish to be tried by God and my country.

House of Commons: 17 February 1800

THE STAKE

The Treaty of Amiens, concluded 25 March 1802, brought a less than fourteen-months' peace; the war which had begun in 1793 against the armed opinions of the Revolution was resumed in 1803 against the military despotism of Buonaparte with its threat to the balance of power and the liberties of Europe. That despotism was not to be overthrown until twelve years later at Waterloo.

Englishmen must look to this as a species of contest from which, by the extraordinary favour of Divine Providence, we have been for a long series of years exempted. If we are now at length called upon to take our share in it, we must meet it with just gratitude for the exemptions we have hitherto enjoyed, and with a firm determination to support it with courage and resolution. We must show ourselves worthy, by our conduct on this occasion, of the happiness which we have hitherto enjoyed and which, by the blessing of God, I hope we shall continue to enjoy. We ought to have a due sense of the magnitude of the danger with which we are threatened; we ought to meet it in that temper of mind which produces just confidence, which neither despises nor dreads the enemy; and while on the one hand we accurately estimate the danger with which we are threatened at this awful crisis, we must recollect on the other hand what it is we have at stake, what it is we have to contend for. It is for our property, it is for our liberty, it is for our independence, nay, for our existence as a nation; it is for our character, it is for our very name as Englishmen, it is for everything dear and valuable to man on this side of the grave.

House of Commons: 22 July 1803

OUR EXULTATION

Let it be remembered that the times in which we live are not ordinary times. When we are called to encounter extraordinary and unprecedented dangers, we must lay our account to submitting to extraordinary and unprecedented difficulties. If we are called on to undergo great sacrifices, we must bear in mind the interesting objects which these sacrifices may enable us to defend and to secure. I need not remind the House that we are come to a new era in the history of nations; that we are called to struggle for the destiny, not of this country alone, but of the civilised world. We must remember that it is not for ourselves alone that we submit to unexampled privations. We have for ourselves the great duty of self-preservation to perform; but the duty of the people of England now is of a nobler and higher order. We are in the first place to provide for our security against an enemy whose malignity to this country knows no bounds: but this is not to close the views or the efforts of our exertion in so sacred a cause. Amid the wreck and the misery of nations, it is our just exultation that we have continued superior to all that ambition or that despotism could effect; and our still higher exultation ought to be, that we provide not only for our own safety, but hold out a prospect to nations now bending under the iron yoke of tyranny of what the exertions of a free people can effect, and that, at least in this corner of the world, the name of liberty is still revered, cherished, and sanctified.

House of Commons: 25 April 1804

MY COUNTRY

News of Trafalgar reached England on 2 November 1805. A week later, at the Lord Mayor's banquet, Nelson's victory was acclaimed, and Pitt's health, as The Saviour of Europe, *was proposed by the Lord Mayor. Pitt's brief reply was his last public speech. In the early hours of 23 January 1806 he died, his last words:* My country! How I leave my country!

I return you many thanks for the honour you have done me; bu
Europe is not to be saved by any single man. England has saved hersel
by her exertions, and will, as I trust, save Europe by her example.

Guildhall, London: 9 November 180.

HENRY ADDINGTON

afterwards first Viscount Sidmouth

1757 – 1844

> *Tory M.P., 1783–1805; Speaker of the House of*
> *Commons, 1789–1800; First Lord of the Trea-*
> *sury and Chancellor of the Exchequer, 1801–4;*
> *Lord President of the Council, 1805, 1806, and*
> *1812; Secretary of State for Home Affairs,*
> *1812–22*

AN HONEST ENGLISH PRIDE

On news of the Battle of Aboukir, which led to the evacuation of Egypt by
Napoleon's forces, Addington moved for a tribute of gratitude to the
memory of Sir Ralph Abercromby (who, in command of the British
troops, had been killed in battle); and to the brave officers and men by
whom the victories before Alexandria had been obtained.

WITHOUT indulging in any unreasonable exultation over the enemy
which at all times is unmanly, we may surely feel an honest English
pride at an event so glorious to this country. There is not a man who
must not feel that every foreign effort of the army adds to our domestic
strength and security. Let us, however, always call to mind that the
great object of every military exertion is the attainment of an honour
able and permanent peace; and let it be understood to be the fixed
purpose of government and of Parliament, as it ought to be of the
people, not to let any victory, however gratifying, induce us to demand
more of the enemy than is necessary for our security; and, on the
other hand, not to allow any amount of disaster to induce us to accept
of less. If such were ever to be the case, we should miserably underrate
the energies and powers of the country; we should render unprofitable
those victories which are its glory; we should diminish the best

esources of the country, consisting, as they do, in that unconquered
and unconquerable public spirit which, when wisely tempered, is the
source of all that is good and great; the pledge of public worth, the
guardian of private honour, and the surest preservative of the glory,
prosperity, and happiness of the country.

House of Commons: 18 May 1801

SANCTUARY FOR JUSTICE

*In 1807, in order to frustrate Napoleon's naval designs, the Danish fleet
had been seized at Copenhagen. At the same time, as a retaliatory
measure against the Napoleonic blockade, Danish merchant ships in
British ports had been detained; it was against this latter action that
Addington's protest was directed.*

The subject on which your lordships have to decide is now before
you: I have been impelled to submit it to your consideration by a sense
of justice towards individuals and by an ardent anxiety for the honour
of the country. The inducements to take this step, I feel to be the more
urgent on account of some new doctrines and opinions, unwarrantable,
I think, in themselves and most dangerous in their tendency, which
are only too likely to gain ground as they appear to be countenanced
by the declared sentiments and evident policy of the Government. It
seems to be imagined that the flagitious conduct of France, and the
consequences which have resulted from it, have absolved us from the
obligation of a strict adherence to those principles of good faith and
justice that have been heretofore considered as necessary to keep
together the great fabric of civil society; and further, that the existence
of a gigantic power, created and maintained by violence and fraud, not
only gives the right of resisting and retaliating upon that power by
means similar to those by which it has been established, but also
justifies us, with a view to our own immediate interests, in employing
the same weapons against unoffending states not parties in our
quarrel: in fine, that, for the purpose of enabling ourselves to maintain
an equal contest with France, and to counteract the danger arising
from her extended dominion, it has become necessary for us to follow
her example.

Against such doctrines I will ever protest, in the name of all that
has hitherto given dignity to our councils or lustre to public or private
character; of all that, by making this country the object of just and
general confidence, has contributed to establish its reputation and to
preserve and extend its influence and power. I well remember that, in
the year 1794, we were exhorted from the Throne, *to render our con-*

duct a contrast to that of our enemies: an exhortation worthy the high
quarter whence it came, and which made upon my mind a deep and
lasting impression. In proportion as our adversary extends his
systematic violation of all the principles of public law and natural
justice, it should be our object, by our conduct towards other states
to manifest more strongly, if possible, our determination to observe
and uphold them. He, indeed, can command nearly the whole population of the Continent: but the spirit by which it is to be actuated may
depend, in a great degree, upon ourselves. Let it therefore be our
endeavour to influence that spirit, by commanding universal confidence in our honour and good faith, as well as respect for our naval
and military power: let it appear that, at least in this country, justice
will find a sanctuary until the storm is overpast and the authority of
public law can again be diffused throughout the civilised world.

House of Lords: 17 May 1804

William Wyndham Grenville, afterwards

LORD GRENVILLE
1759 – 1834

*Whig M.P., 1782–90; Secretary of State for Ire-
land, 1782–83; Joint Paymaster-General of the
Forces, 1784–89; Vice-President of the Board
of Trade, 1786–89; Speaker of the House of
Commons, 1789; President of the Board of
Control for Indian Affairs, 1790–93; Secretary
of State for Foreign Affairs, 1791–1801; First
Lord of the Treasury, in Coalition Ministry,
1806–7*

RESOLUTION

*The peace negotiations of autumn 1797 were rendered abortive by im-
possible demands on the part of France. War was to be waged to the end.*
*   Two days after Grenville had spoken in the Lords, Pitt similarly
addressed the Commons (see page 72) and Grenville's resolution was
adopted by the Commons as that of both Houses.*

EVERY man in this assembly must now see that upon the issue of the
present contest depends, not only whether this country shall exist
any longer as an independent nation, but even exist as a nation

Every man must see that private and public happiness, the honour, the dignity, everything that is dear, even life itself, depend upon the issue of the struggle we have to maintain.

This too is the sentiment with which the public at large are inspired. They are convinced that everything they hold most dear depends upon their exertions to defend the honour and dignity of the country. They feel that a vigorous effort is required to secure that honourable peace which can alone maintain the sources of their happiness; that there is no safety without resistance, no hope but in courage and magnanimity.

I have the fullest confidence in the public spirit and the determined disposition of the people of this country. From you, my lords, I only ask that you will persevere in the sentiments you have expressed and in the conduct you have pursued. I ask you to carry to the foot of the Throne the declaration of this resolution, and that you will give a solemn pledge of your determination to perform the obligation you incur:

Most gracious Sovereign: We, your Majesty's most dutiful and loyal subjects, the lords Spiritual and Temporal, in Parliament assembled . . . feel the duty which we owe, in this great crisis, to God and to our country. Animated by the same sentiments which your Majesty has been pleased to declare to your people and to the world, attached to your Majesty by principle, duty, and gratitude, and sensible that it is only from courage and firmness that we can look either for present safety or permanent peace, we are determined to defend your Majesty's throne, the lives and properties of our fellow subjects, the government and Constitution of our country, and the honour and independence of the British Empire. We know that great exertions are necessary; we are prepared to make them: and placing our firm reliance on that Divine protection which has always hitherto been extended to us, we will support your Majesty to the utmost, and stand or fall with our religion, laws, and liberties.

House of Lords: 8 November 1797

CRIMES AND PUNISHMENTS

Before 1823, when Peel was successful in reforming the criminal law, men could be hanged for over two hundred offences, one of which was shoplifting to the amount of five shillings. When, in 1813, Sir Samuel Romilly made a second unsuccessful attempt to secure the repeal of this statute, both Grey and Grenville spoke in support of his measure.

I have endeavoured to lay before you my opinions on this important subject, as briefly as might be consistent with distinctness. It has always appeared to me that, although the prevention of crimes be

6

the grand object of all penal laws, yet, to some cases, capital punishments must, from the nature of things, be utterly inapplicable. I am convinced that when the offence and the penalty are equally disproportionate the enactment must be either nugatory, inasmuch as human nature will revolt from the application, or, if carried into execution, it must alienate the affections, pervert the judgment, and blunt the sensibility of the people. It must, in such case, either excite in them a feeling of horror and of disgust against their barbarous legislators, or it must tend to confound all those moral sentiments, all those just discriminations between the degrees of crime, which nature and education and experience impress upon the heart of every rational being. From observing the impaired effect which the punishment of death receives, if applied and enforced against minor offences, and from observing the still greater injury which the impunity of offenders and the uncertainty of punishment occasion to the community, where such punishment is ordained and not enforced, I cannot help drawing the inference that it will be much more beneficial to society, as well as more conformable to justice, to apply to minor offences some inferior punishment which may be rigorously enforced.

House of Lords: 2 April 1813

THE CONSTITUTION

It has been the work of ages; formed on no preconcerted plan of human policy; resting on no delusive principles of imagined right; the happy result of a long series of unforeseen and uncontrollable events; the produce of many jarring and contending elements, combined and harmonised by the tried experience, by the unwearied diligence, and by the traditional yet cautious wisdom of a legislature better adapted than any other yet known in the history of mankind, to promote the happiness of the community whose interests it administers. Such is our Government; the boast of Englishmen, the admiration and envy of the world! Such may it long continue!

House of Lords: 30 November 1819

ALGIERS

In 1816, Algiers, which had been the chief stronghold of the Barbary pirates for over three hundred years, was bombarded by a British squadron, under Lord Exmouth, assisted by Dutch men-of-war. The corsairs' fleet was burned and their captives freed.

Grenville's verses, according to his own note, were occasioned by some insulting remarks published in France on the result of the British expedition.

These hands toil-worn, these limbs by fetters galled,
These bodies scarred with many a servile blow,
These spirits wasted by disease and woe,
These Christian souls to miscreant rage enthrall'd,
What band of heroes now recalls to life?
Gives us again to hail our native shores,
And to each fond despairing heart restores
The long-lost parent, the long-widowed wife?
   O Britain! still to lawless power a foe,
Gainst faithless pirate armed, or blood-stained Gaul!
Vain is the taunt, which mocks thy lavish cost,
Thy thankless toil, thy blood poured out for all,
Thy laurels, gained in fight, in treaty lost:
Heaven still shall bless the hand, which lays the oppressor low!

                                Nugæ Metricæ: 1824

SPENCER PERCEVAL

1762–1812

---

*Tory M.P., 1796–1812; Leader of the Opposition
in the House of Commons, 1806–7; Chancellor of
the Exchequer, 1807–12; First Lord of the Treasury, 1809–12*

AERE PERENNIUS

WHEN one sees Tully, hunting amidst fragments and ruins, and
rubbish and weeds, for the lost tomb of Archimedes, one sees how
little the fame of man is indebted to his monuments and how much
more his monuments to his fame.

                 Crown and Rolls *Debating Society.* c. *1795.*

SPIRIT OF ENGLAND

*When the Opposition under Fox attacked the Ministry for resuming the
war with France after the ineffective Peace of Amiens, Perceval replied
with a spirited defence of the Ministry, and of his countrymen.*

  We are told that our country is in a state of siege; and how does it
appear? Why, in our fleets blockading the ports of the enemy! It is

said that we are degraded in the eyes of all Europe. I should be glad to
know the name of that nation which, amongst the surrounding
countries of humiliated Europe, can, from its proud and elevated
dignity, look down upon the present humble prostrate state of
degraded England! If indeed the powers of the Continent felt that
England, crouching with terror within her ports, felt alarm only for
her own safety, they might feel sentiments of contempt for her situation; but, viewing her as the only nation able to cope with the gigantic
power and ambition of France, which had humbled all the rest of
Europe, and the only rallying point to which Europe can turn for the
hopes of its emancipation, I am at a loss to conceive what is meant by
this degradation. I recollect indeed the vaunts of the enemy, the
threats of our annihilation, the *delenda est Carthago,* the assertion that
France and England could not both exist within the same hemisphere,
and the menaces of Buonaparte of our utter destruction; but we have
seen him afterwards crouch to a peace with this country, and purchase
that peace by surrendering the territories of his allies; and how does he
now menace our destruction? Why, by fleets that dare not quit his
shores beyond the protection of those batteries that line his coast from
Dunkirk to Boulogne.

House of ... ...ons: 23 April 1804

Robert Banks Jenkinson, later

Lord Hawkesbury and, afterwards, second

EARL   OF   LIVERPOOL

1770–1828

*Tory M.P., 1790–1803; Secretary of State for
Foreign Affairs, 1801–3, and 1809; Secretary of
State for Home Affairs and Leader of the House
of Lords, 1804–6 and 1807–9; Secretary of
State for War and the Colonies, 1809–12; First
Lord of the Treasury, 1812–27*

SINEWS OF WAR

*The greatest achievement of Pitt's first nine years of power was his
restoration of the national finances; his greatest problem then, to find*

*supplies necessary for the conduct of the war with France. In his budget
speech, 17 December 1796, the year in which Jenkinson's pamphlet was
issued, he asked for a total supply for the year of no less than £27,647,000.*

THE inconveniences to which individuals may be exposed in the
progress of this business, will depend very much on their readiness in
the first instance to come voluntarily to the assistance of the government; but to suppose that the bulk of the public will be backward on
such an occasion is indeed to libel their character. Are they so little
considerate of their reputation as to allow it to be said that, at a time
when we far exceed in commerce and resources all nations that ever
have existed in the world, we are unwilling to lend a part of our wealth
for the support of that Constitution to which we are indebted for it?
We are now in the fourth year of a contest, perhaps the most important in which any country was ever engaged. In the course of this
contest, great and important changes have taken place on the Continent, and we have commenced a negotiation, in which the arrangement
of the most discordant interests is necessarily involved and, in fact, the
settlement of Europe. The work is arduous indeed. To what extent we
may flatter ourselves with success, it would as yet be presumptuous to
decide; but there can be no doubt that our success will in a great
measure depend on the vigour of our exertions, and in our showing
ourselves prepared for either alternative of peace or war. The most
decided advocates for peace are as much called upon for zeal, on this
occasion, as the friends to the prosecution of the war; for, if by peace
is meant peace on secure and honourable terms, the experience of the
last twelve months must be sufficient to convince every unprejudiced
person what are the real dispositions of the French government; and
that every sympton of weakness which shall appear in this country,
will be a ground for more exorbitant demands on the part of our
enemies.

*Reflections on the Present State of the
Resources of the Country: 1796*

INTERVENTION JUSTIFIED

I am aware that objection has been made to the right of interference
with other governments. I cannot conceive on what grounds this
objection is founded. I cannot find any, either in the writings of statesmen, or in recorded treaties, or in the traditionary principles which
regulate the external policy of nations. The great principle of all
government, in its domestic or foreign relations, is self-defence, either

against direct attack, or against probable or premeditated danger. The balance of power if traced to its true source will be found to be derivable from this principle. Certainly it is to be allowed that in common cases the internal concerns of a particular nation ought not to be meddled with by another nation; but if these concerns affect the very existence of other nations, then it becomes a duty to interfere, for the same reasons which justified the interference of a third power between the quarrels of two contending countries. If a house is in flames, does either morality or law require that a man shall wait till his own house catches the conflagration, instead of rushing forward at once to extinguish the danger, even by the demolition of the house whence it issued?

The only question is—is the danger evident? Is there a necessity for self-defence? I will not say that a mere apprehension of danger is sufficient; the danger should be open and apparent; but, in the case of France, I would ask whether the danger has not been felt and experienced for twenty years? One would have thought, indeed, that the French Revolution formed of itself such a case as should be made an example of; that if no precedent had existed which could be applied, a precedent might in this instance have been created.

House of Lords: 10 February 1816

A SATISFACTION

This and the preceding extract are from a speech made on moving for an address to the Prince Regent on the Treaties of 1816, occasioned by the final overthrow of Napoleon at Waterloo, 18 June 1815.

In considering the whole of the great transactions under discussion, I feel the most sincere satisfaction, not only from a review of the object of the great alliance of which we formed a part, but from a reflection upon the result.

The object was to put down the principle of universal empire and military despotism which the power of France was so long employed to promote. I will ever maintain that a project of universal empire filled the mind and actuated the efforts of him against whom this country has so long been compelled to wage war. Views of aggrandizement, utterly inconsistent with the safety of Europe, were pursued by the French government. These were the views of Buonaparte and of that Revolution of which he was the champion; and I believe no rational being can now be found to entertain a doubt that the views of the revolutionists and their principal Captain were alike inconsistent with the general safety of Europe, and the establishment of real liberty.

The defeat of such views must therefore be grateful to every good man, while in the existing state of mental cultivation there is every prospect of the improvement and advance of rational liberty and the happiness of mankind.

Ibid

AN ENGLISH NEUTRALITY

Until we draw the sword, and throw away the scabbard, until we do decide that the policy of Great Britain is war, I trust that our neutrality will be real. If the justice of this be admitted as a general principle, and in ordinary cases, this country is especially bound to take care that its neutrality shall always be fair, honest, and effective; for never was there a country which had more abundant and frequent reason to complain of the faithless and hollow neutrality of other countries than Great Britain. There has not recently been a war in which we have been engaged, in which we have not had to maintain a contest with professed neutrals, as well as with professed belligerents. Having ourselves suffered so much in this respect, and having, very properly, held high language to these aggressors in disguise, I trust that we shall be ready to do unto others as we would they should do unto us; and that in this, as well as in any other contest between the Powers of Europe, to which we may not be parties, we shall set the example of a strict, impartial, and undeviating neutrality.

House of Lords: 14 April 1823

GEORGE CANNING

1770–1827

Tory M.P., 1794–1827; Under-Secretary of State for Foreign Affairs, 1796–1801; Paymaster-General, 1800; Treasurer of the Navy, 1804–6; Secretary of State for Foreign Affairs, 1807–9 and 1822–27; Ambassador Extraordinary to Lisbon, 1814; President of the Board of Control for Indian Affairs, 1816–21; First Lord of the Treasury and Chancellor of the Exchequer, in Coalition Ministry, 1827

PATRIOT OF THE WORLD

On 20 November 1797 appeared the first issue of The Anti-Jacobin or Weekly Examiner, *to be continued every Monday during the sitting of Parliament. It was promoted by Canning and his associates to support Pitt's government in the struggle against France and the Revolution and to counter Jacobin propaganda. The last issue, 9 July 1798, contains Canning's lines on the* New Morality, *a tremendous phillipic informed with his fierce hatred of the Jacobins and their ideas.*

With unsparing hand,
Oh, lash the vile impostures from the land!

First, stern Philanthropy: not she who dries
The orphan's tears, and wipes the widow's eyes;
Not she, who, sainted Charity her guide,
Of British bounty pours the annual tide:
But *French* Philanthropy; whose boundless mind
Glows with the general love of all mankind;
Philanthropy, beneath whose baneful sway
Each patriot passion sinks, and dies away.

Taught in her school to imbibe thy mawkish strain,
Condorcet, filter'd through the dregs of Paine,
Each pert adept disowns a Briton's part,
And plucks the name of England from his heart.

What, shall a name, a word, a sound control
The aspiring thought, and cramp the expansive soul?
Shall one half-peopled Island's rocky round
A love, that glows for all Creation, bound?
And social charities contract the plan
Framed for thy freedom, UNIVERSAL MAN?
No! through the extended globe his feelings run,
As broad and general as the unbounded sun.
No narrow bigot *he*; his reason'd view
Thy interests, England, ranks with thine, Peru!
France at our doors, *he* sees no danger nigh,
But heaves for Turkey's woes the impartial sigh;
A steady patriot of the World alone,
The friend of every country but his own.

New Morality. The Anti-Jacobin: 9 July 1798

THE CANDID FRIEND

Much may be said on both sides. Hark! I hear
A well-known voice that murmurs in my ear,
The voice of CANDOUR. Hail! most solemn sage,
Thou drivelling virtue of this moral age,
CANDOUR, which softens party's headlong rage.
CANDOUR, which spares its foes; nor e'er descends
With bigot zeal to combat for its friends.
CANDOUR, which loves in see-saw strain to tell
Of acting foolishly, but meaning well;
Too nice to praise by wholesale, or to blame,
Convinced that all men's motives are the same;
And finds, with keen discriminating sight,
Black's not so black; nor white so very white.

.   .   .   .

Give me the avow'd, the erect, the manly foe,
Bold I can meet, perhaps may turn his blow;
But of all plagues, good Heaven, thy wrath can send,
Save, save, oh! save me from the *Candid Friend*!

Ibid

THE DELIVERANCE OF EUROPE

WE have great and momentous objects in our view. The most complete
and desirable termination of the conquest would be the deliverance of

Europe. I am told, indeed, that there are persons who affect not to understand this phrase; who think there is something confused, something involved, something of studied ambiguity and concealment in it. I cannot undertake to answer for other gentlemen's powers of comprehension. The map of Europe is before them. I do not admire the intellect of the man who can look over that map without gathering some notion of what is meant by the deliverance of Europe. I do not envy the feelings of that man who can behold the sufferings of Switzerland and who derives from that sight no idea of what is meant by the deliverance of Europe. I do not envy the feelings of that man who can look without emotion at Italy—plundered, insulted, trampled upon, exhausted, covered with ridicule, and horror, and devastation; who can look at all this and be at a loss to guess what is meant by the deliverance of Europe? As little do I envy the feelings of that man who can view the people of the Netherlands driven into insurrection, and struggling for their freedom against the heavy hand of a merciless tyranny, without entertaining any suspicion of what may be the sense of the word deliverance. Does such a man contemplate Holland groaning under arbitrary oppressions and exactions? Does he turn his eyes to Spain trembling at the nod of a foreign master? And does the word deliverance still sound unintelligibly in his ear? Has he heard of the rescue and salvation of Naples by the appearance and the triumphs of the British fleet? Does he know that the monarchy of Naples maintains its existence at the sword's point? And is his understanding, and is his heart, still impenetrable to the sense and meaning of the deliverance of Europe?

House of Commons: 11 December 1798

PORTRAIT OF A DICTATOR

Once more to vex the troubled times,
Flush'd with the triumph of successful crimes,
With Rapine's ravening eagles wide unfurl'd,
Behold! the fell Disturber of the World,
Scourge of the weak, and terror of the strong,
With unresisted legions pours along,
O'er trembling States to stretch his iron reign,
And wrest by force what fraud has fail'd to gain!

Ulm and Trafalgar. 1806

Young as Buonaparte yet is, he has already outlived the love and veneration of mankind. His military successes may yet be admired: he may yet be flattered by those who hope to profit from his power, and obeyed by those who fear it. But his day of esteem and personal attachment has departed never to return. He cannot hope to regain the confidence which he has lost. Nor will he attempt to do so. Despairing of anything like the good opinion of mankind, he will become reckless of it. That which has hitherto been the passion of his mind will be now stimulated to madness. War, devastation, pestilence, and death, will henceforth mark every year of his life. Success will only encourage him to new projects; discomfiture, short of ruin, will only arouse and exasperate him. In his first career of glory, when his power was only budding, and his infant ambition a suitor to popularity, nature had perhaps given him the sympathies of other men, which virtue, which judgment might have cultivated. But they have been suppressed by the selfish pride and insatiable vanity which prosperity has cherished. He has accustomed himself to such strong stimuli of action, that the common sympathies and occurrences of life are like gentle breezes which cannot move his turbid soul. He has no children to attach him to domestic amusements. His wife is not his companion, but his sentinel. He is not fond of literary men, because he fears them. He recoils from familiarity and social intercourse. He likes to be the idol of a temple, sitting abstracted and exalted, seen and worshipped at an awful distance. He must make a chaos of human affairs to employ himself in settling them. He must have the storm and the thunder about him to interest himself and impress others with awe.

Can a character like this, after it has so completely developed itself, be of long duration? Are not the maledictions of mankind every hour ascending, and can the sword of terror intimidate for ever? A morose, hard-hearted, melancholy tyrant, projecting hourly new insults and injuries to mankind; new sacrifices of the interests, the feelings, and the happiness of his fellow-creatures, to his own solitary and boundless despotism; purposing only to carry on the endless wars of ambition under distant climes; making myriads shed their blood for foreign rapine, and incur the curse of annihilating innocent nations; he lives surrounded by the fears and the hatred of his species.

The Austrian State Papers. Quarterly Review: May 1809

MY OWN, MY NATIVE LAND

But let me not be mistaken. Do I, therefore, mean to contend that an absolute monarchy is better than a free government? God forbid! What I mean is this, that, in appreciating the comparative excellence of political institutions, in estimating the force of national spirit and the impulses of national feeling, it is idle to overlook the affections of nature. The order of nature could not subsist among mankind, if there were not an *instinctive* patriotism, I do not say unconnected with, but prior and paramount to, the desire of political amelioration. And surely it is not to be regretted that tyrants and conquerors should have learned, from the lessons of experience, that the first consideration suggested to the inhabitant of any country by a foreign invasion, is not whether the political constitution of the state be faultlessly perfect or not, but whether the altar at which he has worshipped—whether the home in which he has dwelt from his infancy—whether his wife and his children—whether the tombs of his forefathers—whether the palace of the sovereign under whom he was born, and to whom he therefore owes (or, if it must be so stated, fancies that he therefore owes) allegiance—shall be abandoned to violence and profanation.

That, in the infancy of the French Revolution, many nations in Europe were, unfortunately, led to believe and to act upon a different persuasion, is undoubtedly true; that whole countries were overrun by reforming conquerors, and flattered themselves with being prose-lytes till they found themselves victims. Even in this country, there have been times when we have been called upon to consider whether there was not something at home which must be mended before we could hope to repel a foreign invader with success.

It is fortunate for the world that this question should have been tried to a disadvantage; that it should have been tried in countries where no man in his senses will say that the frame of political society is such as, according to the most moderate principles of regulated freedom, it ought to be; where, I will venture to say, without hazard-ing the imputation of being myself a visionary reformer, political society is not such as, after the successes of this war, and from the happy contagion of the example of Great Britain, it is sure gradually to become. It is fortunate for the world that this question should have been tried on its own merits; that, after twenty years of controversy, we should be authorised, by undoubted results, to revert to nature and to truth, and to disentangle the genuine feelings of the heart from the obstructions which a cold, presumptuous, generalising philosophy had wound around them.

One of the most delightful poets of this country, in describing the various proportions of natural blessings and advantages dispensed by Providence to the various nations of Europe, turns from the luxuriant plains and cloudless skies of Italy to the rugged mountains of Switzerland, and inquires whether there also, in those barren and stormy regions, the *patriot passion* is found equally imprinted on the

heart? He decides the question truly in the affirmative; and he says of
the inhabitant of those bleak wilds:

> *Dear is that shed to which his soul conforms,*
> *And dear that hill which lifts him to the storms;*
> *And, as a child, when scaring sounds molest,*
> *Clings close and closer to the mother's breast,*
> *So the loud torrent and the whirlwind's roar,*
> *But bind him to his native mountains more.*

What Goldsmith thus beautifully applied to the physical varieties
of soil and climate has been found no less true with respect to political
institutions. A sober desire of improvement, a rational endeavour to
redress error, and to correct imperfection in the political frame of
human society, are not only natural, but laudable in man. But it is
well that it should have been shown, by irrefragable proof, that these
sentiments, even where most strongly and most justly felt, supersede
not that devotion to native soil which is the foundation of national
independence. And it is right that it should be understood and remembered, that the spirit of national independence alone, aroused where it
had slumbered, enlightened where it had been deluded, and kindled
into enthusiasm by the insults and outrages of an all-grasping invader,
has been found sufficient, without internal changes and compromises
of sovereigns or governments with their people—without relaxation
of allegiance and adjurations of authority, to animate, as with one
pervading soul, the different nations of the Continent; to combine, as
into one congenial mass, their various feelings, passions, prejudices;
to direct these concentrated energies with one impulse against the
common tyrant; and to shake (and, may we not hope? to overthrow)
the *Babel* of his iniquitous power.

Liverpool: 10 January 1814

THE METEOR FLAG OF ENGLAND

The history of Europe for the last twenty-five years, is something
like this. A power went forth, animated with the spirit of evil, to
overturn every community of the civilised world. Before this dreadful
assailant, empires, and monarchies, and republics bowed: some were
crushed to the earth, and some bought their safety by compromise. In
the midst of this wide-spread ruin, among tottering columns and
falling edifices, one fabric alone stood erect and braved the storm; and
not only provided for its own internal security, but sent forth, at every
portal, assistance to its weaker neighbours. On this edifice floated

that ensign, a signal of rallying to the combatant, and of shelter to the
fallen.

Liverpool: 29 June 1818

SUCH IS ENGLAND HERSELF

*When, in November 1823, Canning received the Freedom of Plymouth,
the sight of the ships riding at anchor above the town inspired him to one
of the classic flights of English oratory.*

The end which I confess I have always had in view, and which
appears to me the legitimate object of pursuit to a British statesman,
I can describe in one word. The language of modern philosophy is
wisely and diffusely benevolent; it professes the perfection of our
species a^ ᵗ ᵗ ᵗ ᵗ ᵗ ᵗ ue amelioration of the lot of all mankind. I hope that my
heart beats as high for the general interest of humanity—I hope that
I have as friendly a disposition towards other nations of the earth as
any one who vaunts his philanthropy most highly; but I am contented
to confess that in the conduct of political affairs, the grand object of
my contemplation is the interest of England.

Not that the interest of England is an interest which stands isolated
and alone. The situation which she holds forbids an exclusive selfishness; her prosperity must contribute to the prosperity of other nations
and her stability to the safety of the world. But, intimately connected
as we are with the system of Europe, it does not follow that we are
therefore called upon to mix ourselves on every occasion, with a
restless and meddling activity, in the concerns of the nations which
surround us. It is upon a just balance of conflicting duties and of rival,
but sometimes incompatible, advantages that a government must
judge when to put forth its strength and when to husband it for
occasions yet to come.

Our ultimate object must be the peace of the world. That object may
sometimes be best attained by prompt exertions, sometimes by
abstinence from interposition in contests which we cannot prevent.
But let it not be said that we cultivate peace, either because we fear, or
because we are unprepared for war. The resources created by peace
are means of war. In cherishing these resources, we but accumulate
those means. Our present repose is no more proof of inability to act
than the state of inertness and inactivity in which I have seen those
mighty masses that float in the waters above your town is a proof that
they are devoid of strength and incapable of being fitted out for action.
You well know how soon one of those stupendous masses, now
reposing on their shadows in perfect stillness, how soon, upon any

call of patriotism or of necessity, it would assume the likeness of an animated thing, instinct with life and motion, how soon it would ruffle, as it were, its swelling plumage, how quickly it would put forth all its beauty and its bravery, collect its scattered elements of strength, and awaken its dormant thunder. Such as is one of those magnificent machines when springing from inaction into a display of its might, such is England herself while, apparently passive and motionless she silently concentrates the power to be put forth on an adequate occasion.

THE RULER OF THE WINDS

In December 1826 the Portuguese constitutionalists appealed to Great Britain, under treaty obligations, for assistance against hostile aggression from Spain, who had declared herself in support of the absolutist reactionaries. Canning, aware of all the implications, confirmed the facts, then acted promptly: It was only on last Friday night, *he told Parliament,* that the precise information arrived. On Saturday His Majesty's confidential servants came to a decision. On Sunday that decision received the sanction of His Majesty. On Monday it was communicated to both Houses of Parliament, and this day, at the hour in which I have the honour of addressing you, the troops are on their march for embarkation. *Canning's vigour saved the situation; the Spaniards withdrew, and Portuguese liberty was secured.*

I set out with saying that there were reasons which entirely satisfied my judgment that nothing short of a point of national faith or national honour would justify at the present moment any voluntary approximation to the possibility of war. Let me be understood, however, as not meaning to say that I dread war in a good cause (and in no other may it be the lot of this country ever to engage!) from a distrust of the strength of the country to commence it, or of her resources to maintain it. I dread it, indeed, but upon far other grounds; I dread it from an apprehension of the tremendous consequences which might arise from any hostilities in which we might now be engaged. Some years ago, in the discussion of the negotiations respecting the French war against Spain, I took the liberty of adverting to this topic. I then stated that the position of this country in the present state of the world was one of neutrality, not only between contending nations, but between conflicting principles; and that it was by neutrality alone that we could maintain that balance, the preservation of which I believed to be essential to the welfare of mankind. I then said that I feared that the next war which should be kindled in Europe would be a war not so much of armies as of opinions. Not four years have elapsed, and

behold my apprehension realised! It is, to be sure, within narrow
limits that this war of opinion is at present confined: but it is a war of
opinion, that Spain (whether as Government or as nation) is now
waging against Portugal; it is a war which has commenced in hatred of
the new institutions of Portugal. How long is it reasonable to expect
that Portugal will abstain from retaliation? If into that war this
country shall be compelled to enter, we shall enter into it with a
sincere and anxious desire to mitigate rather than exasperate—and to
mingle only in the conflict of arms, not in the more fatal conflict of
opinions. But I much fear that this country (however earnestly she
may endeavour to avoid it) could not, in such case, avoid seeing
ranked under her banners all the restless and dissatisfied of any
nation with which she might come in conflict. It is the contemplation
of this new power in any future war which excites my most anxious
apprehension. It is one thing to have a giant's strength, but it would be
another to use it like a giant. The consciousness of such strength is,
undoubtedly, a source ˆconfidence and security; but in the situation
in which this country stands, our business is not to seek opportunities
of displaying it, but to content ourselves with letting the professors of
violent and exaggerated doctrines on both sides feel that it is not their
interest to convert an umpire into an adversary. The situation of
England, amidst the struggle of political opinions which agitates more
or less sensibly different countries of the world, may be compared to
that of the Ruler of the Winds, as described by the poet:

> *Celsa sedet Aeolus arce,*
> *Sceptra tenens; mollitque animos et temperat iras;*
> *Ni faciat, maria ac terras coelumque profundum*
> *Quippe ferant rapidi secum verrantque per auras.*

The consequence of letting loose the passions at present chained and
confined would be to produce a scene of desolation which no man can
contemplate without horror; and I should not sleep easy on my couch
if I were conscious that I had contributed to precipitate it by a single
moment.

This, then, is the reason—a reason very different from fear—the
reverse of a consciousness of disability—why I dread the recurrence of
hostilities in any part of Europe; why I would bear much, and would
forbear long; why I would put up with almost anything that did not
touch national faith and national honour, rather than let slip the furies
of war, the leash of which we hold in our hands—not knowing whom
they may reach, or how far their ravages may be carried. Such is the
love of peace which the British Government acknowledges; and such

the necessity for peace which the circumstances of the world inculcate.
I will push these topics no farther.

I return, in conclusion, to the object of the address. Let us fly to the
aid of Portugal, by whomsoever attacked, because it is our duty to do
so; and let us cease our interference where that duty ends. We go to
Portugal, not to rule, not to dictate, not to prescribe constitutions, but
to defend and to preserve the independence of an ally. We go to plant
the standard of England on the well-known heights of Lisbon. Where
that standard is planted, foreign dominion shall not come.

House of Commons: 12 December 1826

Frederick John Robinson, later

VISCOUNT GODERICH

and, afterwards, first Earl of Ripon

1782 – 1859

---

*Tory M.P., 1806–27; Under-Secretary of State
for the Colonies, 1809; Junior Lord of the Admiralty, 1810; Vice-President of the Board of Trade
and Plantations, 1812; Joint Paymaster-General
of the Forces, 1813–17; President of the Board of
Trade, 1818–19 and 1841; Treasurer of the Navy,
1819; Chancellor of the Exchequer, 1823–27;
Secretary of State for War and the Colonies, 1827
and 1830–33; Commissioner for Indian Affairs,
and Leader of the House of Lords, 1827; First
Lord of the Treasury, in Coalition Ministry,
1827–28; President of the Board of Control for
Indian Affairs, 1843–46*

ENGLAND CAME

*In 1808 the Spanish people, looking to English aid, rose in revolt against
the dictatorship of Buonaparte. It was the beginning of the slow overthrow which was to culminate at Toulouse and Waterloo. When Robinson
made his speech news had not yet arrived of Moore's three-days' old
victory at Coruna.*

WHOEVER looks to the situation of affairs in Spain, and the nature of
7

those occurrences that led to the connection with our own, will agree
with the propriety of reducing into practical use the excellent maxim
that vigorous war leads most directly to safe and honourable peace.
Our connection with Spain was formed for the purpose of enabling her
to resist the tyrannous usurpation of France, the injustice of which is
only equalled by the perfidy of the means employed to accomplish that
detestable design. It is indeed difficult to determine which to reprobate
most. I know not in what language to describe the fraud and falsehood
employed by Buonaparte to subdue a people to whom he was united
in the closest bonds of alliance, and who had reposed an ill-founded
confidence in him. In the Declaration he has published, he has told
them that if they refuse to accept his brother Joseph for their king he
will cut out a new kingdom for him, place the crown of Spain upon
his own head, and punish those whom he dares to designate as the
wicked. It would be well for the yet unconquered countries in Europe
(of which I am sorry to say there are now but few) to attend to the first
part of this Declaration, as there are doubtless some to be found from
those territories this embryo kingdom might be formed; and it would
be well for Great Britain to look to the latter part, as she is assuredly
included among the wicked whom the tyrant presumptuously pretends
he has a divine commission to punish.

Some few of my countrymen may think the cause of freedom in
Spain less pure because that country did not agree or participate in
hailing the dawn of liberty which was once thought to illumine the
horizon of France. But surely no sight can be more grand or animating
than such a people, whose character for ages has been famed for so
many virtues and noble qualities, rising against foreign injustice,
tyranny and oppression, resolved to be independent or to perish in the
struggle. Can we wonder at the sympathy which the people of this
country feel, at the energy with which they come forward, and at the
glowing participation of sentiment which they express in a cause so
like their own. Speculative men may differ on points relating to
internal reforms and regulations; but it is evident that the Spanish
people do not think the return of a native king to his legal throne
incompatible with national reform. The cause of Spain has lost none of
its first interest, and Britain is still bound to extend her mighty arm to
save and to succour.

House of Commons: 19 January 1809

ENGLAND: PATRON OF THE ARTS

*The Austrian loan provided a Treasury windfall which Robinson used for
the building of churches, the restoration of Windsor Castle, and, not*

least, the founding of the National Gallery. The purchase of the Anger-
stein collection was followed by the bequests Robinson anticipated and
the present buildings in Trafalgar Square were opened in 1834.

The reference to the king's library is to George IV's presentation to the
British Museum of the magnificent library of George III, the housing of
which inaugurated the Museum rebuilding.

In the course of the last session, during the discussions which took
place on the munificent gift of the king's library, and on the building
which was to be erected for its reception, I think a very general feeling
prevailed in the House that, under the present improving circumstances of the country, we ought not to be niggardly in matters that
regarded the promotion of the arts. As a mere question of money, I do
not say that objections may not be urged against any such proposition
as that which I am about to submit. But taking a more enlarged view
of the subject, looking at the intimate connection of the arts with all
that adorns and ennobles man's nature, it appears to me to be consistent with the true dignity of a great nation, and with the liberal spirit
of a free people, to give a munificent encouragement to the support
and promotion of the fine arts. There being a fund out of which such
an object might be accomplished without any immediate pressure on
the resources of the country, his Majesty's government felt, when a
short time ago an opportunity presented itself of procuring by
purchase an splendid collection of valuable pictures, that many
motives of a high and liberal policy invited us to take advantage of the
opportunity, for the purpose of laying the foundation of a national
gallery of works of art. Accordingly, a negotiation was opened with
the representatives of the late Mr. Angerstein, which terminated in an
agreement for the sale to the public of these pictures for the sum of
£57,000. I have already stated the principles on which his Majesty's
government recommended this grant; and I have not the smallest
doubt that, if a National Gallery had existed in former times, the
liberality of individuals would long ere this have furnished it with as
fine and beautiful specimens of art as can be found in any part of the
world. Should this prove to be the case, I am sanguine in my hope that
the result will be the establishment of a splendid gallery of works of
art worthy of the nation—a gallery on the ornaments of which every
Englishman who paces it may gaze with the proud satisfaction of
reflecting that they are neither the rifled treasures of plundered palaces
nor the unhallowed spoils of violated altars.

House of Commons: 28 February 1824

AND THUS SPAKE ON

This reminiscence of Coleridge's splendid talk is part of a long reference to the poet, who had died in the previous July.

It was not alone his glistening eye and animated features—radiant as they were with the glow of poetic inspiration; nor was it his silver tones, or his varied and expressive elocution, in which the enchantment of his discourse consisted. Equally severe in logical sequence, and as bright· with the changing hues of poetry, but in form less widely discursive, and in style more expressive and simple, his best conversational essays were perhaps in every respect superior to his written works: often has it occurred to the favoured hearer to sigh involuntarily at the close of his flowing periods for some spell that could impart permanency to the words he had been listening to, in the full ~·**h that a book would have been the result to which no rival, in wisdom and eloquence united, exists among the rich products of genius.

And the hearers of Coleridge were many—not at once, but many in succession: it was rare if a visitor came and found Memnon silent; there was no need to wait for the rising of the sun, for the rays which woke that tuneful tongue arose from within and were at all times obedient to the call of friendship or the inquiry of the lover of truth. Hence, few persons of literary habits and taste, resident in London, or visitors, were wholly strangers to Coleridge's wonderful powers of discourse. The young and ingenuous were always greeted with a peculiar welcome. Not a few of those—the best and purest of the rising intellects of the age—were his affectionate pupils; their minds remain indelibly impressed and moulded by him; and thus the bread which day to day he cast upon the waters will be found after many days; transferred by them into the living world of thought and literature, the seed of his wisdom is already scattered abroad, and will yet bear fruit in the busy scenes of social and active life.

                    Presidential Address, *Royal Society of Literature:*
                                                    30 April 1835

Arthur Wellesley, afterwards first

DUKE OF WELLINGTON

1769–1852

Tory M.P., 1790–95 and 1806–9; Chief Secretary for Ireland, 1807–9; Master-General of the Ordnance, with seat in the Cabinet, 1818–27; First Lord of the Treasury, 1828–30 and 1834; Secretary of State for Foreign Affairs, 1834–35; Leader of Opposition in the House of Lords, 1835–41; Minister without Portfolio, 1841–46

When, once rising to reply to a toast, Wellington began: I want words to express—*it was the Prince Regent who interrupted with:* My dear fellow, we know your actions, and we will excuse you your words. *Wellington was no orator; Sir Walter Scott described his Parliamentary efforts as* slicing the argument into two or three parts and helping himself to the best. *He is therefore mainly represented here by extracts from his despatches and campaign letters.*

ARMY POLITICS

IT occurs to me that there is much party in the army in your quarter; this must be put an end to. And there is only one mode of effecting this, and that is for the Commanding Officer to be of no side excepting that of the public, to employ indiscriminately those who can best serve the public, be they who they may or in whatever service. The consequence will be that the service will go on; all parties will join in forwarding it and in respecting him; there will be an end to their petty disputes about trifles; and the Commanding Officer will be at the head of an army instead of a party.

To Colonel Murray. Assye: 16 September 1803

BRITISH GOOD FAITH

I would sacrifice Gwalior, or every portion of India, ten times over, in order to preserve our credit for scrupulous good faith, and the advantages and honour we gained by the late war and the peace: and we must not fritter them away in arguments, drawn from overstrained

101

principles of the laws of nations, which are not understood in this country. What brought me through many difficulties in the war, and the negotiations for peace? The British good faith, and nothing else.

To Major Malcolm. Bombay: 17 March 1804

SOLDIER: SAILOR

This account, taken from the Croker Papers, *was given to Croker 1 October 1834. The meeting it describes took place in September 1805 within a few weeks of Trafalgar.*

Lord Nelson was, in different circumstances, two quite different men, as I myself can vouch, though I only saw him once in my life, and for, perhaps, an hour. It was soon after I returned from India. I went to the Colonial Office in Downing Street, and there I was shown into the little waiting-room on the right hand, where I found, also waiting to see the Secretary of State, a gentleman, whom, from his likeness to his pictures and the loss of an arm, I immediately recognised as Lord Nelson. He could not know who I was, but he entered at once into conversation with me, if I can call it conversation, for it was almost all on his side and all about himself, and in, really, a style so vain and so silly as to surprise and almost disgust me. I suppose something that I happened to say may have made him guess that I was somebody, and he went out of the room for a moment, I have no doubt to ask the office-keeper who I was, for when he came back he was altogether a different man, both in manner and matter. All that I had thought a charlatan style had vanished, and he talked of the state of this country, and of the aspect and probability of affairs on the Continent with a good sense, and a knowledge of subjects at home and abroad that surprised me equally and more agreeably than the first part of our interview had done; in fact he talked like an officer and a statesman. The Secretary of State kept us long waiting, and certainly, for the last half of three-quarters of an hour, I don't know that I ever had a conversation that interested me more. Now, if the Secretary of State had been punctual and admitted Lord Nelson in the first quarter of an hour, I should have had the same impression of a light and trivial character that other people have had, but luckily I saw enough to be satisfied that he was really a very superior man; but certainly a more sudden and complete metamorphosis I never saw.

TENACITY

I conceive that the honour and interests of the country require that we should hold our ground here as long as possible; and, please God,

I will maintain it as long as I can; and I will neither endeavour to shift from my own shoulders on those of the ministers the responsibility of the failure by calling for means which I know they cannot give, and which, perhaps, would not add materially to the facility for attaining our object; nor will I give to the ministers, who are not strong, and who must feel the delicacy of their own situation, an excuse for withdrawing the army from a position which, in my opinion, the honour and interest of the country require they should maintain as long as possible. I think that if the Portuguese do their duty, I shall have enough to maintain it; if they do not, nothing that Great Britain can afford can save the country; and if from that cause I fail in saving it, and am obliged to go, I shall be able to carry away the British army.

To the Right Hon. J. Villiers. Visien: 14 January 1810

SCISSORS

This extract, from a letter written from the Peninsular, has a double interest. In May 1942, General Auckinleck caused copies of it to be sent to all his headquarters officers in the Middle East.

My Lord, if I attempted to answer the mass of futile correspondence that surrounds me, I should be debarred from all serious business of campaigning.

I must remind your lordship—for the last time—that so long as I retain an independent position, I shall see to it that no officer under my command is debarred, by attending to the futile drivelling of mere quill-driving in your lordship's office, from attending to his first duty —which is, as always, to train the private men under his command that they may, without question, beat any force opposed to them in the field.

To Lord Bradford, Secretary of State for War. 1810

SAVE ALL OR NOTHING

Fired by the example of Spain and Portugal, the rest of conquered Europe was stirring in revolt against Napoleonic tyranny. Wellington set such store by the advice in this and a similar letter to Baron Constant that, more than a quarter-of-a-century later, he told Stanhope: I should wish nothing better than to have those letters inscribed upon my tomb.

I have long considered it probable that even *we* should witness a general resistance throughout Europe to the fraudulent and disgusting tyranny of Buonaparte created by the example of what has passed in Spain and Portugal; and that *we* should be actors and advisers in these scenes; and I have reflected frequently upon the measures which should be pursued to give a chance of success.

Those who embark upon projects of this description should be made to understand, or to act as if they understood, that having once drawn the sword they must not return it till they shall have completely accomplished their object. They must be prepared and must be forced to make all sacrifices to the cause. Submission to military discipline and order is a matter of course; but when a nation determines to resist the authority, and to shake off the Government of Buonaparte, they must be prepared and forced to sacrifice the luxuries and comforts of life, and to risk all in a contest which, it should be clearly understood before it is undertaken, has for its objects to save all or nothing.

The first measure for a country to adopt is to form an army and to raise a revenue from the people to defray the expense of the army. Above all, to form a Government of such strength as that army and people can be forced by it to perform their duty. This is the rock upon which Spain has split, and all our measures in any other country which should afford hopes of resistance to Buonaparte should be directed to avoid it. The enthusiasm of the people is very fine and looks well in print, but I have never known it produce anything but confusion. In France, what was called enthusiasm, was power and tyranny, acting through the medium of popular societies, which have ended by overturning Europe, and establishing the most powerful and dreadful tyranny that ever existed. In Spain, the enthusiasm of the people spent itself in *Vivas* and vain-boasting. The notion of its existence prevented even the attempt to discipline the armies; and its existence has been alleged ever since as the excuse for the rank ignorance of the officers, and the indiscipline and constant misbehaviour of the troops.

I therefore earnestly recommend you, wherever you go, to trust nothing to the enthusiasm of the people. Give them a strong and a just and, if possible, a good Government; but above all, a strong one, which shall enforce them to do their duty by themselves and their country; and let measures of finance to support an army go hand in hand with measures to raise it.

> *To Lieutenant-General Lord William Bentinck. Freneda:*
> *24 December 1811*

WATERLOO

Lady Burghesh induced the Duke to give her a full account of the time and mode of his writing that despatch. He had begun it at Waterloo very early on the morning of the 19th, very soon after Dr. Hume had come to him with the news of Gordon's death and other

osses; but when he received the further account of Ponsonby having
fallen, he broke off—feeling that he could not bring himself to write
any more then—and did not go on with his despatch till after he had
rode into Brussels later the same morning.

I observed that this account exactly tallies with the appearance of
the original draft of that despatch which I have seen amongst the
Duke's papers. The first date written upon it is Waterloo, but that is
dashed out and the date Bruxelles substituted.

Conversations with the Duke of Wellington: Earl Stanhope

The position which I took up in front of Waterloo crossed the
highroads from Charleroi and Nivelles, and had its right thrown back
to a ravine near Merke Braine, which was occupied, and its left
extended to a height above the hamlet Ter la Haye, which was likewise
occupied. In front of the right centre, and near the Nivelles road, we
occupied the house and gardens of Hougoumont, which covered the
return of that flank; and in front of the left centre we occupied the
farm of La Haye Sainte. By our left we communicated with Marshal
Prince Blücher at Wavre, through Ohain; and the Marshal had
promised me that, in case we should be attacked, he would support
me with one or more corps, as might be necessary.

The enemy collected his army, with the exception of the 3rd Corps,
which had been sent to observe Marshal Blücher, on a range of heights
in our front, in the course of the night of the 17th and yesterday
morning, and at about ten o'clock he commenced a furious attack
upon our post at Hougoumont. I had occupied that post with a
detachment from General Byng's brigade of Guards, which was in
position in its rear; and it was for some time under the command of
Lieutenant-Colonel Macdonell, and afterwards of Colonel Home; and
I am happy to add that it was maintained throughout the day with the
utmost gallantry by these brave troops, notwithstanding the repeated
efforts of large bodies of the enemy to obtain possession of it.

This attack upon the right of our centre was accompanied by a very
heavy cannonade upon our whole line, which was destined to support
the repeated attacks of cavalry and infantry, occasionally mixed, but
sometimes separate, which were made upon it. In one of these the
enemy carried the farmhouse of La Haye Sainte, as the detachment of
the light battalion of the German Legion, which occupied it, had
expended all its ammunition; and the enemy occupied the only communication there was with them.

The enemy repeatedly charged our infantry with his cavalry, but
these attacks were uniformly unsuccessful; and they afforded oppor-

tunities to our cavalry to charge, in one of which Lord E. Somerset
brigade, consisting of the Life Guards, the Royal Horse Guards, an
1st Dragoon Guards, highly distinguished themselves, as did that o
Major-General Sir William Ponsonby, having taken many prisoner
and an eagle.

These attacks were repeated till about seven in the evening, when th
enemy made a desperate effort with cavalry and infantry, supported b
the fire of artillery, to force our left centre, near the farm of La Hay
Sainte, which after a severe contest was defeated; and, having observe
that the troops retired from this attack in great confusion, and that th
march of General Bülow's corps, by Frischermont upon Planchenoi
and La Belle Alliance, had begun to take effect, and as I could perceiv
the fire of his cannon, and as Marshal Prince Blücher had joined i
person with a corps of his army to the left of our line by Ohain,
determined to attack the enemy, and immediately advanced the whol
line of infantry, supported by the cavalry and artillery. The attac
succeeded in every point: the enemy was forced from his positions o
the heights, and fled in the utmost confusion, leaving behind him, a
far as I could judge, one hundred and fifty pieces of cannon, with thei
ammunition, which fell into our hands.

I continued the pursuit till long after dark, and then discontinued i
only on account of the fatigue of our troops, who had been engage
during twelve hours, and because I found myself on the same roa
with Marshal Blücher, who assured me of his intention to follow th
enemy throughout the night. He has sent me word this morning tha
he had taken sixty pieces of cannon belonging to the Imperial Guard
and several carriages, baggage, etc., belonging to Buonaparte i
Genappe.

I propose to move this morning upon Nivelles, and not to dis
continue my operations.

Despatch to Lord Bathurst, Secretary of State for War.
Waterloo: 19 June 181.

*Uxbridge, to whom the letter from which this is taken was addressed
rode with Wellington at Waterloo. A cannon-shot passed over the
withers of the Duke's horse and took off his companion's leg.* By God!
I've lost my leg! *cried Uxbridge.* Have you, by God! *was all the Duke's
reply.*

I may be wrong, but my opinion is, that we have given Napoleon
his death-blow; from all I hear his army is totally destroyed, the men
are deserting in parties, even the Generals are withdrawing from him.

The infantry throw away their arms, and the cavalry and artillery sell their horses to the people of the country and desert to their homes. Allowing for much exaggeration in this account, and knowing that Buonaparte can still collect, in addition to what he has brought back with him, the 5th Corps d'armée, under Rapp, which is near Strasbourg, and the 3rd Corps, which was at Wavre during the battle, and has not suffered so much as the others, and probably some troops from La Vendée, I am still of opinion that he can make no head against us, *qu'il n'a qu'a se pendre.*

To Lieutenant-General the Earl of Uxbridge. Le Cateau:
23 June 1815

You will have heard of our battle of the 18th. Never did I see such a pounding match. Both were what the boxers call gluttons. Napoleon did not manœuvre at all. He just moved forward in the old style, in columns, and was driven off in the old style. The only difference was, that he mixed cavalry with his infantry, and supported both with an enormous quantity of artillery.

I had the infantry for some time in squares, and we had the French cavalry walking about us as if they had been our own. I never saw the British infantry behave so well.

Boney is now off, I believe, to Rochefort, to go to America. The army, about 40,000 or 50,000, are in Paris. Blücher on the left of the Seine, and I with my right in front of St. Denis, and the left upon the Bois de Bondy. They have fortified St. Denis and Montmartre very strongly. The Canal de l'Ourcq is filled with water, and they have a parapet and batteries on the bank; so that I do not believe we can attack this line. However, I will see.

To Marshal Lord Beresford. Gonesse: 2 July 1815

ADVICE TO AN HISTORIAN

I have received your letter of the 2nd, regarding the Battle of Waterloo. The object which you propose to yourself is very difficult of attainment, and, if really attained, is not a little invidious. The history of a battle is not unlike the history of a ball. Some individuals may recollect all the little events of which the great result is the battle won or lost; but no individual can recollect the order in which, or the exact moment at which, they occurred, which makes all the difference as to their value or importance.

Then the faults or the misbehaviour of some gave occasion for the distinction of others, and perhaps were the cause of material losses;

and you cannot write a true history of a battle without including the faults and misbehaviour of part at least of those engaged.

Believe me that every man you see in a military uniform is not a hero; and that, although in the account given of a general action, such as that of Waterloo, many instances of individual heroism must be passed over unrelated, it is better for the general interests to leave those parts of the story untold, than to tell the whole truth.

If, however, you should still think it right to turn your attention to this subject, I am most ready to give you every assistance and information in my power.

To Sir Walter Scott. Paris: 8 August 1815

These are answers to all your queries; but remember I recommend you to leave the Battle of Waterloo as it is.

To the same. Paris: 17 August 1815

WELLINGTONIANA

A great country cannot wage a little war.

Napoleon was not a personality, but a principle.

A democracy, if a real democracy could be formed, would be the strongest of all governments; but then, remember, the strongest is the most tyrannical.

When one is strongly intent on an object, common sense will usually direct one to the right means.

The Lord's Prayer contains the sum total of religion and morals.

Perhaps there is no man existing who would like to meet me on the field of battle; in that line I am superior. But when the war is over and the troops disbanded, what is your great general more than anybody else. I am necessarily inferior to every man in his own line, though I may excel him in others. I cannot saw and plane like a carpenter, or make shoes like a shoemaker, or understand cultivation like a farmer. Each of these, on his own ground, meets me on terms of superiority.

There is little or nothing in this life worth living for, but we can all of us go straightforward and do our duty.

It is a sort of privilege of modern Englishmen to read in the daily newspapers lies respecting those who serve them. I am really quite indifferent respecting what is read of me.

My consolation for the sacrifices which I am called upon to make, I must find in that hope of honourable fame which is to be acquired only by those who, according to the best of their judgment, fallible at the best, pursue the course which leads to the public good.

If the world were governed by principles, nothing would be more easy than to conduct even the greatest affairs; but in all circumstances, the duty of a wise man is to choose the lesser of any two difficulties which beset him.

Charles Grey, later Viscount Howick

and, afterwards, second

EARL GREY

1764–1845

Whig M.P., 1786–1807; First Lord of the Admiralty, 1806; Secretary of State for Foreign Affairs and Leader of the House of Commons, 1806–7; First Lord of the Treasury, 1830–34

JUST CAUSE OF WAR

THE only just cause of war originates in the principle of self-defence; and no war can be justified on the grounds (to use a fashionable phrase) of political expediency, whatever the consequences of it may be, and however profitable and advantageous it may prove to the State. The principle of self-defence, therefore, being the sole ground on which a war can be justified, the cases in which a war is just may, I conceive, be reduced to three; firstly, when it is undertaken to redeem a right forcibly withheld, and to which we have an irresistible claim; secondly, in providing for future safety; and lastly, in repelling an unjust attack. These are the only three causes that can justify any war, except another which might be included under the third head, and that is, where an ally has been unjustly attacked. I lay particular stress upon the words unjustly attacked, not being willing to admit that when an ally is an aggressor, and refuses to make reparation, the nation with whom he is in alliance, is obliged to support him. A nation is bound to support an ally only in the case of an unjust attack, and

even then only according to the specific meaning of the treaty entere
into between them. The only three causes, therefore, for going to wa
are, to redeem a right, to provide against danger, and to repel a
attack; and any principle of supposed policy that stands in oppositio
to these three causes, and does not come within one or other of them
can never be a just cause of war. *Omnia quae defendi, repeti, repel.
possunt:* the words of Camillus to his soldiers are full of wisdom
policy, and justice.

House of Commons: 12 April 179

MRS. PARTINGTON

But, says the noble and learned lord, I cannot reconcile myself to
support the principle of this measure, because in its operation, or i
being made the precedent for succeeding innovations, it might possibly
or probably, be attended with most mischievous and dangerou
consequences. Really, my lords, it is impossible to answer this argu
ment but by others which have heretofore on many occasions bee
introduced into discussion. If, indeed, such an objection were t
succeed—if the spirit of improvement was to evaporate from th
influence of possible dangers, and probable apprehensions—if error
were not to be corrected, or evils remedied, from an overweenin
dread of innovation—then this country would have to lament th
want of all those great and glorious privileges and securities whicl
constitute so deservedly our national boast and our most essentia
safeguard. For what was Magna Carta but an innovation? What els
the Petition of Right? What else the Revolution, that glorious epocl
when this country obtained a recognition of its liberties? Indeed,
would ask the venerable bench of Bishops, whom, on this occasio
particularly, I see in such formidable numbers arrayed against me
whether if this dislike to innovation, this hostility to improvement, hac
existed some centuries past, this country would have participated ir
the enlightened wisdom and numerous benefits of the Reformation
or whether they themselves would have ever had a seat within thes
walls, with power to decide on this measure of reform, which they ar
now perhaps prepared to oppose.

House of Lords: 180

LIBERTY AND THE LAW

*England was exhausted by the long effort of the Napoleonic wars; the
looked-for revival in trade did not follow upon peace and this, together
with the reduction of the forces, made unemployment widespread at c*

me when bad harvests made bread dear. Riots broke out and in order
ⁱ suppress agitation Habeas Corpus was suspended and the harsh and
npopular Six Acts were passed: in addition the Home Secretary sent
circular letter to all justices of the peace directing them to hold to
ᵃil any persons accused of selling or in any way publishing blas-
ʰemous or seditious libels. It was against this latter action that Grey
ⁱotested.

In all the varieties of writings which may constitute libel, what is
ᵗore difficult to be decided than the question of their guilt or inno-
ₑnce? What more exposed to the influence of undue motives in its
ₑcision? It has been formerly stated by some of the most eminent
ₑrsons in the profession of the law, nay, by almost all of them, to be
ₒ nice and difficult a question that it could not be safely left even to
special jury: that they were only to find the fact of publication, and
ᵗat the criminality of the writing, as a question of law, was exclusively
ₒr the decision of the Court. This was long contended for, and long
ᶜted upon as law; till, happily for the freedom of the press, and for
ᵗe liberty of the country, of which the press is the great palladium,
ᵗat principle was at length exploded, and it was at last established
ᵗat, in prosecutions for libel, both the law and the fact were within
ᵗe province of the jury and to be decided by them.

But what avails this just and beneficent statute, what security is there
ⁱther for the freedom of the press or the liberty of the subject, if,
ʰilst you have imposed this salutary restraint upon the judges, in
ⁱials for libel, you give to them, and to justices of the peace, before
ⁱial, a right to decide that difficult question, and to commit to prison
ᵖon a charge which, after all, may turn out to have had no foundation
ᵘt in the false interpretation of words perfectly innocent by the
ᵘstice before whom the charge was brought? I cannot, I will not
ₑlieve that you can sanction the exercise of such a power. That it is
ₒt law, I think I have already shown, but if it were law, your duty
ᵛould call upon you to lose no time in altering it.

With respect to offences over which this authority is acknowledged,
is ordinarily a simple and intelligible fact of which the magistrate
ᵃs to judge. But upon libel, where the whole guilt or innocence of the
ᶠfence must depend upon the intention, and must be inferred from
ʰe construction and the innuendoes, often difficult for the most
ᵐpartial and unbiased person to decide; where the prejudices,
ⁿterests, or passions of the justice before whom the charge is brought
ⁱe so likely to influence his interpretation of the words; where, in
ᵖolitical or religious libels more especially, his particular opinions and
ᵗtachments must unavoidably have so great a sway; in cases of this

sort, to place, upon the charge of any common informer, the persona
liberty of every writer and publisher on politics, religion, or law, o
any other public question, the unfettered discussion of which is of th
very essence and principle of a free government, at the discretion o
magistrates mixing in all the contests of the time and partaking, on on
side or the other, in all the heats and prejudices, which personal o
party interests engender—if such be the power of the magistrates, an
if this be the law, where, I ask, are all the boasted securities of ou
independence and freedom?

Look, I once more implore you, at the enormous extent an
dangerous tendency of the power now contended for; and with thi
comment upon all that I have argued from the reports of the decisio
of our courts, and the books of our ablest writers, I say once mor
such is not, such cannot be the state of the law in this country, hithert
famed for the sure protection which every individual enjoys agains
the insidious attempts of private malice or the open attacks of power

House of Lords: 12 May 181

THE RIGHTS OF THE PEOPLE

If anything could add to the importance of the question itself, i
would be to be found in the character of the times and in the situatio
of the country. We have been induced to suspend, with respect to
political offences, the operation of a law which forms the chie
bulwark of the Constitution. We have passed other laws, materiall
abridging and restraining the facility of petitioning and the privilege
of free discussion. Even those, who are most impressed with th
necessity of making these new provisions for the security of th
Government by the extension of its powers will, I am sure, admit tha
it is an evil much and deeply to be lamented. But if new laws o
this description are to be enacted—if, when enacted, they are to be
construed to the utmost strictness of their letter, and executed with the
most unrelenting severity, and if, at the same time, interpretations o
the old law are to be adopted and a new practice to be introduced
still further controlling popular rights and privileges and rendering
their exercise difficult and dangerous, what, I ask, is to be the end'
More especially, if this spirit in our legislation is accompanied with
other circumstances operating directly and powerfully in the same
direction—if a great change has taken place in our principles, in ou
policy, in our tastes, in our habits, and in our manners—if we are
become a military and a warlike, from a maritime and pacific people—
if whilst we are increasing the civil powers of the Crown by law, we are

also maintaining an army disproportioned to our population, incompatible with an effective support of our naval superiority, and destructive of the character of a free government—what must be the inevitable tendency of such a system? Its termination cannot be doubtful: one of two things must unavoidably happen; either this free Constitution, the glorious work of a thousand years, must, though its forms may still survive, decline, by no slow degrees, into a military despotism; or—I will not describe the alternative; it would not be less dreadful.

Our best hope of surmounting the evils which surround us must be found in the patience and fortitude of the people, supported and strengthened by a high-minded consciousness of their rights as freemen. Beware, my lords, how you weaken in them this sentiment, the true source of your security and power; how you deprive them of the confidence, so necessary to be cherished and improved, that by Parliament, whose peculiar duty it is to protect them, their interests will not be neglected.

You are indeed sitting in judgment on the rights and liberties of your fellow-subjects; and I earnestly pray that they may sustain no further injury from the proceeding of this night.

Ibid

A MONSTROUS PROPOSITION

The whole political life of Grey, a zealous upholder of the Whig ideal of civil and religious liberty, was dominated by the question of Parliamentary Reform. The constitution of Parliament had been felt to be increasingly unsatisfactory since the Revolution of 1688: many rotten boroughs with few or no inhabitants were represented in Parliament while new industrial districts had no members; seats could be bought and many members sat as the nominees of great lords.

Chatham had stressed the need for Reform. Pitt inherited his father's opinions but veered when faced with the Jacobin excesses of the early French Revolution and with the exigencies of the war with France. Grey moved for Reform as early as 1792 but, unsuccessful on this and two later occasions, he determined to wait until the united opinion of the country should support him. After he went to the Lords, Russell and others continued the cause of Reform in the Commons.

In the post-war years a popular clamour for Reform, held out as the panacea for all political and social woes, swept the country. While in 1830 half Europe was in the throes of bloody revolution, the new industrial England struggled against Tory resistance to enlarge its liberties by fierce agitation for Parliamentary Reform. On 1 March 1841 Russell brought forward a Reform Bill which came to grief in committee

8

after it had passed a second reading, whereupon the ministers forced a dissolution and came back into office on a people's mandate for the whole Bill and nothing but the Bill. By September a new Reform Bill had got through the Commons by a large majority and on 3 October came before the Lords when Grey delivered one of the most memorable speeches ever made in that House.

I have contended, and I must still contend, that the right of nomination, if I may call that usurpation a right, is not only no part of the Constitution but is absolutely inconsistent with the most notorious and most universally acknowledged principles of the Constitution. Among the discoveries of modern times, however, the most remarkable undoubtedly is that the practice of this flagrant and unconstitutional abuse is the only security on which we can confidently rely for the preservation of all those venerable and excellent institutions under which this country has risen to prosperity and power. It has been contended, with all the vehemence and earnestness of sincerity and truth, that albeit the theory of the Constitution is one way, yet that the practice of the Constitution is another and a different way. The theory of the Constitution is admitted to be a full, a fair, and a free representation of the people; but then it is argued that the practice of the Constitution is that the representation shall be neither full, nor fair, nor free, and that by the continuance of this practice, and by the continuance of this practice alone, it is that the country can be securely shielded from dangers of the most appalling character. Men of character and   r   have actually been found elsewhere who have gravely told their auditory that unless members of the House of Commons are allowed to be, not the representatives of the people, but the nominees of peers, of loan contractors, and of speculating attornies, all security for the happiness, the prosperity, and the liberty we enjoy will fall from under us.

I should have supposed that at this hour—in the nineteenth century —when the schoolmaster is abroad and when the growing intelligence of all classes of the community is daily and hourly receiving new light —it would only have been necessary to have such a proposition mentioned in order to have it met with universal derision and contempt. I will not do the intelligent part of the community of this country the injustice to suppose that they can seriously entertain such a monstrous proposition for a moment; but then it has been urged, with so much petulance and pertinacity by the persons with whom the discovery originated, that it becomes necessary to examine it more closely, and particularly to see how far this corrupt system is calculated to preserve, as it is said it does preserve in an eminent degree, this, the aristocratic branch of the legislature. It is singular that in all the writers upon our Constitution—that in all the Acts of Parliament, from the earliest time to the present moment—that in all the works of the able and intelligent expounders of, and commentators upon those Acts—that in all the records of Parliament, as well recent as remote— and, above all, that in the votes, and proceedings, and resolutions of the House of Commons, there is not to be found the slightest trace of a mention of the beneficial effects of this system of representation which is said to be the constant, the ancient, the necessary, and the indisputable practice of the Constitution; but it is still more strange that all our laws, that all the proceedings of Parliament, and that all the resolutions of the House of Commons have been directed—and most properly directed in the opinion of every constitutional writer— to guard, by all possible means, against this practice, which in times past has been considered as pernicious as it is unquestionably corrupt, but which has now, by a rare and unexpected discovery, been found to be the great bulwark of all those liberties and all those institutions which Englishmen hold most dear.

Have your lordships forgotten too, that at the commencement of every new session of Parliament, the House of Commons vote, as one of their standing orders, that it is unconstitutional and illegal, and moreover a high breach of the privileges of the Commons House of Parliament, for any peer to interfere in the election of members to serve in that House? Will your lordships, in the face of such a resolu- tion, declare that it is right for peers to buy and sell seats in the House of Commons; that it is right for peers not only to interfere in elections, but actually to return by their own mere nomination, members to serve in Parliament; and that they should persevere in doing this, not- withstanding that recorded resolution of the other branch of the legislature?

House of Lords: 3 October 1831

CONSIDER AND CONCEDE

Again I would say to your lordships that I ask you not to assent to clamour but I beg of you to consider whether you can with safety reject a measure sanctioned thus by the united voice of the people of England as expressed by their representatives in Parliament, founded so decidedly not on any new theory but on the original and undoubted principles of the Constitution.

But we are told, if there is danger in resistance, there is danger also in concession. It is said, if you once concede, where will you stop ? This is the old doctrine which has led to so much ruin. But is it true

this ruin has been produced by concession? I think not. Was it concession that lost the kingdom of the Netherlands to Philip the Second?
Was it concession that overturned the government of Charles the
First, and led him to the scaffold? No, my lords, it was the faithless
attempt he made to resume those rights which he had reluctantly
granted. Was it concession that created those discontents which
disturbed the end of Charles the Second's reign, and which obliged his
successor to abdicate the throne? Was it concession that lost us
America? I know that some persons make a different application of
those facts of history, and say: *See what are the effects of concession;
when you offered to the Americans all they required, they would not
accept it.* But their refusal is easily explained. All the people of
America desired, in the first instance, was the exercise of their just
rights and privileges. These were pertinaciously and obstinately
refused; and what was the result? An ineffectual offer of those rights
you had refused in the insolence of your strength was forced from you
in the hour of defeat and humiliation. But it was too late, and you were
compelled to sign a treaty of separation and independence.

I say, therefore, my lords, concede in time—concede freely, generously, and not reluctantly; not as if what you granted were an extorted
capitulation rather than an act of mercy and benevolence. I say,
therefore, concede in time—meet the wishes of the people. Look at the
representation of the people; see whether it is liable to those im-
perfections and defects which I have stated, and, if it be so, take a bold,
decisive, and effectual step to remove the complaints of the country
and to place the Constitution upon a rock where it shall be unassailable
and safe from all danger.

Ibid

REFORM NOT REVOLUTION

*At the end of a five-days' debate, on 8 October 1841, the Lords rejected
the second Reform Bill. The country, already tense, was almost flung into
anarchy; riots broke out everywhere. But Grey remained in office; a
third Bill was prepared and, as the country emerged from a dread winter,
was carried through the Commons by Russell. In April, the great debate
in the Lords began and at last, on 4 June 1832, the third reading of the
Bill was carried by a majority of 84. The balance of power in England
had passed from the landed aristocracy to the middle classes. The reforms
had begun which, continued with the measures of 1867, 1884 and 1918,
found their last expression in the Equal Franchise Act of 1928.*

A reform in Parliament supposes a great change in the Constitution
of Parliament, it supposes a great change in the mode in which the
people and their interests are to be represented; but all change is not

evolution, and least of all such change as is proposed by the present Bill. It is to be effected, according to the acknowledged principles of the constitution, by an Act of Parliament, passed by the united will of the legislature, consisting of the King, Lords, and Commons. It may therefore, be fairly considered as effected after sufficient and mature deliberation. It proceeds according to the known forms of the law. I confess, therefore, that I am utterly at a loss to discover how such a measure can, with any show of justice or propriety, be designated as revolutionary. It infringes on none of the ordinary authorities of the land, it violates not one of the regular forms of the Constitution, it invades none of the privileges of this House, it interferes with not one of the prerogatives of the Crown—why then should it be stigmatised as revolutionary? The word revolution has always been used to signify a great change in the political constitution of the state, a change, for example, in the succession to a monarchy or the institutions of a state, carried into effect by a force superior to the law. Neither in character, in terms, nor in principle is this Bill revolutionary; it is truly and substantially a reform, but it is nothing more.

I am acquainted with no way of effecting a reform in Parliament, unless by one of three modes: either by taking away the right of return from decayed and inconsiderable boroughs, which was the ancient practice of the Constitution—and that was disfranchisement; or by giving the right of representation to large, populous, and opulent towns, which had risen into importance but had not the right of returning members to parliament—and that, too, was the practice of the olden times, and that was enfranchisement; or by a great extension of the right of voting—which was also done in the good old times, and which I again say was not revolutionary. In some one of these three ways reform must be effected; and, therefore, all the plans of reform hitherto proposed by the great men who have preceded me, and also that plan of reform which I, too presumptuously, proposed to the House of Commons in 1793, all proceed upon one or all of these three principles united. I trust, therefore, that I stand, upon the present occasion, acquitted of the charge of having strayed beyond the ancient limits of the Constitution and of having proposed to the country a measure revolutionary in its character.

House of Lords: 9 April 1832

FINAL WORDS

My lords, I forbear to press further the consequences of a second rejection. To the country, and to your lordships, the result of this night is important in a degree scarcely paralleled in your records as a legislative assembly. To myself, everything depends upon it. I knew all the difficulties to which I exposed myself when I undertook this measure; a sense of the duty which I owed to my sovereign and my country commanded me to brave them.

Having introduced the measure, I have endeavoured to conduct it through the various embarrassments with which it was beset, with a steady adherence to its principles, and to the views upon which I had originally acted. I have been exposed to much injustice, to many undeserved attacks, to much misrepresentation, and to much suspicion. But I have not been deterred from doing what I thought right, nor allowed myself to be forced and driven into any measures which I could not approve. I have felt the attacks to which I have been exposed, and I know what further I have to expect. In the event of the failure of the Bill, a personal responsibility rests upon me, which, perhaps, was never before sustained by any minister. I may sink under it—that is nothing: I shall have the support of an approving conscience, which has always instructed me to do what is right, and to leave the consequences to God. What I pray for is that I may be the only victim and that the consequences of my failure may affect neither the prosperity nor the peace of my country, nor that union between your lordships and the people on which the welfare of both, together with your lordships' authority, and character, and usefulness, essentially depend.

Ibid

William Lamb, second

LORD MELBOURNE

1774 – 1848

Whig M.P., 1806–12 and 1816–29; Chief Secretary for Ireland, 1827–30; Secretary of State for Home Affairs, 1830–34; First Lord of the Treasury, 1834 and 1835–41

LIBERTY AND FREEDOM

WHILE generation is following generation, while the sceptre of power is passing from the grasp of one nation into that of another; while the dank dews of night are imperceptibly wearing away the monument and the column; while cities are going to decay and stupendous piles of marble and brass moulder into dust; while the material universe bears evident marks of its perishable composition and the astronomer in vain requires the star which his predecessors have observed in the heavens, the mind of man grows more vigorous from time and is ever struggling on with increased energy in pursuit of that perfection which to have sought after, though perhaps it can never be attained, exalts and glorifies human nature. And when we reflect upon what mortal powers have already accomplished, when we remember that the den of the savage has risen into the palace of the monarch and that the forest has been cleared away to make room for the city, that the bowels of the earth have not been inaccessible and that the summits of the mountains protect not their productions, that the unfathomable deep has been made subservient to our convenience and the boisterous wind the minister to our desires, that science has looked through nature and that the laws of heaven have not been hidden from the researches of the philosopher, are we not tempted to exclaim—the creature who has done these things can do more; and if at any time all intellectual faculty could be concentrated to produce one great end, the advancement of truth; if learning would exert itself only to instruct and wit would exercise its lash only on that which is deserving of contempt, what obstacle might not be surmounted, what obscurity might not be dispelled? Such an era may perhaps exist only in the dreams of enthusiasm, but that is no unpleasing nor unprofitable

119

vision which invigorates every generous feeling, arouses every dormant faculty, animates within us the love of virtue, and leads us nearer at last to that model of excellence which it holds forth as the reward of our exertions. That the hope of attaining this reward may ever strongly actuate the human race is surely no dangerous or imprudent prayer. May it pass from the north to the south, from the east to the west; may it civilise the rude millions of Africa, and pour the light of science upon the subterranean darkness of the Laplander; may it abash the proud front of insolent superiority and exalt the meek brow of dependence; may it shower plenty upon the dwellings of penury; may it strike the fetter from the galled limbs of the supplicating slave; may it shame injustice; may it baffle oppression and lighten the load of misfortune wheresoever it lies heavy upon the innocent; may it proceed in this glorious career, promoting throughout the habitable world, wheresoever there exists an intellect to conceive, or a voice to assert the truth, the cause of rational Liberty! Of rational Liberty; not of that grievous despotism, which, generated by luxury, by tyranny, by vice and corruption, has grown up into a monster even more abandoned and abominable than its parents, and still unsated, after the desolation of Europe, crosses the sea in search of new climes, where for ages the peaceful plains have not been wounded by the hoof of the war-horse nor the echoes have reverberated the clang of the trumpet, that other victims may tell, from woeful experience, of its specious appearances and delusive promises, of its open rapine, wanton cruelty, and undisguised injustice. It must be the earnest and incessant supplication of all whose bosoms exult in the joy and grieve for the misery of others, that this sanguinary spirit of ferocity and intolerance which has been permitted, for purposes to us inscrutable, so long and so dreadfully to scourge the world, may fade away before the temperate influence of Freedom; of her whose triumphs are not in cities sacked with fire and sword nor in desolated provinces; whose trophies are raised over subdued ignorance, error and prejudice; whose delight is in the progress of the mind and the amelioration of the heart; whose attributes are benevolence and compassion; whose first great hope is peace perpetual and unbroken, and whose only object is the universal happiness of man.

The Progressive Improvement of Mankind. 1798

A PROPHECY

Hereafter, when great and mighty States, under whatever form of government, insular and continental, shall have arisen in the New

World, when culture shall have covered the face and population spread itself throughout the extent of those vast regions, when armies shall be raised proportionable to that population, when arsenals shall be formed capable of equipping and harbours of containing the fleets which their boundless forests afford the power of building, the affairs of our times and our countries, which appear to us so weighty and gigantic, will be looked on by the philosophers and statesmen of those periods in the same manner as we regard the history of the contests between the States of Greece or of Italy. The violent and desperate religious War of Thirty Years, the War of the Succession, so important in its consequences, and lastly, the overwhelming and devouring War of the French Revolution, will be considered, perhaps, as we consider the Peloponnesian War, as a series of actions in which great virtues were exercised and great talents displayed, but utterly insignificant when compared to the great armies now in motion and the vast territories now in dispute.

From a commonplace book: *c.* 1822,
Lord Melbourne's Papers

OBITER DICTA

The easy-going Melbourne is better revealed in the brief flashes of his obiter dicta than in the long formality of his speeches: thus, to Queen Victoria, pressing for Prince Albert to be made King Consort: For God's sake, let's hear no more of it, ma'am; for if you once get the English people into the way of making kings, you will get them into the way of unmaking them; *and again to the Queen, who records it in her Journal, of Lady Holland:* She has no religion, but every sort of superstition. *Perhaps his best-remembered mot is that made after being the unwilling hearer of an evangelical sermon on sin:* Things have come to a pretty pass when religion is allowed to invade the sphere of private life.

Toleration is the only good and just principle, and toleration for every opinion that can be found.

It is the business of the legislature to remedy practical grievances, not to run after theoretical perfection.

The worst of the present day is that men hate one another so damnably. For my part I love them all.

The people, as well as kings and ministers, are responsible for the exercise of the power committed to their charge.

The middle classes are bad; in the higher and lower classes there's

some good, but the middle classes are all affectation and conceit an
pretence and concealment.

Those who resist improvements as innovations will soon have t
accept innovations that are not improvements.

It is the nature of human things that no man can be free an
independent.

Raphael was employed to decorate the Vatican, not because he wa
a great painter but because his uncle was architect to the Pope.

It is a good thing when these authors die, for then one gets thei
works, and is done with them.

Wealth is so much the greatest good that Fortune has to bestov
that in the Latin and English languages it has usurped her name.

SIR ROBERT PEEL
1788–1850

---

*Tory M.P., 1809–50; Under-Secretary of State
for War and the Colonies, 1810–12; Chief Secretary for Ireland, 1812–18; Secretary of State for
Home Affairs, 1822–27; Secretary of State for
Home Affairs and Leader of the House of
Commons, 1828–30; First Lord of the Treasury
and Chancellor of the Exchequer, 1834–35 and
1841–46*

ONE SENTIMENT

THE nature of the contest in which we are engaged requires that ever
heart and hand should be joined to give strength to the commo
cause. I hope we shall still be able, as we have hitherto been, to ride i
safety through the storm that has destroyed the rest of Europe, an
that we shall still stretch forth a hand to succour those who are ye
struggling for life against the angry waves. To be successful in tha
generous course we must be unanimous; there can be but one senti
ment among the men to whom I address myself, and that sentimen
must be to do honour to themselves and to their country.

House of Commons: 23 January 181

A HOME-SECRETARY'S APOLOGIA

On resigning his first tenure of office as Home-Secretary in April 1827, Peel reviewed the vigorous reforms which an increasingly enlightened public opinion and his own zeal had enabled him to carry through; an overdue reform of the criminal law by which nearly one hundred felonies were removed from the list of capital offences, the law relating to prisons and transportation, and the law relating to juries.

It was during his second tenure of this office, in 1829, that he carried through the Metropolitan Police Act and established the London policeman, quickly called, in Cockney compliment, Bobby *or* Peeler.

I have the satisfaction of reflecting that during the past five years every institution, civil and military, connected with my office has been subject to close inspection and strict review; and that I have been able to make such temperate and gradual reforms as I thought consistent with the general and permanent good. I have also the gratification of knowing that every law found in the Statute-book when I entered office which imposed any temporary or any extraordinary restriction on the liberty of the subject has either been repealed or allowed to expire. There is not a single law connected with my name which has not had for its object some mitigation of the severity of the criminal law; some prevention of abuse in the exercise of it; or some security for its impartial administration.

For all the ancient institutions of my country I have felt a natural prepossession and an earnest desire that they should preserve the veneration which has promoted their continuance; but those prepossessions have not prevented me from inquiring into cases of alleged abuse, and that desire has urged me, in a friendly and temperate spirit, to examine to what degree corruption may have intruded. Where change and restoration were deemed necessary they have been applied, thus recommending those ancient institutions to the long-enduring attachment and veneration of the country.

The confidence of my sovereign, the goodwill of his people, and the approbation of Parliament have been at once the motive and the reward of my exertions.

House of Commons: 1 May 1827

UNITY, PEACE AND CONCORD

The two greatest measures sponsored by Peel, the Catholic Emancipation Act of 1829 and the Repeal of the Corn Laws in 1846, proved his sincerity in that, both demanding a reversal of previous conviction, the one cost him his seat for the University of Oxford, the other lost him office.

The Catholic Emancipation Act freed Catholics from civil disabilities as, in the previous year, the repeal of the Test and Corporation Acts had freed the Nonconformists. It further ended a long agitation by securing Ireland from rule by a Protestant minority.

Objections may be brought forward against the details of every measure of an extensive and complicated nature like the present if considered abstractedly. We shall never settle the Catholic question if every man is determined to settle it in his own way and according to his own peculiar views and wishes. We shall never settle it unless we are prepared to make mutual concessions and sacrifices. I admit the possibility of danger from the grant of Relief; but I ask the Protestants whether there may not be a prospect that, by uniting the Protestant mind on this subject, we shall be able to find new and sufficient securities against any difficulties that may possibly arise out of the settlement of this question. I ask the Roman Catholics to contemplate the extent of privilege that is conferred, and the sacrifices which we make, by consenting to repeal the laws which have given an exclusive character to the legislature and government of the country; let them meet us in the same spirit and manifest an anxious wish to allay every reasonable apprehension. God grant that the sanguine expectations of those who for so many years have advised this settlement may be fulfilled. God grant that the removal of the disabilities which have so long affected our Roman Catholic fellow-subjects may be attended by the desired effect and may assuage the civil contentions of Ireland; that, by the admission of the Roman Catholics to a full and equal participation in civil rights and by the establishment of a free and cordial intercourse between all classes of his Majesty's subjects, mutual jealousies may be removed; and that we may be taught, instead of looking at each other as adversaries and opponents, to respect and value each other and to discover on both sides the existence of qualities that were not attributed to either.

I fully believe that the adjustment of this question in the manner proposed will give better and stronger securities to the Protestant interest and the Protestant establishment than any the present state of things admits of, and will avert evils and dangers impending and immediate. What motive, I ask, can I have for the expression of these opinions but the honest conviction of their truth? I have watched the progress of events. I have seen, day by day, disunion and hatred increasing, the prospect of peace obscured by the gloomy advance of discontent, and suspicion and distrust creeping on *step by step*—to quote the words of Mr. Grattan—*like the mist at the heels of the countryman*. I well know that I might have taken a more popular and

a more selfish course. I might have held language much more accept-
able to the friends with whom I have long acted and to the constituents
I have lately lost. In the course I have taken I have been mainly
influenced by the anxious desire to provide for the maintenance of
Protestant interests and for the security of Protestant establishments:
this is my defence, this is my consolation, this shall be my revenge.

I will hope for the best. God grant that the moral storm may be
appeased, that the turbid waters of strife may be settled and composed,
and that having found their just level they may be mingled with equal
flow in one clear and common stream.

House of Commons: 5 March 1829

A CHANCELLOR'S CHALLENGE

*Peel as Chancellor of the Exchequer in 1842 was faced with an accumu-
lation of yearly deficits in the country's finances. Further general
taxation including the lower classes, in face of their prevalent distress
contrasting with an increase in middle-class prosperity, would have been
harsh and injudicious. Peel therefore courageously met the situation by
taxing those classes from which his own party was mainly recruited; by
a property-tax hitherto only imposed in time of war, by an income-tax
(of sevenpence in the pound), and by tariff-reductions, as main features of
a budget which extensively changed our system of national finance and
was, in conjunction with Peel's success in maintaining peace, the prelude
to the era of Victorian commercial prosperity.*

We live in an important era of human affairs. There may be a
natural tendency to overrate the magnitude of the crisis in which we
live, or those particular events with which we are ourselves conversant;
but I think it impossible to deny that the period in which our lot and
the lot of our fathers has been cast—the period which has elapsed
since the first outbreak of the French Revolution—has been one of the
most memorable that the history of the world will afford. That period
may be divided into two parts, of almost equal duration; a period of
twenty-five years of continued conflict—the most momentous which
ever engaged the energies of a nation—and twenty-five years of
profound European peace, produced by the sacrifices made during the
years of war.

The course which England has pursued during that period will
attract for ages to come the contemplation and, I trust, the admiration
of posterity. There will be a time when those countless millions that
are sprung from our loins, occupying many parts of the globe, living
under institutions derived from ours, speaking the same language in

which we convey our thoughts and feelings—for such must be the ultimate results of our wide-spread colonisation—will view with pride and admiration the example of constancy and fortitude which our fathers set during the momentous period of war. They will view with admiration our previous achievements by land and sea, our determination to uphold the public credit, and all those qualities by the exhibition of which we were enabled ultimately, by the example we set to foreign nations, to ensure the deliverance of Europe. In this review of the period, the conduct of our fathers during the years of war will be brought into close contrast with the conduct of those of us who have lived only during the years of peace.

I am now addressing you after the duration of peace for twenty-five years. I am now exhibiting the financial difficulties and embarrassments in which you are placed; and my confident hope and belief is that, following the example of those who preceded you, you will look those difficulties in the face, and not refuse to make similar sacrifices to those which your fathers made for the purpose of upholding the public credit. You will bear in mind that this is no casual or occasional difficulty. You will bear in mind that there are indications amongst all the upper classes of society of increased comfort and enjoyment—of increased prosperity and wealth, and that concurrently with these indications there exists a mighty evil which has been growing up for the last seven years, and which you are now called upon to meet. If you have, as I believe you have, the fortitude and constancy of which you have been set the example, you will not consent with folded arms to view the annual growth of this mighty evil. You will not reconcile it to your consciences to hope for relief from diminished taxation. You will not adopt the miserable expedient of adding, during peace, and in the midst of these indications of wealth and of increasing prosperity, to the burdens which posterity will be called upon to bear. You will not permit this evil to gain such gigantic growth as ultimately to place it far beyond your power to check or to control.

If you do permit this evil to continue, you must expect the severe but just judgment of a reflecting and retrospective posterity. Your conduct will be contrasted with the conduct of your fathers, under difficulties infinitely less pressing than theirs. I believe that you will not subject yourselves to an injurious or an unworthy contract. It is my firm belief that you will feel the necessity of preserving inviolate the public credit—that you will not throw away the means of maintaining the public credit by reducing in the most legitimate manner the burden of the public debt. My confident hope is that now, when I devolve the responsibility upon you, you will prove yourselves worthy of your mission as the representatives of a mighty people; that you will not tarnish the fame which it is your duty to cherish as the most glorious inheritance and that you will not impair the character for fortitude and good faith which, in proportion as the empire of opinion supersedes and predominates over the empire of physical force, constitutes for every people, but above all for the people of England, the main instrument by which a powerful nation can repel hostile aggressions and maintain extended empire.

House of Commons: 11 March 1842

ADVANCE OR RECEDE?

This night is to decide between the policy of continued relaxation of restriction or the return to restraint and prohibition. This night you will select the motto which is to indicate the commercial policy of England. Shall it be advance or recede? Which is the fitter motto for this great empire? Survey our position; consider the advantage which God and nature have given us, and the destiny for which we are intended. We stand on the confines of Western Europe, the chief connecting link between the Old World and the New. The discoveries of science, the improvement of navigation have brought us within ten days of St. Petersburg, and will soon bring us within ten days of New York. We have an extent of coast greater, in proportion to our population and the area of our land, than any other great nation, securing to us maritime strength and superiority. Iron and coal, the sinews of manufacture, give us advantages over every rival in the great competition of industry. Our capital far exceeds that which they can command. In ingenuity, in skill, in energy, we are inferior to none. Our national character, the free institutions under which we live, the liberty of thought and action, an unshackled press spreading the knowledge of every discovery and of every advance in science, combine with our natural and physical advantages to place us at the head of those nations which profit by the free interchange of their products. And is this the country to shrink from competition? Is this the country to adopt a retrograde policy? Is this the country which can only flourish in the sickly artificial atmosphere of prohibition? Is this the country to stand shivering on the brink of exposure to the healthful breezes of competition. I counsel you to set the example of liberality to other countries. Act thus, and it will be in perfect consistency with the course you have hitherto taken. Act thus, and you will provide an additional guarantee for the continued contentment, and happiness, and well-being of the great body of the people. Act thus, and you will

have done whatever human sagacity can do for the promotion o▮
commercial prosperity.

House of Commons: 9 February 184▮

FAREWELL TO OFFICE

Peel ranked country above party; his honesty moved him to declare, i▮
the face of party prejudice, his change of conviction from protection t▮
free-trade and his courage led him to move for the repeal of the Cor▮
Laws when convinced by Cobden's arguments that they should go. Pee▮
lost office but the people gained cheap bread.

Within a few hours, probably, that power which I have held for a
period of five years will be surrendered into the hands of another—
without repining—without complaint on my part—with a mor▮
lively recollection of the support and confidence I have received
during several years, than of the opposition which during a recen▮
period I have encountered. In relinquishing power I shall leave a nam▮
severely censured, I fear, by many who, on public grounds, deeply
regret the severance of party ties—deeply regret that severance, no▮
from interested or personal motives, but from the firm conviction tha▮
fidelity to party engagements, the existence and maintenance of a
great party, constitutes a powerful instrument of government. I shal▮
surrender power severely censured also by others who, from n▮
interested motive, adhere to the principle of Protection, considering
the maintenance of it to be essential to the welfare and interests of the
country. I shall leave a name execrated by every monopolist, who
from less honourable motives, clamours for protection because i▮
conduces to his own individual benefit. But it may be that I shall leav▮
a name sometimes remembered with expressions of goodwill in the
abodes of those whose lot it is to labour and to earn their daily brea▮
by the sweat of their brow, when they shall recruit their exhauste▮
strength with abundant and untaxed food, the sweeter because it is n▮
longer leavened by a sense of injustice.

House of Commons: 29 June 184▮

THE KEYSTONE OF OUR FOREIGN POLICY

The principle for which I contend is the principle for which ever▮
statesman of eminence in this country for the last fifty years ha▮
contended, namely, non-interference with the domestic affairs o▮
other countries, without some clear and undeniable necessity arising
from circumstances affecting the interests of your own country. Tha▮

THE DUKE OF WELLINGTON AND SIR ROBERT PEEL
From a painting by F. X. Winterhalter at Windsor Castle

LORD JOHN RUSSELL
From a mezzotint by James Bromley after the portrait by Sir
George Hayter painted in 1836 when Russell was Secretary of
State for Home Affairs

must ever be the very keystone of our foreign policy, for if we did not accept the principle, if we should claim to concern ourselves with the internal affairs of other states, on what principle could we deny a similar right to other powers?

It is my firm belief that you will not advance the cause of constitutional government by attempting to dictate to other nations. If you do, your intentions will be mistaken—you will rouse feelings upon which you do not calculate—you will invite opposition to government; and beware that the time does not arrive when, frightened by your own interference, you withdraw your countenance from those whom you have excited, and leave upon their minds the bitter recollection that you have betrayed them. If you succeed, I doubt whether or no the institutions that take root under your patronage will be lasting. Constitutional liberty will be best worked out by those who aspire to freedom by their own efforts. You will only overload it by your help, by your principle of interference, against which I remonstrate—against which I enter my protest—to which I to-night will be no party. You are departing from the established policy of England—you are involving yourselves in difficulties the extent of which you can hardly conceive— you are bestowing no aid on the cause of constitutional freedom, but are encouraging its advocates to look to you for aid, instead of those efforts which can alone establish it, and upon the successful exertion of which alone it can be useful. For all these reasons I give my dissent, my reluctant dissent, from the motion, the carrying of which I believe would give a false impression with respect to the dignity and honour of this country, and would establish a principle which you could not carry into execution without imminent danger to the best interests of the country.

House of Commons: 28 June 1850

LORD JOHN RUSSELL

afterwards first Earl Russell

1792 – 1878

Whig M.P., 1813–61; Paymaster-General of·the Forces, 1831–34; Secretary of State for Home Affairs and Leader of the House of Commons, 1835–39; Secretary of State for the Colonies, 1839–41 and 1859–65; First Lord of the Treasury, 1846–52 and 1865–66; Secretary of State for Foreign Affairs and Leader of the House of Commons, 1852–53, and Minister without Portfolio until 1854; Lord President of the Council, 1854–55

ONE WORD MORE

I HAVE but one word more. It is to entreat the Government, whether they accept these resolutions or not, to adopt some measure tending to conciliate the people. The history of all free states, and particularly of that one on which Machiavel has thrown the light of his genius, demonstrates that they have a progress to perfection, and a progress to decay. In the former of these we may observe that the basis of the government is gradually more and more enlarged and a larger portion of the people are admitted to a share of the power. In the latter, the people, or some class of the people, make requests which are refused, and two parties are created, both equally extravagant and equally incensed. In this state, when the party which supports the Government loses all love and respect for liberty, and the party which espouses liberty loses all attachment and reverence for the Government, the Constitution is near its end. Without any common attraction to the established laws of their country, each is ready to call in force to subdue the other; and it is in the power of an ambitious king, an ambitious general, or an ambitious demagogue, to extinguish the liberties of his country as easily as these lights above our heads will be put out after the debate.

House of Commons: 14 December 1819

THE UNION OF LIBERTY WITH ORDER

The union of liberty with order, then, is the last stage of civilisation and the perfection of civil society. It is in proportion as these two qualities are combined that the merit and the value of different governments are to be estimated; the larger portion they have of both, the more adapted they are to diffuse happiness among their subjects. Thus, in Athens, where liberty was the chief object of the constitution. order was no better observed than in the absolute government of France, and the democracy there were often to the full as tyrannical as Richlieu. On the other hand, Venice, which professed to be a free government, kept admirable order, but to attain this point it sacrificed liberty, and was, in its way, perfectly arbitrary. Thus, whichever way the balance is overthrown, the interests of the community suffer, and freedom itself is impaired—for a free man ought to be able to do all that is not forbidden b the laws, and to be enabled by those laws to do all that is not absolutely necessary for the welfare of society he should be restrained from doing—nor does it matter whether the government is called despotism, or monarchy, or republic; whatever arbitrary power exists, there is tyranny. For this reason it was that Mr. Fox said, in the height of the French Revolution: *I dislike absolute monarchy, I dislike absolute aristocracy, I dislike absolute democracy.* All these kinds of government leave the passions of man their full sway, and are consequently marked with injustice and oppression towards the individual members of the community.

Preface; *An Essay on the History of the English Government and Constitution: 1821*

ABOVE ALL LIBERTIES

The press does nothing more than afford a means of setting forth, in good and able language, the opinions of large classes of society. For if these opinions, however well sustained, are paradoxes confined to the individual who utters them, they fall as harmless in the middle of sixteen millions of people as they would do in a private party of three or four. Nor is it the sentiment of the editor of one newspaper or of another, which controls the course of government. These gentlemen are little if at all known: with one or two exceptions, their names are never mentioned. It is their skill in embodying in a daily journal the feelings and the reasonings which come home to the business and the bosoms of large numbers of their countrymen that obtains for their writings fame and general acceptance. But it would be vain for these persons, powerful as the daily press is, to endeavour to make the people permanently discontented with laws which they loved and a minister whom they revered. They would not be dreaded or even read. Equally vain would it be for a vicious, oppressive, and odious government to suppress the liberty of printing. It was not the press which overturned Charles I, nor could the Inquisition preserve to Ferdinand VII his despotic power. The dark cabal, the secret conspirator, the sudden tumult, the solitary assassin, may all be found where the liberty of printing has never existed. And were a government to suppress it where it does exist, without taking away the matter of sedition, more crime and less security would probably be the result of their foolish panic and powerless precaution.

In looking at the celebrated governments of antiquity and those of modern times which have not admitted a free press, it must strike everyone that they have declined, not from any vice inherent in the institutions by which they were governed, but by the gradual decay of national virtue and the corruption of the people themselves as well as of their leaders. In Sparta, and in Rome, this corruption may, in the beginning, be attributed to an influx of wealth acting upon a nation whose liberties and whose morals were founded upon poverty and the contempt of riches. But the precipitate fall of a state, like that of Rome, into an abyss of profligacy and venality, can only happen when the whole people, stained by political and moral vices, are delivered from a sense of shame by the want of any effectual restraint upon their actions. In both these circumstances, England has the advantage of Rome. Her institutions are not founded on the postulate that her manners must be rude and her legislators poor. Commerce and industry of every kind have been favourites of the law from the commencement. Nor is it easy to emancipate our rulers or our elective body from the sense of shame. Their actions are not submitted to the opinions of a single city, but scanned publicly by sixteen millions of people, nay, by Europe, by America, by the whole globe.

In ordinary times, it is evident the exercise of this censorship must be beneficial to the country. No statesman can hope that his corrupt practices, his jobs, his obliquities, his tergiversations, can escape from a vigilance that never slumbers and an industry that never wearies. Nor is it an important obstacle to truth that the daily newspapers are the advocates of party rather than searchers after truth; they act like lawyers pleading in a great national cause; and the nation, like a jury, after hearing both sides, may decide between them.

The greatest benefit, however, that we derive from publicity is that it corrects and neutralises the vices of our institutions, even when they are not immediately amended by it. Thus, to come at once to the greatest instance of this; the House of Commons is at present so composed, that were it shut up, and admitted no influence from without, the people would soon find that its spirit was so gone, its organs so decayed, its acts so unpalatable, that they would submit to such a government no longer. The House of Commons, too, cannot fail to be influenced on great questions by the general opinion of the people out of doors. If they could meet and discuss measures of state day after day, expose their whole conduct and arguments to the country, and yet pay no attention to the feelings of that country, they would be more or less than human.

An Essay on the History of the English Government and Constitution: 1821

THE NATURE OF ENGLISH LIBERTY

It is my persuasion that the liberties of Englishmen, being founded upon the general consent of all, must remain upon that basis, or must altogether cease to have any existence. We cannot confine liberty in this country to one class of men: we cannot erect here a senate of Venice, by which a small part of the community is enabled to lord it over the majority; we cannot in this land, and at this time, make liberty the inheritance of a caste. It is the nature of English liberty that her nightingale notes should never be heard from within the bars and gratings of a cage; to preserve anything of the grace and the sweetness they must have something of the wildness of freedom.

House of Commons: 25 April 1822

LET TYRANTS FEAR

We are perpetually asked if the nations at present declaring their independence, or reforming their institutions, are fit to be free. It would be lamentable indeed if this plea were to be allowed to prevail in bar to the generous efforts of countries long oppressed by tyranny. It would indeed be a hopeless case for mankind if despotism were thus allowed to take advantage of its own wrong and to bring the evidence of its crimes as the title-deeds of its right. It would indeed be a strange perversion of justice if absolute governments might say: *Look how ignorant, base, false, and cruel, our people have become under our sway; therefore we have a right to retain them in eternal subjection and everlasting slavery.* But no. When I am asked if such or such a nation is fit to be free, I ask in return: *Is any man fit to be a despot?* The answer must be: *None whatever*. It is the proved effect of despotism that wherever her horrid head appears she creates the evils she affects to deplore. And although those who first shake off the chain may bear upon their frame the marks of the degrading links, yet these impressions will wear out and the first fury of the released captive once over, the vengeance of a slave will give way to the virtues of a freeman.

Again, we are told that it is desirable indeed to reform the absolute monarchies of Europe but that revolutions are accompanied by acts of violence and outrage. To be sure they are; but on whom lies the blame of their excesses? Upon those who have risen in arms for liberty but have not been able to restrain the violence of a people suddenly delivered from intolerable restraint, or upon those who have gone on from year to year and from day to day adding to the cruel injuries they inflicted on the most numerous classes of a nation and sustaining by force the monstrous acts of injustice which they perpetrated from wantonness and caprice? On those who have long and patiently borne what no man ought to inflict, or on those who have inflicted what no man ought to suffer? On those who desire the improvement and happiness of mankind, or on those who set up the image of insolent rapacity, and call it a government? Undoubtedly upon the heads of those who provoke a people to rebellion must fall the crimes of that rebellion; he who gives an example of cruelty and injustice must not complain if it rebounds upon himself.

Let it be observed, moreover, that the excesses of a people in revolution are marked down and magnified; they spread indefinite alarm at the time and are recorded to future ages. The crimes of despotism, on the other hand, are the greater part of them performed in darkness; the same hand which takes the life of the patriot arrests the pen of the historian. The surface of despotism is smooth; the world knows not how many victims are languishing in its prisons, or how many of its subjects are swept away by its unjust decrees. Thousands of human beings may have sacrificed their lives to the fears of a tyrant and no one have known it; let a revolution take place, and a convicted conspirator suffer without the forms of law, the whole world resounds with complaint and indignation.

Let the friends of freedom, however, endeavour as much as is in their power to curb the vengeance of the people. Let their magnanimity be worthy of the great cause of which they are the defenders. I fear, however, that now the conquest is begun, the wise and the good can no longer arrest its fury. It is fortunate for the philanthropist who can weave dreams of universal peace, the offspring of universal freedom! My eyes can perceive no such visions. I trust that a happier era is preparing for Europe than any that she has seen since the rise of the Roman Empire, but I anticipate with sad certainty that the contests now carrying on will display to the end a due proportion of those crimes and vices to the recording pen of history, and the reflective observation of philosophy, that seem to be the inseparable companions of aspiring and imperfect man.

Introduction; *Memoirs of the Affairs of Europe from the*
Peace of Utrecht: 1824

BY THE PEOPLE AND FOR THE PEOPLE

In the same spirit which had prompted his abortive Reform measures of 1819 and 1822, Russell, under Grey, was largely responsible for framing the Reform Bill which he brought forward as a Government measure in the Commons on 1 March 1831.

The real question is whether, without some large measure of Reform, the business of the country can be carried on with the confidence and the support of the people? I shall not ask whether you can resist Reform, but I say that it has become a question whether or not the Constitution would now perish if Reform be deferred. This House, in its unreformed state, has nothing to look to but the sympathy, confidence, and support of the nation. If it now refuses Reform, that sympathy will be withheld—that support will be denied. I ask you, then, whether, when his Majesty's Ministers are convinced that Reform is necessary, and when they have the approbation of their gracious sovereign for bringing this proposition before the House; when they declare that Reform is indispensable; when multitudes of petitions pour upon your table, and myriads of voices out of doors put forth a just request for Reform—will this House say: *We are the judges of our own honesty, we despise the advice of the Crown, and disregard at once the warning of ministers and the demands of the people whom we profess to represent?* Will this House say: *We will keep our power, keep it how we may; we regard not the petitions of the people, and are ready to abide by all the consequences of our refusal?*

I appeal, in my turn, to the aristocracy. The gentlemen of England have never been found wanting in any great crisis. When the country was engaged in war against the national enemy, when the honour and security of the country were assailed, they were ever foremost. When burthens were to be borne, they were ever as ready to bear their share as any other class of the community. I ask them now, when a great sacrifice is to be made, to show their generosity, to convince the people of their public spirit, and to identify themselves for the future with the people. Upon the gentlemen of England, then, I call. I ask them to come forward and, by their conduct on this occasion, to give security to the Throne, stability to Parliament and the Constitution, and strength and peace to the country. The question is to be decided by this House.

Whatever may be the result of this proposition, the king's ministers will feel that they have done their duty. They have hitherto pursued an even and straightforward line, consulting no particular class or party, but acting according to the dictates of what they considered their duty. Wherever the line has led them they have not hesitated to encounter any difficulties by which they were met. I therefore think I am justified in saying that we are to be believed when we come forward and state that we consider some effectual measure of Reform to be necessary. I say that we have a right to be believed when we assert that it is not for any sinister end of our own we bring forward the present measure, but because we are interested in the future welfare of this country, which welfare we conceive to be best consulted by the adoption of a timely and an effective Reform—because we think, that by such a course alone we shall be enabled to give a permanency to that Constitution which has been so long the admiration of nations, on account of its popular spirit, but which cannot exist much longer unless strengthened by an additional infusion of popular spirit, commensurate with the progress of knowledge and the increased intelligence of the age. To establish the Constitution on a firm basis, you must show that you are determined not to be the representatives of a small class, or of a particular interest; but to form a body who, representing the people, springing from the people, and sympathising with the people, can fairly call on the people to support the future burthens of the country, and to struggle with the future difficulties which it may have to encounter; confident that those who call upon them are ready to join them heart and hand: and are only looking, like themselves, to the glory and welfare of England.

House of Commons: 1 March 1831

PEACE WITH HONOUR

This and the following extract are from speeches made in the shadow of the Crimean War.

I trust we shall none of us forget that this country holds an important position among the nations of the world—that not once, but many times she has stood forward to resist oppression, to maintain the independence of weaker nations, to preserve to the general family of nations that freedom, that power of governing themselves of which others have sought to deprive them. I trust that character will not be forgotten, will not be abandoned by a people now stronger in means, more populous, and more healthy than it ever has been at any former period. This, then, is not the period to abandon any of those duties towards the whole of mankind, which Great Britain has hitherto performed. Let us perform them, if possible, by our moral influence; let us perform them, if possible, while we maintain the inestimable blessings of peace. But while we endeavour to maintain peace, I certainly should be the last to forget that if peace cannot be maintained with honour, it is no longer peace. It becomes no longer peace, but a truce—a precarious truce—to be denounced by others whenever they may think fit—whenever they think that an opportunity has occurred to enforce by arms their unjust demands upon us or upon our allies.

Greenock: 19 September 1853

For my part, if most unexpectedly the Emperor of Russia should recede from his former demands, we shall all rejoice to be spared the pain, the efforts, and the burdens of war. But if peace is no longer consistent with our duty to England, with our duty to Europe, with our duty to the world, we can only endeavour to enter into this contest with a stout heart. May God defend the right! And I, for my part, shall be willing to bear my share of the burden and the responsibility.

House of Commons: 17 February 1854

TRUTH IS ONE

It is then to Christian principles, Christian morals, and a Christian spirit that we must look for a better and a higher civilisation than any that has been attained. Before many years are passed, there will be in Great Britain and the United States of America, sixty, seventy, or eighty millions of free people. May we not hope that these kindred nations—each speaking the English language—each deriving its pedigree of liberty from a common ancestry—each inheriting the English Bible—each reading Shakespeare and Milton—each divided into many denominations of Christians, but each allowing complete liberty of worship—will unite in the glorious task of a peaceful conquest and bloodless victory? At least let us indulge in this high hope. If we do not arrive at, or even approximate to, perfection, we may look at least to uninterrupted progress towards a far better social organisation than any we have yet enjoyed.

To each one of us belongs a portion of the noble task of speeding our country on her great and glorious way, by walking steadfastly in the full light of such truths as we already possess, and by hastening the noonday brightness of such as are only dawning. Let it not be the reproach of any one of us that, born in a land where the laws acknowledge that thought and speech are free, we have yet ever lent the helping hand of custom, folly, or intolerance to extinguish one spark of that Divine flame which we call the soul, or ever turned away from a righteous and peaceable endeavour to loosen the fetters that still bind it throughout the world.

Some there are who shut their eyes to one truth lest it should impair another they deem more sacred. But one truth can no more quench another truth than one sunbeam can quench another sunbeam. Truth is one, as God is one. Go forward to meet her in whatever garb, welcome her from whatever corner she comes, till at last, beyond the grave, you shall hail her in a blaze of glory which mortal eye can only strain in vain to contemplate. Truth is the gem for which the wise man digs the earth, the pearl for which he dives into the ocean, the star for which he climbs the heavens—the herald and the guardian of moral and political progress.

The Obstacles which have retarded Moral and Political progress:
A lecture. Exeter Hall: November 1853

SALUTE TO SPAIN: 1808

Here was indeed a crisis in the affairs of Europe. The cause of national independence, which in the first portion of the war was defended by France, was now about to be upheld by the other nations of Europe. No matter how ignorant, how ill-armed, how ill-led the Spanish people might be, here was a nation animated by a real enthusiasm; ready to fight in the field of battle, in the town, in the village, in the farm-yard, and in the peasant's cottage for the sacred cause of national independence.

It behoved England, therefore, to welcome this reviving spirit, to expend her growing treasures, to employ her extensive credit, to dispatch her most skilful officers, to marshal her bravest troops in defence of this sacred cause. England might be exhausted in the struggle, but by lifting up her heart to meet the mighty danger, and by an attempt to free herself and other nations from intolerable slavery, she could never be disgraced.

Recollections and Suggestions: 1874

THE LINES OF TORRES VEDRAS: 1810

Never was I more struck than with the physical, military, and political spectacle which lay before me. Standing on the highest point, and looking around him on every side, was the English General, his eyes bright and searching as those of an eagle, his countenance full of hope, beaming with intelligence, as he marked with quick perception every movement of troops and every change of circumstance within the sweep of the horizon. On each side of the fort of Sobral rose the entrenchments of the Allies, bristling with guns and alive with the troops who formed the garrison of this fortified position. Far off, on the left, the cliffs rose to a moderate elevation, and the line of Torres Vedras was prominent in the distance.

Below us, over a large extent of hill and valley, plain and eminence, was the position of the French army. The villages were full of their soldiers; the white sails of the Portuguese windmills were actively in motion for the supply of flour to the invading army. There stood the advanced guard of the conquering legions of France; here was the living barrier of England, Spain, and Portugal prepared to stay the destructive flood, and to preserve from the deluge the liberty and independence of three armed nations. The sight filled me with admiration, with confidence, and with hope.

Recollections and Suggestions: 1874

Edward Geoffrey Stanley, later

Lord Stanley and, afterwards, fourteenth

EARL OF DERBY

1799 – 1869

*Whig M.P., 1832–35; Conservative M.P.,
1835–44; Under-Secretary of State for the
Colonies, 1827–28; Chief Secretary for Ireland,
1830–33; Secretary of State for War and the
Colonies, 1833–34 and 1841–45; First Lord of
the Treasury, 1852, 1858–59 and 1866–68*

AN ENGLISHMAN LOOKS AT AMERICA: 1824

*The United States had enjoyed less than half-a-century of independence
when, in 1824–25, Stanley made a nine-months' tour in North America.
The spirit which prompted his visit is shown in this extract from the
early pages of his journal.*

THE peculiar circumstances which rendered America an object of
controversy have in a great measure died away, and to an unprejudiced Englishman she must be a subject of great and increasing
interest. Her history, though short, is identified with that of his own
country—her constitution, though yet but a bold experiment, offers
a practical commentary upon his own, and involves in its progress, in
its prosperity, in its very existence, the dearest and deepest principles
of that of England. The effect of every deviation from it, every modification, may be watched as it effects religion, morals, manners, national
and individual happiness. She affords subjects of momentous inquiry
to the statesman, the philosopher, and the moralist: and the greater
heights to which she is daily rising in the scale of nations, makes it of
more importance to know and estimate her real situation. But in
drawing practical conclusions, it is of the first necessity not to deceive
ourselves by fancied resemblance, and to study well all the various
points of difference, all the modifying circumstances which produce in
America very different results from those which would be effected in
Europe by apparently the same causes. It would be an interesting
speculation for a man of leisure and reflection, to contemplate the
various effects which have been produced by all the various com-

140

inations of climate, origin, accidental circumstances, and positive
institutions upon the national character of each several state, and to
consider how the genius of the constitution is constantly at work,
amalgamating the whole, and gradually reducing them all to the
uniform hue of equalising democracy.

Journal of a Tour in America, 1824–25

NEW YORK: 1824

On Wednesday July 21 after an average passage of thirty-seven days,
we first made land, which was ascertained to be the Highlands of
Neversink (a corruption from Navesank, the name of an Indian tribe)
on the Jersey shore, and at eleven the same night we took on board a
pilot. If we had been gratified the night before by the fresh smell of the
pinewoods and the sounds of land, we were far more so the next
morning, as we worked up with fine summer weather and a gentle
breeze just sufficient to carry us through the ebb tide. The approach to
New York, near thirty miles from Sandy Hook, is one of great beauty,
though possessing no very striking features. Long Island, on our right,
is a low and flat but well wooded shore; on our left and before us lay
Staten Island and the Jersey shore, the former intervening, with a
coast of no great height, but the surface prettily tumbled. The houses
are all white, and at a distance look neat and comfortable, though
built chiefly if not entirely of wood. The face of the country is covered
with immense woods of uncleared pine, to an extent which I had not
anticipated, but which results from the poorness of the soil. After
passing the Narrows, defended by a fort on each side, the magnificent
bay opens to view, presenting a prospect in its style perhaps unequalled.
Its charms, however, consist in the constant undulation of the surrounding shores, the abundance of wood, the happy mixture of sea
and land, the partial cultivation interspersed amid the natural wildness, all as unlike as possible to that with which the inhabitants are
fond of comparing it—the Bay of Naples—with which it has no one
feature in common.

The first view of the city of New York is very striking—lying in a
small island, formed by the confluence of two great rivers, its buildings
interspersed with trees, and presenting at one *coup d'oeil* land, water,
wood, town, country and sea. This position, however, is unfavourable
for displaying the extent and commercial importance of the city, as the
approach is to a very narrow point, occupied by a public walk called
the Battery, neither of great extent nor of great beauty. The houses too
in the neighbourhood are low, irregular, and mean looking—and

perhaps to our prejudices their very cleanliness, the absence of smoke
and the circumstance of their being painted of all colours, convey
ideas different from our notions of a great commercial town. These
impressions, however, would be far from correct as there is perhaps no
city in the world which is increasing in commercial importance with
such rapidity as New York. Houses have been built for the last two
years at the rate of from three to four thousand each year—the
population is estimated at about a hundred and thirty thousand—and
it is curious enough that for many years, both increasing with great
rapidity, it has nearly maintained its proportion of one: eleven to the
population of the whole state.

                                                                                    Ibid

AS BROTHER MEN

*The Emancipation Act which finally abolished slavery in British posses-
sions was introduced by Stanley, as Colonial Secretary, in May and
passed in August 1833. It both secured the freedom of the slaves and
indemnified the planters.*

The whole of this argument amounts to saying that the negroes are
not fit for emancipation and that we must wait until they are. The
argument goes too far; for it proceeds to the indefinite conclusion that
we must postpone emancipation, not for ten or twenty or thirty years,
but to some period no one can say how remote. I know that people
will tell me we do not wish to perpetuate slavery—we merely wish to
postpone emancipation till the negroes are fit for freedom—till they
manifest a disposition for laborious industry sufficient to qualify them
for the privileges of free men. That argument, if it proves anything,
proves too much. Do men ever show a disposition to labour until
population presses upon food; and will that ever take place so long as
the depopulating influence of slavery prevails? We are told that the
negroes own no domestic ties; nor will they, so long as you keep them
in that state of slavery which debases their principles, and which
deprives them of foresight, and which takes away from them the
motives to industry. The slaves have no education, and you deny them
any; for as slaves they can have none. They have hitherto been treated
as chattels attached to the soil—do you think they can be made fit for
freedom till freedom has exercised its influence upon their minds and
upon their moral character?

But I entertain a hope that from the day on which the act passes
there will be secured to the country, to the colonies, and to all classes
of his Majesty's subjects, the benefits of a virtual extinction of all the
horrors attendant upon a state of slavery; and that, at no very distant

period, by no uncertain operation, but by the effect of that machinery which the proposed plan will put in motion, the dark stain which disfigures the fair freedom of this country will be wholly wiped out.

I conclude with offering up an ardent prayer, that by the course which the House may adopt, it will for a second time set the world a glorious example of a commercial nation, weighing commercial advantages light in the balance against justice and religion; that they will achieve the great object of extinguishing slavery, gradually, safely, but at the same time completely; a result the more to be desired, if accomplished by a yielding on one side and the other, which may make both sides forget extreme opinion; and which will exhibit a great and proud example of a deliberative assembly, reconciling conflicting interests, liberating the slave without inflicting hardship on his master, gratifying the liberal and humane spirit of the age, without harming even those who stand in its way, and vindicating their high functions by acting in a manner on this important question which will afford a sure pledge of a successful termination of the glorious career on which they are about to enter.

House of Commons: 14 May 1833

THE BEGINNING OF WISDOM

But most of all, to you I say, if such there be among you, who are panting even now with generous ambition to enter upon the stormy career of political life, whose young imaginations are even now picturing to themselves ardent hopes of swaying the destiny of nations, and exercising their talents for the benefit of mankind—to you I say, quench not those high aspirations, check not those noble energies; but amid the cares and vexations which I warn you to expect, but bid you not to shrink from encountering, amid the embarrassments and anxieties inseparable from your destined course, the wearying disgust, the thwartings of ignorance or selfishness, the doubts and perplexities, the misconstructions to which your every word and action will be subject—believe me, when I say that to guide you, and to cheer you, and to support you, you will need some higher incentive than that of human praise—some nobler reward than that of human ambition— some principle more fixed than that of human honour—you will require the daily conviction that you are treading steadfastly your allotted path of duty, under the guidance of One with whom is the result of all your labours, and under a deep responsibility to One with whom there is no misconstruction and no change.

Rectorial Address, University of Glasgow: 17 December 1834

LET HIS GREAT EXAMPLE STAND

*On 18 November 1852 all that was mortal of the Duke of Wellingto,
was,* to the noise of the mourning of a mighty nation, *laid to rest i,
St. Paul's Cathedral.*

When, amidst solemn and mournful music, slowly and inch b`
inch, the coffin which held the illustrious dead descended into its las`
long resting place, I was near enough to see the countenances of many
of the veterans who were companions of his labours and of hi
triumphs; I was near enough to hear the suppressed sobs and to se`
the hardly-checked tears, which would not have disgraced the cheek:
of England's greatest warriors, as they looked down for the last time
upon all that was mortal of our mighty hero. Honour, my lords, to the
people who so well knew how to reverence the illustrious dead
Honour, my lords, to the friendly visitors—especially to France, the
great and friendly nation that testified by the presence of their repre
sentatives their respect and veneration for his memory whom they
regarded as a foe worthy of their steel!

His object was neither fame nor glory, but a lasting peace. We have
buried in our greatest hero the man among us who had the greates
horror of war, the great object of whose country is to maintain peace
To do that, however, a nation must possess the means of self-defence
I trust that we shall bear this in mind, not in words only, but in our
actions and policy, setting aside all political and party considerations
and that we shall concur in this opinion—that, in order to be peaceful
England must be powerful; but that, if England must be powerful
she ought to be so in order that she should be more secure of peace.

House of Lords: 19 November 185.

NOBLESSE OBLIGE

I have had ancestors who, for their loyalty to the throne, and their
fidelity to their country, have died on the field of battle, and, harde,
still, upon the scaffold. Though I cannot pretend to emulate their high
claims, yet, if loyalty to the Crown or faithfulness to my country ca,
upon me, I trust I shall not disgrace their name by refusing to purchase
the safety of the one or the other by the sacrifice of my heart's bes
blood.

On installation as Chancellor of the University, *Oxford:*
7 June 185:

GLORY UNTARNISH'D

Men are born to die on the battlefield as well as upon the bed of sickness.

House of Lords: 3 December 1857

> O friend! if we, survivors of this war,
> Could live, from age and death forever free,
> Thou shouldst not see me foremost in the fight,
> Nor would I urge thee to the glorious field:
> But since on man ten thousand forms of death
> Attend, which none may 'scape, then on, that we
> May glory on others gain, or they on us!

The Iliad of Homer, translated by Edward, Earl of Derby: 1864

George Gordon, afterwards

George Hamilton-Gordon, fourth

EARL OF ABERDEEN

1784 – 1860

Scotch representative peer, Tory, 1806–14; Ambassador-Extraordinary at Vienna, 1813; Chancellor of the Duchy of Lancaster, with seat in Cabinet, 1828; Secretary of State for Foreign Affairs, 1828–30 and 1841–46; Secretary of State for War and the Colonies, 1834–35; First Lord of the Treasury, in Coalition Ministry, 1852–55

'TWAS A FAMOUS VICTORY

Aberdeen accompanied the Emperor Francis throughout the Leipsic campaign of 1813. Though not under fire, he was in the immediate neighbourhood of the battle of Leipsic and entered the city on the day after its capture. The searing sights of carnage and destruction left him with an

10

abhorrence of any but defensive war which greatly influenced his futur policy.

HOW shall I describe the entrance into this town? For three or fou miles the ground is covered with bodies of men and horses, many no dead. Wretches wounded unable to crawl, crying for water amids heaps of putrefying bodies. Their screams are heard at an immens distance, and still ring in my ears. The living as well as the dead ar stripped by the barbarous peasantry, who have not sufficient charit to put the miserable wretches out of their pain. Our victory is mos complete. It must be owned that victory is a fine thing, but one shoul be at a distance.

To his sister-in-law, Lady Maria Hamilton, from Leipsic:
22 October 181.

This town has been burnt and ravaged by the French in thei retreat.

The most affecting sight I think that I ever beheld, I have seer to-day. Houses were burning; the owners of these cottages in the deepest misery, and their children were playing around, and were quite delighted with the fire which consumed the whole property of their parents, and condemned them to cold and hunger. Here is a mixture of innocence and wretchedness which goes to the heart! I do not know when I have felt more severely the wretchedness of mankind.

To the same from Schulchtern: 3 November 1813

CRIMEAN WAR EFFORT

Early in 1854 England drifted into the two-years' Crimean War, before the end of which the unhappy Aberdeen was out of office.

When it pleased her Majesty to place me in the situation in which I now have the honour to stand, I thought it my duty explicitly to declare the principles on which the Government would be carried on. On that occasion, I felt it my duty to declare that the policy of the Government was a policy of peace. I believe it will be admitted that to that policy we have endeavoured to adhere. Nay, more, I am satisfied that the great and universal support we now meet with throughout the country in the war in which we are engaged, is due to the belief that we sincerely did our utmost to avoid the calamities of war. The moment it became necessary to declare war, although I can truly say that I clung to the hope of peace with an almost desperate tenacity, I declared that, so far as I was concerned, it should be carried on with the utmost vigour and energy of which the Government was capable. Perhaps the moment is not inopportune to ask whether that pledge has been fulfilled? If you will only consider what has been done in the course of six short months, I think you will admit that this country never made an exertion at all comparable with that she has just made. An army has been collected, and transported from the shores of this country, such as never left them in preceding history—an army such as the Duke of Wellington never commanded, and appointed in all its parts in a manner which, humanly speaking, is calculated to ensure its success. Conceive what the extent of preparation must have been when you are told that not less than seven hundred vessels were engaged in the same operation. The difficulties connected with it and the time required indispensably for such an undertaking must strike every man of common candour; and yet we hear people talk of delay, as if there had been delay! Such an effort was never before in the history of the world made in so short a time. Our army has gone forth and has achieved its first great victory in conjunction with our gallant allies, our strict concord and union with whom have been fully established from the very first moment, and which hold out the most encouraging prospects to all Europe.

I have said that the war would be continued with the utmost vigour and energy of which the country was capable, but in this I do not abandon a pacific policy. I believe that, to carry on the war in this manner affords the best prospect of arriving at an early and a satisfactory conclusion. I believe that peace, although sought by different means, is sought as effectually under present circumstances, by this course, as it would be by written negotiations or diplomatic discussions. Let me observe that, in carrying on the war with this vigour and this energy, we have nevertheless done something to deprive war of its horrors, to humanise its operations, and to mitigate those atrocities with which it is inevitably accompanied. At the risk and at the sacrifice of some belligerent rights, we have admitted the commerce of neutrals, and we have by our example put an end to privateering, a most dreadful relic of a barbarous age, which the world will probably now never see revived. I say, then, that we have endeavoured to mitigate the horrors of war even while carrying it on with the utmost vigour, and, in so carrying it on, I repeat, that I for one shall never lose sight of the only legitimate object of all war, that of arriving at a stable, just, and honourable peace. War, when it ceases to be a necessity, becomes a crime. I should consider any one who had prolonged the horrors of war for a single day, when it was in his power to make a just, safe, and honourable peace, would be greatly guilty in the eyes of God and man.

Aberdeen: 9 October 1854

CONFLICT

How troubled Aberdeen was by his share in the responsibility for war is shown, even more than in this note written after his resignation in 1853, by his declining to rebuild the parish church of Methlick without apparent reason, until after his death were found various scraps of paper on which he had written out the seventh and eighth verses of 1 Chronicles xxii.

I have never entertained the least doubt of the justice of the war in which we are at present engaged. It is unquestionably just, and it is also strongly marked by a character of disinterestedness. But although just and disinterested, the policy and the necessity of this war may perhaps be less certain. It is possible that our posterity may form a different estimate on this head from that at which we have arrived.

The policy, or necessity, of any war must always be more or less the subject of doubt, and must vary according to a change of circumstances. This is not matter of immutable principle, but may be affected by an infinite variety of considerations. It is true that every necessary war must also really be a just war; but it does not absolutely follow that every just war must also be a necessary war.

Be this as it may, it is perfectly clear that a vast majority of the people of this country entertain no doubt on the subject, but are thoroughly convinced that the war is both just and necessary, and, as such, are prepared to give it their cordial support.

Now, with the existence of so strong and general a feeling, it seems almost to partake of arrogance to demur in any degree to these conclusions, and to resist the weight of the popular voice.

But a reference to history may prevent us from subscribing implicitly to such demonstrations of opinion. It is enough to recall to recollection that, when Sir Robert Walpole was reluctantly drawn into his Spanish war, the country was quite as unanimous as—perhaps more so than—at the present moment. Yet, in spite of such unanimity, there is no man who would now hesitate to declare that the war in question was both unjust and unnecessary.

The national feeling at that period was excited under circumstances in some degree similar to the present. At that period a peace of thirty years had rendered the minds of men more easy to be roused by appeals which had all the character of novelty; and at the present day

I believe that our forty years' peace has rendered the nation more ready to receive the excitement and to encounter the unknown evils of a state of war. I am very far from meaning to assert that the people did not entertain a strong feeling of indignation against injustice and of sympathy for the oppressed. Their natural feelings are always generous; but I doubt if this impulse would have led to the same results if it had been called into action at an earlier period after the conclusion of the late war.

We hear great apprehensions expressed on all sides lest this war should be terminated by an ignominious peace. But although we should share in the feeling, it may not be so easy to avoid the imputation of such a result. For in every contest in which this country has been engaged during the last century we may presume that it has been the determination of each succeeding Government, loudly declared, to obtain the conditions of a just and honourable peace. It is remarkable, however, that with a single exception every treaty concluded at the termination of our great wars has been stigmatised as humiliating and degrading, ignominious, hollow, and unsafe.

Such has been the sentence of the patriots of the day. It was the case at the Peace of Utrecht in 1713, at the Peace of Aix-la-Chapelle in 1748, at the Peace of Paris in 1763, at the Peace of Versailles in 1783, and at the Peace of Amiens in 1801. The single exception was the Peace of Paris in 1814; and, although severely criticised in other respects, it would have been difficult in this case for patriotism or faction to have discovered humiliation and disgrace in a treaty dictated at the head of a victorious army in the capital of an enemy.

But although such has been the contemporaneous condemnation of our treaties of peace, I do not think that this severe verdict has been ratified by a more impartial posterity.

Henry John Temple, third

VISCOUNT PALMERSTON

1784 – 1865

Tory M.P., 1807–30; Whig and Liberal M.P., 1830–65; Junior Lord of the Admiralty, 1808–09; Secretary of State at War, 1809–28; Secretary of State for Foreign Affairs, 1830–34, 1835–41 and 1846–51; Secretary of State for Home Affairs, 1852–55; First Lord of the Treasury, 1855–58 and 1859–65

THE PRICE OF FREEDOM

THE honourable gentleman has alluded to the distresses and financial embarrassments of the country. I should be the last man to speak of those distresses in a slighting manner; but in considering the amount of our burdens, we ought not to forget under what circumstances those difficulties have been incurred. Engaged in an arduous struggle, single-handed and unaided, not only against all the powers of Europe, but with the confederated forces of the civilised world, our object was not merely military glory—not the temptation of territorial acquisition—not even what might be considered a more justifiable object, the assertion of violated rights and the vindication of national honour; but we were contending for our very existence as an independent nation. When the political horizon was thus clouded, when no human foresight could point out from what quarter relief was to be expected, when the utmost effort of national energy was not to despair, I would put it to the honourable gentleman whether, if at that period it could have been shown that Europe might be delivered from its thraldom, but that this contingent must be purchased at the price of a long and patient endurance of our domestic burdens, we should not have accepted the burdens with gratitude? I lament as deeply as the honourable gentleman the burdens of the country; but it should be recollected that they were the price which we agreed to pay for our freedom and independence.

House of Commons: 16 May 1820

HENRY JOHN TEMPLE, VISCOUNT PALMERSTON
From a lithograph by J. S. Templeton after the portrait painted
in 1840 by W. C. Ross, A.R.A., when Palmerston was Secretary
of State for Foreign Affairs

THE JUNIOR AMBASSADOR

From a carricature of Lord Beaconsfield published in *Vanity Fair*, 2 July 1878, during his absence with Lord Salisbury at the Congress of Berlin from which they brought back *Peace with Honour*

THE RIGHTS OF CATHOLIC PATRIOTS

This extract is from Palmerston's speech on the second reading of the 1829 Catholic Relief Bill. Unhappily Palmerston proved a false prophet when, speaking for the measure, he declared that it would open a career of happiness to Ireland which for centuries she had been forbidden to taste.

The honourable baronet stated yesterday that his objections to the admission of Catholics into Parliament were founded, not upon their general conduct as subjects, but upon the incompatibility of their religious tenets with the safety of the Constitution. I presume it is not to the speculative tenets of the Catholics that he objects; that it is not because they believe in transubstantiation, and in the efficacy of the invocation of saints, that he would exclude them from these walls; it must be that in his opinion they hold some doctrines applicable to worldly actions and temporal affairs, which are incompatible with their duties in a Protestant country.

The Catholics deny such doctrines, and I believe their denial; but if everything which has been asserted on this subject were true, it would not alter the practical conclusion to which I should be disposed to come.

If the question, indeed, were whether we should or should not have any Catholics, these arguments would be applicable and conclusive, and I should say, let Ireland be Protestant, and let us have no Catholics in any part of the Empire. But that decision is beyond the reach of human control: there they are, be their religion good or bad: there they are, be their tenets wholesome or objectionable: there they are, five or six millions of Catholics in the heart of the Empire; and the only question is, what shall we do with them? Whether by kind treatment and conciliation we shall make them into our friends, or by exclusion and coercion convert them into enemies? Even if their doctrines were thus objectionable, and the hold which we have over them by abstract principle, and a mere sense of duty, were but slight, the more expedient it would be, since extermination is impossible, to win them to us by kindness, and to bind their hearts to ours by the ties of a common interest; and, therefore, though I utterly disbelieve that the Catholics are guided by the objectionable doctrines which are imputed to them, yet, for the sake of argument, I would concede this assertion, and upon that very basis contend for the policy of emancipation.

What are these doctrines? The only one which is important to the present question is that which relates to their allegiance; for I am sure the honourable baronet is much too liberal and enlightened to give countenance to the vulgar prejudice that Catholics do not deem themselves bound to keep faith with heretics. It is said that the Catholic renders to a Protestant sovereign only a divided allegiance. Now the Catholic utterly denies this charge. Let the most zealous Protestant devise any form of words which shall, in terms the most unequivocal and explicit, adjure any division of that allegiance, which a faithful subject owes to his temporal prince, and that oath the Catholic is prepared to take in the utmost sincerity of heart; and if it is said that oaths are words, and words are empty air, he refers you to the exploits of your navy and army, and appeals to Catholic actions to satisfy Protestant doubts. What more can man do? What fuller refutation can human ingenuity desire? But with what marvellous inconsistency is this objection advanced!

Suppose, for argument's sake, that the allegiance of the Catholic could not be depended upon, and that he were liable to be swayed by foreign influence to betray his country and forswear his king; what is the situation in which such a man would be most dangerous? What is the last situation in which it would be wise to place him? Why, beyond a doubt, in naval or military command. But in naval or military command the law allows the Catholic to be placed; and that law is of recent enactment, and sanctioned, or, at least, unopposed by those very men who cast in the teeth of the Catholic this charge of divided allegiance. Upon what rational ground then can this charge be made an objection to his admission into Parliament? Can you trust a man to stand sentinel at the very gates of your fortress, in actual contact with the enemy, and yet distrust him in the midst of your garrison and surrounded by your guards? A Catholic may lead the fleet of England into fight; a Catholic may command the army of his country in the day of battle. In that perilous hour, when the interests, the honour, perhaps even the safety of England may hang upon the workings—ay, the secret workings of one single mind; when one single act treacherously done, or one single act treacherously omitted, may bring with it irretrievable disaster; in that perilous hour, we are content to commit our fortunes to the hands of the Catholic, confident in his patriotism, his honour, and his faith. But when the question is as to a seat in this House, where he is one among a great number—where little can depend upon individuals—where every word that he utters, and everything that he does, are public as the art of man can make them, and are borne, by the next morning's dawn, upon the wings of the wind, to every corner of the Empire—here, forsooth, we tremble at the dangers that would befall the State if this man of divided allegiance were permitted to vote in a Committee for Supply.

House of Commons: 18 March 1829

MIND OVER MIGHT

There are two great parties in Europe; one which endeavours to bear
sway by the force of public opinion, the other by the force of physical
control. The principle on which the system of this party is founded is,
in my view, fundamentally erroneous. There is in nature no moving
power but mind; all else is passive and inert: in human affairs this
power is opinion; in political affairs it is public opinion; and he who
can grasp the power, with it will subdue the fleshly arm of physical
strength, and compel it to work out his purpose. Look at one of those
floating fortresses which bear to the farthest regions of the globe the
prowess and the glory of England; see a puny figure at the helm,
commanding the winds of heaven and the waves of the ocean, and
enslaving even the laws of nature as if, instead of being ordained to
hold the universe together, they had only been established for his
particular occasion. And yet the merest breath of those winds which
he has yoked to his service, the merest drop of that fathomless abyss
which he has made into his foot-stool, would, if ignorantly encountered, be more than enough for his destruction; but the powers of his
mind have triumphed over the forces of things, and the subjugated
elements are become his obedient vassals. And so also it is with the
political affairs of empires; and those statesmen who know how to
avail themselves of the passions and the interests and the opinions of
mankind are able to gain an ascendancy, and to exercise a sway over
human affairs, far out of all proportion greater than belong to the
power and resources of the state over which they preside; while those,
on the other hand, who seek to check improvement, to cherish abuses,
to crush opinions and to prohibit the human race from thinking,
whatever may be the apparent power which they yield, will find their
weapon snap short in their hand when most they need its protection.

House of Commons: 11 June 1829

THE POLICY OF ENGLAND

I hold that the real policy of England—apart from questions which
involve her own particular interests, political or commercial—is to be
the champion of justice and right; pursuing that course with moderation and prudence, not becoming the Quixote of the world but giving
the weight of her moral sanction and support wherever she thinks that
justice is, and wherever she thinks that wrong has been done. In
pursuing that course, and in pursuing the more limited direction of our
own particular interests, my conviction is that as long as England keeps

herself in the right, as long as she wishes to permit no injustice, as long as she wishes to countenance no wrong, as long as she labours at legislative interests of her own, and as long as she sympathises with right and justice, she never will find herself altogether alone. She is sure to find some other state of sufficient power, influence and weight to support and aid her in the course she may think fit to pursue. Therefore I say that it is a narrow policy to suppose that this country or that is to be marked out as the eternal ally or the perpetual enemy of England. We have no eternal allies, and we have no perpetual enemies. Our interests are eternal and perpetual, and those interests it is our duty to follow. When we find other countries marching in the same course, and pursuing the same objects as ourselves, we consider them as our friends, and we think for the moment that we are on the most cordial footing; when we find other countries that take a different view, and thwart us in the object we pursue, it is our duty to make allowance for the different manner in which they may follow out the same objects. It is our duty not to pass too harsh a judgment upon others, because they do not exactly see things in the same light as we; and it is our duty not lightly to engage this country in the frightful responsibilities of war, because from time to time we may find this or that power disinclined to concur with us in matters where their opinions and ours may fairly differ. That has been, so far as my faculties have allowed me to act upon it, the guiding principle of my conduct. And if I might be allowed to express in one sentence the principle which I think ought to guide an English Minister, I would adopt the expression of Canning, and say that with every British Minister the interests of England ought to be the shibboleth of his policy.

House of Commons: 1 March 1848

CIVIS ROMANUS SUM

This peroration to Palmerston's most famous speech, eulogised even by his political opponents, was spoken in defence of the Ministry's conduct of foreign policy; the speech was concerned with the degree of protection to be afforded British subjects abroad. Palmerston's contention was that, if our subjects abroad have complaints against individuals, or against the Government of a foreign country, if the courts of law of that country can afford them redress, then, no doubt, to those courts of justice the British subject ought in the first instance to apply; and it is only on a denial of justice, or upon decisions manifestly unjust, that the British Government should be called upon to interfere.

I believe that the principles on which we have acted are those which are held by the great mass of the people of this country. I am convinced these principles are calculated, so far as the influence of England may properly be exercised with respect to the destinies of other countries, to conduce to the maintenance of peace, to the advancement of civilisation, to the welfare and happiness of mankind.

I do not complain of the conduct of those who have made these matters the means of attack upon her Majesty's Ministers. The government of a great country like this is, undoubtedly, an object of fair and legitimate ambition to men of all shades of opinion. It is a noble thing to be allowed to guide the policy and to influence the destiny of such a country; and if ever it was an object of honourable ambition, more than ever must it be so at the moment at which I am speaking. For while we have seen the political earthquake rocking Europe from side to side; while we have seen thrones shaken, shattered, levelled, institutions overthrown and destroyed; while in almost every country of Europe the conflict of civil war has deluged the land with blood, from the Atlantic to the Black Sea, from the Baltic to the Mediterranean, this country has presented a spectacle honourable to the people of England and worthy of the admiration of mankind.

We have shown that liberty is compatible with order; that individual freedom is reconcilable with obedience to the law. We have shown the example of a nation in which every class of society accepts with cheerfulness the lot which Providence has assigned to it, while at the same time every individual of each class is constantly striving to raise himself in the social scale, not by injustice and wrong, not by violence and illegality, but by preserving good conduct, and by the steady and energetic exertion of the moral and intellectual faculties with which his Creator has endowed him. To govern such a people as this is indeed an object worthy of the ambition of the noblest man who lives in the land, and therefore I find no fault with those who may think any opportunity a fair one for endeavouring to place themselves in so distinguished and honourable a position; but I contend that we have not in our foreign policy done anything to forfeit the confidence of the country. We may not, perhaps, in this matter or in that have acted precisely up to the opinions of one person or of another; and hard indeed it is, as we all know by our individual and private experience, to find any number of men agreeing entirely in any matter on which they may not be equally possessed of the details of the facts, circumstances, reasons, and conditions which led to action. But, making allowance for those differences of opinion which may fairly and honourably arise among those who concur in general views, I maintain that the principles which can be traced through all our foreign transactions, as the guiding rule and directing spirit of our proceedings, are such as deserve approbation.

I therefore fearlessly challenge the verdict which this House, as representing a political, a commercial, a constitutional country, is to give on the question now brought before it; whether the principles on which the foreign policy of her Majesty's Government has been conducted, and the sense of duty which has led us to think ourselves bound to afford protection to our fellow-subjects abroad, are proper and fitting guides for those who are charged with the government of England; and whether, as the Roman in days of old held himself free from indignity when he could say *Civis Romanus sum*; so also a British subject, in whatever land he may be, shall feel confident that the watchful eye and the strong arm of England will protect him against injustice and wrong.

House of Commons: 25 June 1850

POSTBAG

Palmerston's very characteristic official correspondence abounds in lively examples of the sound sense with which he invested his problems and which earned him his great popularity.

In 1850 the Austrian general, Haynau, newly-notorious for the atrocities he had permitted in Italy and Hungary, paid a visit to London where, sightseeing at Barclay and Perkins' brewery, he was set upon by the indignant and muscular draymen and had to take refuge until his rescue by the police. The Austrian ambassador, Koller, protested and pressed for prosecution of the draymen.

I told Koller that it was much better that no prosecution should take place, because the defence of the accused would necessarily be a minute recapitulation of all the barbarities committed by Haynau in Italy and Hungary, and that would be more injurious to him and to Austria than any verdict obtained against the draymen could be satisfactory.

I must own that I think Haynau's coming here, without rhyme or reason, so soon after his Italian and Hungarian exploits, was a wanton insult to the people of this country, whose opinion of him had been so loudly proclaimed at public meetings and in all the newspapers. But the draymen were wrong in the particular course they adopted. Instead of striking him, which, however, by Koller's account they did not do much, they ought to have tossed him in a blanket, rolled him in the kennel, and then sent him home in a cab, paying his fare to the hotel.

To Sir George Grey, Home Secretary: 1 October 1850

On the outbreak of cholera in 1853 the Presbytery of Edinburgh wrote to Palmerston, then Home Secretary, suggesting that a national fast be appointed on Royal authority.

Lord Palmerston would, therefore, suggest that the best course which the people of this country can pursue to deserve that the further progress of the cholera should be stayed, will be to employ the interval that will elapse between the present time and the beginning of next spring in planning and executing measures by which those portions of their towns and cities which are inhabited by the poorest classes, and which, from the nature of things, must most need purification and improvement, may be freed from those causes and sources of contagion which, if allowed to remain, will infallibly breed pestilence and be fruitful in death, in spite of all the prayers and fastings of a united but inactive nation. When man has done his utmost for his own safety, then is the time to invoke the blessing of Heaven to give effect to his exertions.

To the Moderator, Presbytery of Edinburgh: 19 October 1853

I cannot agree with you as to the principle on which the grass in the park should be treated. You seem to think it a thing to be looked at by people who are to be confined to the gravel walks. I regard it as a thing to be walked upon freely and without restraint by the people, old and young, for whose enjoyment the parks are maintained; and your iron hurdles would turn the parks into so many Smithfields, and entirely prevent that enjoyment. As to people making paths across the grass, what does that signify? When I see the grass worn by foot traffic, I look on it as a proof that the park has answered its purpose, and has done its duty by the health, amusement, and enjoyment of the people.

To Sir Benjamin Hall, First Commissioner of Works:
31 October 1857

OLD ENGLAND

Those persons and those parties who wish to improve the institutions of a great country like this are bound to go slowly and deliberately, or they are sure to meet with great resistance at every step which they take. I do not complain of that resistance. It belongs to the character of the country, and it has this advantage, that it prevents sudden and ill-considered alterations, and that measures proposed as improvements receive the due consideration and discussion which renders them ultimately better adapted to the conditions of the people to whom they apply. A love and affection for ancient practices and institution is an honourable and peculiar characteristic of the people of thi country, and I am the last to wish that that honourable and usefu sentiment should ever be discarded from their minds. Nationa character is often evinced by circumstances apparently trifling ii themselves, and there are some of the nations of the Continent who are more volatile and more apt to change. In many parts of the Continent if an innkeeper wishes to recommend his inn, he hangs up a sign of *The New White Horse*, or *The New Golden Cross*. The las novelty is that which is considered the most attractive. Here a contrary course is pursued, and, if the owner of a country alehouse wishes to draw custom, he hangs up the sign of *The Old Plough New Revived* There is at a place called Hanwell, not far from London, an inn to which gentlemen who were fond of pigeon-shooting used to resort to practise their skill. What is the sign of that inn? It is *The Old Hats* Not that anybody was thought to prefer an old hat to a new one, bu it was expected that gentlemen would come to *The Old Hats* ii preference to *The New Hats*. A rival inn was set up, and what was it sign? Why, *The Old Old Hats*, and much it profited by that superlative designation. The people of this country, too, when they wish to express their attachment to the land they live in, call it, with affection ate endearment, Old England; but that does not prevent them from repairing what may have got into decay, or from improving, o ornamenting, or embellishing that which is still good, but may be made better.

Tiverton: July 185.

THIS ENGLAND NEVER DID

There is no man with an English heart in his bosom who does no feel that England is worth defending, and that he ought to make an sacrifice rather than allow his country to be conquered. This countr is the heart of civil and political liberty, and its conquest would no only be one of the greatest calamities to the country itself, but woul be a misfortune to the whole of the civilised world. Campbell, in line describing the fate of Poland, says that

> *Hope for a season bade the world farewell,*
> *And Freedom shrieked when Kosciusko fell;*

but hope would indeed for ever bid adieu to the world and freedom would die if England were to be conquered.

Ibi

THE HEAVENS DECLARE

The study of the mechanism of that great universe of which our solar system forms but a comparatively insignificant part and of which, on a starlight night, we see some portion exposed, is one which leads the mind to the most exalted thoughts, which expands our considerations more than any other, and excites our wonder and our admiration. Let it not be said these studies divert the mind from the practical precepts of religion; on the contrary, I maintain that they tend to strengthen and confirm the faith which is inculcated by revealed religion. For when we contemplate those marvellous arrangements extending over space indefinite and comprising worlds innumerable, with order and system which nothing but the most supreme wisdom could have established; when we consider the multitudes of suns and worlds even beyond the range of telescopic power, we are made sensible of the comparative insignificance of everything that belongs to this earth; and if there is any man who, in the consciousness of genius, in the enjoyment of wealth, in the possession of station, is inspired by feelings of vanity and pride, when he reflects that the world upon which he treads is a mere speck in creation and he himself but an immeasurable atom in that speck, these thoughts must tend to lower that pride, to divest him of that vanity, and to teach him veneration and humility.

But when he turns his thoughts, when he considers the infinite variety, the ingenuity, and the wisdom with which everything on this earth has been adapted to specific purposes and for the enjoyment of created beings; when he sees even in the smallest and most minute creation the most admirable adaptation of every detail; when he reflects on the constitution of his own frame; when he reflects upon all the faculties with which his mind has been endowed and when he considers the powers which have been given to man, to extend his ken far away from the globe which he inhabits, and to acquire knowledge of things so distant that millions of years are required to bring to us the light which flows from their centre—he must be persuaded that those arrangements were not intended in vain. He must be convinced that those moral and intellectual powers with which he has been endowed have not been given simply for the purpose of a day, and that day the life of man. He must be convinced that they are designed to fit him for some better and future state, and therefore I say that these great, exalted, and sublime contemplations are calculated to strengthen and encourage that faith of which it is said that, panting for a happier state, it deems death but nature's signal for retreat.

Rectorial Address, University of Glasgow: 30 March 1863

BENJAMIN DISRAELI

afterwards Earl of Beaconsfield

1804–1881

Conservative M.P., 1837–76; Chancellor of the Exchequer and Leader of the House of Commons, 1852, 1858–59 and 1866–68; Leader of Conservative Opposition in House of Commons, 1852–58, 1859–66 and 1868–73; First Lord of the Treasury, 1868 and 1874–80

OF MAGNA CARTA

IT is the fashion nowadays to depreciate the value of the Great Charter—an ominous sign of the times, in my belief. For he runs a slight chance of being ultimately counted among the false prophets of the realm who predicts that, when the mention of that blessed deed does not command the reverential gratitude of every Briton, evil fortunes are impending for this society. Despots may depreciate it whether they assume the forms of crowned monarchs or popular tribunes, for it stands alike in their way; but he who really loves freedom and his fatherland will never forget that the signet of the tyrant sealed alike our civil liberty and our national independence. They were great men, my lord, that Archbishop of Canterbury and that Earl of Pembroke who, in the darkness of feudal ages, laid this bold and broad foundation of our national liberties; they were great men, and they were great statesmen. They did not act upon abstract principles, luckily for us—principles which the next age might have rejected and the first schoolman hired by the King might have refuted; they acted upon positive conventional right. They set up no new title; they claimed their inheritance. They established the liberties of Englishmen as a life estate which their descendants might enjoy, but could not abuse by committing waste, or forfeit by any false and fraudulent conveyance. They entailed our freedom.

A Vindication of the English Constitution, in a Letter to a
Noble and Learned Lord: 1835.

THE ENGLISH CONSTITUTION

The English nation, to obtain the convenience of monarchy, have established a popular throne, and, to enjoy the security of aristocracy, have invested certain orders of their fellow-subjects with legislative functions: but these estates, however highly privileged, are invested with no quality of exclusion; and the Peers and the Commons of England are the trustees of the nation, not its masters. The country where the legislative and even the executive office may be constitutionally obtained by every subject of the land is a democracy, and a democracy of the highest character. If neither ancient ages nor the more recent experience of our newer time can supply us with a parallel instance of a free government, founded on the broadest basis of popular rights, yet combining with democratic liberty aristocratic security and monarchical convenience; if the refined spirit of Greece, if the great Roman soul, if the brilliant genius of feudal Italy, alike failed in realising this great result, let us cling with increased devotion to the matchless creation of our ancestors, and honour, with still deeper feelings of gratitude and veneration, the English Constitution. That Constitution, my lord, established civil equality in a rude age, and anticipated by centuries in its beneficent practice the sublime theories of modern philosophy; having made us equal, it has kept us free. If it has united equality with freedom, so also it has connected freedom with glory. It has established an Empire which combines the durability of Rome with the adventure of Carthage. It has, at the same time, secured us the most skilful agriculture, the most extended commerce, the most ingenious manufactures, victorious armies, and invincible fleets. Nor has the intellectual might of England under its fostering auspices been less distinguished than its imperial spirit, its manly heart, or its national energy. The authors of England have formed the mind of Europe, and stamped the breathing impression of their genius on the vigorous character of a new world. Under that Constitution the administration of justice has become so pure, that its exercise has realised the dreams of some Utopian romance. That Constitution has struggled successfully with the Papacy, and finally, and for the first time, proved the compatibility of sectarian toleration and national orthodoxy. It has made private ambition conducive to public welfare, it has baffled the machinations of factions and of parties; and when those more violent convulsions have arisen, from whose periodic visitations no human institutions can be exempt, the English Constitution has survived the moral earthquake and outlived the mental hurricane, and been sedulous that the natural course of our

11

prosperity should only be disturbed and not destroyed. Finally, it has secured for every man the career to which he is adapted, and the reward to which he is entitled; it has summoned your lordship to preside over Courts and Parliaments, to maintain law by learning, and to recommend wisdom by eloquence; and it has secured to me, in common with every subject of this realm, a right—the enjoyment of which I would not exchange for

> *The ermined stole,*
> *The starry breast and coronetted brow—*

the right of expressing my free thoughts to a free people.

Ibid

THE HIGHEST DELIGHT

The idea that human happiness is dependent on the cultivation of the mind and on the discovery of the truth, is, next to the conviction of our immortality, the idea the most full of consolation to man; for the cultivation of the mind has no limits, and truth is the only thing that is eternal. A man who knows nothing but the history of the passing hour, who knows nothing of the history of the past, who in a moment of despondency or gloom has no hope in the morrow, because he has read nothing that has taught him that the morrow has any changes—that man, compared with him who has read the most ordinary abridgement of history or the most common philosophical speculation, is as distinct and different an animal as if he had fallen from some other planet, was influenced by a different organisation, working for a different end, and hoping for a different result. It is knowledge that influences and equalises the social condition of man; that gives to all, however different their political position, passions which are in common, and enjoyments which are universal. Knowledge is like the mystic ladder in the patriarch's dream. Its base rests on the primeval earth, its crest is lost in the shadowy splendour of the empyrean; while the great authors who for traditionary ages have held the chain of science and philosophy, of poesy and erudition, are the angels ascending and descending the sacred scale, and maintaining, as it were, the communication between man and heaven. This feeling is so universal that there is no combination of society in any age in which it has not developed itself. It may indeed be partly restrained under despotic governments, under peculiar systems of retarded civilisation, but it is a consequence as incidental to the spirit and the genius of the

Christian civilisation of Europe as that the day should follow night, and the stars should shine according to their laws and order.

*The Value of Literature to Men of Business: an address to members
of the Manchester Athenæum. 23 October 1844*

TWO NATIONS

This is a new reign, said Egremont, *perhaps it is a new era.*

I think so, said the younger stranger.

I hope so, said the elder one.

Well, society may be in its infancy, said Egremont, slightly smiling; *but say what you like, our Queen reigns over the greatest nation that ever existed.*

Which nation? asked the younger stranger, *for she reigns over two.*

The stranger paused; Egremont was silent, but looked inquiringly.

Yes, resumed the younger stranger, after a moment's interval. *Two nations; between whom there is no intercourse and no sympathy; who are as ignorant of each other's habits, thoughts and feelings as if they were dwellers in different zones, or inhabitants of different planets; who are formed by a different breeding, are fed by a different food, are ordered by different manners, and are governed by the same laws.*

You speak of . . . said Egremont, hesitatingly.

THE RICH AND THE POOR.

And yet, said Egremont, *a great family, rooted in the land, has been deemed to b an element of political strength.*

I'll tell you what, said Gerard, *there is a great family in this country, and rooted in it, of which we have heard much less than they deserved, but of which I suspect we shall very soon hear enough to make us think a bit.*

In this country?

Ay; in this country and every other one: I mean the PEOPLE.

Sybil. 1845

YOUNG ENGLAND

There is a whisper rising in this country that Loyalty is not a phrase, Faith not a delusion, and Popular Liberty something more diffusive and substantial than the profane exercise of the sacred rights of sovereignty by political classes.

That we may live to see England once more possess a free Monarchy, and a privileged and prosperous People, is my prayer; that these great consequences can only be brought about by the energy and devotion of our Youth is my persuasion. We live in an age when to be young and to be indifferent can be no longer synonymous. We must prepare for the coming hour. The claims of the Future are represented by suffering millions; and the Youth of a Nation are the trustees of Posterity.

Ibid

I LOOK TO THE PEOPLE

We have been told that we shall derive from this great struggle, not merely the repeal of the Corn Laws, but the transfer of power from one class to another—to one distinguished for its intelligence and wealth—the manufacturers of England. My conscience assures me that I have not been slow in doing justice to the intelligence of that class; certain I am that I am not one of those who envy them their wide and deserved prosperity; but I must confess my deep mortification that in an age of political regeneration, when all social evils are ascribed to the operation of class interests, it should be suggested that we are to be rescued from the alleged power of one class, only to sink under the avowed dominion of another. If this is to be the end of all our struggles —if this is to be the great result of this enlightened age—I, for one, protest against the ignominious catastrophe. I believe that the monarchy of England, its sovereignty mitigated by the acknowledged authority of the estates of the realm, has its root in the hearts of the people, and is capable of securing the happiness of the nation and the power of the State. But if this be a worn-out dream—if, indeed, there is to be a change, anxious as I am to maintain the present polity of this country, ready to make as many sacrifices as any man for that object— I, for one, hope that the foundation of it may be deep, the scheme comprehensive, and that instead of falling under such a thraldom, under the thraldom of capital—under the thraldom of those who, while they boast of their intelligence, are more proud of their wealth— if we must find a new force to maintain the ancient throne and immemorial monarchy of England, I hope that we may find that novel power in the invigorating energies of an educated and enfranchised people.

House of Commons: 20 February 1846

OUR DEBT TO JEWRY

The words on the true faith of a Christian *occurring in the form of oath required to be sworn by every member necessarily excluded practising Jews from Parliament. In 1833 a Commons proposal to dispense with*

*this phrase was rejected by the Lords as it was again in 1847 when
Disraeli, speaking on Lord John Russell's motion, sought to remind
Christendom of its debt to the members of his race. He himself, at the
instance of his father, had been baptized into the Anglican Church in
1817, but for which fact his political career would have been impossible.*

*In 1858 this Jewish disability was removed on a compromise allowing
each House to determine the form of oath to be taken by its members and
in 1866, on Catholic representation, a new oath which omitted the
offending phrase was drawn up.*

In Europe—that Europe which you have baptized Christendom—
how stands the Jew in relation to the Church of Christ? What possible
object can the Jew have to oppose the Christian Church? Is it not the
first business of the Christian Church to make the population whose
minds she attempts to form, and whose morals she seeks to guide,
acquainted with the history of the Jews? Has not the Church of
Christ—the Christian Church, whether Roman Catholic or Protestant
—made the history of the Jews the most celebrated history in the
world? On every sacred day you read to the people the exploits of
Jewish heroes, the proofs of Jewish devotion, the brilliant annals of
past Jewish magnificence. The Christian Church has covered every
kingdom with sacred buildings, and over every altar we find the tables
of the Jewish law. Every Sunday—every Lord's day—if you wish to
express feelings of praise and thanksgiving to the Most High, or if
you wish to find expression of solace in grief, you find both in the
words of the Jewish poets. All the early Christians were Jews. The
Christian religion was first preached by men who had been Jews until
they were converted; every man in the early ages of the Church by
whose power, or zeal, or genius, the Christian faith was propagated,
was a Jew.

In exact proportion to your faith ought to be your wish to do this
great act of national justice. If you had not forgotten what you owe to
this people, if you were grateful for that literature which for thousands
of years has brought so much instruction and so much consolation to
the sons of men, you as Christians would be only too ready to seize
the first opportunity of meeting the claims of those who profess this
religion. But you are influenced by the darkest superstitions of the
darkest ages that ever existed in this country. It is this feeling that has
been kept out of this debate; indeed, that has been kept secret in
yourselves—enlightened as you are—and that is unknowingly influencing you as it is influencing others abroad.

I cannot sit in this House with any misconception of my opinion on
the subject. Whatever may be the consequences on the seat I hold—

and I should not have referred to such a consideration unless other gentlemen had done so—I cannot give a vote which is not in deference to what I believe to be the true principles of religion. Yes, it is as a Christian that I will not take upon me the awful responsibility of excluding from the legislature those who are of the religion in the bosom of which my Lord and Saviour was born.

House of Commons: December 1847

LIBERTY TO KNOW, TO UTTER, AND TO ARGUE FREELY

It is unnecessary for me to say that it is not probable I shall ever say or do anything which would tend to depreciate the influence or diminish the power of Parliament or the press. My greatest honour is to be a member of this House, in which all my thoughts and feelings are concentred; and as for the press, I am myself a gentleman of the press, and I bear no other scutcheon. I know well the circumstances under which we have obtained in this country the blessing of a free press. It is only a century and a half ago since we got rid of the censorship; and when we had got rid of the censorship we had a law of libel which, for nearly a century, rendered that freedom of the press a most perilous privilege. Until Mr. Fox's great Act upon the law of libel, no public writer could have been said to be safe in this country, and the House will recollect that during the interval—not a very long interval, little more than half a century—that liberty of the press has been often modified, often interfered with by British ministers; and that modification and that interference have always been sanctioned by British Parliaments. I hope we live in happier times than those which preceded us in that respect. I hope we have arrived at a conclusion in this country that if the press is free it should enjoy a complete freedom; that the best protection against the excesses of the press is the spirit of discussion, which is the principle upon which our society at present depends; and I think that all parties in this country have come to the conclusion that the liberty of the press is the most valuable of our public privileges, because, in fact, it secures and guarantees the enjoyment of all the rest.

With all my love of the liberty of the press, with all my confidence that we have arrived at a state of security in England which will prevent any minister at any time ever again attempting to interfere with that liberty, I am still conscious that we enjoy it in this country on certain conditions which do not, in my opinion, prevail in other countries: namely, of a long established order, a habit of freedom of discussion, and, above all, an absence of all those circumstances and of all those causes, many of which are disturbing society in other countries.

House of Commons: 18 February 1853

SCHOOL FOR HEROES

We may draw at least this conclusion from the war which has broken out. I think what has occurred has shown that the arts of peace, practised by a free people, are not enervating. I think that the deeds which have been referred to, both of the commanders and the common soldiers, have shown that education has not a tendency to diminish, but to refine and raise the standard of the martial character. In these we may proudly recognise the might and prowess of a free and ancient people. These are all the circumstances and conditions which are favourable to our confidence in the progress of civilisation and flattering to the consciousness of every Englishman.

House of Commons: 15 December 1855

THE NATION IN ADVERSITY

I think there is no mistake so grave on the part of a Minister as to undervalue public peril. The English nation is never so great as in adversity. In prosperity it may be accused, and perhaps justly, of being somewhat ostentatious, and, it may be, even insolent: in middle fortunes it may often prove itself unreasonable, but there never has been a time when a great sense of responsibility has been thrown upon the people of this country, when they have not answered the occasion and shown that matchless energy which has made and will maintain their po sition as the leading nation of the world.

House of Commons: 11 August 1857

THE OLD WORLD AND THE NEW

The day is coming, if it has not already come, when the question of the balance of power cannot be confined to Europe alone. You have on the other side of the Atlantic vigorous and powerful communities, who will no longer submit to your circumscribed theory of authority. The Australian colonies, though now in their youth, but in the youth of giants, have already, as it were, thrown their colossal shadow over Europe. And it is for old Europe I lament, that she is exhausting her energies and her resources in these wars. I could wish that she would rather prepare for that awful competition which in coming times she must encounter. I would rather see France and Germany and Russia develop their resources, improve their agriculture, increase their population, and cultivate the arts of life, social and scientific, instead of wasting their strength, risking their stability, and sinking, when the era to which I have referred arrives, by their own mismanagement and want of prescience, into an inferior and exhausted position. Remember always that England, though she is bound to Europe by tradition, by affection, by great similarity of habits, and all those ties which time alone can create and consecrate, is not a mere Power of the Old World. Her geographical position, her laws, her language and religion, connect her as much with the New World as with the Old. And although she has occupied not only an eminent, but, I am bold to say, the most eminent, position among European nations for ages, still, if ever Europe by her shortsightedness falls into an inferior and exhausted state, for England there will remain an illustrious future. We are bound to the communities of the New World, and those great States which our own planting and colonising energies have created, by ties and interests which will sustain our power and enable us to play as great a part in the times yet to come as we do in these days, and as we have done in the past. And therefore, now that Europe is on the eve of war, I say it is for Europe, not for England, that my heart sinks.

Aylesbury: 1859

A TEMPERED PEOPLE

Patriotism depends as much on mutual suffering as on mutual success, and it is by that experience of all fortunes and all feelings that a great national character is created.

House of Commons: 18 March 1862

THE CHURCH OF ENGLAND

For deep and fervid feeling, there is no race in the world equal to the English; the notes on the gamut of their feeling are few, but they are deep. Industry, Liberty, Religion, form the solemn scale. Industry, Liberty, Religion—that *is* the history of England. Now, upon these three subjects, they have periods of exaltation. They have had periods of deep feeling within our own experience, alike with regard to *toil* and with regard to *freedom*; and it is not impossible there are many in this room who may witness a period of exaltation with regard to religion, that has certainly not been equalled in our times, or in the times of our fathers. But what an opportunity is that for the Church. When great bodies of the nation, who have never been in communion with the Church, have their minds, their feelings, their passions, all exalted in the direction of religion, and influenced by the religious principle, what an opportunity for the Church, with her learning, her organisation, and the ineffable influences of her tradition, with her sacred services, her divine offices, with all the beauty of holiness in which she worships, to advance and address them. What an immense field for any Church. But what a field for a corporation which is not merely a Church, but which is the Church of England; blending with divine instruction the sentiment of patriotism, and announcing herself, not only as the Church of God, but as the Church of the Country. With these views, instead of supposing that the relations which exist between a large body of our fellow subjects and the Church—relations at this moment of indifference and even of alienation—are causes why the Church should not assert her Nationality, they are causes and circumstances which peculiarly call upon the Church to exert herself; and to prepare for a coming future which will demand her utmost energies, as I believe it will yield her greatest rewards.

High Wycombe: 30 October 1862

DIRE FORECAST

This passage is from Disraeli's greatest speech on behalf of the Church. It was delivered in the Sheldonian Theatre, on the invitation of Bishop Wilberforce, and after denouncing the latitudinarianism of the Broad Church, Disraeli turned on the evolutionists to flash one of his most famous epigrams: What is the question now placed before society with a glib assurance the most astounding? The question is this—*Is man an ape or an angel?* My lord, I am on the side of the angels.

Why, my lord, man is a being born to believe. And if no Church comes forward with its title-deeds of truth, sustained by the tradition of sacred ages and by the conviction of countless generations, to guide him, he will find altars and idols in his own heart and his own imagination. But observe this. What must be the relations of a powerful Church, without distinctive creeds, with a being of such a nature? Why, of course, the chief principle of political economy will be observed. Where there is a great demand there will be a proportionate supply; and commencing, as the new school may, by rejecting the principle of inspiration, it will end by every priest becoming a prophet; and beginning as they do by repudiating the practice of miracles,

before long, rest assured, we shall be living in a flitting scene o
spiritual phantasmagoria. There are no tenets however extravagant
and no practices however objectionable, which will not in time
develop under such a state of affairs; opinions the most absurd and
ceremonies the most revolting—

> *Qualia demens*
> *Aegyptus portenta colat—*

perhaps to be followed by the incantations of Canidia and the Cory
bantian howl.

But consider the country in which all this may take place. Dangerous
in all countries, it would be yet more dangerous in England. Ou
empire is now unrivalled for its extent; but the base—the material
base—of that empire is by no means equal to the colossal super
structure. It is not our iron ships; it is not our celebrated regiments; i
is not these things which have created, or indeed really maintain, our
empire. It is the character of the people. Now, I want to know where
that famous character of the English people will be if they are to be
influenced and guided by a Church of immense talent, opulence, and
power, without any distinctive creed. You have in this country
accumulated wealth that never has been equalled, and probably it will
still increase. You have a luxury that will some day peradventure riva
even your wealth. And the union of such circumstances with a Church
without a distinctive creed will lead, I believe, to a dissoluteness o:
manners and of morals rarely equalled in the history of man, bu
which prepares the tomb of empires.

Oxford: 25 November 186

ENGLAND IS SAFE

For my part, I do not believe that the country is in danger. I think
England is safe in the race of men who inhabit her; that she is safe in
something much more precious than her accumulated capital—her
accumulated experience; she is safe in her national character, in her
fame, in the traditions of a thousand years, and in that glorious future
which I believe awaits her.

House of Commons: 15 July 1867

A STATESMAN'S CREED

It is not true that the only real happiness is physical happiness; it is
not true that physical happiness is the highest happiness; it is not true

hat physical happiness is a principle on which you can build up a flourishing and enduring commonwealth. A civilised community must rest on a large realised capital of thought and sentiment: there must be a reserved fund of public morality to draw upon in the exigencies of national life. Society has a soul as well as a body. The traditions of a nation are part of its existence. Its valour and its discipline, its venerable laws, its science and erudition, its poetry, its art, its eloquence and its scholarship are as much portions of its life as its agriculture, its commerce, and its engineering skill.

If it be true, as I believe, that an aristocracy distinguished merely by wealth must perish from satiety, so I hold it equally true that a people who recognise no higher aim than physical enjoyment must become selfish and enervated. Under such circumstances, the supremacy of race, which is the key of history, will assert itself. Some human progeny, distinguished by their bodily vigour or their masculine intelligence, or by both qualities, will assert their superiority, and conquer a world which deserves to be enslaved. It will then be found that our boasted progress has only been an advancement in a circle, and that our new philosophy has brought us back to that old serfdom which it has taken ages to extirpate.

But the still more powerful, indeed the insurmountable, obstacle to the establishment of the new opinions will be furnished by the essential elements of the human mind. Our idiosyncrasy is not bounded by the planet which we inhabit. We can investigate space, and we can comprehend eternity. No considerations limited to this sphere have hitherto furnished the excitement which man requires, or the sanctions for his conduct which his nature imperatively demands. The spiritual nature of man is stronger than codes or constitutions. No Government can endure which does not recognise that for its foundation, and no legislation last which does not flow from that fountain. The principle may develop itself in manifold forms, in the shape of many creeds and many churches; but the principle is divine. As time is divided into day and night, so religion rests upon the Providence of God and the responsibility of man. One is manifest, the other mysterious; but both are facts. Nor is there, as some would teach you, anything in these convictions which tends to contract our intelligence or our sympathies. On the contrary, religion invigorates the intellect and expands the heart. He who has a due sense of his relations to God is best qualified to fulfil his duties to man.

Rectorial Address, University of Glasgow: 19 November 1873

172   ENGLAND IS HER

THE EMPIRE

No Cæsar or Charlemagne ever presided over a dominion s
peculiar. Its flag floats on many waters; it has provinces in every zone
they are inhabited by persons of different races, different religions
different laws, manners, and customs. Some of these are bound to u
by the ties of liberty, fully conscious that without their connectio
with the metropolis they have no security for public freedom and self
government; others are bound to us by flesh and blood and by materia
as well as moral considerations. There are millions who are bound t
us by our military sway, and they bow to that sway because they kno
that they are indebted to it for order and justice. All these communitie
agree in recognising the commanding spirit of these islands that ha
formed and fashioned in such a manner so great a portion of th
globe. My lords, that Empire is no mean heritage; but it is not a
heritage that can only be enjoyed; it must be maintained. And it ca
only be maintained by the same qualities that created it—by courage
by discipline, by patience, by determination, and by a reverence fo
public law and respect for national rights.

House of Lords: 8 April 187

WILLIAM EWART GLADSTONE
1809–1898

Conservative M.P., 1832–65; Liberal M.P., 1865–95; Junior Lord of the Treasury and afterwards Under-Secretary of State for War, 1834–35; Vice-President of the Board of Trade, 1841–43; President of the Board of Trade, 1843–44; Secretary of State for the Colonies, 1845–46; Chancellor of the Exchequer, 1852–55 and 1859–66; First Lord of the Treasury, 1868–74, 1880–85, 1886, and 1892–94

ST. PAUL'S

AMIDST the unceasing din, and the tumult of men hurrying this way and that for gold, or pleasure, or some self-desire, the vast fabric thrusts itself up to heaven and firmly plants itself on soil begrudged to an occupant that yields no lucre. But the city cannot thrust forth its cathedral; and from thence arises the harmonious measured voice of intercession from day to day. The church praying and deprecating continually for the living mass that are dead while they live, from out of the very centre of that mass; silent and lonesome is her shrine, amidst the noise, the thunder of multitudes. Silent, lonesome, motionless, yet full of life; for were we not more dead than the stones, which, built into that sublime structure witness continually to what is great and everlasting—did priest or chorister, or the casual worshipper but apprehend the grandeur of his function in that spot—the very heart must burst with the tide of emotions gathering within it.

Diary: 20 March 1841

FREEDOM AND AUTHORITY

Miserable indeed would be the prospect of the coming times, if we believed that authority and freedom were simply conflicting and contradictory elements in the constitution of a community, so that whatever is given to the one must be deducted from the other. But no Briton who has devoted any portion of his thoughts to the history of his country, or the character of its inhabitants, can for a moment be ensnared into that, for him, false and degrading belief. It has been providentially allotted to this favoured isle that it should show to all

173

the world, how freedom and authority, in their due and wise develop ments, not only may co-exist in the same body, but may, instead of im pairing, sustain and strengthen one another. Among Britons, it is th extent and security of freedom which renders it safe to entrust larg powers to Government, and it is the very largeness of those powers an the vigour of their exercise, which constitute, to each individual of th community, the great practical safeguard of his liberties in return. Th free expression of opinion, as our experience has taught us, is the safety valve of passion. That noise of the rushing stream, when it escapes alarms the timid; but it is the sign that we are safe. The concession o reasonable privilege anticipates the growth of furious appetite.

Regularity, combination, and order, especially when joined wit publicity, have of themselves a marvellous virtue; they tend t subordinate the individual to the mass, they enlarge by healthy exercis the better and nobler parts of our nature, and depress the poorer an meaner; they make man more a creature of habits, and less of mer impulse; they weaken the relative influence of the present, by streng thening his hold upon the future and the past, and their hold upo him. By gathering, too, into organised forms the various influence that bear sway in a mixed community, and leaving them to wor within prescribed channels, those which are good acquire the multi plied strength of union, while the bad neutralise one another b reciprocal elimination. It is a great and noble secret, that of con stitutional freedom, which has given to us the largest liberties, wit the steadiest throne, and the most vigorous executive in Christendom I confess to my strong faith in the virtue of this principle. I have live now for many years in the midst of the hottest and noisiest of it workshops, and have seen that amidst the clatter and the din ceaseless labour is going on; stubborn matter is reduced to obedience and the brute powers of society, like the fire, air, water, and mineral o nature, are with clamour indeed, but also with might, educated an shaped into the most refined and regular forms of usefulness for man I am deeply convinced that, among us, all systems, whether religious o political, which rest on a principle of absolution, must of necessity be not indeed tyrannical, but feeble and ineffective systems; and tha methodically to enlist the members of a community, with due regar to their several capacities, in the performance of its public duties, the way to make that community powerful and healthful, to give firm seat to its rulers, and to engender a warm and intelligent devotio to those beneath their sway.

*A Letter to the . . . Bishop of Aberdeen . . . On the Functions
of Laymen in the Church.* 185.

WILLIAM EWART GLADSTONE
From a steel engraving after a photograph taken *c.* 1855 when
Gladstone was Chancellor of the Exchequer

SOME STATESMEN OF THE GREAT WAR, 1914–18

From a painting by Sir James Guthrie, P.R.S.A. The group includes five Prime Ministers of Britain: Mr. Lloyd George (third seated figure from left), Mr. Churchill (seated centre), Balfour (standing with outstretched hand), Asquith (last seated figure on right), and Bonar Law (second standing figure from right)

ENGLAND AND HER COLONIES

Experience has proved that if you want to strengthen the connection between the colonies and this country—if you want to see British law held in respect and British institutions adopted and beloved in the colonies, never associate with them the hated name of force and coercion exercised by us, at a distance, over their rising fortunes. Govern them upon a principle of freedom. Defend them against aggression from without. Regulate their foreign relations. These things belong to the colonial connection. But of the duration of that connection let them be the judges, and I predict that if you leave them the freedom of judgment it is hard to say when the day will come when they will wish to separate from the great name of England. Depend upon it, they covet a share in that great name. You will find in that feeling of theirs the greatest security for the connection. Make the name of England yet more and more an object of desire to the colonies. Their natural disposition is to love and revere the name of England, and this reverence is by far the best security you can have for their continuing, not only to be subjects of the crown, not only to render it allegiance, but to render it that allegiance which is the most precious of all—the allegiance which proceeds from the depths of the heart of man.

Chester: 12 November 1855

LOUD WAR

It is indeed true that peace has the moral perils and temptations for degenerate man, as has every other blessing, without exception, that we can receive from the hand of God. It is, moreover, not less true that, amidst the clash of arms, the noblest forms of character may be reared, and the highest acts of duty done; that these great and precious results may be due to war as their cause; and that one high form of sentiment in particular, the love of country, receives a powerful and general stimulus from the bloody strife. But this is as the furious cruelty of Pharaoh made place for the benign virtue of his daughter; as the butchering sentence of Herod raised without doubt many a mother's love into heroic sublimity; as plague, as famine, as fire, as flood, as every curse and every scourge that is wielded by an angry Providence for the chastisement of man, is an appointed instrument for tempering human souls in the seven-times heated furnace of affliction, up to the standard of angelic and archangelic virtue.

War, indeed, has the property of exciting much generous and noble feeling on a large scale; but with this special recommendation it has in its modern forms especially, peculiar and unequalled evils. As it has a wider sweep of desolating power than the rest, so it has the peculiar quality that it is more susceptible of being decked in gaudy trappings and of fascinating the imagination of those whose proud and angry passions it inflames. But it is, on this very account, a perilous delusion to teach that war is a cure for moral evil, in any other sense than as the sister tribulations are. The eulogies of the frantic hero in *Maud*, however, deviate into grosser folly. It is natural that such vagaries should overlook the fixed laws of Providence. Under these laws the mass of mankind is composed of men, women, and children who can but just ward off hunger, cold, and nakedness; whose whole ideas of Mammon-worship are comprised in the search for their daily food, clothing, shelter, fuel; whom any casualty reduces to positive want, and whose already low estate is yet further lowered and ground down when *the blood-red blossom of war flames with its heart of fire*. But what is a little strange is, that war should be recommended as a specific for the particular evil of Mammon-worship. Such it never was, even in the days when the Greek heroes longed for the booty of Troy, and anticipated lying by the wives of its princes and its citizens.

Still it had, in times now gone by, ennobling elements and tendencies of the less sordid kind. But one inevitable characteristic of modern war is that it is associated throughout, in all its particulars, with a vast and most irregular formation of commercial enterprise. There is no incentive to Mammon-worship so remarkable as that which it affords. The political economy of war is now one of its most commanding aspects. Every farthing, with the smallest exceptions conceivable, of the scores or hundreds of millions which a war may cost, goes directly and very violently, to stimulate production, though it is intended ultimately for waste or for destruction. Even apart from the fact that war suspends, *ipso facto*, every rule of public thrift, and tends to sap honesty itself in the use of the public treasure for which it makes such unbounded calls, it therefore is the greatest feeder of that lust of gold which we are told is the essence of commerce, though we had hoped it was only its occasional besetting sin. It is, however, more than this; for the regular commerce of peace is tameness itself compared with the gambling spirit which war, through the rapid shiftings and high prices which it brings, always introduces into trade. In its moral operation it more resembles, perhaps the finding of a new gold-field, than anything else.

Tennyson: The Quarterly Review: October 1855

TRIBUTE

In this peroration to one of his famous budget speeches, Gladstone paid tribute to his countrymen groaning under an expenditure for the previous year of £72,840,000 with income tax at 9d. Earlier in his speech he had suggested if the country is content to be governed at the cost of between £60,000,000 and £62,000,000 a year, there is not any reason why it should not be governed without the income tax.

We have seen this country during the last few years without European war, yet placed under a burden of taxation such as, out of a European war, it never was before called upon to bear; we have also seen it last year under the pressure of a season of blight, such as hardly any living man can recollect. Yet, on looking abroad over the face of England, no one is sensible of any signs of decay. Least of all can such an apprehension be felt with regard to those attributes which are perhaps highest of all, and on which most of all depends our national existence—the spirit and courage of the country. It is needless to say that neither the sovereign upon the Throne, nor the nobles and the gentry that fill the place of the gallant chieftains of the Middle Ages, nor the citizens who represent the invincible soldiery of Cromwell, nor the artisans or peasantry who are the children of those sturdy archers that drew the crossbows of England in the fields of France— that none of these betray either inclination or tendency to depart from the tradition of their forefathers. The spirit of the people is excellent. There never was a nation in the whole history of the world more willing to bear the heavy burdens under which it lies—more generously disposed to overlook the errors of those who have the direction of its affairs. And for my own part I hold that, if this country can steadily and constantly remain as wise in the use of her treasure as she is unrivalled in its production, and as moderate in the exercise of her strength as she is rich in its possession, then we may well cherish the hope that there is yet reserved for England a great work to do on her own part and on the part of others, and that for many a generation to come she will continue to hold a foremost place among the nations of the world.

House of Commons: 15 April 1861

YOU CANNOT FIGHT AGAINST THE FUTURE

You cannot fight against the future. Time is on our side. The great social forces which move onwards in their might and majesty, and which the tumult of our debates does not for a moment impede or disturb—those great social forces are against you: they are marshalled

12

on our side; and the banner which we now carry in this fight, though perhaps at some moment it may droop over our sinking heads, yet it soon again will float in the eye of Heaven, and it will be borne by the firm hands of the united people of the three kingdoms, perhaps not to an easy, but to a certain, and to a not far distant victory.

House of Commons: 27 April 1866

A NEW LAW OF NATIONS

We have ceased, or are fast ceasing, from the feverish contest for influence all over the world; and we are learning that that influence which is least courted, and least canvassed for, comes the quickest, and lives the longest. If we no longer dream of foreign acquisitions, we are content in having treaties of mutual benefit with every nation upon earth; treaties not written on parchment, but based on the permanent wants and interests of man, kept alive and confirmed by the constant play of the motives which govern his daily life, and thus inscribing themselves, in gradually deepening characters, on the fleshly tablets of the heart. We may well ask, and in a happier sense,

Quae regio in terris nostri non plena laboris

One accomplishment yet remains needful to enable us to hold without envy our free and eminent position. It is that we should do as we would be done by; that we should seek to found a moral empire upon the confidence o. the several peoples, not upon their fears, their passions, or their antipathies. Certain it is that a new law of nations is gradually taking hold of the mind, and coming to sway the practice, of the world; a law which recognises independence, which frowns upon aggression, which favours the pacific, not the bloody settlement of disputes, which aims at permanent and not temporary adjustments; above all, which recognises, as a tribunal of paramount authority, the general judgment of civilised mankind. It has censured the aggression of France; it will censure, if need arise, the greed of Germany. *Securus judicat orbis terrarum.* It is hard for all nations to go astray. Their ecumenical council sits above the partial passions of those, who are misled by interest, and disturbed by quarrel. The greatest triumph of our time, a triumph in a region loftier than that of electricity and steam, will be the enthronement of this idea of Public Right, as the governing idea of European policy; as the common and precious inheritance of all lands, but superior to the passing opinion of any. The foremost among the nations will be that one which by its conduct shall gradually engender in the mind of the others a fixed belief that it is just. In the competition for this prize, the bounty of Providence has given us a place of vantage; and nothing save our own fault or folly can wrest it from our grasp.

Germany, France and England: Edinburgh Review: October 1870

A GREAT AND NOBLE PRIZE

The Balkan peoples had long suffered under the hideous oppression of Turkish misrule when in 1875 Bosnia and Herzegovina rose in revolt, followed in 1876 by Bulgaria, by Serbia and Montenegro. Each sought a national independence which, after the failure of the European Concert had involved the Russo-Turkish War, was at last secured to them in 1878 by the Treaty of Berlin.

That solution to the Eastern question had been foreseen by Gladstone. Horrified, as indeed were his countrymen generally, by the news of the Bulgarian atrocities in 1876, he poured out speech after speech in eloquent appeal to humanity and justice for support to the Balkan peoples in their struggle for independence, and, to quote his famous pamphlet, for clearing the Turks out of Europe, bag and baggage.

There were other days when England was the hope of freedom. Wherever in the world a high aspiration was entertained, or a noble blow was struck, it was to England that the eyes of the oppressed were always turned—to this favourite, this darling home of so much privilege and so much happiness, where the people that had built up a noble edifice for themselves would, it was well known, be ready to do what in them lay to secure the benefit of the same inestimable boon for others. You talk to me of the established tradition and policy in regard to Turkey. I appeal to an established tradition, older, wider, nobler far—a tradition not which disregards British interests, but which teaches you to seek the promotion of these interests in obeying the dictates of honour and justice. And what is to be the end of this? Are we to dress up the fantastic ideas some people entertain about this policy and that policy in the garb of British interests, and then, with a new and base idolatry, fall down and worship them? Or are we to look not at the sentiment but at the hard facts of the case, which Lord Derby told us fifteen years ago; namely, that it is the populations of those countries that will ultimately possess them, and that will ultimately determine their abiding condition? It is to this fact, to this law, that we should look. There is now before the world a glorious prize. A portion of those unhappy people are still as yet making an effort to retrieve what they have lost so long, but have not ceased to love and desire. I speak of those in Bosnia and Herzogovina. Another portion —a band of heroes such as the world has rarely seen—stand on the

rocks of Montenegro, and are ready now, as they have ever been
during the four hundred years of exile from their fertile plains, to
sweep down from their fastnesses and meet the Turks at any odds for
the re-establishment of justice and of peace in those countries.
Another portion still, the five millions of Bulgarians, cowed and
beaten down to the ground, hardly venturing to look upwards, even
to their Father in heaven, have extended their hands to you; they have
sent you their petition, they have prayed for your help and protection.
They have told you that they do not seek alliance with Russia, or with
any foreign power, but that they seek to be delivered from an intolerable burden of woe and shame. That burden of woe and shame—the
greatest that exists on God's earth—is one that we thought united
Europe was about to remove; but to removing which, for the present,
you seem to have no efficacious means of offering even the smallest
practical contribution. But the removal of that load of woe and shame
is a great and noble prize. It is a prize well worth competing for. It is
not yet too late to try to win it. I believe there are men in the Cabinet
who would try to win it, if they were free to act on their own beliefs
and aspirations. It is not yet too late, I say, to become competitors for
that prize; but be assured that whether you mean to claim for yourselves even a single leaf in that immortal chaplet of renown, which
will be the reward of true labour in that cause, or whether you turn
your backs upon that cause and upon your own duty, I believe, for
one, that the knell of Turkish tyranny in these provinces has sounded.
So far as human eye can judge, it is about to be destroyed. The
destruction may not come in the way or by the means that we should
choose; but come this boon from what hands it may, it will be a noble
boon, and as a noble boon will gladly be accepted by Christendom and
the world.

House of Commons: 7 May 1877

ENGLAND AND AMERICA IN CONCORD

They alike prefer the practical to the abstract. They tolerate opinion,
with only a reserve upon behalf of decency; and they desire to confine
coercion to the province of action, and to leave thought, as such,
entirely free. They set a high value on liberty for its own sake. They
desire to give full scope to the principles of self-reliance in the people,
and they deem self-help to be immeasurably superior to help in any
other form; to be the only help, in short, which ought not to be continually, or periodically, put upon its trial, and required to make good
its title. They mistrust and mislike the centralisation of power; and

they cherish municipal, local, even parochial liberties, as nursery grounds, not only for the production here and there of able men, but for the general training of public virtue and independent spirit. They regard publicity as the vital air of politics, through which alone, in its freest circulation, opinions can be thrown into common stock for the good of all, and the balance of relative rights and claims can be habitually and peacefully adjusted. It would be difficult, in the case of any other pair of nations, to present an assemblage of traits at once so common and so distinctive.

Kin beyond Sea: North American Review: September 1878

THE NECESSITY FOR WAR

However much you may detest war—and you cannot detest it too much—there is no war—except one, the war for liberty—that does not contain in it elements of corruption, as well as of misery, that are deplorable to recollect and to consider; but however deplorable wars may be, they are among the necessities of our condition; and there are times when justice, when faith, when the welfare of mankind, require a man not to shrink from the responsibility of undertaking them. And if you undertake war, so also you are often obliged to undertake measures that may lead to war.

Edinburgh: 17 March 1880

A PEOPLE'S INHERITANCE

Another period has opened and is opening still—a period possibly of yet greater moral dangers, certainly a great ordeal for those classes which are now becoming largely conscious of power, and never heretofore subject to its deteriorating influences. These have been confined in their actions to the classes above them, because they were its sole possessors. Now is the time for the true friend of his country to remind the masses that their present political elevation is owing to no principles less broad and noble than these—the love of liberty, of liberty for all without distinction of class, creed or country, and the resolute preference of the interests of the whole to any interest, be it what it may, of a narrower scope.

Letter to Sir John Cowan: 17 March 1894

Robert Gascoyne-Cecil, third

MARQUIS OF SALISBURY

1830–1903

*Conservative M.P., 1853–68; Secretary of State
for India, 1866–67 and 1874–78; Secretary of
State for Foreign Affairs, 1878–80; Prime Minister and Secretary for Foreign Affairs, 1885–92 and
1895–1900; Prime Minister and Lord Privy Seal,
1900–2*

A CHARACTER OF PITT

THE lapse of years only brings out in brighter lustre the grandeur of his intellect and the loftiness of his character. In the combined gentleness and firmness of his administration he was a typical English statesman. No man was ever so yielding without being weak, or so stern without being obstinate. In ordinary times he followed after peace more anxiously than Walpole, and often offended his friends by his willingness to compromise and concede. When revolutionary passions had made gentleness impossible, he could be as rigorous as Strafford or as Cromwell. As a legislator, the experience of years has tended more and more to confirm his wisdom. Most of the evils under which we suffer are evils of which he warned us; and where we have averted or softened them, it has been by remedies of his devising. The policy, both at home and abroad, in commerce and in government, which all parties now by common consent pursue, follows very closely the maxims which he laid down. He was the first Parliamentary statesman, unless an exception be made in favour of his father, who represented not a section, but the whole of England—monarchical, aristocratic, agricultural, commercial. The king justly prized him, as his wisest and truest champion. The aristocracy, after he had overthrown the clique which had domineered over them for so long, rallied gradually round his standard. The country gentlemen long toasted him as the impersonation of loyal and patriotic statesmanship, and the commercial classes clung to him as their special protector. England may well cherish his fame, and look upon his greatness with an interest which no other single image in modern political history can claim. She owes it to him that she was rescued from the deep degradation into which corruption and imbecility had plunged her. She owes to him the policy which, planned and commenced by him, and perfected by his disciples, placed her on a pinnacle of greatness which no modern nation had attained before. But she owes to him a greater benefit than all these—an example of pure and self-denying patriotism, and the elevation of public feeling which it has worked. If corruption has been driven from our politics altogether—if faction is being daily more discredited—if our public men, even the worst of them, are more patriotic in their conduct than the statesmen of the Coalition—these results are in no small degree due to the spectacle with which Pitt's long career familiarised the nation's eyes, of stainless purity and lofty forgetfulness of self.

Stanhope's Life of Pitt: Quarterly Review: April 1861

THE STATE: A CONTRAST IN IDEALS

There are sentiments and emotions attaching to the idea of a State which have nothing commercial in their nature. The self-sacrifice and heroism that it can evoke when it is threatened show that it is the object of emotions far higher than self-interest. The glory which it has won, or hopes to win, centres round it affections and aspirations which would not be felt for an organisation that only existed to foster the material well-being of those who belonged to it. But this sentimental aspect is not the one in which our advanced school of Reformers love to look at it. Their efforts are unceasingly directed to the task of stripping off these poetical trappings. They tell us that such follies are the heritage of darker times; that it is a delusion to give a personality to the State; to attribute to it moral duties, or to employ its powers for the gratification of lofty aims and feelings. Their constant struggle is to present it nakedly as a Joint-Stock Company for the preservation of life and property; and they are estopped by their own philosophy from appealing to the loftier views of it which have descended from less business-like times.

The House of Commons: Quarterly Review: July 1864

CATCHWORDS AND DEMOCRACY

There is no science in which the wholesome ordeal of definition is more needed than in politics. So little of exact reasoning and so much of *ad captandum* declamation is employed in political discussions, that words are of much more importance in it than thoughts. The man who can discover a phrase by which the desired argument or assertion is hinted, without being formally laid down, does far more for his cause than the keenest reasoner. A falsehood stated may be disproved; a fallacy elaborately worked out may be easily exposed. But it is difficult to deal with falsehood or fallacy which exist only in suggestion and have not passed in any distinct shape upon the mind of the person who is influenced by them. A deceptive word or phrase does not seem to convey an argument and disarms antagonism, while the trouble of analysing the arguments contained indisposes the hearer for scrutiny. A new error can never be said to have secured its footing, or to be furnished with the proper apparatus for conquering the popular mind, until its most important fallacies have been disguised in the form of catchwords or party cries. The man who first connected the words freedom and progress with the word democracy, did this inestimable service to the democratic cause.

There is no *a priori* justification for such a connection. There is nothing in the nature of things to make us suppose that the freedom of those who are not on the side of the Government will be better observed where the Government is the creature of a multitude than where it is in the possession of one. In other words, there is no obvious ground for assuming that masses of men are calmer and more free from passion than individuals. Such an assumption, if not founded in the nature of things, is certainly not countenanced by history. The Athenian people were not remarkable for clemency or self-restraint, and played the tyrant in their time as bloodily as any Persian or Macedonian king. Rome had scarcely approached to the condition of a true democracy before it became anarchical. The pure democratic forms, which from the very birth of their community the canton of Uri has enjoyed, in no way hindered them from laying upon their conquered neighbours of what is now Ticino as heavy a yoke as was imposed by any feudal baron. The feverish interval during which France enjoyed the blessings of pure democracy will not be upheld, even by the most advanced Liberal, as a period remarkable for the respect that was paid to individual freedom. There is nothing, therefore, in experience, and nothing in theory, to authorise the connection of the two ideas. But it has been done systematically and perseveringly; and perseverance has been rewarded with the success which generally awaits it. The two have been put together until people have come to believe that they are connected.

The juxtaposition of the ideas of progress and democracy, which has been established with equal success, has been more curious still. It is more utterly at variance with the teaching of history. It is quite true that the history of the human race has been the record of a continual progress; but it is not true that that progress has been identified with a movement towards democracy, or that it has been the most strikingly displayed in countries where that form of government prevailed. For the future it is, of course, impossible to speak; but, as regards the past, it is a simple matter of fact that the human race have not progressed towards democracy. During the experience of the living generation there may have been a movement, not intentionally towards democracy, but towards a larger development of popular power out of which democracy may possibly grow. But this movement has only been the flow of a tide, whose alternate rise and fall has been recorded ever since the dawn of civilised polity. Democratic equality of political power was as much developed among several nations of classical antiquity, and among the Teutons before the feudal system began to grow up amongst them, as in any part of Europe at the present moment, with the exception, perhaps, of some of the Swiss cantons. If there is any lesson which a general survey of history teaches us, it is that the preponderance of power in a State seldom remains in the same hands for any length of time. But the doctrine that all States have been and are intending to entrust this preponderance finally to the multitude is one that cannot be supported by any evidence whatever.

The United States as an Example: Quarterly Review:
January 1865

THE NECESSITY FOR RELIGIOUS BELIEF

It is the result, not the essence, of Christianity, that is of importance to the politician. From a purely secular point of view, there would certainly be an advantage if we could have the purity of Christian morality and the benefits of Christian zeal without its stubborn and inflexible creed. In the same way, it would be a great saving of trouble if it were possible to cut down oaks without the tedious necessity of planting them first. These theorists need to be taught by hard experience, as theorists scarcely more presumptuous have been taught before, that Christian morality is a blessing which can only be enjoyed by the world as a consequence of Christian faith. What misleads them is that this rule is true of a community, but it is not necessarily true of an individual. Some of the brightest examples of what a Christian life should be have been, and still are, men who have renounced all but the mere pretence of Christian faith. The fact in their case is that their morality was formed before their intellect went astray. Virtue had become easy to them before faith had become difficult. Thus it has come to pass that Christianity has been reproached with her own success, and the morality which her preaching has produced has been employed to discredit its truth. But what the world has not yet seen is a society in which the dogmas these gentlemen despise have lost their hold upon all classes and both sexes, and which yet retains its morality or even its civilisation through two or three generations. The virtuous heretic or infidel, the child of believing parents, brought up in a believing community, is not difficult to understand. But in order to prove the disconnection between the *objects of a Christian life* and *dogmatic teaching*, which is the cardinal principle of this new school, it is necessary to produce a generation born of unbelieving parents, nurtured amid an unbelieving community, and which yet has grown up even to that measure of Christian self-restraint which we are able to recognise in our own lukewarm age. These will be the only conditions under which it can be fully ascertained by experiment whether Christian morality can be produced by mere sentimental admiration, or whether it needs for its sustenance the love of an historic Saviour and the fear of a genuine retribution. No impartial reader of history, ancient or modern, can doubt of the calamitous issue to which the experiment, if it should be ever tried, will come. The dream of undogmatic religion is too baseless to impose long upon educated minds. Either the philosophic caprice of the day will melt silently away, and the mass of our countrymen will be left in the undisturbed enjoyment of the reverence for the great doctrines of their faith which they have always cherished, or we shall return to the same starting-point by a more circuitous and more disastrous route. We shall either cling to our articles of faith in spite of rationalist and unsectarian teaching, or we shall learn, by a cruel experience, that men will not be moral without a motive, and that a motive can only be furnished by religious belief.

The Church in her Relations to Political Parties: Quarterly Review:
July 1865

THE NEIGHBOURLY VIEW

A nation like ours should behave to other nations just as a man should behave to neighbours and equals among whom he may chance to be dwelling. If you wish to get on with the people with whom you are living you must not look for perpetual opportunities of getting a little advantage over them; you must view your own claims and theirs in a just and neighbourly spirit—on the one hand never sacrificing any important and genuine right in respect to which you think that oppression or encroachment is being attempted, and on the other hand abstaining from erecting small controversies into envenomed disputes and treating every difference as a matter of vital principle. The people who do these things in private life and in diplomacy may secure an advantage or two at first, but directly their temper is discovered by their neighbours they will find that they are opposed by a combination of these neighbours which places them in a worse position than if they had never insisted on their rights. I must add that what I call my neighbourly view of foreign politics extends beyond the mere controversies or disputes or discussions we may have with our neighbours. We must not only deal with them in a spirit of goodwill, recognising the necessity of concessions on the one side or the other, but we must also recognise that the members of every community have duties towards each other. We are part of what has been well called the federation of mankind. We belong to a great community of nations, and we have no right to shrink from the duties which the interests of the community impose upon us. There is all the difference in the world between good-natured, good-humoured effort to keep well with your neighbours and that spirit of haughty and sullen isolation which has been dignified by the name of non-intervention. We are part of the community of Europe, and we must do our duty as such. We must strive to take that place and to obtain that great and just object of foreign policy—the permanence of peace, in which industry and prosperity may thrive.

Carnarvon: 10 April 1888

Archibald Philip Primrose, fifth

EARL OF ROSEBERY

1847 – 1929

Under-Secretary of State for Home Affairs, 1881–83; Lord Privy Seal and First Commissioner of Works, 1885; Secretary of State for Foreign Affairs, 1886 and 1892–94; First Lord of the Treasury, 1894–95

A FAIRER UNION STILL

OUR ancestors put their hand to a mighty work, and it prospered They welded two great nations into one great empire, and moulded local jealousies into a common patriotism. On such an achievement we must gaze with awe and astonishment, the means were so adverse and the result so surprising. But we should look on it also with emulous eyes. Great as that Union was, a greater still remains. We have in our generation, if we would remain a generation, to effect that union of classes without which power is a phantom and freedom a farce. In these days the rich man and the poor gaze at each other across no impassable gulf; for neither is there in this world an Abraham's bosom of calm beatitude. A powerless monarchy, an isolated aristocracy, an intelligent and aspiring people, do not together form the conditions of constitutional stability. We have to restore a common pulse, a healthy beat to the heart of the Commonwealth. It is a great work, the work of individuals as much as of statesmen, alien from none of us, rather pertinent to us all; each in his place can further it.

Each one of us—merchant and clerk, master and servant, landlord and tenant, capitalist and artisan, minister and parishioner—we are all privileged to have a hand in this the most sublime work of all; to restore or create harmony betwixt man and man; to look, not for the differences which chance or necessity has placed between class and class, but for the common sympathies which underlie and connect all humanity. It is not monarchs, or even statesmen, that give to a country prosperity and power. France in 1789 had a virtuous monarch and able statesmen. But the different classes of the community had then become completely estranged, and the upper crust of society was shivered to dust by the volcano beneath. In this country the artificial

188

barriers which separate class from class are high enough, but, thank God, they are not insuperable. Let us one and all prevent their becoming so. A great page records the bloodless and prosperous history of the Scottish Union. A greater page lies vacant before us on which to inscribe a fairer union still.

Edinburgh Philosophical Institution: 3 November 1871

INHERITANCE OF THE PAST

Much is passing away, much more must pass away; and it is well. Your old draperies, your old tapestries, your old banners are clutched by the greedy century, and carded and thrown into the mill, that they may emerge damp sheets for your newspapers; and it is well. Your old bones are pulverised that they may dress the pastures; and it is well. Your abbeys and your castles are quarries for dykes, and prize bothies, and locomotive sheds; and it is well. Your archives cover preserves, your ancestral trees pave roads, you sound for coal under your old tower and it tumbles about your ears, your clan emigrates to Glasgow or to Canada, the glen is silent save for the footfall of the deer; and it is well. The effigies and splendours of tradition are not meant to cramp the energies or the development of a vigorous and various nation. They are not meant to hold in mortmain the proper territory of human intelligence and righteous aspiration. They live and teach their lessons in our annals; they have their own worshippers and their own shrines, but the earth is not theirs nor the fullness thereof. For all that, however, these very annals, and the characters they inspire and describe, are our intangible property; they constitute an inheritance we are not willing to see either squandered or demolished, for they are the title-deeds and heirlooms of our national existence.

Rectorial Address, University of Edinburgh: 4 November 1882

THE COMMONWEALTH OF NATIONS

The phrase, commonwealth of nations, trite enough now, was mint-bright when Lord Rosebery used it to describe an ideal of Imperial relations which he developed in a series of speeches made on a visit to New Zealand and Australia, November 1883–January 1884.

I say that these are no longer colonies in the ordinary sense of the term. I claim that this is a nation—a nation not in aspiration or in the future, but in performance and fact. I claim that this country has established to be a nation, and that its nationality is now and will be henceforward recognised by the world. That is a great position to take, and I think the facts I have stated substantiate it. But there is a further question, and it is this: Does this fact of your being a nation and I think you feel yourselves to be a nation, imply separation from the Empire? God forbid! There is no need for any nation, however great, leaving the Empire, because the Empire is a commonwealth of nations.

It seems to me that hand in hand they may yet follow up a career of usefulness to mankind—led by those common and eternal principles of justice which alone can exalt and sustain a nation, and which we proudly boast and humbly hope have long guided and directed the British Empire; which have been the pillar of cloud by day and the pillar of fire by night that have guided us to so many achievements and through so many troubles. I believe that every day we remain united we shall be less anxious to part. I believe that every day we remain united it will be considered more desirable that we should continue so, not merely for our own selfish interests, but for the interest of humanity at large: because it is on the British race, whether in Great Britain, or the United States, or the Colonies, or wherever it may be, that rest the highest hopes of those who try to penetrate the dark future, or who seek to raise and better the patient masses of mankind. Each year the power and the prerogative of that race appear to me to increase; each year it seems to fill more and more of the world. I believe that the connection of the British Empire will remain, for the reason that it is desirable for civilisation that it should continue to exist. I confess I think that each day that we live we shall be more and more unwilling to see this ancient Empire of ours—raised with so much toil, colonised with so much energy, cemented with the blood and sweat of so many generations—pass away like a camp struck noiselessly in the night, or split into isolated and sterile communities jealous among themselves, disturbed by suburban disputes and parochial rivalries, dwindling possibly, like the Italian States of the Middle Ages, into political insignificance, or degenerating into idle and polite nonentity. And let me remind this assemblage of the fact—that empires, and especially great empires, when they crumble are apt to crumble exceedingly small.

Adelaide: 18 January 1884

OUR COMMON HUMANITY

This noble peroration is from an address given on the centenary of the death of Robert Burns, when glancing at the poet's failings, Lord

Rosebery pleaded Remember, I do not seek to palliate or excuse . . .
but it all seems infinitely little, infinitely remote . . .

I should like to go a step farther and affirm that we have something
to be grateful for even in the weaknesses of men like Burns. Mankind
is helped in its progress almost as much by the study of imperfection
as by the contemplation of perfection. Had we nothing before us in our
futile and halting lives but saints and the ideal, we might well fail
altogether. We grope blindly along the catacombs of the world, we
climb the dark ladder of life, we feel our way to futurity, but we can
scarcely see an inch around or before us. We stumble and falter and
fall, our hands and knees are bruised and sore, and we look up for
light and guidance. Could we see nothing but distant unapproachable
impeccability, we might well sink prostrate in the hopelessness of
emulation and the weariness of despair. Is it not then, when all seems
blank and lightless and lifeless, when strength and courage flag, and
when perfection seems as remote as a star, is it not then that imperfection helps us? When we see that the greatest and choicest of the
images of God have had their weaknesses like ours, their temptations,
their hours of darkness, their bloody sweat, are we not encouraged by
their lapses and catastrophes to find energy for one more effort, one
more struggle? Where they failed we feel it a less dishonour to fail;
their errors and sorrows make, as it were, an easier ascent from infinite
imperfection to infinite perfection. Man after all is not ripened by
virtue alone. Were it so this world were a paradise of angels. No!
Like the growth of the earth, he is the fruit of all the seasons, the
accident of a thousand accidents, a living mystery, moving through the
seen to the unseen. He is sown in dishonour; he is matured under all
the varieties of heat and cold; in mist and wraith, in snow and vapours,
in the melancholy of autumn, in the torpor of winter, as well as in the
rapture and fragrance of summer, or the balmy affluence of the
spring—its breath, its sunshine, its dew. And at the end he is reaped—
the product, not of one climate, but of all; not of good alone, but of
evil; not of joy alone, but of sorrow—perhaps mellowed and ripened,
perhaps stricken and withered and sour. How, then, shall we judge any
one? How, at any rate, shall we judge a giant, great in gifts and great
in temptation; great in strength and great in weakness? Let us glory in
his strength and be comforted in his weakness. And when we thank
heaven for the inestimable gift of Burns, we do not need to remember
wherein he was imperfect, we cannot bring ourselves to regret that he
was made of the same clay as ourselves.

Burns Centenary meeting, Glasgow: 21 July 1896

HYMN

Two stanzas from a hymn written in 1897, for Jubilee Sunday and for Epsom Church.

King of Kings and Lord of Lords,
 Hush the angry nations' rage.
Still the clamour, sheathe the swords,
 And the wrath of man assuage.
Let the archangels of peace
 Compass us with guardian wings,
Unity and faith increase,
 Lord of Lords and King of Kings.

And when to the trumpet's peal,
 At Thy seat of judgement dread,
Sovereigns and subjects kneel,
 Pale battalions of the dead,
Lord, have mercy, purge our taint,
 Sin and wrath, in love divine:
Kingdoms here are shadows faint;
 May we reign with Thee in Thine.

CROMWELL

He comes tramping down through the ages in his great wide boots, a countenance swollen and reddish, a voice harsh, sharp, and untunable, with a country-made suit, a hat with no band, and doubtful linen with a speck of blood upon it. He tramps over England, he tramps over Scotland, he tramps over Ireland, his sword in one hand, his Bible in the other. Then back to London, whence he puts forth that heavy foot into Europe; and all Europe bows before him. When he is not scattering enemies and battering castles he is scattering Parliaments and battering general assemblies. He seems to be the very spirit of destruction, an angel of vengeance permitted to reign for a season to efface what he has to efface and then to disappear. Then comes the end. The prophetic Quaker sees the waft of death go out against that main, there is a terrible storm, and he lies dying in Whitehall, groaning out that his work is done, that he will not drink or sleep, that he wishes to make what haste he can to be gone, and the sun as it rises on his great day, the third of September, the day of Dunbar and of Worcester, finds Cromwell speechless, and, as it sets, leaves him dead. That is the view of Cromwell we get from contemporary portraits.

Yet there is another side; for with all his vigorous characteristic personality there is something impersonal about Cromwell. Outside the battlefield he never seems a free agent, but rather the instrument of forces outside and about him. The crises of nations, like the crises of nature, have their thunderbolts, and Cromwell is one of these; he seems to be impelled, to be projected into the world in the agony of a great catastrophe, and to disappear with it. On the field of battle he is a great captain, ready, resourceful and overwhelming; off the field he seems to be a creature of invisible influences, a strange mixture of a strong practical nature with a sort of unearthly fatalism, with a sort of spiritual mission; and this combination, in my judgement, makes the strength of Cromwell.

Queen's Hall, London: 14 November 1899

AN *IF*

And yet one cannot but pause for a moment to reflect that but for a small incident—the very ordinary circumstance of the acceptance of a peerage—this Empire might have been incalculably greater. Had the elder Pitt, when he became First Minister, not left the House of Commons, he would probably have retained his sanity and his authority. He would have prevented, or suppressed, the reckless budget of Charles Townshend, have induced George III to listen to reason, have introduced representatives from America into the Imperial Parliament, and preserved the thirteen American colonies to the British Crown. Is it fanciful to dwell for a moment on what might have happened? The Reform Bill which was passed in 1832 would probably have been passed much earlier, for the new blood of America would have burst the old vessels of the Constitution. It would have provided for some self-adjusting system of representation, such as now prevails in the United States, by which increasing population is proportionately represented. And at last, when the Americans became the majority, the seat of Empire would perhaps have been moved solemnly across the Atlantic, and Britain have become the historical shrine and the European outpost of the world empire. What an extraordinary revolution it would have been had it been accomplished! The greatest known without bloodshed; the most sublime transference of power in the history of mankind. Our conceptions can scarcely picture the procession across the Atlantic, the greatest sovereign in the greatest fleet in the world, ministers, Government, Parliament departing solemnly for the other hemisphere, not, as in the case of the Portuguese sovereigns emigrating to Brazil, under the

13

spur of necessity, but under the vigorous embrace of the younger world. It is well to bridle the imagination, lest it become fantastic and extravagant. Moreover, it is a result to which we can scarcely acclimatise ourselves, even in idea. But the other effects might have been scarcely less remarkable. America would have hung on the skirts of Britain and pulled her back out of European complications. She would have profoundly affected the foreign policy of the mother country in the direction of peace. Her influence in our domestic policy would have been scarcely less potent. It might probably have appeased and even contented Ireland. The ancient Constitution of Great Britain would have been rendered more comprehensive and more elastic. On the other hand, the American yearning for liberty would have taken a different form; it would have blended with other traditions and flowed into other moulds. And, above all, had there been no separation, there would have been no War of Independence, no War of 1812 with, all the bitter memories that these have left on American soil. To secure that priceless boon, I could have been satisfied to see the British Federal Parliament sitting in Columbia territory. It is difficult, indeed, to dam the flow of ideas in dealing with so pregnant a possibility. But I restrain myself, because I know that I am dreaming . . .

Rectorial Address, University of Glasgow: 16 November 1900

EPSOM

This extract gains in point from the fact that it was Lord Rosebery's fortune to win the Derby twice during his short tenure of office, with Ladas II *in 1894 and with* Sir Visto *in 1895.*

A miracle yet remained to be wrought on behalf of Epsom. In the last quarter of the eighteenth century, a roystering party at a neighbouring country house founded two races, in two successive years, one for three-year-old colts and fillies, the other for three-year-old fillies, and named them gratefully after their host and his house—the Derby and the Oaks. Seldom has a carouse had a more permanent effect. Up to that time Epsom had enjoyed little more than the ordinary races of a market-town. The great Eclipse, himself, who long lived in Epsom, had run there in some obscurity. But now horses, some of them unworthy to draw him in a post-chaise, were to earn immortality by winning on Epsom Downs before hundreds of thousands of spectators. Parliament was to adjourn during the ensuing century, not without debate, to watch the struggle. Ministers and ex-ministers would ride or drive down to the famous race; and in white hats with blue veils discuss the prospects of their favourites. Political leaders would give vent to splendid groans when they realised that they had sold the winner. In the midst of the Crimean War the result of the Derby was to be recorded in General Orders. Crowds would assemble in London, and from London to Epsom, to watch the still greater crowds returning from the contest. For a week Epsom would reek of racing. During that period the eyes of the sporting section of the civilised world would be turned on the little Surrey town. Many indeed, who were in no respect sporting, became sporting for that occasion.

It is much the same now. The Olympian dust is the same, and is still scattered by the flying horses. The world still admires—not perhaps with so concentrated a gaze. And all this excitement, enthusiasm, triumph, whatever you may call it, Epsom and the universe perhaps owe to an extra magnum of Lord Derby's choice claret, or a superfluous bottle of Lord Derby's curious port.

For two weeks, then, or for a part of them, Epsom races and revels; and recovers during the remaining fifty. The recovery is less sweet than it was, for what was once rural is now suburban. But Nature happily, as we know, is not easily expelled. There are still common land and down, still stately trees and vernal blossom, the nightingales still sing.

Preface to *Epsom: Gordon Home: 1901*

ARTHUR JAMES BALFOUR

afterwards Earl Balfour

1848 – 1930

Conservative M.P., 1874–1922; President of the Local Government Board, 1885–86; Secretary for Scotland, 1886–87; Chief Secretary for Ireland, 1887–91; First Lord of the Treasury and Leader of the House of Commons, 1891–92 and 1895–1902; Prime Minister and First Lord of the Treasury, 1902–5; First Lord of the Admiralty, 1915–16; Secretary of State for Foreign Affairs, 1916–19; Lord President of the Council, 1919–22 and 1925–29

MAN

MAN, so far as natural science by itself is able to teach us, is no longer the final cause of the universe, the Heaven-descended heir of all the ages. His very existence is an accident, his story a brief and transitory episode in the life of one of the meanest of the planets. Of the combination of causes which first converted a dead organic compound into the living progenitors of humanity, science, indeed, as yet knows nothing. It is enough that from such beginnings famine, disease, and mutual slaughter, fit nurses of the future lords of creation, have gradually evolved, after infinite travail, a race with conscience enough to feel that it is vile, and intelligence enough to know that it is insignificant. We survey the past, and see that its history is of blood and tears, of helpless blundering, of wild revolt, of stupid acquiescence, of empty aspirations. We sound the future, and learn that after a period, long compared with the individual life, but short indeed compared with the divisions of time open to our investigation, the energies of our system will decay, the glory of the sun will be dimmed, and the earth, tideless and inert, will no longer tolerate the race which has for a moment disturbed its solitude. Man will go down into the pit, and all his thoughts will perish. The uneasy consciousness, which in this obscure corner has for a brief space broken the contented silence of the universe, will be at rest. Matter will know itself no longer. Imperishable monuments and immortal deeds, death itself, and love stronger than death, will be as though they had never been. Nor will anything that *is* be better or be worse for all that the labour, genius, devotion, and suffering of man have striven through countless generations to effect.

Foundations of Belief: 1895

THE ARTIST'S IMMORTALITY

I believe that every impartial observer will admit that, of the æsthetic emotion actually experienced by any generation, the merest fraction is due to the *immortal* productions of the generations which have long preceded it. Their immortality is largely an immortality of libraries and museums; they supply material to critics and historians, rather than enjoyment to mankind; and if it were to be maintained that one music-hall song gives more æsthetic pleasure in a night than the most exquisite compositions of Palestrina in a decade, I know not how the proposition could be refuted.

The ancient Norsemen supposed that besides the soul of the dead, which went to the region of departed spirits, there survived a ghost, haunting, though not for ever, the scenes of his earthly labours. At first vivid and almost life-like, it slowly waned and faded, until at length it vanished, leaving behind it no trace or memory of its spectral presence amidst the throng of living men. So, it seems to me, is the immortality we glibly predicate of departed artists. If they survive at all, it is but a shadowy life they live, moving on through the grada-tions of slow decay to dist int but inevitable death. They can no longer, as heretofore, speak directly to the hearts of their fellow-men, evoking their tears or laughter, and all the pleasures, be they sad or merry, of which imagination holds the secret. Driven from the market-place, they become first the companions of the student, then the victims of the specialist. He who would still hold familiar intercourse with them must train himself to penetrate the veil which, in ever-thickening folds, conceals them from the ordinary gaze; he must catch the tone of a vanished society, he must move in a circle of alien associations, he must think in a language not his own. Need we, then, wonder that under such conditions the outfit of a critic is as much intellectual as emotional, or that if from off the complex sentiments with which they regard the immortal legacies of the past we strip all that is due to interests connected with history, with biography, with critical analysis, with scholarship, and with technique, but a small modicum will, as a rule, remain which can with justice be attributed to pure æsthetic sensibility.

Ibid

SCIENCE, THE INSTRUMENT OF CHANGE

I do not myself believe that this age is either less spiritual or more sordid than its predecessors. I believe, indeed, precisely the reverse. But however this may be, is it not plain that if a society is to be moved by the remote speculations of isolated thinkers it can only be on condition that their isolation is not complete? Some point of contact they must have with the world in which they live; and if their influence is to be based on widespread sympathy, the contact must be in a region where there can be, if not full mutual comprehension, at least a large measure of practical agreement and willing co-operation. Philosophy has never touched the mass of men except through religion. And, though the parallel is not complete, it is safe to say that science will never touch them unaided by its practical applications. Its wonders may be catalogued for purposes of education, they may be illustrated by arresting experiments, by numbers and magnitudes which startle or fatigue the imagination; but they will form no familiar portion of the intellectual furniture of ordinary men unless they be connected, however remotely, with the conduct of ordinary life. Critics have made merry over the naïve self-importance which represented the human race as the centre and final cause of the universe, and conceived the stupendous mechanism of Nature as primarily designed to satisfy its wants and minister to its entertainment. But there is another, and an opposite, danger into which it is possible to fall. The material world, howsoever it may have gained in sublimity, has, under the touch of science, lost (so to speak) in domestic charm. Its profounder secrets seem so remote from the concerns of men that in the majority they rouse no serious interest; while of the minority who are fascinated by its marvels, not a few will be chilled by its impersonal and indifferent immensity.

For this latter mood only religion, or religious philosophy, can supply a cure. But for the former, the appropriate remedy is the perpetual stimulus which the influence of science on the business of mankind offers to their sluggish curiosity. And even now I believe this influence to be underrated. If in the last hundred years the whole material setting of civilised life has altered, we owe it neither to politicians nor to political institutions. We owe it to the combined efforts of those who have advanced science and those who have applied it. If our outlook upon the universe has suffered modifications in detail so great and so numerous that they amount collectively to a revolution, it is to men of science we owe it, not to theologians or philosophers. On these, indeed, new and weighty responsibilities are being cast. They have to harmonise and co-ordinate, to prevent the new from being narrow, to preserve unharmed the valuable essence of what is old. But science is the great instrument of social change, all the greater because its object is not change but knowledge; and its silent appropriation of this dominant function, amid the din of political and religious strife, is the most vital of all the revolutions which have marked the development of modern civilisation.

Decadence: Henry Sedgwick Memorial Lecture, Cambridge:
25 January 1908

A VISION OF EMPIRE

I do not quarrel with those, I do not accuse them either of want of perception, want of imagination, or want of patriotism, who say that the British Empire as we know it is but a transitory arrangement; that it resembles the ordinary family life; that there was a time at which the protection of the Mother Country was necessary to its children in their early stages; that that time must pass in the world of politics and history as it passes in the world of domestic life; and that the time must come, and assuredly will come, when these great and growing communities will feel that all that could be gained from the British Empire as it used to be understood has been gained, and that in all kindness of heart and with every sympathy each member of that great Empire had better go its own way like the adult members of a human family.

That may happen: it is possible. The worldly wise would say that it is probable; and yet I think that there is a higher and a better way. I dream other dreams and have other visions of the future which may be in store for our descendants, whether they be born on this side of the Atlantic or the other, on this side of the world or the Antipodes. I cannot help thinking that as we have now thoroughly realised in every one of these great communities that each is to manage its own affairs—carry out its own life, make its own experiments as freely as if it were an independent political entity—as that is a truth thoroughly understood by every politician of every party in every one of these several communities—I cannot help thinking that upon that solid basis we shall build up something which the world has never yet seen, which political dreamers in the past have never yet dreamed of, a coalition of free and self-governing communities who feel that they are never more themselves, never more masters of their own fate, than when they recognise that they are parts of a greater whole, from which they can draw inspiration and strength, and to which they can give inspiration and strength; and that each lives its own life and is most itself when it feels itself in the fullest sense a self-governing entity which yet has a larger whole to look to, whose interests are not alien to it, on whom it can rest in time of trouble, from whom it can draw experience, to whom it can look, to whom it can give aid, and from whom it can receive aid.

That is an ideal coalition, of free self-governing communities which has never yet existed in the world, but of which we see the beginnings at the present time, and of which only our posterity will see the full fruition.

London: 18 June 1911

DEATH

This passage is from a letter to Lady Desborough, written 5 August 1915, on the death of her two elder sons, Julian and Riversdale Grenfell, killed in action.

I do not pretend to offer consolation; in one very real sense there is no consolation to be offered. The blow, the double blow has fallen, and the shock which threatens the very citadel of life can be softened by nothing that I or perhaps any other can do or utter. Who can measure the pain of separation? Who can deny that, normally at least, death *means* separation? And that between the living and the dead there lies an impassable gulf which no longing and no love is able to bridge? For this there is no remedy; we must bear it as we may; but to me it seems that in many cases the sorrow caused by death is due to something more and other than the cause of separation. It is due perhaps to an unacknowledged feeling that the separation is to be unending. Now if this be the settled conviction of the mourner, there is nothing more to be said. But if this is not the case, if the conviction be the other way, if the certainty or even the possibility of a future life be admitted, then we know that there is something wrong if the agonies of bereavement are more than those which should follow on a severance which though complete is temporary.

For myself, I entertain no doubt whatever about a future life. I deem it at least as certain as any of the hundred-and-one truths of the framework of the world, as I conceive the world. It is no mere theological accretion, which I am prepared to accept in some moods and reject in others. I am as sure that those I love and have lost are living to-day, as I am that yesterday they were fighting heroically in the trenches. The bitterness lies not in the thought that they are really dead, still less in the thought that I have parted with them for ever; for I think neither of these things. The bitterness lies in the thought that *until I also die* I shall never again see them smile or hear their voices. The pain is indeed hard to bear, too hard it sometimes seems for human strength. Yet measured on the true scale of things it is but brief; death cannot long cheat us of love.

AN ENGLISHMAN TO CONGRESS

On 5 May 1917, Mr. Balfour, then in the United States at the head of a Mission from Great Britain, spoke before Congress. It was the first time that an Englishman had addressed the House and the occasion was made more significant by President Wilson's presence in one of the galleries.

Mr. Speaker, ladies, and gentlemen of the House of Representatives, will you permit me, on behalf of my friends and myself, to offer you my deepest and sincerest thanks for the rare and valued honour which you have done us in receiving us here to-day? We all feel the greatness of the honour, but I think to none of us can it come home so closely as to one who, like myself, has been for forty-three years in the service of a free assembly like your own. I rejoice to think that a member of the British House of Commons has been received here to-day by this great sister assembly with such kindness as you have shown to me and my friends.

These two assemblies are the greatest and oldest of the free assemblies now governing the great nations of the world. The history, indeed, of the two is very different. The beginnings of the British House of Commons go back to the dim historic past, and its full rights and status have only been secured after centuries of political struggle. Your fate has been a happier one. You were called into existence at a much later stage of social development. You came into being complete, perfected, and with all your powers determined, your place in the Constitution secured beyond chance of revolution.

But, though the history of these two great assemblies is different, each of them represents the great democratic principle to which we look forward as security for the future peace of the world. All the free assemblies now to be found governing the great nations of the earth have been modelled either upon your practice, or upon ours, or upon both combined.

The compliment paid to the Mission from Great Britain by such an assembly upon such an occasion not one of us is ever likely to forget, but there is something, after all, of even deeper significance in the circumstances under which I now have the honour to address you than any which arise out of an interchange of courtesies, however sincere, between two great friendly nations. We all, I think, feel instinctively that this is one of the great moments in the history of the world, and that what is now happening on both sides of the Atlantic represents a drawing together of great and free peoples for mutual protection against the aggression of military despotism.

I am not one of those who are such bad democrats as to say that democracies make no mistakes. All free assemblies have made blunders and sometimes have committed crimes. Why is it, then, that we look forward to the spirit of free institutions throughout the world, and especially among our present enemies, as one of the greatest guarantees of the future peace of the world? I will tell you, gentlemen, how it seems to me. It is quite true that a people and the representatives of a people may be betrayed by some momentary gust of passion into a policy which they ultimately deplore, but it is only a military despotism of the German type that can through generations, if need be, pursue steadily, remorselessly, unscrupulously, and appallingly the object of dominating civilisation and mankind.

And, mark you, this evil, this menace under which we are now suffering, is not one which will diminish with the growth of knowledge and the progress of material civilisation, but, on the contrary, increases with it. When I was young we used to flatter ourselves that progress inevitably meant peace and that growth of knowledge was always accompanied as its natural fruit by the growth of goodwill among the nations of the earth. Unhappily we know better now. We know that there is such a thing in the world as a power which can with unvarying persistency force all the resources of knowledge and of civilisation into the one great task of making itself the moral and material master of the world.

It is against that danger that we free peoples of the Western civilisation have bound ourselves together. It is in that great cause that we are going to fight, and are fighting at this very moment, side by side. In that cause we shall surely conquer, and our children will look back on this fateful date as the one from which democracies can feel secure. Their progress, their civilisation, and their rivalry, if need be, will be conducted not on German lines, but in the free and friendly spirit which really befits the age in which we live.

JEWRY

Balfour's lifelong interest in Jewish problems found a culminating expression in the Declaration *of November 1917 which eventually secured* the restoration of Palestine to the civilising forces of Jewish national endeavour. *In 1922, a Palestinian settlement of about five*

hundred Jews, supported by the American Zion Commonwealth, was
founded and named Balfouria in his honour.

My noble friend told us that he has no prejudice against the Jews.
I think I may say that I have no prejudice in their favour. But their
position and their history, their connection with world religion and
with world politics, is unique. There is no parallel to it in any other
branch of human history. Here you have a small race originally
inhabiting a small country, at no time in its history wielding anything
that can be described as material power, sometimes crushed in between
great Oriental monarchies, its inhabitants deported, then scattered,
then driven out of the country altogether into every part of the world,
and yet maintaining a continuity of religious and racial tradition to
which we have no parallel elsewhere.

That is sufficiently remarkable, but consider how they have been
treated during long centuries, which in some parts of the world extend
to the minute and the hour in which I am speaking; consider how they
have been subjected to tyranny and persecution; consider whether the
whole culture of Europe, the whole religious organisation of Europe,
has not from time to time proved itself guilty of great crimes against
this race. I quite understand that some members of the race may have
given occasion for much ill-will, and I do not know how it could be
otherwise, treated as they were; but, if you are going to lay stress on
that, do not forget what part they have played in the intellectual, the
artistic, the philosophic and scientific development of the world. I say
nothing of the economic side of their energies, for on that Christian
attention has always been concentrated.

You will find them in every university, in every centre of learning;
and at the very moment when they were being persecuted, when some
of them, at all events, were being persecuted by the Church, their
philosophers were developing thoughts which the great doctors of the
Church embodied in their religious system. As it was in the Middle
Ages, as it was in earlier times, so it is now. And yet, is there anyone
here who feels content with the position of the Jews? They have been
able, by this extraordinary tenacity of their race, to maintain this
continuity, and they have maintained it without having any Jewish
home.

Surely it is in order that we may send a message to every land where
the Jewish race has been scattered, a message that will tell them that
Christendom is not oblivious of their faith, is not unmindful of the
service they have rendered to the great religions of the world, and,
most of all, to the religion that the majority of your lordships' House

profess, and that we desire to the best of our ability to give them that
opportunity of developing, in peace and quietness under British rule,
those great gifts which hitherto they have been compelled from the
very nature of the case only to bring to fruition in countries which
know not their language and belong not to their race?

House of Lords: 21 June 1922

Henry Campbell-Bannerman, afterwards

SIR HENRY CAMPBELL-BANNERMAN

1 8 3 6 – 1 9 0 8

---

*Liberal M.P., 1868–1908; Financial Secretary to
the War Office, 1871–74 and 1880–82; Parliamentary Secretary to the Admiralty, 1882–84;
Chief Secretary for Ireland, 1884–85; Secretary
of State for War, 1886 and 1892–95; Prime
Minister and First Lord of the Treasury, 1905–8*

THE TWO IMPERIALISMS

WE hear a great deal nowadays of Imperialism, and there are those who
seem to think that by calling themselves Imperialists they have added
a cubit to their stature. But the meaning of the word varies infinitely
according to the disposition of the man who uses it. If an Imperialist
means a man who would maintain by land and sea the power of the
Empire at the highest pitch; who would secure perfect safety for these
islands from hostile attack, but who is not content to confine his view
to these islands alone; who would preserve the territorial integrity and
interests of the Empire; who would guard our rights of trade either
within the Empire or beyond its bounds; and who would strengthen by
every means in his power the ties that bind us to our kinsmen in every
quarter of the globe—if that is to be an Imperialist, then there is not a
man here who is not as unflinching an Imperialist as those who have
the word always on their lips. We are not afraid of the responsibilities

of Empire, we are proud to be the guardians of the heritage handed down by our fathers, nay, we do not shrink from adding to it if duty or honour compels us; but we abjure the vulgar and bastard Imperialism of irritation, and provocation, and aggression, of clever tricks and manœuvres against neighbours, and of grabbing everything even if we have no use for it ourselves.

National Liberal Federation, Hull: 8 March 1899

FOEMEN INTO FRIENDS

Campbell-Bannerman, though inclined to that section of his party which believed war in South Africa might have been averted, accepted its necessity when once engaged upon. But his acceptance was tempered with a brave generosity of attitude towards our antagonists which found a fine reciprocation not only at the time of reconciliation and when, in 1907, his ministry conferred self-government on the Transvaal and Orange Free State, but later still when brave foemen of 1899–1902 became staunch friends of 1914 and 1939.

War is not a mere game, a trial of skill between two players to be continued until the board is cleared of pieces on one side or the other. It is an instrument, odious and horrible, but in this imperfect world a necessary instrument for the accomplishment of great political objects. What is the political object here? It is the peace, the harmony, the contentment of South Africa under the predominant power of Great Britain. Now the cardinal fact upon which the whole problem turns is that this is of the nature of a civil war. We are not fighting with a foreign foe whom we are to overcome and then abandon. These men are to be our neighbours—nay, they are to be our fellow-citizens. Whatever be their faults, whatever be their offences against us, if we are to stay in South Africa at all they will be there; they are indistinguishable from the great majority of our own citizens in our own colonies; they are indeed so intermixed with them by sympathies and by blood-relationship that they are practically one community from end to end. Now what will anyone who rightly appreciates these facts say are to be our objects in the war we have undertaken? The first should be to impose upon our antagonists a military superiority. But the second is to impress upon them our ultimate and essential friendliness towards them; and this is no false representation of our feelings. It is founded upon truth, because the large-hearted British people, whatever may be their anger, indignation, and prejudice, have no animosity or antipathy against the Boers, and no desire for their subjection. When I think of these things, some words echo in my recollection; words which appear in one of the lyrics which Henry Lushington wrote at the commencement of the Crimean war. He describes the departure of the Grenadier Guards for the East, where they are to fight side by side with our old traditional enemies, the French. On their way to the station they march over Waterloo Bridge:

> *name of happy omen,*
> *For the staunchest friends are wrought*
> *Out of the bravest foemen.*

There is an object, a worthy object, for a great and far-seeing statesman, for a large-hearted statesman, to turn brave foemen into staunch friends.

Stirling: 25 October 1901

MIRAGE

Campbell-Bannerman was not the last politician whose faith in peace, disarmament and international goodwill was betrayed by events. Less than a year after this speech, von Bülow announced Germany's veto on any proposals for disarmament at The Hague Conference of 1907.

On the one hand we find the reasoned opinion of Europe declaring itself more and more strongly for peace, and, on the other hand, preparations for war which in their extent and effectiveness suggest that a lust for blood is the actuating principle of modern society. It is this sinister paradox which baffles the will and lowers the self-respect of the Western world, and when we ask ourselves, as we are bound to do, whether the object of these preparations is attained, we encounter another paradox. The other day Lord Lansdowne, discussing the growth of armaments, said: *The moment may come when the people of this country will prefer to eat their daily bread in fear rather than starve in security.* But can any of us say that as a result of such overwhelming sacrifices of money, of men, of ideals, and of civil dignity the sense of security has been attained? Is it not evident that a process of simultaneous and progressive arming defeats its own purpose? Scare answers to scare, and force begets force, until at length it comes to be seen that we are racing one against another after a phantom security which continually vanishes as we approach. If we hold that war is the most futile and ferocious of human follies, what are we to say to the surpassing futility of expending the strength and substance of nations on preparations for war, possessing no finality, amenable to no alliances that statesmanship can devise, and for ever consuming the reserves—the well-being and vitality of its people—on which a State must ultimately rely when the time of trial comes, if come it must?

Do not imagine that I wish to discourage you by contrasting the hard facts of the situation with the aspirations we all share. That is the last thing that I have in mind. I am not despondent about the future. It is only a few short years since peace was a wanderer on the face of the earth, liable at any moment to be trampled upon and despitefully used; and if wars and preparations for wars have not ceased since she found a rest for the sole of her foot at the Hague, remember that time is needed for the growth of confidence in the new order of things, and that allowance must be made for the momentum of the past which thrusts the old regime forward upon the new. Remember, too, that the people are on your side. I know it is said that democracy is as prone to war as any other form of Government. But democracy, as we know it, is a late comer on the world's stage, where it has barely had time to become conscious of its characteristic powers, still less to exert them effectively in its external relations. The bonds of mutual understanding and esteem are strengthening between the peoples, and the time is approaching when nothing can hold back from them the knowledge that it is they who are the victims of war and militarism; that war in its tawdry triumphs scatters the fruits of their labour, breaks down the paths of progress, and turns the fire of constructive energy into a destroying force.

Inter-Parliamentary Congress, London: 23 July 1906

HIGH TRUCE OF GOD

It should perhaps be noted that the spirit of the Lakes Agreement extends not only to the water frontier but to the whole length of the boundary between Canada and the United States.

On those great inland seas which lie between Canada and the United States—over which every year passes a traffic greater than that of the Mediterranean—not a single warship floats. This water frontier of three thousand miles was neutralised by agreement between this country and the United States of America in 1817. The treaty provided for the maintenance of a nominal naval force. Yet what did Mr. Cobden say before a Parliamentary Committee in 1850? He said that from the moment of the existence of that treaty, *both parties have totally disregarded the maintenance of the force; there is not at the present moment more than one crazy English hulk on all those lakes.*

And now even the crazy English hulk has long disappeared, and the waters that unite the two countries are not disfigured by a single ship o war. What could be finer than this high truce of God, under which two free and sister nations have resolved to live within the security of tha defenceless barrier and to banish those symbols of strife, prejudice and suspicion on their highway frontier? Is the relationship so estab lished less noble than those which subsist between the nations of the Old World, the nations which still hug the ancient blasphemy tha armed force is the only title to respect and the only guarantee o security? I think not. I believe that the New World has shown us a more excellent way. Heaven help the great federations of free people t continue to prosper and go on in all that makes the real strength of State and maintain in all its radiance their bright example.

Manchester: 9 May 190

HERBERT HENRY ASQUITH

afterwards Earl of Oxford and Asquith

1 8 5 2 – 1 9 2 8

Liberal M.P., 1886–1918 and 1920–24; Secretary of State for Home Affairs, 1892–95; Chancellor of the Exchequer, 1905–8; Prime Minister in Liberal Ministry, 1908–15 and in Coalition Minis- try, 1915–16

THE SPIRIT OF OUR CONSTITUTION

In 1909 Mr. Lloyd George sought to make his Budget an instrument o social reform; but his measures which exasperated the Conservatives resulted in its rejection by the House of Lords. Thereupon Asquith dissolved Parliament and, returning with a majority, not only secured the passing of the Budget by a people's mandate, but also, by the threa of creating three hundred new peers from among his supporters (one o

whom was Thomas Hardy), contrived the passage of the Parliament Act
of 1911, thus limiting the future power of the Lords.

THE purpose of my motion to-day is not to complain of the financial
and administrative hardship which the House of Lords has so heed-
lessly caused, and still less to defend against the criticisms of noble
persons in another place the principles and the methods of the Budget.
These are not, in our view, a matter for these gentlemen, but for this
House alone to decide.

No, mine is a totally different purpose. It is the vindication of the
first principles of the Constitution and the assertion of this House's
immemorial right, and to enter a prompt and solemn protest against the
whole proceeding. In this country we live, and have lived for centuries
past, under an unwritten Constitution. It is true that we have on the
Statute-book great instruments like Magna Carta, the Petition of
Right, and the Bill of Rights which define and secure many of our
rights and our privileges; but the great bulk of our constitutional
liberties—and I will add of our constitutional practices—do not derive
their validity and sanction from any Bill which has received the formal
assent of the King, Lords, and Commons. They rest on usage, custom,
convention, often of slow growth in their early stages, not always
uniform, but which in course of time received universal observance and
respect. Let me point out further that it is the essential incident of such
an unwritten Constitution that there should be powers which are legal
powers in the sense that their exercise cannot be questioned in any
Court of law, yet which in the course of time and by the effect of such
usages as I have described, first of all fitfully and intermittently used,
finally in the progress of our development become dormant, moribund,
and for all practical purposes dead. The familiar illustration which is
well known to every one is the veto of the Crown. There is nothing
whatever to prevent me or any other Minister from advising his
Majesty to refuse his assent to a Bill which has been passed both by the
House of Commons and by the House of Lords; and if his Majesty
accepted that advice and refused his assent that Bill could not take its
place on the Statute-book and would not have the effect of law. Yet
the Minister who gave such advice would deserve to be impeached,
because although in point of law the right of the Crown to veto a Bill
is as unquestioned to-day as it was in the time of Queen Elizabeth, two
hundred years of desuetude and contrary practice have made a legal
right which is not constitutionally exercised or followed.

I read a speech the other day in which was derided the distinction
drawn by the Lord Chancellor between that which is legal and that
14

which is constitutional, and he said that it was the antiquarianism and pedantry of lawyers which left him quite cold. It was pedantry of this kind, the pedantry which realises and dwells upon the distinction between the genius and the spirit of our Constitution on the one side, and the bare and barren letter of the law on the other, it was pedantry of this kind that made and saved the liberties of England. It was pedants like Pym, Selden, and Somers who rescued this House largely through the power of the purse from the domination of the Crown; and we need not be ashamed to be called by the same name and to bear the same reproach while acting in the same spirit and using largely the same methods we put an end to the usurpations of the House of Lords.

House of Commons: 2 December 1909

THE ENGLISH BIBLE

The three-hundredth anniversary of the Authorised Version of the Bible was commemorated at the Albert Hall on 29 March 1911. Mr. White-law Reid, United States ambassador, read a message from President Taft: This Book of Books has not only reigned supreme in England for three centuries, but has bound together, as nothing else could, two great Anglo-Saxon nations, one in blood, in speech, and in a common religious life. Our laws, our literature, and our social life owe whatever excellence they possess largely to the influence of this our chief classic, acknowledged as such equally on both sides of the sea.

Americans must, therefore, with unfeigned satisfaction join in thanksgiving to the God of the Bible, who has thus bound together the Old and the New World by so precious a tie . . .

There is a celebrated retort reported to have been made to an obscurantist critic by Tyndale himself—Tyndale, confessor and martyr, in the greatest campaign ever waged by the soldiers of freedom against the yoke of intellectual and spiritual tyranny—a celebrated retort in which he said, *If God spare my life, ere many years I will cause a boy that driveth the plough to know more of the Scriptures than thou dost.* Never has what looked like a hazardous prediction, if not a vain-glorious boast, been more amply or richly fulfilled. To the common people of England, when Tyndale began to translate the New Testament, the Bible was a collection of oracles in a dead language. Their interpretation was the monopoly of a sacerdotal caste. Even Sir Thomas More himself thought that an English translation should not be hazarded except with a safeguard, the safeguard that all the copies should be entrusted to the Bishops, and doled out at their discretion only to such as the Bishops should perceive to be *honest, sad, and virtuous*. The circulation of the Bible in English, first surreptitiously, then with the connivance, and at last with the open approval, of the State, as Tyndale's and Coverdale's translations, the Great Bible, the Bishops' Bible, the Geneva Bible, finally our Authorised Version— the circulation of the Bible in English was in a far truer sense than the legislation of Henry and Elizabeth, the moving force of the Reformation.

It delivered our people from a yoke to which they will never again submit. It opened to one and all, small and great, poor and rich, learned and ignorant, the treasure-house of the Divine wisdom. It gave to each in the daily round of labour and care, as well as in the supreme and testing moments of life, an equal and unstinted share in the teachings which inspire, the consolations which soothe, the faith which can move mountains, the hope which endures to the end.

1914–18

The war which is now shaking to its foundations the whole European system, originated in a quarrel in which this country had no direct concern. We strove with all our might, as every one now knows, to prevent its outbreak, and, when that was no longer possible, to limit its area. It is all-important that it should be clearly understood when it was and why it was that we intervened. It was only when we were confronted with the choice between keeping and breaking solemn obligations, between the discharge of a binding trust and of shameless subservience to naked force, that we threw away the scabbard. We do not repent our decision. The issue was one which no great and self-respecting nation, certainly none bred and nurtured like ourselves in this ancient home of liberty, could, without undying shame, have declined. We are bound by our obligations, plain and paramount, to assert and maintain the threatened independence of a small and neutral State. Belgium had no interest of her own to serve, save and except the one supreme and overriding interest of every State, great or little, which is worthy of the name—the preservation of her integrity and of her national life. History tells us that the duty of asserting and maintaining that great principle which is, after all, the well-spring of civilisation and of progress, has fallen once and again at the most critical moments in the past to States, relatively small in area and in population, but great in courage and resolve—to Athens and Sparta, the Swiss Cantons, and, not least gloriously, three centuries ago, to the Netherlands. Never has the duty been more clearly and bravely acknowledged, and never has it been more strenuously and heroically discharged than during the last weeks by the Belgian King and the Belgian people. They have won for themselves the immortal glory which belongs to a people who prefer freedom to ease, to security, to life itself. We are proud of their alliance and their friendship. We salute them with respect and with honour. We are with them heart and soul, because by their side and in their company we are defending at the same time two great causes—the independence of small States and the sanctity of international covenants.

House of Commons: 27 August 1914

The Germans asked themselves what interest, direct or material, had the United Kingdom in this conflict. Could any nation, least of all the cold, calculating, phlegmatic, egotistic British nation embark upon a costly and bloody contest from which it had nothing in the hope of profit to expect? They forgot that we, like the Belgians, had something at stake which cannot be translated into *the lore of nicely calculated less or more.* What was it we had at stake? First and foremost, the fulfilment to the small and relatively weak country of our plighted word, and behind and beyond that the maintenance of the whole system of international goodwill, which is the moral bond of the civilised world. Here again they were wrong in thinking that the reign of ideas, old world ideas, like those of duty and good faith, had been superseded by the ascendancy of force. War is at all times a hideous thing, at the best an evil to be chosen in preference to worse evils and at the worst little better than the letting loose of hell upon earth. Great ndeed is the responsibility of those who allow their country—as we have done—to be drawn into such a welter. But there is one thing much worse than to take such a responsibility, and that is upon a fitting occasion to shirk it. Our record in the matter is clear. We strove up to the last moment for peace, and only when we were satisfied that the price of peace was the betrayal of other countries and the dishonour and degradation of our own did we take up the sword.

Mansion House, Dublin: 25 September 1914

I should like, beyond this inquiry into causes and motives, to ask your attention and that of my fellow-countrymen to the end which, in this war, we ought to keep in view. Forty-four years ago, at the time of the war of 1870, Mr. Gladstone used these words: *The greatest triumph of our time will be the enthronement of the idea of public right as the governing idea of European politics.* Nearly fifty years have passed. Little progress, it seems, has yet been made towards that good and beneficent change, but it seems to me to be as good a definition as we can have of our European policy—the idea of public right. What does it mean when translated into concrete terms? It means first and foremost, the clearing of the ground by the definite repudiation of militarism as the governing factor in the relation of States and in the future moulding of the European world. It means next that room must be found and kept for the independent existence and the free development of the smaller nationalities each with a corporate consciousness of its own. And it means finally, or it ought to mean, perhaps, by a slow and gradual process, the substitution for force, for the clash of competing ambition, for groupings and alliances and a precarious equipoise, of a real European partnership based on the recognition of equal right and established and enforced by a common will.

Ibid

As the war has developed it has been realised by all thinking men that it has a far wider range of significance than could have been foreseen or even imagined when it first began. It arose, so far as we here are concerned, in the violation of treaty obligations and the contemptuous setting aside of the rights of the smaller nationalities in the European order. But it soon became apparent that higher and deeper issues than these were at stake, which according as they were decided in one sense or the other, would affect the whole future of civilisation. It took time, as the contest swayed this way and that, to discern through the smoke and the poisoned fumes of the battlefield the true character and the ultimate aims of the forces that are arrayed against one another. The Germans have made it more and more clear that the triumph of their cause would be the death-knell of all democratic ideals. And at the same time their new methods of warfare, at first incredible, and, indeed, inconceivable, have demonstrated that for the attainment of that end they hold themselves absolutely free to dispense with the old restraints, whether of honesty or of humanity.

It was the realisation of these things and of the consequence which followed from them that not merely local but world-wide interests, moral as well as material, were in jeopardy that led our American kinsmen to decide that they could not hold aloof from the struggle. But that is still not a complete account of the case. The Allied cause is now plainly seen by all men to have what by implication it had from the first—a positive as well as a negative purpose. Its aim is not merely to repel aggression, to vindicate public faith, to clip the wings of militarism, to defeat the ambitious and frustrate the designs of what the Germans call their world polity. It is determined to provide against the recurrence of the horrors which are scourging mankind and devastating the world, not merely by repression and punishment, but by bringing into life and into effective action the corporate judgment, the sense of common interests and common duties, the reconciling, and if need be, the restraining and constraining forces of the whole family of nations. These, stripped of what is transient and superficial, are the features that, measured by the true scale of significance, show the real stature of the two causes now engaged in mortal strife. There is none of us in this room, in this country, in this Empire, who does not pray for peace as the world's paramount need. But the only peace worth the making or the taking, is one which will open a new road, free of toll, to all peoples, whether great or small, safeguarded by the common will, and, if need be, by the common power, for the further progress of humanity.

Connaught Rooms, London: 14 June 1918

There is nothing that we can do in conditions so unexampled as these than as a House and on behalf of the nation to acknowledge our gratitude to Almighty God.

House of Commons: Armistice Day, 11 November 1918

When history comes to tell the tale of these four years, it will recount a story the like of which is not to be found in any epic in any literature. It is and will remain by itself as a record of everything Humanity can dare or endure—of the extremes of possible heroism and, we must add, of possible baseness, and above and beyond all, the slow moving but in the end irresistible power of a great ideal. The Old World has been laid waste. Principalities and Powers, to all appearances inviolable and invincible, which seemed to dominate a large part of the families of mankind, lie in the dust. All things have become new. In this great and cleansing purging it has been the privilege of our country to play her part, a part worthy of a people who themselves have learned beforehand the lesson to practise the example of ordered freedom.

House of Commons: 18 November 1918

VALEDICTORY

Lord Oxford's last public speech was made at York, when, 19 October 1927, he received the Freedom of that city, an honour previously bestowed on only two of his predecessors—Chatham in 1758 and Wellington in 1827.

However uncertain may appear to be the prospects of the immediate future, never lose faith and hope. Never allow yourselves to be ensnared in sombre and paralysing generalities and shallow pessimism. There are moments when the most sanguine among us are tempted to be depressed by the spectacular follies and stupidities of mankind, and as we survey this disillusioning panorama, to say to ourselves, *As it was in the beginning, is now, and ever shall be, world without end.* That is not a wholesome mood, nor is it, in the long run, justified by reason or by experience. One of the greatest theologians and thinkers of the English Church, Bishop Butler, is reported in a moment of gloom to have expressed the belief that nations, like individuals, are subject to an access of fits of madness. And he added that on no other hypothesis was it possible to explain some of the most surprising and yet most stubborn facts of history. That may be true or not. It is, at any rate, the part of wisdom not to let one's vision be obscured by the clouds of dust which from time to time are raised in the course of its progress by the chariot of human destiny. It is more inspiring, and, I am persuaded a better founded and indeed a safer faith, when men's thoughts—and not only their thoughts in an intellectual sense, but their ideals and their purposes—are, as one of our great Victorian poets taught us *widened by the process of the suns.*

DAVID LLOYD GEORGE

1 8 6 3 –

Liberal M.P. since 1890; President of the Board of Trade, 1905–8; Chancellor of the Exchequer, 1908–15; Minister of Munitions, 1915–16; Secretary of State for War, 1916; Prime Minister and First Lord of the Treasury in Coalition Ministry, 1916–22

THE BETTERMENT OF THE PEOPLE

This is from one of the great series of speeches made by Mr. Lloyd George in the Budget crisis of 1909. See note on page 208.

WE are raising money by means that make it no more difficult for men to live, we are raising it for making provision for hundreds of thousands of workmen in the country who have nothing between them and starvation in old age except the charity of the parish. We propose a great scheme in order to set up a fund in this country that will see that no man suffers hunger in the dark days of sickness, breakdown in health, and unemployment which visit so many of us. That is what we are going to do. We cannot get these schemes for the betterment of the people without effort, and they will not be worth getting without effort. Freedom does not descend like manna from Heaven. It has been won step by step, by tramping the wilderness, fighting enemies, crossing Jordan, and clearing Jebusites out of the land. I do not regret that we cannot obtain these blessings except by fighting. The common people have taken no step that was worth taking without effort, sacrifice and suffering.

I cannot pretend to regret this conflict with which we are now confronted. It is well that democracies should now and again engage in these great struggles for a wider freedom and a higher life. They represent stages in the advance of the people from the bondage of the past to the blessings of the future. Those who dread these political convulsions, who apprehend from them nothing but destruction and danger, have read their history in vain. The race has nothing to fear except from stagnation. Against our will, we have been precipitated into this tumult. For all that, we mean to win our way through it to a better time. The people may not secure all they seek, but if they bear

216

SALUTE TO AMERICA: 1917

*America declared war on Germany, 6 April 1917. Six days later Lloyd
George spoke at a Savoy Hotel meeting of the American Luncheon Club:*

I am the first British Minister of the Crown who, speaking on
behalf of the people of this country, can salute the American nation as
comrades in arms. I am glad. I am proud. I am glad not merely because
of the stupendous resources which this great nation can bring to the
succour of the Alliance, but I rejoice as a democrat that the advent of
the United States into this war gives the final stamp and seal to the
character of the conflict as a struggle against military autocracy
throughout the world. *A fight for human liberty.* That was the note
which rang through the great deliverance of President Wilson. The
United States of America have a noble tradition of having never
engaged in a war except for liberty. This is the greatest struggle for
liberty upon which they have ever embarked.

R.F.C.

The heavens are their battlefield; they are the cavalry of the clouds.
High above the squalor and the mud, so high in the firmament that
they are not visible from earth, they fight out the eternal issues of
right and wrong. Their daily, yea, their nightly struggles, are like the
Miltonic conflict between the winged hosts of light and of darkness.
They fight the foe high up and they fight him low down; they skim like
armed swallows, hanging over trenches full of armed men, wrecking
convoys, scattering infantry, attacking battalions on the march.
Every flight is a romance; every report is an epic. They are the knight-
hood of this war, without fear and without reproach.

House of Commons: 29 October 1917

LIBERTY

It is all very well to worship at the shrine of liberty, but you cannot
defend it with garlands.

Birkenhead: 7 September 1917

Liberty is not merely a privilege to be conferred; it is a habit to be
acquired.

House of Commons: 10 May 1928

Liberty has restraints but no frontiers.

International Liberal Conference: July 1928

JEW BAITING

Of all the bigotries that savage the human temper there is none so stupid as the anti-Semitic. It has no basis in reason; it is not rooted in faith; it aspires to no ideal; it is just one of those dank and unwholesome weeds that grow in the morass of racial hatred. How utterly devoid of reason it is may be gathered from the fact that it is almost entirely confined to nations who worship Jewish prophets and apostles, revere the national literature of the Hebrews as the only inspired message delivered by the Deity to mankind, and whose only hope of salvation rests on the precepts and promises of the great teachers of Judah. Yet, in the sight of these fanatics the Jews of to-day can do nothing right. If they are rich they are birds of prey. If they are poor they are vermin. If they are in favour of a war, it is because they want to exploit the bloody feuds of the Gentiles to their own profit. If they are anxious for peace, they are either instinctive cowards or traitors. If they give generously—and there are no more liberal givers than the Jews—they are doing it for some selfish purpose of their own. If they do not give—then what could one expect of a Jew but avarice? If labour is oppressed by great capital, the greed of the Jew is held responsible. If labour revolts against capital, the Jew is blamed for that also. If he lives in a strange land he must be persecuted and pogrommed out of it. If he wants to go back to his own, he must be prevented. Through the centuries in every land, whatever he does, or intends or fails to do, he has been pursued by the echo of the brutal cry of the rabble of Jerusalem against the greatest of all Jews—*Crucify Him!*

Is it Peace? 1923

HOMAGE TO LINCOLN

One of Mr. Lloyd George's earliest recollections is of a portrait of Lincoln that hung on the wall of the cottage at Llangstumdwy, where he was brought up by his uncle, Richard Lloyd, whose hero Lincoln was. Thus from early childhood the future Prime Minister was familiar with every detail of a life paralleled by his own in its progress from poverty to leadership.

I have come here to-day with one purpose, and one purpose only; to pay my humble and reverent tribute of respect to the memory of one of the great men of the world. It is difficult for me to express the feelings with which I visited the home and the last resting-place of one of the noblest figures in the history of mankind. There have been many great men whose names have been inscribed on the scroll of human history; there are only a few whose names have become a legend amongst men. Amongst these conspicuously stands the name of Abraham Lincoln. His fame is wider to-day than it was at the date of his tragic death, and it is still widening. His influence is deeper, and it is still deepening.

Even if this were the occasion, I do not feel competent to pronounce any judgment on the qualities that made him great, and on the deeds and words that will make his name endure for evermore. Least of all would I presume to do so in the city where there are men still living who remember and knew him. All I know about him is that he was one of those rare men whom you do not associate with any particular creed or party, or even country, for he belongs to mankind in every race, in every clime, and in every age.

There are the great men of a party, and the great men of a creed. There are the great men of their time, and there are the great men of all time for their own native land; but Lincoln was a great man of all time, for all parties, for all lands and for all races of men. He was the choice and champion of a party, but his lofty soul could see over and beyond the bounds of party the unlimited terrain beyond. His motto was: *Stand with anybody who stands right. Stand with him while he is right and part with him when he goes wrong.* Those are his own words. No pure partisan would ever assent to so discriminating and disintegrating a proposition.

His career—from the wretched log cabin at Kentucky, on to the official residence of the President of the greatest republic on earth— seems a triumphal march enough for any ambition. And yet, his life is in many ways one of the saddest of human stories, and even the tragic end comes as a relief.

He once said, *I have not willingly planted a thorn in any man's bosom.* Yet, as soon as he reached the height of his ambition, this man, who shunned hurt and scattered kindness on his path, was doomed by a cruel destiny to send millions of his own fellow-countrymen through the torturing experiences of a prolonged and fierce war against their own kith and kin. The tenderest soul who ever ruled over men was driven for five years by an inexorable fate to pierce the gentle hearts of mothers with anguish that death alone can assuage.

And in this, the greatest and most poignant task of his life, he was worried, harassed, encumbered, lassoed at every turn by the vanities, the jealousies, the factiousness and the wiles of swarms of little men. He was misrepresented, misunderstood, maligned, derided, thwarted in every good impulse, thought, or deed. No wonder his photographs became sadder and sadder and more and more tragic year by year up to the tragic end.

His example and his wise sayings are the inheritance of mankind, and will be quoted and used to save it from its follies to the end of the ages. The lessons of his statesmanship are as applicable to-day as they were sixty years ago. They will be as applicable a thousand years hence as they are to-day. Being dead, he still speaketh. He has messages of moment for this present hour. I will give you two of them.

The first message of Abraham Lincoln to this day and this moment and this emergency in the life of man is: *Clemency in the hour of triumph*. The doctrine of Abraham Lincoln was *Reconcile the vanquished*. It is a time for remembering that vengeance is the justice of the savage, and that conciliation is the triumph of civilisation over barbarism. Lincoln is the finest product of the Christian civilisation in the realm of statesmanship, and the wise counsel he gave to his own people in the day of their triumph he gives to-day to the people of Europe in the hour of their victory over the forces that menace their liberties.

What is his next message? *Trust the common people*. He believed in their sincerity, he believed in their common sense, he believed in their inherent justice, he believed in their ultimate unselfishness. The first impulse of the people may be selfish. Their final word is always unselfish. That was the doctrine of Abraham Lincoln, and to-day, when democracy is in greater peril than it has probably been in your lifetime or mine, his message carries across the waves, and will, I hope, be heard in Europe and will impel the democracies of Europe to fight against the wave of autocracy sweeping over their continent. It is the hour for Abraham Lincoln's doctrine to be preached in the countries of Europe. His influence upon our democracy in England is deep, and I believe permanent, and if the peril reaches our shores, the words of Abraham Lincoln will be an inspiration and a strength to those who will be battling for the cause of the people. The principles of Abraham Lincoln will yet save the world for liberty, for peace, for goodwill and honest men.

Springfield, Illinois: 17 October 1923

ANDREW BONAR LAW

1858–1923

Conservative M.P., 1900–23; Parliamentary Secretary of the Board of Trade, 1902–6; Leader of the Opposition, 1911–15; Secretary of State for the Colonies, 1915–16; Chancellor of the Exchequer, 1916–18; Lord Privy Seal and Leader of the House of Commons, 1919–21; Prime Minister and First Lord of the Treasury, 1922–23

OUR STAND

When, at the time of the Agadir crisis, war between Great Britain and Germany threatened, Bonar Law, 27 November 1911, had said: If, therefore, war should ever come between these two countries, which Heaven forbid! it will not, I think, be due to irresistible natural laws, it will be due to the want of human wisdom.

On 6 August 1914, two days after the outbreak of war, the House of Commons went into Committee of Supply and Bonar Law, as Leader of the Opposition, spoke immediately after the Prime Minister.

I FEEL that I am bound to make it clear to the Committee and to the country what is the attitude of His Majesty's Opposition on this question. There are two things which I desire to impress upon the Committee. The first is that we have dreaded war and have longed for peace as strongly as any section of this Committee; and the second is that in our belief we are in a state of war against our will, and that we, as a nation, have done everything in our power to prevent such a condition of things arising. When this crisis first arose I confess that I was one of those who had the impulse to hope that even though a European conflagration should take place, we might be able to stay out. I had that hope strongly. But in a short time I became convinced that into this war we should inevitably be drawn and that it really was a question only whether we should enter it honourably or be dragged into it with dishonour.

I remember an occasion when I said that if ever war arose between Great Britain and Germany it would not be due to inevitable causes, for I did not believe in an inevitable war. I said it would be due to

223

human folly. It is due to human folly and to human wickedness, but neither the folly nor the wickedness is here.

We are fighting for the honour and, what with the honour is bound up always, the interest of our nation. But we are fighting also for the whole basis of the civilisation for which we stand and for which Europe stands. I do not wish to inflame passion. I only ask the House to consider a report that the city of Liége is invaded by German troops and that civilians, as in the days of the Middle Ages, are fighting for their hearths and homes against trained troops. In a state of war, war must be waged; but remember that this plan has been long matured; that the Germans were ready to take the course which they took the other day of saying to Belgium: *Destroy your independence. Allow our troops to go through, or we will come down upon you with a might impossible for you to resist.* If we had allowed that to be done, our honour and our position as one of the great nations of the world would have been gone for ever. This is no small struggle. It is the greatest, perhaps, in which this country has ever been engaged. It is Napoleonism once again. Thank Heaven, so far as we know, there is no Napoleon.

House of Commons: 6 August 1914

AT OUR SIDE

It is fitting that tribute to the Empire's loyalty should be paid by the first colonial-born Prime Minister of Great Britain. It is from a preface contributed, 6 December 1915, to Canada in Flanders, *a record by his fellow-Canadian, Sir Max Aitken, M.P., now Lord Beaverbrook.*

We have a right to feel very proud of the part which is being played in the terrible tragedy of this war by the great Dominions of the British Crown. We had no power to compel any one of them to contribute a single penny, or to send a single man, but they have given of their best; not to help us, though I think they would have done that also, but to defend the Empire which is theirs as much as ours.

Led by a General who a few years ago was in arms against us and is now Prime Minister of South Africa, the Union Government has wrested from Germany a territory larger than the whole German Empire; and a South African contingent is now in England ready to play their part on the battlefields of Flanders.

The Australians and New Zealanders have shown in the Dardanelles that in courage, resourcefulness, and tenacity better troops have never existed in the world. Whatever the final result of that operation may be, the blood which has been shed there has not been shed in vain. Not to Australians and New Zealanders alone, but to men of every race throughout the British Empire, the Peninsula of Gallipoli will for ever be sacred ground because of the brave men who lie buried there.

In glory will they sleep, and endless sanctity.

To what Canada has done, and is doing, higher praise could not be given than was contained in the despatch of the Commander-in-Chief after the battle of Ypres: *In spite of the danger to which they were exposed, the Canadians held their ground with a magnificent display of tenacity and courage, and it is not too much to say that the bearing and the conduct of these splendid troops averted a disaster which might have been attended with most serious consequences.*

Our enemies said, and probably they believed, that the outbreak of war would be the signal for the breaking-up of the British Empire. They have been mistaken. After this war the relations between the great Dominions and the Mother Country can never be the same again. The pressure of our enemies is welding us together, and the British Empire is becoming in reality, as well as in name, a united nation.

THRONE AND PEOPLE

On 18 November 1918, Bonar Law as Leader of the Opposition, in the absence of an indisposed Prime Minister, moved an Address congratulating His Majesty on the conclusion of the Armistice.

Nature, as a great writer said, rests everywhere on true foundations; governments, societies, and civilisation itself rest only upon a crust which has grown hard by custom and habit. This war has broken through that crust, and as a consequence Europe is seething with revolution to-day. Yet here we can look forward to the future with hope, with courage, and with confidence because the institutions which habit has created with us are based on the strongest of all foundations—the consent of the nation which is subjected to them. Of these institutions none rests on more secure foundations than the Throne. The Throne is the link which has kept the British Empire together, which has enabled it to play a glorious part in this terrible struggle, and which will make the union closer and closer. But the Throne as an institution would have been much less strong but for the character of its occupant. Government knows, and the people know too, that from the first day of this war until this hour no man has devoted himself more wholeheartedly or more unselfishly to the great

15

task in which as a nation we have been engaged. And in that work he has been nobly helped by his Royal Consort. They have shared the sacrifices; they have delighted in the joys, and they have sympathised with the sorrows of their people; and at this time when kings like shadowy phantoms are disappearing from the scene our Sovereign passes daily without an escort through the streets of the centre of the Empire, and is everywhere met with tributes of respect, of devotion, and of affection. The phantom kings have fallen because they based their claims on an imaginary divine right. Our King rests secure because the foundation of his Throne is the will of his people.

House of Commons: 18 November 1918

STANLEY BALDWIN

afterwards Earl Baldwin of Bewdley

1867 –

Conservative M.P., 1908–37; Financial Secretary to the Treasury, 1917–21; President of the Board of Trade, 1921–22; Chancellor of the Exchequer, 1922–23; Prime Minister and First Lord of the Treasury, 1923–24, 1924–29, and 1935–37; Lord President of the Council, 1931–35; Lord Privy Seal, 1932–34

ENGLAND

TO me, England is the country, and the country is England. And when I ask myself what I mean by England, when I think of England when I am abroad, England comes to me through my various senses—through the ear, through the eye, and through certain imperishable scents.

The sounds of England, the tinkle of the hammer on the anvil in the country smithy, the corncrake on a dewy morning, the sound of the scythe against the whetstone. The sight of a plough team coming over the brow of a hill, the sight that has been seen in England since England was a land, and may be seen in England long after the Empire has perished and every works in England has ceased to function, for centuries the one eternal sight of England; the wild anemones in the woods in April, the last load at night of hay being drawn down a lane as the twilight comes on, when you can scarcely distinguish the figures of the horses as they take it home to the farm. And above all, most subtle, most penetrating and most moving, the smell of wood smoke coming up in an autumn evening, or the smell of the scutch fires: that wood smoke that our ancestors, tens of thousands of years ago, must have caught on the air when they were coming home with the result of the day's forage, when they were still nomads, and when they were still roaming the forests and the plains of the continent of Europe. These things strike down into the very depths of our nature, and touch chords that go back to the beginning of time and the human race, but they are chords that with every year of our life sound deeper in our innermost being.

Royal Society of St. George, London: 6 May 1924

THE EMPIRE

It stands in the sweep of every wind, by the wash of every sea, a witness to that which the spirit of confidence and brotherhood can accomplish in the world. It is a spiritual inheritance which we hold in trust not only for its members, but for all the nations which surround it. Let us see to it that we hand it on to our successors with untarnished glory.

Broadcast: 24 May 1927

THE ABBEY

Westminster Abbey is linked with the history of the English-speaking peoples as is no other building in the world. Built by English kings, with the craftsmanship of English workmen, this great church provided the Chapel of the Pyx for the Treasury, her Chapter House for the sittings of Parliament and her chapels for the burying of kings.

It is hard for us to realise the Westminster of the thirteenth century. Where the omnibuses swing round by St. Margaret's Church and along that busy road to Lambeth Bridge, Henry III, the founder of the Abbey as we know it, planted an orchard of pear trees that he might see the white walls rising through the blossom as he watched his masons at work from his palace in the spring. The monastery is gone, the fields are gone, but the Abbey is ours, darkened with age, with a beauty against which Time is powerless, the spectator of six centuries of ceaseless striving, of splendid successes, of splendid failures, of dreams and of achievement. By her altar our kings have been crowned; under her roof we have given thanks for our victories; under her roof we have mourned our dead.

Abbey Appeal for Funds: 1 July 1927

SERVICE OF DEMOCRACY

The whole world to-day, with one or two exceptions, is singing loudly the praises of democracy. The whole world renders lip-service to democracy. It has learned that cry from the English-speaking peoples. Our great task in the future is to show the world what democracy can mean. There have been democracies in the past. There are democracies to-day. I like to think that no democracy to-day is even a shadow of the democracies that our children's children may see in years to come.

Freedom can be maintained only by constant vigilance. A democracy can be maintained only when every man, woman and child in that democracy mean to do everything in their power to make that community better, stronger, freer. The reason so many democracies in the past have perished is because democracy is always, in the Old World, on a knife edge. Or, as I have often expressed it, it is a certain point on the circumference of a wheel. How frequently has mankind travelled on the circumference of that wheel, working its way, with infinite labour, to a point that you would call democracy. Go but a little further than that point and democracy becomes licence, licence becomes anarchy, and then the wheel goes full circle and anarchy comes back to tyranny, and man has to fight his way back out of tyranny once again.

We stand on that part of the wheel called democracy, secure at the moment from either licence on the one hand or tyranny on the other. It is our task to keep the wheel in that position. We cannot keep it there without an educated people—educated not only in letters, but in those deep and profound moral truths on which our forefathers first of all built up the British Islands and then went out to build up the Empire. You are the children of those men. Resolve, every one of you, that you will give your best thought, your best work, not only to the furthering of your individual interests, which of course is necessary, but also to that greater community of which each of us is but a unit. Work for yourself, work for Canada, work for the whole Empire, and determine that so long as we speak the same tongue, obey the same God, obey the same laws, wherever we be situated, we remain to the end of time one people as the only hope of this world.

Toronto: 6 August 1927

SERVICE OF OUR LIVES

In the Abbey I saw our young King and his Queen dedicating their lives to the service of their people, a service that can only be ended by death.

As I drove through the streets of London I saw the faces of the crowds eager to see and greet their newly crowned King and Queen, and listening to the ringing cheers, the cheers of the warmest-hearted, kindliest people in the world, I thought there was only one way in which we could all of us make permanent that deep impression of what we have seen and heard this day.

Let us dedicate ourselves—afresh if need be—to the service of our fellows, a service in widening circles, service to the home, to our neighbourhood, to our county, our province, to our country, to the

Empire, and to the world. No mere service of our lips, service of our lives, as we know will be the service of our King and Queen. God bless them!

Broadcast: Coronation Day, 12 May 1937

PATRIOTISM AND CHARACTER

I would remind you of the words used by Ennius: *Moribus stat res Romana*—On character the Roman State is founded. It was because these words were forgotten, because the Roman character perished, that the Empire perished, and the world was plunged again into barbarism.

Character is the foundation of the British Empire. Unless we build on the ancient virtues of duty, truth and patriotism, our experiment in democracy will fail and the dissolution of our Empire ..ill be a question of years.

I have used the word patriotism on purpose because, rightly used, it is a potent force for good. At its best it is a noble virtue. It derives strength from the fact that it is a fundamental primitive instinct, an instinct common to higher and lower civilisations, attaching itself to the earliest memories of childhood, to the fields and woods and streams amongst which we grew up. The highest form of human altruism has been inspired by patriotism. Not only with soldiers and sailors, but with scholars, engineers and business men, service of their country has been the deepest motive of their work. The world is enriched by the several contributions of nations, and it seems to me that depreciation of patriotism cannot really help but may rather hinder international co-operation. You cannot make the world better by abandoning one of the most powerful motives to noble action that the world has yet known . . .

But we must never forget that patriotism is not an intellectual concept. It is an emotion, and is therefore capable of being enlisted or exploited for ignoble ends. It is indeed the last refuge of a scoundrel when it is used as a cloak of avarice and in the spirit of domination. Pure patriotism, which asks nothing and seeks nothing, which gives service because it can no other, is a necessary ingredient in the character upon which a great democracy is built. Indeed, if the word be used in its widest sense and in its highest, it comprises the whole duty of man as a citizen.

Rectorial Address, University of Glasgow: 20 January 1930

THE TORCH I WOULD HAND TO YOU

In this the last speech I shall make before a great audience as Prime Minister of this country let me proclaim my faith, which is the faith of millions of all races from end to end of the British Empire. Here we have ceased to be an island, but we are still an Empire. And what is the secret? Freedom, ordered freedom within the law, with force in the background and not in the foreground; a society in which authority and freedom are blended in due proportion, in which State and citizen are both ends and means.

It is an Empire organised for peace and for the free development of the individual in and through an infinite variety of voluntary associations. It deifies neither the State nor its rulers. The old doctrine of the divine right of kings has gone, but we have no intention of erecting in its place a new doctrine of the divine right of States. No State that ever was is worthy of a free man's worship.

The young King and Queen, whom we have delighted to honour in these memorable days, are the servants of the sovereign people. To them they have dedicated themselves. That is the magic of monarchy, which is everlasting. The King is the symbol of the union, not only of an Empire, but of a society which is held together by a common view of the fundamental nature of man. It is neither the worship of a tribe nor a class. It is a faith, a value placed upon the individual, derived from the Christian religion.

The Christian State proclaims human personality to be supreme; the servile State denies this. Every compromise with the infinite value of the human soul leads straight back to savagery and the jungle. Expel this truth of our religion, and what follows? The insolence of dominion, and the cruelty of despotism. Denounce religion as the opium of the people, and you swiftly proceed to denounce political liberty and civil liberty as opium. Freedom of speech goes, tolerance follows, and justice is no more.

The association of the peoples of the Empire is rooted, and their fellowship is rooted, in this doctrine of the essential dignity of the individual human soul. That is the English secret, however feebly and faintly we have at times and places embraced and obeyed it.

The torch I would hand to you, and ask you to pass from hand to hand along the pathways of the Empire, is a Christian truth rekindled anew in each ardent generation. Use men as ends and never merely as means; and live for the brotherhood of man, which implies the Fatherhood of God. The brotherhood of man to-day is often denied and derided and called foolishness, but it is, in fact, one of the foolish

things of the world which God has chosen to confound the wise, and
the world is confounded by it daily.

We may evade it, we may deny it; but we shall find no rest for our
souls, nor will the world until we acknowledge it as the ultimate
wisdom.

Empire Rally of Youth, Royal Albert Hall, London: 18 May 1937

JAMES   RAMSAY   MACDONALD
1866–1937

---

*Labour M.P., 1906–18 and 1922–31; National
Labour M.P., 1931–35 and 1936–37; Prime
Minister, First Lord of the Treasury and Secretary
of State for Foreign Affairs, 1924; Prime Minister
and First Lord of the Treasury, 1929–31 and, in
Coalition Ministry, 1931–35; Lord President of
the Council, 1935–37*

PORTRAIT OF A LABOUR LEADER

*Keir Hardie, born 1856, son of a ship's carpenter, at seven years old
a Glasgow errand-lad and from ten to twenty at work in the Ayrshire
coal-mines, became the founder of the Independent Labour Party,
previous to which working-men candidates for Parliament had fought
under the Liberal banner. Hardie became M.P. for West Ham in 1892.*

WHAT then was the secret of the man? I who have seen him in all
relationships, at the height of triumph and in the depths of humiliation,
on the platform and at the fireside, dignified among strangers and
merry amongst friends, generally fighting by his side but sometimes in
conflict with him, regard that secret as first of all his personality and
then his proud esteem for the common folk and his utter blindness to
all the decorations of humanity. He was a simple man, a strong man,
a gritty man.

Hardie was of the *old folk*. Born in a corner of Scotland where there
still lingered a belief in the uncanny and superhuman, he went out a
strong man in heart and in backbone, with the spirit of great tradition
in him; nurtured by a mother who faced the hard world like a woman
of unconquerable soul, whose tears were followed by defiance and

whose sighs ended with challenge, he went out like a knight armed with a sword which had the magic of conquest tempering its steel. That was his birthright, and that birthright made him a gentleman, whether running errands for a baker in Glasgow, or facing the *overfed beasts* on the benches of the House of Commons. Such men never fear the face of men and never respect their baubles.

From the same sources came his comfort in the common folk. Hardie had those native qualities which never became incompetent to value the honour and the worth of a kitchen fireside, of a woman who, like his mother, toiled in the fields, of a man who earned his living by the sweat of his brow, subduing Heaven the while. When he became famous, his world widened and he mixed with people in different circumstances. But he met them as the self-respecting workman, all unconscious of difference and with neither an attempt nor a desire to imitate them.

Experience in the world strengthened this part of his nature. Whether as a baker's messenger forced to pass moral judgment on the man of substantial respectability, or as a Trade Union official studying the results of the work of directors, managers, and such like, or as a politician in touch with the political intelligence and general capacity of the ruling classes, he saw no inferiority in his fellow workmen. He found them careless, disorganised, indifferent; but their lives remained real and their common interests were the true interests. They were the robust stem upon which every desirable thing had to be grafted.

Thus it was that the sober people, the people prepared for idealistic effort, the people whose ears detected the ring of a genuine coin and had become tired of the spurious or ill-minted thing, the people who were laying the foundations of their new cities on the rock of human worth, were drawn to him, honoured him, believed in him and loved him. It is very difficult for a man made of that material to do justice to *the classes* in these times—to their qualities, their lives, their interests, and even their worship—but Hardie was catholic, and rarely have his friends heard from his lips an unjust condemnation of these people. Charity lay even in his most emphatic condemnations.

Of Hardie's work it is easy to judge even at this early day, so distinctive was it. He will stand out for ever as the Moses who led the children of labour in this country out of bondage—out of bondage, not into Canaan, for this is to be a longer job. Others had described that bondage, had explained it, had told what ought to come after it. Hardie found the Labour Movement on its industrial side narrowed to a conflict with employers, and totally unaware that that conflict, if successful, could only issue in a new economic order; on its political side, he found it only thinking of returning to Parliament men who came from the pits and workshops to do pretty much the same work that the politicians belonging to the old political parties had done, and totally unaware that Labour in politics must have a new outlook, a new driving force of ideas and a new standard of political effort. When he raised the flag of revolt in Mid-Lanark, he was a rebel proclaiming civil war: when he fought the old Trade Union leaders from the floor of Congress, he was a sectary; when the Independent Labour Party was formed in Bradford, it was almost a forlorn hope attacked by a section of Socialists on the one hand and by the Labour leaders in power on the other. What days of fighting, of murmuring, of dreary desert trudging were to follow, only those who went through them know. Through them, a mere handful of men and women sustained the drudgery and the buffetings. Hardie's dogged—even dour—persistence made faint-heartedness impossible. One has to think of some of those miraculous endurances of the men who defied hardship in the blank wilderness, the entangled forest, the endless snowfield, to get an understanding of the exhaustion of soul and mind and body which had to be undergone between 1890 and 1900, in order to create a Labour Movement.

Preface to *The Life of Keir Hardie: W. Stewart, 1921*

AND WIDER

In the generations that have gone we launched our exploring ships upon many a venturesome voyage, and to-day our people, our institutions, our traditions, and our methods are to be found over all the earth. Our days of voyaging are not over. The world of mind and idea lies around us in unexplored tracts more vast by far than this earth was to our seamen, and the Commonwealth of Nations centring in this Motherland still hears the call to go out in an Elizabethan spirit of gallantry and doughtiness in search of liberty, justice and peace.

Broadcast: Empire Day, 24 May 1924

TO AMERICA

In October 1929 Macdonald visited the United States, his expressed aims being the need for establishing friendship between Great Britain and America; to make misunderstanding impossible; and to discuss the high and deep problems of international peace.

You, representing the United States, and I, representing Great Britain, feel that looking forward into the future we must be inspired by a new faith of fraternity, with a new courage to follow large and stirring moral aims and supplement all our material achievements by things that belong to the spiritual excellencies of the peoples of the world.

Through this gateway, the gateway of New York, have passed generation after generation, millions of people seeking new worlds, not only seeking worlds that yield riches to their labour, but seeking worlds that offer peace, comfort and nourishment to their minds and their souls. America, the United States, is not merely a geographical or a materialistic expression.

My friends, in the traditions that you will always cherish are the traditions of the exile, are the traditions of the seekers, are the traditions of the men and women who lifted up their eyes to the hills, who looked to the west, and finding in the old lands the dead hand of tradition too strong, the hand of the past too powerful, set sail across the inhospitable waters of the Atlantic, seeking happiness, peace and comfort, not only to their bodies but to their minds and their souls. Your skyscrapers can soar high, your millions can mount up to untold numbers, your prosperity may go on by leaps and bounds, but America, most precious of all your possessions, is your own soul. And I come here on this mission to meet your President not to advance material interests, but in order that we two great nations, who can look behind with pride and before with hope, shall shake hands and shall pledge ourselves not to any alliances—these belong to the old bad order of things—but shall pledge ourselves to common aspirations; pledge ourselves that our two flags, wherever the work of God is to be done in this world, will be flying side by side in the doing of that work; give a pledge, not to each other as it used to be, but to causes, standing side by side, straining our ears to listen to inspiring calls, ambitious of nothing, competitive in nothing, except which shall be first to obey and to carry them to successful issue.

City Hall, New York: 4 October 1929

THE BURDEN OF LABOUR

I have come over as a missionary of peace, and where should I come to receive inspiration for that mission rather than to the ranks of Labour? Labour—you supply the army, you supply the munitions, you supply the national credit, you are used for incurring the debts, and you have to pay them in the fullness of time. All classes in a war share in its sacrifices. Every mother from the highest in the land to the most poverty-stricken has to face the anxieties, the dangers, the pains and, ultimately, the sacrifices; but taken in the mass, Labour bears the burdens, Labour bears the pains, Labour bears the sacrifices. And if there should be another war the circumstances of it will be such that the pains and sacrifices of Labour will be infinitely greater than they have been in past wars.

In days gone by the fighting took place on the front lines. The men who were killed were the men who were within the range of the guns, but in the next war, should there be a next war, death will be dealt out not only on the battlefield, destruction will rise from the bottom of the sea, destruction will descend from the heavens themselves, destruction will meet your wives, your children, yourselves in the workshops.

I never have been and I never shall be one of those who believe that class this and class that alone are there to help us. My appeal has always been a national appeal, whether fighting my party battles at home or trying to lead the whole world on the smoother and better roads of reason and moral righteousness. Nevertheless, the well springs that give enthusiasm and power to go on and fight live in the secret corners of my heart sacred to the worker's fireside, the worker's life, the worker's wife and the worker's child. When I think of war, when I think of national enmity, when I think of strife, those are the people that come first and bear me companionship in my thoughts.

Annual Convention of the American Federation of Labour, Toronto:
19 October 1929

DISCIPLINE IS NOT ENOUGH

The ever-active test imposed upon every political structure like the British Commonwealth is, can it keep the balance between its continuing existence and the maintenance of liberty in the federated groups?

We have bred in our very bones the conviction that the sense of liberty and responsibility in the citizen is the foundation-stone of the State. The real defence of the State is the character and spirit of its people, and for the development of this, discipline is not enough. Freedom is essential. Freedom used by an enlightened people yields the highest discipline. We have shown the whole world how a free democracy has withstood intact the strains and stresses of this generation. We have had our crises—crises of war, and crises of economic catastrophe—but in none of them, neither here nor in any of our self-governing Dominions, has the regime collapsed, the constitutional system proved inadequate, or the people been found incapable within the framework of their constitution and without surrender of their liberties, of meeting and dealing with their difficulties.

We must strive that that will remain so. We must be in the truest sense conservative of all that is best in our heritage, but at the same time remember that that heritage has not been given to us as a treasure to be buried in a napkin, but one to be enriched by our own efforts in using it for good.

Broadcast: Empire Day, 24 May 1933

NEVILLE CHAMBERLAIN
1869-1940

Conservative M.P., 1918-40; Postmaster-General, 1922-23; Paymaster-General, 1923; Minister of Health, 1923, 1924-29, and 1931; Chancellor of the Exchequer, 1923-24 and 1931-37; Prime Minister and First Lord of the Treasury, 1937-40; Lord President of the Council, 1940

HEY! HO!

Chamberlain was an open-air man—a keen fisherman and shot, and, in his early years in the Bahamas, sufficiently enthusiastic an entomologist to discover a new species of butterfly, now known as Terias Chamberlainii; *his interest in bird-life is shown in these notes contributed to the* Daily Telegraph, 8 August 1936.

ONE of the pleasantest features of No. 11 Downing Street is it outlook on the old L-shaped garden that lies between it and the Horse Guards Parade, with its ancient shaded wall, its marvellous turf, and its venerable ilex and hawthorn. When I came to it first, it was mid-winter; the trees, save the ilex, were leafless, the birds silent. Yet it was pleasant to look on, and full of promise.

As, later in the year, the spring brought up the sap, and the green began to show in the tips of the lime-buds, the first sound that came through the open window of my bedroom in the morning was the song of a thrush. *Hey! Ho! Hey! Ho!* he sang so joyously and vigorously that his exuberant spirits were infectious, and I got into the habit of listening for him in the daytime as well as in the early morning.

It was only after a long time that I began to remark to myself that never had I heard a thrush put so little variety into its song. Thrushes generally repeat notes, often many times in succession, but then they will break off and improvise. This fellow seemed to have nothing more to say than his *Hey! Ho! Hey! Ho!* exhilarating as he made them sound.

Could it, I wondered, be a missel thrush? But no! there was none of that piercing, breathless phrasing of the storm-cock. This was clearly and decidedly a song thrush.

Often, curiously enough, the opening notes were followed by the unmistakable mellow drawling whistle of a blackbird. But it was only gradually that the truth dawned across me.

I had never seen a thrush in the garden, though blackbirds were often on the lawn, and sometimes came to drink at my bird-bath. Could this be a blackbird which had picked up those two notes from a thrush singing in St. James's Park? I determined to solve the mystery by observation, but I had to wait long before I could find an opportunity.

At last, one week-end in July, when I had to be in London, I was working in my room when I heard the well-known cry. I ran into the garden: the bird was concealed in the thick foliage of a plane tree by the Foreign Office steps. I waited patiently, motionless, on the lawn, and presently a shadow passed across the trees. *Hey! Ho! Hey! Ho!* came from the interior of the plane opposite, and in another minute the singer emerged at the very top of the tree, shouting out his little song of gladness.

No mistake about it this time—a blackbird imitating the habit as well as the notes of the song thrush, and proud of his accomplishment.

August has come, and the blackbird's song is ended. But I fancy that whenever in future my thoughts turn to the garden of No. 11 I shall hear again that *Hey! Ho! Hey! Ho!*

A MAN OF PEACE

It fell to Neville Chamberlain in one of the supreme crises of the world to be contradicted by events, to be disappointed in his hopes, and to be deceived and cheated by a wicked man.

Mr. Churchill: House of Commons, 12 November 1940

What sort of future are we trying to create for ourselves and for our children? Is it to be better or worse than that which we have inherited? Are we trying to make a world in which the peoples that inhabit it shall be able to live out their lives in peace of mind and in the enjoy-ment of a constantly rising standard of all that makes life worth living, of health and comfort, of recreation and of culture? Or are we preparing for ourselves a future which is to be one perpetual night-mare, filled with the constant dread of the horrors of war, forced to bury ourselves below ground and to spend all our substance upon the weapons of destruction?

One has only to state these alternatives to be sure that human nature, which is the same all the world over, must reject the nightmare with all its might, and cling to the old prospect which can give happi-ness. And for any Government deliberately to deny to their people what must be their plainest and simplest right would be to betray their trust, and to call down upon their heads the condemnation of all mankind.

I do not believe that such a Government anywhere exists among civilised peoples. I am convinced that the aim of every statesman worthy the name, to whatever country he belongs, must be the happi-ness of the people for whom and to whom he is responsible, and in that faith I am sure that a way can and will be found to free the world from the curse of armaments and the fears that give rise to them, and to open up a happier and a wiser future for mankind.

Guildhall, London: 9 November 1937

Do not let us forget that freedom has come down to us from the past, bought for us at a price. If we wish to keep it we must pay the interest on that price in each succeeding generation, but there is no need to look forward to the future with apprehension, and still less with de-spair. Whatever differences there may be between us and other nations, do not forget that we are all members of the human race and subject to the like passions and affections and fears and desires. There must be something in common between us if only we can find it, and perhaps by our very aloofness from the rest of Europe we may have some special part to play as conciliator and mediator. An ancient historian once wrote of the Greeks that they had made gentle the life of the world. I do not know whether in these modern days it is possible for any nation to emulate the example of the Greeks, but I can imagine no nobler ambition for an English statesman than to win the same tribute for his own country.

Birmingham: 8 April 1938

When I think of those four terrible years and I think of the seven million young men who were cut off in their prime, the thirteen

million who were maimed and mutilated, the misery and the suffering
of the mothers and the fathers, the sons and the daughters, and the
relatives and the friends of those who were killed, and the wounded,
then I am bound to say again what I have said before, and what I say
now, not only to you, but to all the world—in war, whichever side may
call itself the victor, there are no winners, but all are losers.

It is those thoughts which have made me feel that it was my prime
duty to strain every nerve to avoid a repetition of the Great War in
Europe. And I cannot believe that anyone who is not blinded by party
prejudice, anyone who thinks what another war would mean, can fail
to agree with me and to desire that I should continue my efforts.

Kettering: 2 July 1938

I am a man of peace to the depths of my soul. Armed conflict
between nations is a nightmare to me; but if I were convinced that any
nation had made up its mind to dominate the world by fear of its force,
I should feel that it must be resisted. Under such a domination life for
people who believe in liberty would not be worth living; but war is a
fearful thing, and we must be very clear, before we embark on it, that
it is really the great issues that are at stake, and that the call to risk
everything in their defence, when all the consequences are weighed, is
irresistible.

For the present I ask you to await as calmly as you can the events of
the next few days. As long as war has not begun, there is always hope
that it may be prevented, and you know that I am going to work for
peace to the last moment.

Broadcast, after his return from a second visit to Hitler at Bad
Godesberg: 27 September 1938

My good friends, this is the second time in our history that there has
come back from Germany to Downing Street peace with honour.

I believe it is peace for our time.

To the crowd outside 10 Downing Street after his return
from Munich: 30 September 1938

THE CONFLICT OPENS

This flower safety quickly faded. On 24 August 1939, the House of
Commons was summoned to cope with the immediate threat of war. On
1 September it was announced that German troops had crossed the
Polish frontier, and that the bombing of open towns had begun. Even then

a last chance to suspend aggression was afforded the German Govern-ment. On 3 September the British and French Empires were at war with Germany.

If, despite all our efforts to find the way of peace—and God knows I have tried my best—if in spite of all that, we find ourselves forced to embark upon a struggle which is bound to be fraught with suffering and misery for all mankind and the end of which no man can foresee, if that should happen, we shall not be fighting for the political future of a far-away city in a foreign land; we shall be fighting for the pre-servation of those principles of which I have spoken, the destruction of which would involve the destruction of all possibility of peace and security for the peoples of the world. This issue of peace or war does not rest with us, and I trust that those with whom the responsibility does lie will think of the millions of human beings whose fate depends upon their actions. For ourselves, we have a united country behind us, and in this critical hour I believe that we, in this House of Commons, will stand together, and that this afternoon we shall show the world that, as we think, so we will act, as a united nation.

House of Commons: 24 August 1939

The time has come when action rather than speech is required. Eighteen months ago in the House I prayed that the responsibility might not fall upon me to ask this country to accept the awful arbitra-ment of war. I fear that I may not be able to avoid that responsibility. But I could not wish for conditions in which such a burden should fall upon me in which I should feel clearer than I do to-day as to where my duty lies. No man can say that the Government could have done more in trying to keep open the way for an honourable and equitable settle-ment of the dispute between Germany and Poland. Nor have we neglected any means of making it crystal clear to the German Govern-ment that if they insisted on using force again in the manner in which they have used it in the past we were resolved to oppose them by force. Now that all the relevant documents are being made public we shall stand at the bar of history knowing that the responsibility for this terrible catastrophe lies on the shoulders of one man—the German Chancellor, who has not hesitated to plunge the world into misery in order to serve his own senseless ambitions.

House of Commons: 1 September 1939

It now only remains for us to set our teeth and to enter upon this struggle, which we ourselves earnestly endeavoured to avoid, with
16

determination to see it through to the end. We shall enter it with a clear conscience, with the support of the Dominions and the British Empire, and the moral approval of the greater part of the world. We have no quarrel with the German people, except that they allow themselves to be governed by a Nazi Government. As long as that Government exists and pursues the methods it has so persistently followed during the last two years, there will be no peace in Europe. We shall merely pass from one crisis to another, and see one country after another attacked by methods which have now become familiar to us in their sickening technique. We are resolved that these methods must come to an end. If out of the struggle we again re-establish in the world the rules of good faith and the renunciation of force, why, then even the sacrifices that will be entailed upon us will find their fullest justification.

House of Commons: 1 September 1939

This is a sad day for all of us, and to none is it sadder than to me. Everything that I have worked for, everything that I have hoped for, everything that I have believed in during my public life, has crashed into ruins. There is only one thing left for me to do; that is, to devote what strength and powers I have to forwarding the victory of the cause for which we have to sacrifice so much. I cannot tell what part I may be allowed to play myself; I trust I may live t᷍ see the day when Hitlerism has been destroyed and a liberated F᷍rope has been re-established.

House of Com᷍᷍᷍s: 3 September 1939

Now may God bless you all. May He defend the right. It is the evil things that we shall be fighting against—brute force, bad faith, injustice, oppression, and persecution—and against them I am certain that the right will prevail.

Broadcast: 3 September 1939

WINSTON SPENCER CHURCHILL

1874–

*Conservative M.P., 1900–3 and since 1924;
Liberal M.P., 1903–22; Under-Secretary of State
for the Colonies, 1906–8; President of the Board
of Trade, 1908–10; Secretary of State for Home
Affairs, 1910–11; First Lord of the Admiralty,
1911–15; Chancellor of the Duchy of Lancaster,
1915; Minister of Munitions, 1917; Secretary of
State for War and for the Air, 1918–21; Secretary
of State for the Colonies, 1921; Chancellor of the
Exchequer, 1924–29; Prime Minister, First Lord of
the Treasury, and Minister of Defence since 1940*

THE CHARGE AT OMDURMAN

*Lieutenant W. S. Churchill, attached to the 21st Lancers, took part in
that regiment's famous charge at Omdurman, 2 September 1898.*

TWO hundred and fifty yards away the dark-blue men were firing
madly in a thin film of light-blue smoke. Their bullets struck the hard
gravel into the air, and the troopers, to shield their faces from the
stinging dust, bowed their helmets forward, like the Cuirassiers at
Waterloo. The pace was fast and the distance short. Yet, before it was
half covered, the whole aspect of the affair changed. A deep crease in
the ground—a dry watercourse, a *khor*—appeared where all had
seemed smooth level plain; and from it their sprang, with the sudden-
ness of a pantomime effect and a high-pitched yell, a dense white mass
of men nearly as long as our front and about twelve deep. A score of
horsemen and a dozen bright flags rose as if by magic from the earth.
Eager warriors sprang forward to anticipate the shock. The rest stood
firm to meet it. The Lancers acknowledged the apparition only by an
increase of pace. Each man wanted sufficient momemtum to drive
through such a solid line. The flank troops, seeing that they overlapped,
curved inwards like the horns of a moon. But the whole event was a
matter of seconds. The riflemen, firing bravely to the last, were swept
head over heels into the *khor*, and jumping down with them, at full
gallop and in the closest order, the British squadrons struck the fierce
brigade with one loud furious shout. The collision was prodigious.

Nearly thirty Lancers, men and horses, and at least two hundred
Arabs were overthrown. The shock was stunning to both sides, and for
perhaps ten wonderful seconds no man heeded his enemy. Terrified
horses wedged in the crowd, bruised and shaken men, sprawling in
heaps, struggled, dazed and stupid, to their feet, panted and looked
about them. Several fallen Lancers had even time to remount. Meanwhile the impetus of the cavalry carried them on. As a rider tears
through a bullfinch, the officers forced their way through the press;
and as an iron rake might be drawn through a heap of shingle, so the
regiment followed. They shattered the Dervish array, and, their pace
reduced to a walk, scrambled out of the *khor* on the further side,
leaving a score of troopers behind them, and dragging on with the
charge more than a thousand Arabs. Then, and not till then, the
killing began; and thereafter each man saw the world along his lance,
under his guard, or through the back-sight of his pistol; and each had
his own strange tale to tell.

Stubborn and unshaken infantry hardly ever meet stubborn and
unshaken cavalry. Either the infantry run away and are cut down in
flight, or they keep their heads and destroy nearly all the horsemen by
their musketry. On this occasion two living walls had actually crashed
together. The Dervishes fought manfully. They tried to hamstring the
horses. They fired their rifles, pressing the muzzles into the very bodies
of their opponents. They cut reins and stirrup-leathers. They flung
their throwing-spears with great dexterity. They tried every device of
cool determined men practised in war and familiar with cavalry; and,
besides, they swung sharp heavy swords which bit deep. The hand-to-
hand fighting on the further side of the *khor* lasted for perhaps one
minute. Then the horses got into their stride again, the pace increased,
and the Lancers drew out from among their antagonists. Within two
minutes of the collision every living man was clear of the Dervish
mass. All who had fallen were cut at with swords till they stopped
quivering, but no artistic mutilations were attempted.

Two hundred yards away the regiment halted, rallied, faced about,
and in less than five minutes were re-formed and ready for a secon
charge. The men were anxious to cut their way back through the
enemies. We were alone together—the cavalry regiment and
Dervish brigade. The ridge hung like a curtain between us and e
army. The general battle was forgotten, as it was unseen. This v a
private quarrel. The other might have been a massacre; but he the
fight was fair, for we too fought with sword and spear. Inde the
advantage of ground and numbers lay with them. All prep ed to
settle the debate at once and for ever. But some realisation of the cost

of our wild ride began to come to those who were responsible. Riderless horses galloped across the plain. Men, clinging to their saddles, lurched helplessly about, covered with blood from perhaps a dozen wounds. Horses, streaming from tremendous gashes, limped and staggered with their riders. In a hundred-and-twenty seconds five officers, sixty-five men, and one-hundred-and-nineteen horses out of fewer than four hundred had been killed or wounded.

The Dervish line, broken by the charge, began to re-form at once. They closed up, shook themselves together, and prepared with constancy and courage for another shock. But on military considerations it was desirable to turn them out of the *khor* first and thus deprive them of their vantage ground. The regiment again drawn up, three squadrons in line and the fourth in column, now wheeled to the right, and, galloping round the Dervish flank, dismounted and opened a heavy fire with their magazine carbines. Under the pressure of this fire the enemy changed front to meet the new attack, so that both sides were formed at right angles to their original lines. When the Dervish change of front was completed, they began to advance against the dismounted men. But the fire was accurate, and there can be little doubt that the moral effect of the charge had been very great, and that these brave enemies were no longer unshaken. Be this as it may, the fact remains that they retreated swiftly, though in good order, towards the ridge of Surgham Hill, where the Khalifa's Black Flag still waved, and the 21st Lancers remained in possession of the ground—and of their dead.

The River War: 1899

PROLOGUE

A European war cannot be anything but a cruel, heartrending struggle, which, if we are ever to enjoy the bitter fruits of victory, must demand, perhaps for several years, the whole manhood of the nation, the entire suspension of peaceful industries, and the concentrating to one end of every vital energy in the community.

In former days, when wars arose from individual causes, from the policy of a minister or the passion of a king, when they were fought by small regular armies of professional soldiers, and when their course was retarded by the winter season, it was possible to limit the liabilities of the combatants. But now, when mighty populations are impelled against each other, each individual severally embittered and inflamed—when the resources of science and civilisation sweep away everything that might mitigate their fury, a European war can only end in

the ruin of the vanquished and the scarcely less fatal commercial
dislocation and exhaustion of the conquerors. Democracy is more
vindictive than cabinets. The wars of peoples will be more terrible
than those of kings.

House of Commons: 12 May 1901

ARMS AND THE COVENANT

Arm and stand by the Covenant of the League of Nations *was Mr.
Churchill's reiterated message in the between-war years:* Never till now
have great communities afforded such ample means of measuring their
approaching agony. Never have they seemed less capable of taking
effective measures to prevent it.

The life of Britain, her glories and message to the world, can only be
achieved by national unity, and national unity can only be preserved
upon a cause which is larger than the nation itself. However we may
differ in political opinion, however divergent our party interests,
however diverse our callings and stations, we have this in common.
We mean to defend our island from tyranny and aggression, and so
far as we can, we mean to hold out a helping hand to others who may
be in even more immediate danger than at this moment we are ourselves. We repudiate all ideas of abject or slothful defeatism. We wish
to make our country safe and strong—she can only be safe if she is
strong—and we wish her to play her part with other parliamentary
democracies on both sides of the Atlantic Ocean in warding off from
civilisation, while time yet remains, the devastating and obliterating
horrors of another world war. We wish to see inaugurated a reign of
international law, backed, as it must be in these turbulent times, by
ample and, if possible, superabundant strength.

At this moment in history the broad, toiling masses in every
country have for the first time the opportunity of a fuller and less
burdened life. Science is at hand to spread a more bountiful table than
has ever been offered to the millions and to the tens of millions.
Shorter hours of labour, greater assurances against individual misfortune, a wider if a simpler culture, a more consciously realised sense of
social justice, an easier and more equal society—these are the treasures
which after all these generations and centuries of impotence and
confusion, are now within the reach of mankind.

Are these hopes, are these prospects, are all the secrets which the
genius of man has wrested from Nature to be turned only by tyranny,
aggression and war to his own destruction? Or are they to become the
agencies of a broadening freedom, and of an enduring peace?

Never before has the choice of blessings or curses been so plainly, vividly, even brutally offered to mankind. The choice is open. The dreadful balance trembles. It may be that our island and all the commonwealths it has gathered around it will, if we are worthy, play an important, perhaps even a decisive part in turning the scales of human fortune from bad to good, from fear to confidence, from miseries and crimes immeasurable to blessings and gains abounding.

We make ourselves the servants of this cause, but it is no use espousing a cause without having also a method and a plan by which that cause may be made to win. I would not affront you with generalities. There must be the vision. There must be a plan, and there must be action following upon it. We express our immediate plan and policy in a single sentence: *Arm and stand by the Covenant.* In this alone lies the assurance of safety, the defence of freedom, and the hope of peace.

Manchester: 9 May 1938

LET US TO THE TASK

We cannot tell what the course of the struggle will be, into what regions it will carry us, how long it will last, or who will fall by the way. But we are sure that in the end right will win, that freedom will not be trampled down, that a truer progress will open, and a broader justice will reign. And we are determined to play our part worthily, faithfully, and to the end.

Come, then; let us to the task, to the battle, to the toil. Each to our part, each to our station. Fill the armies, rule the air, pour out the munitions, strangle the U-boats, sweep the mines, plough the land, build the ships, guard the streets, succour the wounded, uplift the downcast, and honour the brave. Let us go forward together in all parts of the Empire, in all parts of this island. There is not a week, nor a day, nor an hour to be lost.

Manchester: 27 January 1940

BLOOD, TOIL, TEARS AND SWEAT

Mr. Churchill assumed office 10 May 1940 and three days later addressed the Commons for the first time as Prime Minister.

I would say to the House, as I said to those who have joined this Government: *I have nothing to offer but blood, toil, tears and sweat.*

We have before us an ordeal of the most grievous kind. We have before us many, many long months of struggle and of suffering. You ask what is our policy. I will say: It is to wage war, by sea, land and air, with all our might and with all the strength that God can give us; to wage war against a monstrous tyranny, never surpassed in the dark, lamentable catalogue of human crime. That is our policy. You ask what is our aim. I can answer in one word: Victory. Victory at all costs, victory in spite of all terror, victory, however long and hard the road may be; for without victory, there is no survival. Let that be realised; no survival for the British Empire, no survival for all that the British Empire has stood for, no survival for the urge and impulse of the ages, that mankind will move forward towards its goal. But I take up my task with buoyancy and hope. I feel sure that our cause will not be suffered to fail among men. At this time I feel entitled to claim the aid of all, and I say: *Come then, let us go forward together in our united strength.*

House of Commons: 13 May 1940

UNDER MENACE OF INVASION

I have full confidence that if all do their duty, we shall prove ourselves once again able to defend our island home, to ride out the storm of war, and to outlive the menace of tyranny, if necessary for years, if necessary alone. That is the resolve of His Majesty's Government. That is the will of Parliament and the nation. Even though large tracts of Europe and many old and famous States have fallen or may fall into the grip of the Gestapo and all the odious apparatus of Nazi rule, we shall not flag nor fail. We shall go on to the end. We shall fight in France, we shall fight on the seas and oceans, we shall fight with growing confidence and growing strength in the air. We shall defend our island, whatever the cost may be. We shall fight on the beaches, we shall fight on the landing grounds, we shall fight in the fields and in the streets, we shall fight in the hills. We shall never surrender, and even if, which I do not for a moment believe, this island or a large part of it were subjugated and starving, then our Empire beyond the seas, armed and guarded by the British Fleet, would carry on the struggle, until, in God's good time, the New World, with all its power and might, steps forth to the rescue and the liberation of the Old.

House of Commons: 4 June 1940

THE BATTLE OF BRITAIN

The Battle of France is over. The Battle of Britain is about to begin. Upon this battle depends the survival of Christian civilisation. Upon it depends our own British life, and the long continuity of our institutions and our Empire. The whole fury and might of the enemy must very soon be turned on us. Hitler knows that he will have to break us in this island or lose the war. If we can stand up to him all Europe may be free and the life of the world may move forward into broad sunlit uplands. But if we fail, then the whole world, including the United States, and all that we have known and cared for, will sink into the abyss of a new Dark Age made more sinister, and perhaps more prolonged, by the light of a perverted science. Let us therefore brace ourselves to our duties, and so bear ourselves that, if the British Commonwealth and Empire lasts a thousand years, men will still say, *This was their finest hour*.

House of Commons: 11 June 1940

R.A.F

The gratitude of every home in our Island, in our Empire, and indeed throughout the world, except in the abodes of the guilty, goes out to the British airmen who, undaunted by odds, unwearied in their constant challenge and mortal danger, are turning the tide of world war by their prowess and by their devotion. Never in the field of human conflict was so much owed by so many to so few.

House of Commons: 20 August 1940

LET IT ROLL

We have to think not only for ourselves but for the lasting security of the cause and principles for which we are fighting and of the long future of the British Commonwealth of Nations. The principle of association of interests for common purposes between Great Britain and the United States had developed even before the war. Undoubtedly this means that these two great organisations of the English-speaking democracies, the British Empire and the United States, will have to be somewhat mixed up together in some of their affairs for mutual and general advantage. For my own part, looking out upon the future, I do not view the process with any misgivings. I could not stop it if I wished; no one can stop it. Like the Mississippi, it just keeps rolling along. Let it roll. Let it roll on full flood, inexorable, irresistible, benignant, to broader lands and better days.

House of Commons: 20 August 1940

A NEW MAGNA CARTA

In a broadcast message to President Roosevelt, 9 February 1941, Mr. Churchill exclaimed: Put your confidence in us. Give us your faith and your blessing and under Providence all will be well. We shall not fail or falter. We shall not weaken or starve. Neither the sudden shock of battle nor the long-drawn trials of vigilance and exertion will wear us down. Give us the tools and we will finish the job.

The Lease-Lend Bill received the President's signature on 11 March.

The most powerful democracy has, in effect, declared in solemn Statute that they will devote their overwhelming industrial and financial strength to ensuring the defeat of Nazism in order that nations, great and small, may live in security, tolerance and freedom. By so doing, the Government and people of the United States have in fact written a new Magna Ca. not only has regard to the rights and laws upon which a healthy and advancing civilisation can alone be erected, but also proclaims by precept and example the duty of free men and free nations, wherever they may be, to share the responsibility and burden of enforcing them.

In the name of His Majesty's Government and speaking, I am sure for Parliament and for the whole country, and indeed, in the name of all freedom-loving peoples, I offer to the United States our gratitude for her inspiring act of faith.

House of Commons: 12 March 1941

ORDEAL BY FIRE

In mid-April 1941 Mr. Churchill went to some of our great cities and seaports which had been most heavily bombed and to some of the places where the poorest people had got it worst. *Moved by the people's exaltation of spirit he broadcast a tribute on his return:*

The British nation is stirred and moved as it never has been at any time in its long, eventful, and famous history, and it is no hackneyed figure of speech to say that they mean to conquer or to die. What a triumph the life of these battered cities is over the worst that fire and bomb can do! What a vindication of the civilised and decent way of living we have been trying to work for and work towards in our island! What a proof of the virtues of free institutions, what a test of the quality of our local authorities, and of customs and societies so sturdily built!

This ordeal by fire has in a certain sense even exhilarated the manhood and the womanhood of Britain. The sublime but also terrible experiences and emotions of the battlefield, which for centuries have been reserved for the soldiers and sailors, are now shared for good or ill by the entire population. All are proud to be under the fire of the enemy.

Old men, little children, the crippled, the veterans of former wars, aged women, the ordinary hard-pressed citizen, the sturdy workman with his hammer in the shipyard or who loads the ships, and the skilful craftsman, the members of every kind of A.R.P. service, are proud to feel that they stand in the line together with our fighting men when one of the greatest causes is being fought out, as fought out it will be, to the end. This, indeed, is a grand, heroic period of our history, and the light of glory shines upon all.

Broadcast: 27 April 1941

ATLANTIC CHARTER

In a special broadcast from Downing Street, 14 August 1941, Mr. Attlee, Lord Privy Seal and Deputy Prime Minister, made the dramatic announcement that Mr. Churchill and Mr. Roosevelt had met at sea.

One of the results of their conference was the following joint declaration, the Atlantic Charter:

The President of the United States and the Prime Minister, Mr. Churchill, representing His Majesty's Government in the United Kingdom, being met together, deem it right to make known certain common principles in the national policies of their respective countries on which they base their hopes for a better future for the world.

FIRST, *their countries seek no aggrandizement, territorial or other.*

SECOND, *they desire to see no territorial changes that do not accord with the freely expressed wishes of the people concerned.*

THIRD, *they respect the right of all peoples to choose the form of Government under which they will live; and they wish to see sovereign rights and self-government restored to those who have been forcibly deprived of them.*

FOURTH, *they will endeavour, with due respect for their existing obligations, to further enjoyment by all States, great or small, victor or vanquished, of access, on equal terms, to the trade and to the raw materials of the world which are needed for their economic prosperity.*

FIFTH, *they desire to bring about the fullest collaboration between all nations in the economic field, with the object of securing for all improved labour standards, economic advancement, and social security.*

SIXTH, *after the final destruction of Nazi tyranny, they hope to see established a peace which will afford to all nations the means of dwelling in safety within their own boundaries, and which will afford assurance that all the men in all the lands may live out their lives in freedom from fear and want.*

252 ENGLAND IS HERE

SEVENTH, *such a peace should enable all men to traverse the high seas and oceans without hindrance.*

EIGHTH, *they believe all of the nations of the world, for realistic as well as spiritual reasons, must come to the abandonment of the use of force. Since no future peace can be maintained if land, sea, or air armaments continue to be employed by nations which threaten, or may threaten, aggression outside of their frontiers, they believe, pending the establishment of a wider and permanent system of general security, that the disarmament of such nations is essential. They will likewise aid and encourage all other practicable measures which will lighten for peace-loving peoples the crushing burden of armament.*

On his return, the Prime Minister broadcast to the nation, describing his meeting with President Roosevelt as symbolic of the deep underlying unities which stir, and at decisive moments rule, the English-speaking peoples throughout the world.

And thus we come back to the quiet bay somewhere in the Atlantic, where misty sunshine plays on great ships which carry the White Ensign or the Stars and Stripes. We had the idea when we met there—the President and I—that, without attempting to draw final and formal peace aims and war aims, it was necessary to give all peoples, and especially the oppressed and conquered peoples, a simple, rough-and-ready, war-time statement of the goal towards which the British Commonwealth and the United States mean to make their way; and thus make a way for others to march with them upon a road which will certainly be painful, and may be long.

There are two distinct and marked differences in this joint declaration from the attitude adopted by the Allies during the latter part of the last War, and no one should overlook them. The United States and Great Britain do not now assume that there will never be any more war again. On the contrary, we intend to take ample precautions to prevent its renewal in any period we can foresee, by effectively disarming the guilty nations while remaining suitably protected ourselves.

The second difference is this: that instead of trying to ruin German trade by all kinds of additional trade barriers and hindrances, as was the mood of 1917, we have definitely adopted the view that it is not in the interests of the world and of our two countries that any large nation should be unprosperous or shut out from the means of making a decent living for itself and its people by its industry and enterprise. These are far-reaching changes of principle upon which all countries should ponder.

Above all, it is necessary to give hope and assurance of final victory to those many scores of millions of men and women who are battling for life and freedom, or who are already bent down under the Nazi yoke. Hitler and his confederates have for some time been adjuring, bullying, and beseeching the populations whom they have wronged and injured to bow to their fate, to resign themselves to their servitude, and for the sake of some mitigations and indulgences, to collaborate—that is the word—in what is called the new order in Europe.

What is this new order which they seek to fasten first upon Europe and if possible—for their ambitions are boundless—upon all the continents of the globe? It is the rule of the *Herrenvolk*, the master-race, who are to put an end to democracy, to parliaments, to the fundamental freedoms and decencies of ordinary men and women, to the historic rights of nations, and give them in exchange the iron rule of Prussia, the universal goose-step, and a strict, efficient, discipline enforced upon the working classes by the political police, with the German concentration camps and firing parties, now so busy in a dozen lands, always handy in the background. There is the new order.

Napoleon in his glory and genius spread his empire far and wide. There was a time when only the snows of Russia and the white cliffs of Dover with their guardian fleets stood between him and the dominion of the world. Napoleon's armies had a theme: they carried with them the surges of the French Revolution—*Liberty, equality, and fraternity*, that was the cry.

There was a sweeping away of outworn medieval systems and aristocratic privilege: the land for the people, a new code of laws. Nevertheless, Napoleon's empire vanished like a dream. But Hitler— Hitler has no theme, naught but mania, appetite, and exploitation. He has, however, weapons and machinery for grinding down and holding down conquered countries which are the product, the sadly perverted product, of modern science. The ordeals, therefore, of the conquered peoples will be hard. We must give them hope. We must give them the conviction that their sufferings and their resistances will not be in vain. The tunnel may be dark and long, but at the end there is light.

That is the symbolism and that is the message of the Atlantic meeting. Do not despair, brave Norwegians, your land shall be cleansed, not only from the invader, but from the filthy quislings who are his tools. Be sure of yourselves, Czechs, your independence shall be restored. Poles, the heroism of your people standing up to cruel oppressors, the courage of your soldiers, sailors, and airmen, shall not be forgotten. Your country shall live again and resume its rightful part in the new organisation of Europe.

Lift up your heads, gallant Frenchmen; not all the infamies of

Darlan and of Laval shall stand between you and the restoration of your birthright. Tough, stout-hearted Dutch, Belgians, Luxemburgers; tormented, mishandled, shamefully castaway peoples of Yugoslavia; glorious Greece, now subjected to the crowning insult of the rule of the Italian jackanapes; yield not an inch. Keep your souls clean from all contact with the Nazi; make them feel, even in the fleeting hour of brutish triumph, that they are the moral outcasts of mankind. Help is coming; mighty forces are arming in your behalf. Have faith, have hope; deliverance is sure.

Broadcast: 24 August 1941

THESE THINGS SHALL BE

On 22 December 1941 Mr. Churchill arrived in the U.S.A. to discuss concerted war efforts with the President. Four days later he was privileged to address both houses of Congress: The fact that my American forebears of so many generations played their part in the life of the United States and that here I am, an Englishman, welcomed in your midst, makes this experience one of the most moving and thrilling in my life.

Members of the Senate and members of the House of Representatives, I turn from the turmoil and convulsions of the present to the broader basis of the future. Here we are together facing a group of mighty foes, who seek our ruin; here we are together defending all that which to free men is dear. Twice in a single generation the catastrophe of world war has fallen upon us; twice in our lifetime has the long arm of fate reached across the ocean to bring the United States into the forefront of the battle itself. If we had kept together after the last War if we had taken common measures for our safety, then this renewal of the curse need never have fallen upon us.

Do we not owe it to ourselves, to our children and to mankind tormented, to make sure that these catastrophes do not engulf us for the third time? It has been proved that pestilences may break out in the Old World, from which, once they are afoot, the New World cannot escape. Duty and prudence alike command first that the germ-centres of hatred and revenge should be constantly and vigilantly purged and treated in good time, and that an adequate organisation should be set up to make sure that the pestilence can be controlled at its earliest beginnings before it spreads and reaches throughout the entire earth.

Five or six years ago it would have been easy, without shedding a drop of blood, for the United States and Great Britain to have insisted on the fulfilment of the disarmament clauses of the treaties which

Germany signed after the Great War; and that also would have been the opportunity for assuring to the Germans those raw materials which we declared in the Atlantic Charter should not be denied to any nation, victor or vanquished. That chance has passed. It is gone. Prodigious hammer-strokes have been needed to bring us together again. If you will allow me to use other language, I will say that he must indeed have been a blind soul who cannot see that some great purpose and design is being worked out here below, of which we have the honour to be faithful servants. It is not given to us to peer into the mysteries of the future. Still, I avow my hope and faith, sure and inviolate, that in the days to come the British and American peoples will for their own safety and for the good of all walk together in majesty, in justice, and in peace.

BLUEPRINT

In a broadcast, 21 March 1943, Mr. Churchill assumed that the defeat of Nazi tyranny and Prussian militarism would precede the ending of the war against Japan.

On this assumption it would be our hope that the United Nations, headed by the three great victorious Powers, the British Commonwealth of Nations, the United States and Soviet Russia, should immediately begin to confer upon the future world organisation which is to be our safeguard against further wars by effectually disarming and keeping disarmed the guilty States, by bringing to justice the grand criminals and their accomplices, and by securing the return to the devastated and subjugated countries of the mechanical resources and artistic treasures of which they have been pillaged. We shall also have a heavy task in trying to avert widespread famine in the ruined regions.

We must hope and pray that the unity of the three leading victorious Powers will be worthy of their supreme responsibility and that they will think not only of their own welfare but of the welfare and future of all.

One can imagine that under a world institution embodying or representing the United Nations, and some day all nations, there should come into being a Council of Europe and a Council of Asia. As, according to the forecast I am outlining, the war against Japan will still be raging, it is upon the creation of the Council of Europe and the settlement of Europe that the first practical task will be centred.

Now this is a stupendous business. In Europe lie most of the causes which have led to these two world wars. In Europe dwell the historic parent races from whom our Western civilisation has been so largely derived. I believe myself to be what is called a good European, and I should deem it a noble task to revive the fertile genius and restore the true greatness of Europe.

I hope we shall not lightly cast aside all the immense work which was accomplished by the creation of the League of Nations. Certainly we must take as our foundation the lofty conception of freedom, law, and morality, which was the spirit of the League.

We must try to make the Council of Europe into a really effective League, with all the strongest forces concerned woven into its texture, with a High Court to adjust disputes, and with forces, armed forces, national or international or both, held ready to enforce these decisions and prevent renewed aggression and the preparation of future wars.

This Council when created must eventually embrace the whole of _____ all the main branches of the European family must some day be partners in it. Side by side with the great Powers there should _____ groupings of States or confederations which would express themselves through their own chosen representatives the whole making a Council of great States and groups of _____.

It is my earnest hope, though I can hardly expect to see it fulfilled in my lifetime, that we shall achieve the la_____ measure of the integrated life of Europe that is possible without destroying the individual characteristics and traditions of its many ancient and historic races.

All this will, I believe, be found to harmonise with the high permanent interests of Britain, the United States and Russia. It certainly cannot be accomplished without their cordial and concerted agreement and direct participation. Thus and thus only will the glory of Europe rise again.

WORDSWORTH'S VIEW OF NATURE

To
W. P. T.

WORDSWORTH'S
VIEW OF NATURE

And its Ethical Consequences

By

NORMAN LACEY, M.A.

ARCHON BOOKS

HAMDEN, CONNECTICUT

1965

First published 1948

Reprinted, 1965, by arrangement with
CAMBRIDGE UNIVERSITY PRESS
in an unaltered and unabridged edition

Library of Congress Catalog Card Number: 65-14190
Printed in the United States of America

PREFACE

To come forward with yet another book on Wordsworth, in view of the several and valuable studies of the poet which have appeared in recent years, would seem to require some justification. My defence is that, as it seems to me, the full importance of Wordsworth is only slowly making itself felt. His value does not lie solely in the undoubted excellence of much of his poetry, nor in his attempt at a philosophy of Nature. It rests also upon the fact that he, our national poet of the years 1798–1815, and perhaps the greatest of the Romantic poets, is the only one in whom it is possible to study the transition from Romantic into Victorian. The understanding of this transition appears to me of great importance for the study of the Victorian age, and therefore, indirectly, of the present time, since the nineteenth century was the psychological field in which so many of our present troubles took root.

The book here presented makes no claim to be a comprehensive study of Wordsworth from this angle. It is simply a short expedition into the field, in which some of the larger questions are briefly indicated. My immediate purpose has been to show that, as I believe, there are certain events in Wordsworth's experience which bear a significance other than that which he assigned to them. He was at certain moments in possession of a secret—which he lost because he did not fully understand it. If my view is correct, if we can see Wordsworth's experience in this different light, I believe we may have glimpses of 'Nature' which will point forward to a truer authority, a more substantial basis for the good life than the Nature which Wordsworth extolled.

PREFACE

The first task must clearly be to establish Wordsworth's views. A general discussion of Nature in the *Lyrical Ballads* serves as introduction to a close study of the 1805 text of *The Prelude*, which brings to light Wordsworth's leading ideas and attitudes. These are submitted to review, and some of their consequences noticed. Wordsworth's difficulties, and subsequent modifications of his views, are considered in a chapter on the later poems. A final section attempts to draw together the results, and to make some estimate of the value of Wordsworth's writings.

The studies of Wordsworth from which I have received enlightenment are too numerous to mention in detail, though for their interest and stimulus, Mr Herbert Read's *Wordsworth* and Mr H. I'A. Fausset's *The Lost Leader* deserve separate notice. But, as for all students of Wordsworth, my chief debt of gratitude is to the late Professor Ernest de Selincourt for his indefatigable labour upon the Wordsworth texts, and in particular for making available the 1805 text of *The Prelude*.

Finally, I should like to acknowledge my indebtedness to the several people who have helped in the publication of this book. My thanks are especially due to Dr R. E. Priestley, Mr J. F. Waterhouse, and Professor H. G. Wood, of the University of Birmingham, for their advice and assistance, and also to Professor Basil Willey for his sympathetic and valuable criticism.

7.1.47.   N.L.

CONTENTS

ABBREVIATIONS AND REFERENCES

L.B. = *Lyrical Ballads*, 1798–1805. Methuen and Co. 8th edition, with an introduction by George Sampson.

L.W. = *Letters of William and Dorothy Wordsworth*. Edited by E. de Selincourt. Oxford Press, 1935.

O.W. = *Poetical Works of William Wordsworth*. Edited by T. Hutchinson. Oxford Press, 1939.

All references to *The Prelude* are to the text of 1805, edited by E. de Selincourt. Oxford Press, 1936.

All references to *The Excursion* are to the final text (1850) as printed in the Oxford edition of the *Poetical Works*.

CHAPTER ONE

NATURE IN THE *LYRICAL BALLADS*

'This great grandmother of all creatures bred
Great Nature ever young yet full of eld
Still moving, yet unmoved from her sted
Unseen of any, yet of all beheld.'

(*Faerie Queene*, Book VII, Canto 13)

Wordsworth first comes forward as the poet of Nature in
the volume which he wrote jointly with Coleridge, published in 1798 and called *Lyrical Ballads*. In this book
Wordsworth makes a double declaration of faith in Nature.
In the poems he tries to show the power and the blessings
of Nature in the life of man, and in the introduction he
declares that the natural language of simple people is a
suitable vehicle for poetic pleasure. With certain exceptions the poems fall into two classes, which may for convenience be called poems of experience and poems of
experiment, corresponding to this twofold declaration. We
may note in passing, a paradox. It is that, whereas the
poems of experiment in which Wordsworth was trying to
justify his theory of poetic diction always leave some doubt
of their success, the poems of experience in which he was
not trying to do anything other than record his faith and his
feelings, triumphantly vindicate his theory of poetic diction.

Can we from these poems of Wordsworth's experience
establish his view of Nature without incurring his charge
of 'murdering to dissect'? Ballad is not philosophy and
it is no criticism of the *Lyrical Ballads* that their philosophy
is incoherent. But Wordsworth himself said that each of
his poems would be found to have a worthy purpose, so
we can hardly be thought to offend if we try to discover
his purpose and his teaching even in his lyrics.

The *Lines written above Tintern Abbey* are a fitting
conclusion to the first volume of the *Lyrical Ballads*, for they

L
I
I

were written at the close of the happy period of collaboration between the two authors. After leaving Somerset, Wordsworth went to the Wye Valley with his sister for a few days. On the last evening of their tour, as they were travelling down from Tintern into Bristol, there came to Wordsworth in rapid succession the lines of a remarkable poem. Probably no poem of equal length was ever so completely given to a poet. In the well-known lines of *Tintern Abbey,* which stand almost word for word as they were first conceived, all Wordsworth's deepest experiences of Nature are gathered up and given succinct expression. Wordsworth rightly hesitated to call the poem an ode; it is better described as a lyrical meditation on the theme of Nature, and so effective is it that after reading it we feel hardly surprised that Wordsworth should give his faith to a power which had so enriched his life.

In looking at this poem we notice at the outset that he does not mean by nature the totality of the physical universe, he means a selection of natural forms once present to his eye, and almost certainly forms radiant in sunshine. These forms of beauty have given him 'sensations sweet' such as have restored him when jaded, when surrounded by ugliness. He thinks they may also have had some direct social effect in making him perform unconsciously, little acts of kindness and love. But more important, he feels that these forms of beauty may be connected in some way with a certain mystical experience—with rare occasions when

Our human blood
Almost suspended, we are laid asleep
In body and become a living soul:
While with an eye made quiet by the power
Of harmony, and the deep power of joy,
We see into the life of things.[1]

[1] L.B. p. 172.

2

However, he is not certain what kind of connection
there is, if any, between nature and his mystical experience,
and he returns to what he knows for certain—that in the
fret and fever of the world he has often turned for relief
to his memory of the beautiful scene in the Wye Valley.
It is the pure spirit of the young man searching through
all things for a kindred purity. We hear it in the line
'O sylvan Wye! Thou wanderer through the woods'.

Nature through her beautiful forms can restore the
spirit of man. Wordsworth had not always regarded Nature
in this way. He could remember a time in his youth, when
Nature's forms, the tall rock and the gloomy wood were
for him simply, 'an appetite, a feeling and a love'. But
now, at twenty-eight, he hears in their presence 'the still
sad music of humanity' and it is for a spiritual influence
which appears to come from them that he gives praise.
It is in the presence of nature that he has had an experience
that is really the threshold of that 'gift of aspect more
sublime' which he has already described.

> And I have felt
> A presence that disturbs me with the joy
> Of elevated thoughts; a sense sublime
> Of something far more deeply interfused,
> Whose dwelling is the light of setting suns,
> And the round ocean and the living air,
> And the blue sky, and in the mind of man
> A motion and a spirit, that impels
> All thinking things, all objects of all thought,
> And rolls through all things.[1]

Because this experience has occurred to him in the
presence of nature he reasonably expects that it may so
occur to him again, and thus he sees in nature 'the anchor
of my purest thoughts, the guide, the guardian of my
heart and soul of all my moral being'. The poem continues
with a paean of praise to Nature in language which suggests

[1] L.B. p. 173.

a biblical parallel. Who shall separate us from the blessings of Nature? Shall evil tongues, or rash judgements, or greetings where no kindness is? No. For

> Nature never did betray
> The heart that loved her; 'tis her privilege,
> Through all the years of this our life, to lead
> From joy to joy:

Thus Wordsworth makes Nature the author and finisher of his faith. We shall see whether Nature will bear the weight which he tried to put upon her.

What then are the characteristics of Nature and how are we to approach her? We gain some further insight from the shorter poems.

> She has a world of ready wealth,
> Our minds and hearts to bless—
> Spontaneous wisdom breathed by health,
> Truth breathed by cheerfulness.[1]

Stop analysing with the mind, says Wordsworth. Give up attending to science and art: come forth into the open air and let Nature be your teacher. The intellect is not to be trusted. Nature will feed our minds if we can learn a wise passiveness. This does not mean doing nothing. We are to bring to Nature 'a heart that watches and receives'. These two verbs are equally active. We are to watch, not with the intention of judging or comparing but simply to take in deliberately what we see. It is not quite clear what the results of this process are likely to be. Perhaps the restoration of pure thoughts: perhaps 'the harvest of a quiet eye' is some random truths 'In common things that round us lie'.[2] Can such random truths, appearing haphazard, help us in our so furiously active world? Wordsworth would have replied: 'Perhaps not; then so much the

---

[1] *The Tables Turned.* L.B. p. 45.
[2] *A Poet's Epitaph.* L.B. p. 297.

worse for your world.' And in his criticism of our speed he would have been entirely right. Whether he was right to make physical nature the sole object of our watchful contemplation is to us questionable. It was not so to Wordsworth in 1798. The famous or notorious stanza:

> One impulse from a vernal wood,
> May teach you more of man,
> Of moral evil and of good,
> Than all the sages can.[1]

sounds like the hyperbole of exultation. But it is not necessarily so. Wordsworth is on the whole cautious and, as we have seen in *Tintern Abbey*, is not willing to commit himself to what he has not experienced. This verse is often misunderstood because it is misquoted. The operative word of the second line is 'may' not 'will' or 'can'. One impulse may, if it is the right impulse, teach you if you are teachable. He does not say that any and every impulse can and will teach everybody. Wordsworth's point is that when the right impulse comes it carries an unquestionable authority, and the knowledge it brings is received immediately into our whole being, so that at one bound we are carried further than years of mere head-knowledge, not felt upon our pulses, will ever bring us.

Similarly in the *Lines written at a small distance from my house.*

> Some silent laws our hearts may make
> Which they shall long obey.[2]

the 'may' implies a contingency as well as an option. If when we are out walking Nature should confer a special impulse, it may seem to us to have a binding force. Then, and only then, shall we be committed to obey.

These poems are instinct with an idea of the universe which was quite new in English poetry at that time. The

---

[1] *The Tables Turned.* L.B. p. 46.   [2] L.B. p. 85.

life of man and the life of nature are felt to be inextricably bound up with one another. Earth and man are animated by the same forces. Furthermore, man's mind and his body are felt to be so connected with one another as to be hardly separable.

> Love, now an universal birth,
>   From heart to heart is stealing,
>   From earth to man, from man to earth:
>   —It is the hour of feeling.
>
> One moment now may give us more
> Than fifty years of reason:
> Our minds shall drink at every pore
> The spirit of the season.[1]

Could any lines convey more powerfully the sense of mind and body as one living whole? This attitude is a striking change from that which we find only a few years earlier in Dr Johnson. In *Rasselas* (published 1759), Imlac declares: 'all the conclusions of reason enforce the immateriality of mind, and all the notices of sense and investigations of science concur to prove the unconsciousness of matter', and later: 'All that we know of matter is inert, senseless and lifeless.'[2] Wordsworth's view was a complete revolution from the Cartesian attitude in which mind was wholly immaterial and contemplated matter which was entirely material.

The three short poems *Lines written at a small distance from my house*, *Expostulation and Reply*, *The Tables Turned*, read like parts of one poem. They breathe the gladness of the spirit deeply interfused in the creation. But this spirit may also act monitorially, as Wordsworth shows in *Nutting*. The silent trees and the intruding sky seemed by the very quiet of their acceptance of his childish ravage, to admonish him. Nature can be law as well as impulse. In the beautiful

---

[1] *Lines written at a small distance from my house.* L.B. p. 85.
[2] *Rasselas* (ch. XLVIII).

lyric *Three years she grew in sun and shower,* Nature is to the maiden 'An overseeing power to kindle or restrain'. In *Hartleap Well* the idea which is hardly more than hinted in *Nutting,* receives stronger expression. The poem tells the story of a hart hunted to death for sport. The huntsman builds a pleasure house on the spot where the hart died, but after his own death the summer-house falls into ruin, and the place seems accursed. Nature seems to have excommunicated the spot. Decay and gloom prevail, and it is said that the animals will not drink the water there. The poet, in conversation with a shepherd, concludes that

> This Beast not unobserved by Nature fell;
> His death was mourned by sympathy divine.
>
> The Being, that is in the clouds and air, . . .
> Maintains a deep and reverential care
> For them the quiet creatures whom he loves,[1]

and he draws the moral that we are

> Never to blend our pleasure or our pride
> With sorrow of the meanest thing that feels.[1]

But 'the quiet creatures whom he loves' is ambiguous. Does the Being only love certain quiet creatures? Are they then favourites, and if so what is the attitude of the Being to other creatures—lions, vultures, spiders, for example? We get little help from Wordsworth in this; the range of animals in his poetry includes only certain more attractive and lovable creatures. And he is apt to romanticize even these. It may be true in some sense as yet beyond our comprehension, that 'with Nature never do they wage a foolish strife'; it is manifestly not true that 'their old age is beautiful and free'.[2] The permanent longing of the human mind to gain control of life, by reducing the puzzling variety of phenomena to intellectual order, leads to the habit of

---

[1] *Hartleap Well.* L.B. p. 191.
[2] *The Fountain.* L.B. p. 270.

7

making generalizations. In the lines just quoted, Wordsworth has mentally projected his experience of the moment of blessing in the gentle breeze on to nature everywhere and always, which shows that his intellect was meddling, in the sense of falsifying, his experience. Nature's overseeing power had momentarily forgotten to restrain him.

But Wordsworth does at least realize that nature is not everywhere as it is in the Lake District, and in the poem *Ruth* he presents a young man who has experienced nature in the tropics. In this poem he is in difficulties. He does not want to blame Nature if he can help it. So we are told that the fair forms of Nature in the tropics must have given the young man some good intentions, and that Ruth when she has been deserted, does not tax 'the engines of her pain, the rocks and pools, and airs that gently stir the vernal leaves', with the ill which has been done to her. But how has the ill been done? Wordsworth concedes that whatever in those climes the young man found

> Irregular in sight or sound
> Did to his mind impart
> A kindred impulse,...
>
> The tumult of a tropic sky,
> Might well be dangerous food
> For him, a Youth to whom was given
> So much of earth so much of Heaven,
> And such impetuous blood.[1]

So perhaps Nature is not always a wise nurse or a safe guide. If the case stands doubtful with the young man who visits the tropics, it is not at all doubtful with some of those who live there. They are wild, vicious men. In fact, the existence of evil and the insufficiency of Nature to be a law, are implicit in many of the *Lyrical Ballads*. The desertion of Martha in *The Thorn*, the pursuit of the hart to death in *Hartleap Well* are contrary to Nature in the

[1] L.B. p. 257.

Wordsworthian use of the word. And even Luke, the son of Michael and child of the mountains, whose mind, by the time he left home at eighteen, must have been peopled with lovely forms, when he gets among the people of the city, falls away into dissolute conduct.

We may conclude this somewhat discursive account of Nature in the *Lyrical Ballads* with a brief summary. It is difficult to discover exactly Wordsworth's view and probable that it had no very clear outline in the poet's mind. But this much is certain. Nature is the source of great blessing to mankind, the bringer of life and gladness to all creatures. Nature is trustworthy. The human intellect is not trustworthy. Faust is invited to leave his dusty study and to come out into the light of Nature which will both rejuvenate him and teach him immediate truth. The universe is a living universe throughout. Earth and man, mind and body are felt to be animated by the same spirit, a spirit which gives man not only physical vitality but also pure feelings and ennobling thoughts. Whether this spirit is 'Nature' or some other spirit, apprehended through natural forms, is not clear. The lines quoted above (page 7) seem to justify the identification of the spirit with 'Nature'.

Wordsworth recognizes evil only by implication in the *Lyrical Ballads*, but he had met it in his life. This world was often a weary weight and unintelligible (again the attempt to control it intellectually is implied), but the remarkable mystical experience which he had had at times in the presence of nature convinced him entirely that if the mystery was often a burden, there was nevertheless an ultimate solution of it, and a deep meaning in life. It was because of this that he based his faith on Nature and tried to develop that faith into a comprehensive philosophy. He made his first attempt to do this in *The Prelude*, which he finished in its original form in 1805. To that poem we now turn for a clearer exposition of his ideas.

9

CHAPTER TWO

NATURE IN *THE PRELUDE*,
BOOKS I–VIII[1]

In 1798, fired by Coleridge with enthusiasm for the project, Wordsworth began what he intended to be his master work, a great philosophic poem on Nature, Man and Society. But, as he explained in the Introduction to *The Prelude*, doubts of his capacity for his task soon assailed him, and therefore, partly as a preparation for the longer poem, he chose a theme 'of single and determined bounds', the history of the growth of his own mind. This poem was not published, and received no definite title during his lifetime. It was usually known as the 'poem to Coleridge'; it was only after Wordsworth's death that Mrs Wordsworth named it *The Prelude*.

Wordsworth began to write *The Prelude* in 1798 and completed Books I and II by 1799. Thereafter it was laid aside entirely until 1804, when he took it up again, bringing it to completion in its first form, which we shall study, in 1805. He may at the outset have thought of it as no more than an overture to his philosophic poem, but actually he achieved in it a major work, complete in itself and remarkable in its strength and unity. It has, incidentally, its own small overture in *Tintern Abbey* in which he briefly indicated the phases of his love for Nature, and in a few memorable lines gave account of his mystical experiences.

The Prelude does not set out to be autobiography; it only claims to be the story of the growth of a poet's mind. We shall see it better in its setting if we briefly remind ourselves of the actual history of Wordsworth's youth.

---

[1] All quotations from *The Prelude* are from the 1805 text.

Born at Cockermouth on 7 April, 1770, he was the second of five children of a middle-class family. They lived at Cockermouth until his mother's death in 1778, when the family were dispersed. William then went to school at Hawkshead and lodged there during the vacations. He was at school until 1787 when he went up to St John's College, Cambridge. He took his B.A. degree in January 1791. If we except his journey to Switzerland in 1790 with his friend Robert Jones, his life was outwardly uneventful. Of his character we know little, though that little is significant. His mother is reported to have said that he was the only one of her children about whom she was in the least anxious; she predicted that William would be remarkable for good or evil. He tells us himself that he was of 'a stiff, moody and violent temper'. He was self-willed and reticent. So far as we can trace, with the possible exception of Jones, he made no deep friendships in his first twenty-one years. Certainly he was never seriously influenced, much less dominated, by any other person or by any creed or system of ideas. He was brought up in the Anglican Church, and although his life and his poetry show a knowledge of Christian teaching, Christianity never vitally gripped his imagination. His childhood and youth are an uninterrupted development of his own nature. In all those formative years, there was for him but one over-mastering influence, one great educating force, the power of Nature. It was not surprising therefore, that he should dedicate *The Prelude* to Nature. It was a worthy tribute to her—'an orphic song to its own music chanted' was Coleridge's judgement.

The 1805 text of *The Prelude* is the fullest exposition of Wordsworth's view of Nature that we have. In it he comes nearer than in any other work to formulating a philosophy of Nature and of Man, and on the whole his treatment of his theme is consistent. We shall get the best introduction to his ideas if we follow his own chronology and observe what he has to say about Nature at each stage of his life.

At the outset we must observe that if Nature is the object of his worship, the main object of his interest is that on which Nature acts, the mind of man. As we have seen from the *Lyrical Ballads* his attitude to the mind was almost without precedent at that time. He, more than any other of the romantic poets, was the prophet of modern psychology. It is a part of the new degree of self-conciousness which came upon the world at that time, that the human mind appears as a new dark continent inviting exploration. There is a recognition that mental events are frequently of an extreme complexity and that there is much in the mind's workings which cannot be understood. Wordsworth is fascinated and awed by this prospect.

> The mind of Man is fram'd even like the breath
> And harmony of music. There is a dark
> Invisible workmanship that reconciles
> Discordant elements,   (Bk i, ll. 351–4)

And from *The Recluse*

> ...Not Chaos, not
> The darkest pit of lowest Erebus,
> ...can breed such fear and awe
> As fall upon us often when we look
> Into our Minds, into the Mind of Man—
>   (Lines prefaced to *The Excursion*, ll. 35–40)

The Prelude then is a study of the working of Nature upon this mysterious mind or, more strictly, of the interaction of Nature and mind,

> And the creation (by no lower name
> Can it be called) which they with blended might
> Accomplish: (Preface to *The Excursion*, ll. 69–71)

Nature to Wordsworth in his youth was both religion and education. It will make for clarity to consider these aspects separately.

NATURE AS EDUCATION

Nature is manifold in form, but one in spirit. Man has diverse powers of mind and body, but the man educated by Nature develops as a whole. Nature keeps all his powers in a healthy state of integration.

This beneficent process begins in the cradle. The child of Nature is predisposed to see life steadily and to see it whole. His awakening sense impressions are not simply a dance of atoms, a series of camera shots of an alien world; they group themselves significantly—in other words a child of Nature has imagination. Wordsworth does not often use the word imagination until he comes to speak of the more fully conscious mind of the young man, but it is clear that it is the imaginative faculty which Nature is educating, from the beginning.

> This faculty [imagination] hath been the moving soul
> Of our long labour; we have traced the stream
> From darkness and the very place of birth
>
> (Bk xiii, ll. 171–3)

The beginning of the imaginative life is due to the mother's love; the child responds with love and 'in mute dialogues with his mother's heart' (Bk ii, l. 283) receives:

> A virtue which irradiates and exalts
> All objects through all intercourse of sense.
>
> (Bk ii, ll. 259–60)

The passage (Bk ii, ll. 237–80) in which Wordsworth speaks of babyhood, taken by itself, might be misleading. It looks as though he were saying that the mother's love helps to make the infant babe at home in 'the very world which is the world of all of us, the place in which we find our happiness or not at all'. Certainly he does mean that a child so loved, takes his place naturally and gladly in *this* world, his new home—'No outcast he, bewildered and depressed'—rather, 'An inmate of this active universe';

13

but we know from other passages in *The Prelude* that 'in that twilight when we first begin to see this dawning earth', the child is sometimes bewildered by Nature—bewildered and delighted by 'gleams like the flashing of a shield', by parts of objects which 'by chance collisions and quaint accidents' coalesce into extraordinary appearances. He inherits both blessings, the aspects of things in their normal perspective, and as they sometimes are, 'circumfused with light divine'.

We notice again as in the *Lyrical Ballads* that Nature is thought of as a power of love, though as yet that term is vague in outline. We gain some idea of its meaning from Wordsworth's portrait of his mother. He shows her to have been a woman of quiet dignity and simple religious faith. Benign herself, she believed that Nature was benevolent. The God of Nature would provide alike for the bodies and minds of her children. Her trustfulness was the source of many blessings; it kept her free from over-anxiety, from pride and restless ambition. And it gave her children that sense of security and leisure which enabled them to be active but not restless, to enjoy to the full the beauty of the natural scenes in which they grew up.

Wordsworth does not examine the source of the kindliness of his mother; he only records that it was:

> not from faculties more strong
> Than others have, but from the times, perhaps,
> And spot in which she liv'd, and through a grace
> Of modest meekness,   (Bk v, ll. 285–8)

To him it seemed natural. But it is important to notice that it is to this good beginning that he attributes the right direction of his own life; by it he was

> furnish'd with that kind
> Of prepossession without which the soul
> Receives no knowledge that can bring forth good,
> No genuine insight ever comes to her: (Bk viii, ll. 458–61)

14

Granted this advantage, Nature can develop all the powers of the child. So well does Wordsworth show the wholeness of Nature's influence that it is difficult to separate the different aspects of her working. All natural thought is steeped in feeling; all natural feeling leads to true knowledge. But it is possible to make some separation of the emotional and intellectual aspects of the natural education.

NATURAL DEVELOPMENT OF THE EMOTIONS

The main effect of Nature's education on the emotions is that the feelings are both purified and enlarged.

The first two books of *The Prelude* are a record of tumult and peace; of the hurrying feet of the young schoolboy, bird-snaring, running, rowing or skating on Windermere, 'glad animal movements' and excitements set in the midst of peace and grandeur. We gain the impression that the beauty and serenity of Nature in the Lake country is acting upon him with gentle and persistent power:

> On the heights
> Scudding away from snare to snare, I plied
> My anxious visitation, hurrying on,
> Still hurrying, hurrying onward; moon and stars
> Were shining o'er my head; I was alone
> And seemed to be a trouble to the peace
> That was among them. (Bk i, ll. 318–24)

At nightfall, returning from a noisy schoolboy expedition to the further shore of Windermere, they return over the dusky lake—

> Oh! then the calm
> And dead still water lay upon my mind
> Even with a weight of pleasure and the sky
> Never before so beautiful, sank down
> Into my heart and held me like a dream.
> (Bk ii, ll. 176–80)

The purifying effect of this natural beauty works upon all the schoolboys. They race their boats to the islands on Windermere. Their goal is so beautiful a place that:

> In such a race
> So ended, disappointment could be none,
> Uneasiness, or pain, or jealousy:
> We rested in the shade, all pleas'd alike,
> Conquer'd and Conqueror. Thus the pride of strength,
> And vain-glory of superior skill
> Were interfus'd with objects which subdu'd
> And temper'd them, and gradually produc'd
> A quiet independence of the heart.   (Bk ii, ll. 65–73)

Nature purifies the feelings by beauty and by fear. The young bird-snarer, when he steals another's prey, hears low breathings coming after him, and when he rows out into the lake in a stolen boat, he knows a more terrifying kind of pursuit. As he moves farther from the shore, first the summit, and then the mass of a huge cliff come into his view. But it appears to him as though this cliff is stalking him, pursuing him with huge strides for every stroke of his oars. He turns back trembling, and goes homeward with serious thoughts. For days afterwards, in his mind:

> There was a darkness, call it solitude,
> Or blank desertion, no familiar shapes
> Of hourly objects, images of trees,
> Of sea or sky, no colours of green fields:
> But huge and mighty Forms that do not live
> Like living men mov'd slowly through the mind
> By day and were the trouble of my dreams.
> (Bk i, ll. 421–7)

Wordsworth's purpose in narrating this incident seems to be twofold. First that the ministry of fear has a direct ethical effect. Not that Nature created his conscience about stealing (but we note that he has not so far inquired into the source of conscience)—before he begins to row he knows it is 'an act of stealth and troubled pleasure'—but

16

Nature reinforces the admonition of conscience. More
important to Wordsworth, however, as the next passage
reveals, was his desire to show that the child, being made
unusually receptive by his sense of misdoing, receives an
impression of the terrifying immensity of Nature. He feels
awe, almost terror, before the grandeur of Nature, but this
feeling takes on the greatness of that which inspires it, so
that his pain and fear are ennobled, and the adventure of
human life is raised in dignity by the grandeur of its setting.

So he ends the account of his school-days with praise to
his native mountains and lakes for their gift of purity:

> Ye Mountains and Ye Lakes,
> And sounding Cataracts! Ye Mists and Winds
> That dwell among the hills where I was born.
> If, in my youth, I have been pure in heart,
> If, mingling with the world, I am content
> With my own modest pleasures, and have liv'd
> With God and Nature communing, remov'd
> From little enmities and low desires,
> The gift is yours;   (Bk ii, ll. 440–8)

And Nature also enlarges the feelings. She transforms
her first gift, 'the gloomy and severe scatterings of childhood'—the natural awe of the child before the immensity
of the universe—into a human-heartedness for his fellow-
beings:

> 'Twas thy power
> That rais'd the first complacency in me,
> And noticeable kindliness of heart,
> Love human to the Creature in himself
> As he appear'd, a stranger in my path,
> Before my eyes a Brother of this world;
>   (Bk viii, ll. 74–9)

At the same time Nature was preparing in him the mature
love of mankind which came to him in his twenty-second
year. Often during childhood he had been surprised by the
sudden appearance of a shepherd emerging from the

mountain mist, who had appeared 'in size like a giant
stalking through the sky'. At other times he had seen him
at a distance, his form 'glorified by the deep radiance of
the setting sun' (Bk viii, ll. 403–4).

Thus, man too took on something of the grandeur of his
setting, and unconsciously the boy was led to love and
reverence for human nature. Once again we observe that
he is predisposed to think well before he thinks ill of man.
And to this, in part, he attributes his moral safety when he
is in London "'mid the crowded deformities of city life'.

Wordsworth's claim is that it is the man whose feelings
have been purified and developed by Nature who feels
distress at the sight of human vice. It is the whole man
educated by Nature, who at the sight of

> Woman as she is to open shame
> Abandon'd and the pride of public vice,
>
> (Bk vii, ll. 418–19)

feels acutely that the human race is thereby split in twain.
He himself is kept safe from

> those ensuing laughters and contempts
> Self-pleasing, which if we would wish to think
> With admiration and respect of man
> Will not permit us; but pursue the mind
> That to devotion willingly would be rais'd
> Into the Temple and the Temple's heart.
>
> (Bk viii, ll. 465–70)

Thus it is Nature and not any moral teaching in
school or church which gives him a moral standard of
judgement. The natural education produces the man of
true feeling. And Nature, he will tell us, prepares the man
of true knowledge.

NATURE IN *THE PRELUDE*, BOOKS I-VIII

NATURAL DEVELOPMENT OF THE INTELLECT

Wordsworth's theory is that Nature is the author of our best intellectual blessings:

> Attention comes,
> And comprehensiveness and memory,
> From early converse with the works of God
> Among all regions; chiefly where appear
> Most obviously simplicity and power.
> By influence habitual to the mind
> The mountain's outline and its steady form
> Gives a pure grandeur, and its presence shapes
> The measure and the prospect of the soul
> To majesty; such virtue have the forms
> Perennial of the ancient hills; nor less
> The changeful language of their countenances
> Gives movement to the thoughts, and multitude,
> With order and relation.   (Bk vii, ll. 716–29)

(Nature's)

But her chief blessing is the bringing to birth of the faculty known as the Imagination, the organ of the mind by which man seeks, seizes upon and even creates true knowledge.

Wordsworth's life as a child was hardly intellectual at all. Up to the age of ten he was receiving sensations and impressions, some of which, he tells us, slept until maturer seasons called them forth. But as a boy he becomes conscious of Nature and begins to seek her for her own sake. From this time forward his education is a reciprocal process, in which he gives love, and Nature gives knowledge:

> The seasons came,
> And every season to my notice brought
> A store of transitory qualities
> Which, but for this most watchful power of love
> Had been neglected, left a register
> Of permanent relations, else unknown.
>   (Bk ii, ll. 307–12)

He perceives differences in things 'where to the common eye no difference is'. He certainly had an uncommon eye, but this perception of difference was almost certainly sharpened by the intellectual education he was receiving at school. Luke, the son of Michael in the poem of that name, also grew up in the love of Nature and no doubt he also perceived differences in things, but without having the same power to express them.

Wordsworth, throughout his school life, goes on raising

> . . . that interminable building rear'd
> By observation of affinities .
> In objects where no brotherhood exists
> To common minds.   (Bk ii, ll. 402–5)

—and carries on the process into his Cambridge days.

The University does not cause any major intellectual awakening in him. The only immediate effect of this first removal to a completely new environment, is to make him more distinctly aware of his own habits and of the blessings of his native region. His senses are delighted with the unusual scenes, but

> When the first glitter of the show was pass'd,
> And the first dazzle of the taper light,
> As if with a rebound my mind return'd
> Into its former self.   (Bk iii, ll. 94–7)

And his verse only becomes fully alive where he is describing Nature's growing influence upon him.

> I look'd for universal things; perus'd
> The common countenance of earth and heaven;
> And, turning the mind in upon itself,
> Pored, watch'd, expected, listen'd;   (Bk iii, ll. 110–13)

He is not seeking knowledge in the ordinary sense, and certainly not for any utilitarian purpose; he is seeking rather 'the signature of all things'. It is the powers of Nature's various forms and their interaction which fascinate him:

From deep analogies by thought supplied,
Or consciousnesses not to be subdued,
To every natural form, rock, fruit or flower,
Even the loose stones that cover the high-way,
I gave a moral life, I saw them feel,
Or link'd them to some feeling; the great mass
Lay bedded in a quickening soul, and all
That I beheld respired with inward meaning.

(Bk iii, ll. 122–9)

As consciousness grows, bringing into view more and more phenomena, he is busy with mind and spirit trying to weld all his knowledge into a whole. Even so he does not entirely succeed. His inner knowledge,

was oft in depth
And delicacy like another mind
Sequester'd from my outward taste in books,

(Bk vi, ll. 114–16)

As to books he tells us he followed no settled plan of reading. His prescribed studies were to Nature in his mind as Faust's lamp to the sun:

Those lovely forms
Had also left less space within my mind,
Which, wrought upon instinctively, had found
A freshness in those objects of its love
A winning power, beyond all other power.

(Bk iii, ll. 366–70)

In literature as in life, he seeks Nature, and he therefore reads poetry—in several languages—history and travel, rather than ethics, logic or philosophy.

His defence of this apparently random process of education as against planned studies, is

That in the unreasoning progress of the world
A wiser Spirit is at work for us,
A better eye...more prodigal
Of blessings, and more studious of our good
Even in what seem our most unfruitful hours.

(Bk v, ll. 384–8)

He uttered a prophetic warning to all teachers in an age which was to be ever more dominated by the worship of efficiency, against being too skilled in the usury of time, against trying to manage and shape in every detail the design of the child's future. They are thereby only too likely to produce a child, or rather a dwarf man, whose knowledge is both wrong in content and sought for the wrong reason—out of vanity not out of interest. A mass of names, phrases, information on heterogeneous subjects, is not true knowledge, it does not belong to the child's true nature and it can bring forth no good.

Wordsworth does not despise knowledge; he himself says

> Many are the joys
> Of youth; but oh! what happiness to live
> When every hour brings palpable access
> Of knowledge, when all knowledge is delight,
> And sorrow is not there. (Bk ii, ll. 303–7)

He even admits the pleasure and value of geometry, quite abstract intellectual knowledge, to 'a mind beset with images and haunted by itself'. He sees in it another province of Nature, where her laws are set forth for man's instruction. But he comes to it, as to other knowledge, with the right attitude of 'Indian awe and wonder'. The child who looks upon the world in this way does not lack mental occupation. There is no need to fear that the devil will find work for his idle hands; rather will Nature give him

> ...child-like fruitfulness in passing joy,
> [and] ...steady moods of thoughtfulness, matur'd
> To inspiration. (Bk iii, ll. 148–50)

Such steady moods will develop into a constant activity—

> I had an eye
> Which in my strongest workings, evermore
> Was looking for the shades of difference
> As they lie hid in all exterior forms,

22

Near or remote, minute or vast, an eye
Which from a stone, a tree, a wither'd leaf,
To the broad ocean and the azure heavens,
Spangled with kindred multitudes of stars,
Could find no surface where its power might sleep,
Which spake perpetual logic to my soul.

(Bk iii, ll. 156–65)

'Outward things done visibly for other minds, words, signs, symbols or actions'—these are not important. It is the education of this inward eye which is important. Wordsworth calls it the Imagination. Here we see the difficulty of attempting to separate feeling and intellect, for to Wordsworth the imagination is not a purely intellectual faculty—it is the organ of intellectual love. It is Nature's representative in the mature man, the master light of all his seeing. In place of a burden of mere information it gives him a vital principle, which selects, meditates upon, and recombines the phenomena presented to it, according to Nature's standards, thereby creating in the mind a true picture of the world. It is the Imagination exercising Nature's standards, giving him 'among least things a sense of greatest' which helps him to find meaning in 'the blank confusion' 'the perpetual flow of trivial objects melted and reduced to one identity' (Bk vii, ll. 701–3) with which London presents him.

The object of the Imagination, then, is Truth. But Wordsworth recognizes that another faculty has been almost equally active with him since his school-days. Sometimes the 'plastic power' which he possessed was not 'subservient strictly to the external things with which it commun'd' but was 'rebellious, acting in a devious mood, a local spirit of its own'. It was then in the service of a faculty whose object was not truth but pleasure, and this faculty he called the Fancy. But Nature saw to it that Fancy did not get out of hand, and that he recognized the difference

23

between it and 'the plain imagination and severe'. In his early attempts at literary creation, when he found himself adding

> the pangs of disappointed love
> And all the long Etcetera of such thought
>
> (Bk VIII, ll. 613–14)

to the woodman's illness—which was actually due to exposure—it was 'Nature's solid images' which steadied him, and never allowed him to confuse fancy with fact.

So the natural education gives intellectual as well as emotional standards of judgement. It produces the man of true knowledge and true feeling—the Imaginative Man.

Wordsworth writes of himself as he was at eighteen, at the University:

> Unknown, unthought of, yet I was most rich
> I had a world about me; 'twas my own,
> I made it; for it only liv'd to me,
> And to the God who look'd into my mind.
>
> (Bk III, ll. 141–4)

Outwardly at the time and for some years afterwards there was not a little of the supercilious undergraduate about Wordsworth. He admits it and his letters reveal it. Many incompatibles can live together in the flood of youth's energy. But the real man was alive; alive with the true humility and the true riches. Nature had helped him to find 'the points. . .where all stand single' and thus all the knowledge he had was vitally his own. He had not allowed himself to be driven at high speed through a hundred provinces of knowledge, gathering tabulated information about each. He was not up to the minute, a punctual presence, he was in all probability ignorant and inept for practical affairs. But at his age that was as it should be. The oak was but yet a yearling, growing not at man's pace but Nature's and delving its roots deep.

NATURE IN *THE PRELUDE,* BOOKS I-VIII

NATURE AS RELIGION

The greatness of *The Prelude* is, so to speak, not in its light but in its darkness, in the sense of a spirit immanent in the universe but transcendent to it. The young Wordsworth was aware of this spirit; it was the source of his deepest joy. When as a man he had given his love to mankind and was suffering with every setback to Man's hopes in the course of the French Revolution, he grieved at the shifts to which his new allegiance put him, compared to the free blessings of his former worship of Nature.

> When I began at first, in early youth
> To yield myself to Nature, when that strong
> And holy passion overcame me first,
> Neither day nor night, evening or morn
> Were free from the oppression;...
> ...to serve was high beatitude
> The tumult was a gladness, and the fear
> Ennobling, venerable; sleep secure,
> And waking thoughts more rich than happiest dreams.
>
> (Bk x, ll. 382–6, 398–401)

The word 'oppression' is significant. It is a word used by a man whose religion leaves him no reserved areas, demands all his thoughts, subjects him to a discipline not always welcome. Even as a boy he obscurely understood that he must maintain his own 'creative sensibility',[1] must not allow himself to be 'subdued by the regular action of the world'.[1] His 'local spirit' stood out against conventional behaviour mainly because of its need to be 'subservient strictly to the external things with which it communed'.[1]

> ...whatsoe'er of Terror or of Love
> Or Beauty, Nature's daily face put on
> From transitory passion, unto this
> I was as wakeful, even, as waters are
> To the sky's motion: in a kindred sense
> Of passion was obedient as a lute
> That waits upon the touches of the wind. (Bk iii, ll. 132–8)

[1] Bk ii, ll. 377–87.

25

The picture he gives of his youth is no doubt slightly idealized, but in the main it is true. It required devotion as well as a certain toughness to hold to his faith in Nature, when it led him to no aptitude for practical affairs and brought in no fruits of any kind recognized by his conventionally-minded uncles.

To say that Nature was his religion is not quite to say that he worshipped nature. As we shall see, his attitude is curiously mixed; he sometimes seems to worship nature and sometimes to be giving worship to a spirit animating nature. He is a nature lover but of a special kind. He has none of the instinctive wordless kinship with animals which characterizes hunters like Selous or Baden-Powell. Nor has he the detailed knowledge of the botanist or of an ardent entomologist like Fabre. He is an accurate observer, but in all his observation it is the *moods of Nature* of which he is most intently aware. Nature for him is something living, and living not merely organically but spiritually, disclosing spiritual meanings to those who walk faithfully with her.

> The great mass
> Lay bedded in a quickening soul, and all
> That I beheld respired with inward meaning.
> (Bk III, ll. 127–9)

He 'pored, watch'd, expected, listen'd' and Nature spoke to him rememberable things. He is sensitive not only to variations in Nature's daily appearances, but also to the variations, even down to quite small changes, which Nature makes in his own condition.

When he returns from his first term at Cambridge, and makes again the circuit of Esthwaite Lake 'at a sober hour, not winning or serene' he finds that

> a comfort seem'd to touch
> A heart that had not been disconsolate,
> Strength came where weakness was not known to be,
> At least not felt; (Bk IV, ll. 143–6)

26

He notes on another occasion when walking

> Along the public Way, when, for the night
> Deserted, in its silence it assumes
> A character of deeper quietness
> Than pathless solitudes.　　　　(Bk iv, ll. 365–9)

that his mind is exhausted:

> worn out by toil,
> And all unworthy of the deeper joy,
> Which waits on distant prospect, cliff, or sea.
> 　　　　　　　　　　　　(Bk iv, ll. 381–3)

a recognition similar to that made by the author of *The Cloud of Unknowing*:

> For I tell thee truly that this work [loving God] asketh a full great restfulness and a full whole and a clean disposition, as well in body as in soul. (Ch. 41.)

The kind of sensitiveness which these passages reveal is one of the marks of a religious mind.

He has recorded in *The Prelude* two occasions on which his fellowship with Nature was consummated in mystical experience. As in the experiences given in *Tintern Abbey* his normal life seemed to be suspended, and he became alive in a different dimension in which he saw 'into the life of things'. One of these occasions is connected with his crossing of the Alps. His journey across France to Switzerland was the real climax of his education. After the long time of his novitiate the priest of Nature went on pilgrimage to Nature's great cathedral—the High Alps. We know from the letter which he wrote to Dorothy from Switzerland[1] that he was deeply stirred by the grandeur of the scenes which met him there. The hour in which he and Jones discovered that they had actually crossed the Alps and were descending the road to Italy was probably not of

---

[1] L.W. *Early Letters*, p. 33.

any unusual significance. It was almost certainly when he was recollecting the occasion that the unusual occurred. This I take to be the significance of his address to the Imagination at this point. He was probably about to transcribe in blank verse the account he had already given in *Descriptive Sketches*[1] when suddenly:

> Imagination! lifting up itself
> Before the eye and progress of my Song
> Like an unfather'd vapour; here that Power
> In all the might of its endowments, came
> Athwart me; I was lost as in a cloud,
> Halted, without a struggle to break through.
> And now recovering, to my Soul I say
> I recognise thy glory; in such strength
> Of usurpation, in such visitings
> Of awful promise, when the light of sense
> Goes out in flashes that have shewn to us
> The invisible world, doth Greatness make abode,
> There harbours whether we be young or old.
> Our destiny, our nature, and our home
> Is with infinitude, and only there;
> With hope it is, hope that can never die,
> Effort, and expectation, and desire,
> And something evermore about to be.
> The mind beneath such banners militant
> Thinks not of spoils or trophies, nor of aught
> That may attest its prowess, blest in thoughts
> That are their own perfection and reward,
> Strong in itself, and in the access of joy
> Which hides it like the overflowing Nile.
>
> (Bk vi, ll. 525–48)

This passage is quoted in full because it shows both the similarity of this experience to that given in *Tintern Abbey* and a significant difference in Wordsworth's attitude to it. There is an element of humility before the grandeur of the invisible world, but it is not to that world that his first lines

[1] *Descriptive Sketches* (text of 1793), l. 130 appears as Bk vi, l. 561 and ll. 245–52 appear in ll. 562–4. O.W. p. 604 and p. 606.

are addressed, but to the greatness of the Soul. By implication that greatness is conferred by 'infinitude' but his first thoughts are directed to the human and not to the Godward side of the experience. As we shall see later this attitude may help to explain the puzzles of his later development.

The flash of revelation appears to have shown him more distinctly than at other times, the relation of the visible to the invisible, for the lines quoted are followed almost immediately by lines which express a quite coherent philosophy of Nature.

> The immeasurable height
> Of woods decaying, never to be decay'd,
> The stationary blasts of water-falls,
> And everywhere along the hollow rent
> Winds thwarting winds, bewilder'd and forlorn,
> The torrents shooting from the clear blue sky,
> The rocks that mutter'd close upon our ears,
> Black drizzling crags that spake by the wayside
> As if a voice were in them, the sick sight
> And giddy prospect of the raving stream,
> The unfetter'd clouds, and region of the Heavens,
> Tumult and peace, the darkness and the light
> Were all like workings of one mind, the features
> Of the same face, blossoms upon one tree
> Characters of the great Apocalypse,
> The types and symbols of Eternity
> Of first and last, and midst, and without end.
>
> (Bk vi, ll. 556–72)

Yet notwithstanding the vigour of this passage, there is a doubt at the heart of it. Nature's images were 'all *like* workings of one mind'—or were they actually its workings? As image rushes upon image, the certainty seems to grow, and yet the doubt is never quite dispelled. This view of the universe, breath-taking in its grandeur and its simplicity, momentous in its consequences both for poetry and for life, was it reality or dream? And the poet's attitude—belief or only willing suspension of disbelief?

Wordsworth was not quite certain—which is perhaps why he sometimes seems to give his allegiance to nature, to the beautiful forms presented to him, and sometimes to the eternal spirit. There are moreover, certain passages which imply that God and Nature are not distinguished. In one of his note-books the following lines are found:

> One interior life
> In which all beings live with God, themselves
> Are God, existing in the mighty whole,
> As undistinguishable as the cloudless east
> Is from the cloudless west, when all
> The hemisphere is one cerulean blue.

Bk v, l. 16 of *The Prelude* speaks of 'a soul divine which we participate' and in Bk ii, ll. 418–31, particularly ll. 430–1:

> I saw one life, and felt that it was joy.
> One song they sang,

—can be read in the same sense.

But it is not accurate to describe the young Wordsworth as a pantheist. There is too much evidence that he separated the Creator from the creation. He does so quite distinctly in *Descriptive Sketches* published in 1793,[1] as well as in the text we are considering. His mother did not

> by habit of her thoughts mistrust
> Our Nature; but had virtual faith that he,
> Who fills the Mother's breasts with innocent milk,
> Doth also for our nobler part provide,
> Under his great correction and controul,
> As innocent instincts, and as innocent food.

(Bk v, ll. 270–5)

---

[1] L. 3: 'Sure, Nature's God that spot to man had given', also ii, ll. 551–4:
'He holds with God himself communion high,
When the dread peal of swelling torrents fills
The sky-roof'd temple of the eternal hills,
And savage Nature humbly joins the rite.'

When later he is in the depths of trouble, the light which guided and cheered him was

> The life of nature, by the God of love
> Inspired, celestial presence ever pure. (Bk xi, ll. 99–100)

In one passage he keeps a perfect balance between the praise of God and the praise of nature. Addressing the Italian lakes which he visited after crossing the Alps, he writes:

> Like a breeze
> Or sunbeam over your domain I pass'd
> In motion without pause; but Ye have left
> Your beauty with me, an impassion'd sight
> Of colours and of forms, whose power is sweet
> And gracious, almost might I dare to say
> As virtue is, or goodness, sweet as love
> Or the remembrance of a noble deed,
> Or gentlest visitations of pure thought
> When God, the Giver of all joy, is thank'd
> Religiously, in silent blessedness. (Bk vi, ll. 605–15)

But he speaks of Nature so much more frequently, and in such terms of rapture, that it is clear that Nature is in the forefront of his mind and God in the background. He does sometimes, as the quoted lines show, appear to think of God as possessing human qualities, but more often he speaks of Him in impersonal and universal terms. He is 'infinitude'. He is 'wisdom and spirit of the Universe'. He is Eternity; He is the

> Upholder of the tranquil Soul,
> Which underneath all passion lives secure
> steadfast life. (Bk iii, ll. 116–18)

(Notice the impersonal relative.) God is a vital principle of Being, immanent in the Universe, creating ever new forms of beauty, speaking to men if at all, by silent blessings and silent warnings. That other conception of God, the inspiration of the Jewish race from earliest times, of God as primarily a God of righteousness rather than of beauty, as supra-personal rather than impersonal, standing over against man in the awful majesty of ethical perfection, speaking to man by a succession of definite words in his mind: 'I set before thee this day life and death'—such an idea of God, though implicit here and there in *The Prelude*, was far from being Wordsworth's main thought. But, as we have seen from this study of Nature as education, his religion was not without ethical value, and on that other occasion of his mystic experience which we have not yet touched upon, Nature and ethics were brought into vital connection.

On his first vacation from Cambridge, after a night of gaiety and dancing, he walked home in the early dawn, and the glory of Nature that was set before him took hold of him as never before. His spirit was uplifted in adoration. But in the midst of his joy there was a shadow of warning. He knew that a seal had been set upon him; that thenceforward, though he had not chosen the moment, he was committed to hold to whatever in conduct seemed akin to the beauty which possessed him.

> I made no vows, but vows
> Were then made for me; bond unknown to me
> Was given, that I should be, else sinning greatly,
> A dedicated Spirit. (Bk iv, ll. 341–4)

This was the origin of his feeling that he was a chosen son, a feeling which upheld him through years of difficulty and isolation. That in itself was no small blessing, and undoubtedly the experience must also have had a strong influence for good on his conduct. He does not always make explicit the connection between Nature and his sensitiveness to good and evil, but the whole tenor of *The Prelude* is that Nature has led him to the true standards of judgement against which conduct is measured.

had not as yet come into serious collision with his self-will. She had demanded service, but 'high beatitude' had always quickly followed. So far his religion had brought him only joy. And if it was in fact a superstructure built upon his inherited 'religious dignity of mind', what was to happen if that were overthrown, his predisposition towards the truth set aside? Could Nature restore it to him? Of more general interest, what hope could Nature offer to all the thousands in whom that religious dignity of mind seemed to be 'a function never lighted up'?

The young Wordsworth, who set out light-heartedly on his second journey to France in the late autumn of 1791, did not know how severely the ensuing years were to test his faith in Nature.

CHAPTER THREE

NATURE IN *THE PRELUDE,*
BOOKS IX–XIII

The years 1791–5 are the critical years of Wordsworth's life. Unfortunately, they are also the most obscure. There are tracts of months in which we do not know what he was doing, and concerning the whole period it is difficult to be certain what he was thinking.

In November 1791 he went to France again—

> Led chiefly by a personal wish
> To speak the language more familiarly,
> (Bk ix, ll. 36–7)

he tells us. This reason was no doubt partly an unconscious rationalization. History was being made in France. A movement of the human spirit destined to influence the course of life for centuries was gathering momentum there. It is hardly fanciful to suggest that Nature led him thither.

He went to Orleans, rather than Paris, in order to be less under temptation to speak English. In his search for suitable lodgings he made the acquaintance of Annette Vallon, a girl four years his senior, who had come from Blois on a visit to her brother, Paul Vallon, a notary clerk in the town. Annette was willing to give Wordsworth lessons in French. Student and teacher became friends, and very soon fell in love.

At the same time Wordsworth began to take an interest in the progress of the Revolution. He was chiefly stimulated at first by a group of Royalist officers who defended aristocracy and privilege, and were bent on thwarting all the aims of the Revolution. This came as a challenge to him.

Brought up in the plain equalitarianism of the dalesmen, in a country where no one

> Was vested with attention or respect
> Through claims of wealth or blood;   (Bk ix, ll. 224–5)

—an equality which he had found continued, though in a different way, at Cambridge, where all stood upon equal ground

> And wealth and titles were in less esteem
> Than talents and successful industry, (Bk ix, ll. 234–5)

—to him the Revolution seemed nothing unusual. It was a blessing come late rather than soon, and in the name of 'the government of equal rights and individual worth' he rebuked these defenders of the old regime, and to judge by his own account, with considerable success.

But the great positive awakening of his interest in Man and government, the event which caused him to stretch the sinews of his mind and to take up his political responsibilities as the proper concern of a man, was his meeting with Michel Beaupuis. This man, also an army officer but a fervent Republican, might be said to wear his equality like a courtier. Enthusiastic as he was for the triumph of the common people, for just government, and the ending of social abuse, he was no harsh doctrinaire. His love was not only for mankind but for each individual man of whatever class. He rendered service to all with meekness and with a kind of gallantry. A character so gracious was naturally attractive to Wordsworth, and he readily caught from him the revolutionary enthusiasm. It aroused all that was generous in his nature. During his later days at Cambridge, when he had given himself to the easy stream of social life, his early promise of dedication had often been forgotten, but here in the cause of the young Republic he saw and felt an object worthy of his entire loyalty and service. He plunged eagerly into political discussion with Beaupuis and felt, in that expectant hour in history, that their 'heart-bracing colloquies'

> of civil government, and its wisest forms,
> Of ancient prejudice and chartered rights,
> Allegiance, faith, and law by time matured,
>
> (Bk ix, ll. 328–30)

were not academic, but momentous for future action. To the young lover of Annette they seemed his appropriate service, an earnest preparation for life. Nature retired to a second place; all his love was now given to the cause of Man. All his youth seemed to have been a preparation for this time which now

> Rush'd in as if on wings,....
> The pulse of Being everywhere was felt,
> When all the several frames of things, like stars
> Through every magnitude distinguishable,
> Were half confounded in each other's blaze,
> One galaxy of life and joy.   (Bk viii, ll. 625–30)

He was supremely happy; much too happy to live for more than the immediate hour and the great promise of the time. And so the consummation of his love for Annette may have seemed only the natural response to the generous hour in which they lived.

Just when his eyes were opened to the future we do not know. Later in the year his movements begin to grow obscure. Beaupuis had left to join his regiment in July. Wordsworth went to Paris in October and was there until he received news of the birth of his daughter (15 December). He then returned to England, compelled, he tells us, by nothing less than absolute want of funds—a state of affairs which was not remedied by his hasty publication of his youthful poems, *An Evening Walk* and *Descriptive Sketches*, nor by application to his guardians. They regarded his French liaison as only further proof of his worthlessness. But on top of these personal disappointments came a severer blow. An event occurred which, he tells us, was the first serious shock to his nature. France, goaded to anger by the constant plotting of England and Austria, declared war on England, and a few days later (11 February 1793) England declared war on France. Not only Wordsworth but many another ardent young Republican was thrown into a state of consternation and perplexity. And to Wordsworth it meant also that he would be separated from his lover.

Wordsworth admits that this declaration of war was not unforeseen, but it was felt as a shock nevertheless, and it was the beginning of a long period of trouble for him, a period which was to be the making of him both as a poet and a sympathetic human being. He began to take upon himself the burden of human affairs. From his rather intellectual approach to men—as we have observed, he had seen them hitherto from a distance and somewhat idealized—he came close to the sufferings of individuals. He was to witness the gradual breakdown of all his hopes for the French Revolution and the failure of his own love affair. He had to face these difficulties entirely alone. The war separated him from Annette and her child, and knowing the Royalist sympathies of the Vallon family he was in some anxiety about them. He was in disgrace with his uncles, and they had forbidden him to call on his sister. He was alienated from the majority of his countrymen by his political views, he was without the support of any religious creed or church, and he had as yet no achievements of his own to give him self-confidence. He had only the generosity of youth and his faith in Nature and Man to support him.

Nature had led him to the love of mankind. All the energy and devotion he had previously given to her, he now gave to Man. As he tells us, he approached the shield of human nature from the golden side and was prepared to stake everything on the quality of its metal. The course of affairs in France alone was bound to have caused him pain, but his sympathy was deepened and rendered more imaginative by his personal crisis. In the fate to which, against his will, he found that he had committed Annette he saw and felt the case of thousands of women separated from their husbands or lovers by the war.

In the summer of 1792, in the first flush of his enthusiasm for the Revolution, the earth seemed 'an inheritance new-fallen' to Man, a Kingdom soon to be ruled in justice and perfect harmony by the common people. He confessed he was half glad of its obvious blemishes in the joyful anticipation of seeing them disappear. But even by October his joy was tempered by serious anxiety. He saw the political inexperience of the young Republic and he longed that men might arrive—

> From the four quarters of the wind to do
> For France what without help she could not do,
> A work of honour; (Bk x, ll. 123–5)

and he even considered offering himself for such service. From then onward the Revolution dealt blow after blow at his hopes, compelling him constantly to bring up new reserves of strength and ingenuity to defend his faith. It is not too much to say that he was tied to the wheels of the Revolution and dragged through the dust and blood of it with ever greater suffering.

> It was a lamentable time for man
> Whether a hope had e'er been his or not,
> A woeful time for them whose hopes did still
> Outlast the shock; most woeful for those few,
> They had the deepest feeling of the grief,
> Who still were flattered, and had trust in man.
> (Bk x, ll. 356–61)

He could to some extent allow for the violence of the French. He knew that throwing off oppression was not peaceable work. But England's hostility to France, and the severe measures of repression taken against all sympathizers with the Revolution were a more serious blow to his belief in Man. And yet he could not rejoice at the thought that Englishmen were dying in the war against France, even though his sympathies were all with France. The situation produced, as he said, 'a conflict of sensations without name'.

After the death of Robespierre his hopes revived once more. That sinister figure removed, he felt there was a chance for the establishment of true liberty at last. His belief was akin to the illusion that if once the sea can be made perfectly smooth there need never be any more waves. But within two months the Thermidoreans, rather than face rebellion from their starving armies, had sent them to plunder other countries. They overran Spain and Holland. Wordsworth was now in serious difficulties. He could no longer pretend that France was fighting a war of self-defence. His belief in the inherent goodness of man's feelings seemed to have proved insupportable. But he was loyal and stubborn, and he did not give up hope in Man. When about this time, he lighted on Godwin's *Enquiry Concerning Political Justice* and found there a philosophy which set men's hopes above the vagaries of feeling, in the clear dispassionate light of the intellect, his hopes rose once more. He thought he had at last found 'secure intelligence, a firm foundation for society'. He began to test all things by this new measuring-rod—the intellect—only to find that this kind of analysis merely filled his mind with a jumble of inchoate arguments and unrelated speculations. He lost all feeling of conviction and eventually gave up all his problems in despair.

So much we learn from *The Prelude*. Whether he suffered more through the Revolution or through his love affair is difficult to say. The course of his relationship to Annette we can only infer from his actions, and its significance only from his poems. The likeliest explanation of his behaviour towards Annette seems to me as follows. The shock of England's declaration of war on France caused him to realize fully, that he was an Englishman. It set in motion a long process of introspection by which he gradually came to recognize his own nature and powers. At some point in this process he discovered with fear and dismay that an inner voice was opposing his marriage with Annette. It told him that the chosen son had been chosen for a different destiny—although as yet that destiny was maddeningly obscure. He realized it was useless to deny this voice because it was the voice of his real self. At the same time he also knew that to desert an unmarried mother and her child was dishonourable. Hence a state of misery which was increased by such letters as came through from Annette, with their heart-rending appeals to him to come and marry her. There is to my mind no question that Wordsworth suffered acutely and for many years on this account. The frequency of the theme of the deserted mother in his early poems cannot, I think, be set aside as mere coincidence. If I read correctly the earliest text of the poem later called *Guilt and Sorrow*[1] it seems to reveal that acutely sensitive Wordsworth whom we have seen in the early books of *The Prelude*. The sailor is distracted with misery on account of his crime. When he is at last brought face to face with his dying wife, he beseeches her to pity and forgive him. She does so gladly, but he cannot receive forgiveness. He feels he is too deeply stained with guilt. At the table he looks at his own hands in misery, and cannot break bread with them. Wordsworth was certainly of

> . . .a conscience nice
> And over tender for the trial which
> His fate had call'd him to.

[1] *Wordsworth's Poetical Works: Early Poems*, p. 125. Edited by E. de Selincourt. Oxford, 1940.

And so

> Through dark and shapeless fear of things to come,
> And...through strong compunction for the past
> He suffer'd breaking down in heart and mind.
>
>   (*The Prelude*, Bk ix, ll. 721–3, 747–9)

Thus at the end of 1794 he was in a condition of almost complete despair and bewilderment. Gone for ever were his original hopes for mankind, and his personal hopes of ever achieving anything worth while had also broken down. The chosen son had been chosen—for what? He could not tell.

It would be unfair to lay the entire blame for this condition on his faith in Nature. He had stepped over from Nature's kingdom to Man's, from the private happy world of the adolescent to the noisy arena of politics and war, and in this unfamiliar territory he had made mistakes. Nevertheless, the inadequacy of the natural education alone as a preparation for life among men was apparent. The forms of Nature had not kept him from intellectual errors, from endlessly

> disjoining, joining things
> Without the light of knowledge.
>
>   (Bk viii, ll. 608–9)

Nature could apparently give him no kind of direction for his life, nor any very clear light on the problems of conduct. It would be distasteful to speculate on the meaning of his saying that Vaudracour in his relationship to Julia trusted 'to Nature for a happy end of all' (Bk ix, l. 602) beyond saying that if Nature gave him an intimation of right conduct, she did not also confer on him the power to follow it. Nature had taught him to see Man as 'a creature great and good'. But he had painfully discovered a root of evil in himself, and the Revolution had taught him that in mankind there was a 'reservoir of guilt filled up from age to age'. How was it then, after he had been led to this

43

knowledge, that he could return to his faith in Nature and build his whole philosophy upon it? *The Prelude* does not explain why, and only in part how, it came about.

The year 1795 saw a change in Wordsworth's fortunes. His blessings, like his troubles, did not come singly. In January of that year he found himself the inheritor of a legacy of £900 under the will of a certain Raisley Calvert to whom he had been a companion for some months in 1794. This gift enabled him to carry out a plan which he and Dorothy had had in mind since early 1794. As the guests of Calvert they had then made an experiment to see how economically they could live. The results of this experiment were such that Wordsworth knew that he could safely anticipate happiness from their permanent settlement together. He had an additional stroke of good fortune in the offer at a reasonable rent of an attractive country house on the Somerset-Dorset border, called Racedown. Small wonder that as he set out from Bristol for Racedown in September 1795 'trances of thought and mountings of the mind came fast upon him'. He wrote:

> ...it is shaken off,
> As by a miraculous gift 'tis shaken off,
> That burthen of my own unnatural self
> The heavy weight of many weary day
> Not mine, and such as were not made for me.
> Long months of peace...
> ...and undisturb'd delight
> Are mine in prospect.   (Bk 1, ll. 21–9)

And so it proved. The next three years were for him a period of recovery of health and power culminating in the wonderful years 1797 and 1798 when he and Dorothy and Coleridge freely rambled the Quantock Hills discussing everything that interested them from politics to poetry, and composing between them the *Lyrical Ballads*. For Wordsworth it was a second spring-time.

At first it was Dorothy who was the main force in his restoration. Through her affection he knew that there was at least one person in the world by whom he was not despised, nor ostracized. She encouraged him to believe in himself and to believe in himself as a poet. And her understanding of the situation with Annette, though it could not take away his sense of guilt, assuaged the pain of it. He admitted that it was Dorothy and Coleridge and *lastly* 'Nature's Self by (their) human love assisted' which,

> Revived the feelings of my earlier life,
> Gave me that strength and knowledge full of peace,
> Enlarged, and never more to be disturb'd, (Bk x, ll. 925–7)

This was already an admission that Nature was insufficient for his needs. But certainly Nature had helped him. Even at the lowest point when his soured being was apt to destroy everything it touched with critical acids, he still had a secret joy in Nature. He could not deny his pleasure in the return of spring. But his trouble had affected even his love of Nature. His old deep enjoyment had gone and instead he found that he was merely comparing scene with scene, seeking greedily ever new combinations of form and colour in a 'transport of the sense, vivid but not profound'.

He saw, however, that Dorothy was free from this critical attitude. Like her mother she did not glance on the hour or on the place in restless pride:

> Nor with impatience from the season ask'd
> More than its timely produce.   (Bk v, ll. 281–2)

> Whatever scene was present to her eyes
> That was the best, to that she was attuned
> Through her humility and lowliness,
> And through a perfect happiness of soul.
>   (Bk xi, ll. 208–11)

He felt his critical superiority silently rebuked. His restlessness began to give way, and he breathed to a deeper rhythm. He felt that natural graciousness of mind which had been his in youth, gradually returning.

> On all sides day began to reappear,
> And it was proved indeed that not in vain
> I had been taught to reverence a Power
> That is the very quality and shape
> And image of right reason, that matures
> Her processes by steadfast laws, gives birth
> To no impatient or fallacious hopes,
> No heat of passion or excessive zeal,
> No vain conceits, provokes to no quick turns
> Of self applauding intellect, but lifts
> The Being into magnanimity.   (Bk xii, ll. 22–32)

The fever of youth's search for power was shaken off. The sign of it is that he no longer looked everywhere in Nature for grandeur and immensity. As he showed in *The Borderers* these aspects of Nature may be used to minister to pride. He was willing now to look on humble things

> To look with feelings of fraternal love
> Upon those unassuming things that hold
> A silent station in this beauteous world.   (Bk xii, ll. 50–2)

And he turned the same eye on the realm of man. 'Triumphs of unambitious peace at home and noiseless fortitude' he saw to be of more value than showy political successes. He turned from the vanity and thoughtlessness of politicians to the wisdom of peasants.

But it was undoubtedly Dorothy's influence which helped him to look on life and Nature in this way.

No doubt in Wessex he also saw frequently—

> Only a man harrowing clods
> In a slow silent walk
> With an old horse that stumbles and nods
> Half asleep as they stalk
>
> Only thin smoke without flame
> From the heaps of couch-grass[1]

[1] Thomas Hardy, *In Time of the Breaking of Nations*.

46

and also felt

> Yet this will go onward the same
> Though Dynasties pass.[1]

By such contrasts between country and town, Nature may have helped him to 'settling judgements now of what would last and what would disappear'.

But there was no particular reason why Nature should have caused him to look on 'silent unassuming things' rather than upon any other of her creatures. He may have been right to feel Nature as a power that can 'lift the Being into magnanimity' but it is evident that human love was helping him to feel it. He saw in Nature 'the pervading grace that has been, is, and shall be' but Dorothy, his 'companion, never lost through many a league' on their country walks, helped him to see it.

He was again living in the country, in Dorothy he saw his former self, and by Calvert's gift he was restored to the same frugal independence that he had known as a boy. Thus circumstances combined to encourage him to do what he most desired to do—to forget the dark years and to try to step back into the wholeness of his earlier life. It may really have seemed to him, as he suggests in *The Prelude*, that this was his right course. In his youth he had also been 'Nature's Inmate' and being within her life he was not separated from

> Those mysteries of passion which have made,
> And shall continue evermore to make,...
> One brotherhood of all the human race.
>
> (Bk xi, ll. 84–8)

It seemed to him that those mysteries of passion were Nature's holiest places, and as he considered the life of Dorothy, it appeared to him that they should be kept

[1] Thomas Hardy, op. cit.

inviolate and not assailed by the analytical reason. Nature was the holy ground in which Man's life stood; the proper attitude to her was one of worship and unquestioning acceptance, not of scepticism. His arrival at this position explains in some measure his renewed faith in Nature; it also shows how he came to put into Nature that content which we have noted in the earlier books of *The Prelude*— a power of similar benignity to his mother's and his sister's love.

In trying to go back to the wholeness of his earlier life, he was in fact attempting a psychological impossibility; there is evidence even in *The Prelude* that he was not entirely happy about it. The full review of this position occupies the next chapter; we here follow *The Prelude* and notice the immediate consequences of his attitude.

He had become afraid of the analytical use of the intellect, but after he had come to know Coleridge, he saw that he might use the intellect not destructively but creatively, to build up his earlier knowledge of Nature into a philosophy. In Coleridge's *Religious Musings* Wordsworth heard lines which confirmed his own intimations of the significance of natural objects. Coleridge saw

> ...all visible things
> As steps that upward to their Father's throne
> Lead gradual. (*Religious Musings*, ll. 51–3)

Also, Coleridge introduced him to the philosophy of David Hartley and interpreted Hartley to mean that all things, man, plant and animal were symbols of reality, 'monads of the infinite mind'. Wordsworth could see that much of his earlier experience might be co-ordinated by Hartley's philosophy, or rather, by Coleridge's version of it, and that it might thus form the basis of a work which should be on a scale commensurate with his former hopes and resolutions.

So it was that he began with enthusiasm on the poem which eventually became *The Prelude*. He also wrote at the time those lines which still stand as a prospectus to *The Excursion*, and express what he hoped to do in his great philosophical poem. They express what was to be the moving spirit of all his work—

> Paradise and Groves
> Elysian, Fortunate Fields—like those of old
> Sought in the Atlantic Main—why should they be
> A history only of departed things,
> Or a mere fiction of what never was?
> For the discerning intellect of Man,
> When wedded to this goodly universe
> In love and holy passion, shall find these
> A simple produce of the common day.
> —I, long before the blissful hour arrives,
> Would chant, in lonely peace, the spousal verse
> Of this great consummation.
>
> (Preface to *The Excursion*, ll. 47–58)

As he got to work on this new task, he began to feel more secure. Some of his earlier questions were revived. He felt called on to make good search

> If man's estate, by doom of Nature yoked
> With toil, is therefore yoked with ignorance
>
> (*The Prelude*, Bk xii, ll. 174–5)

and so he returned to his love of wandering upon the roads and questioning the country folk he met. He renders a worthy tribute to the countryman. These men are

> ...their own upholders, to themselves
> Encouragement, and energy and will,
> Expressing liveliest thoughts in lively words
> As native passion dictates.   (Bk xii, ll. 261–4)

Some are shy and meek men 'unpractised in the strife of phrase'. But they too have a true imaginative life:

> Theirs is the language of the heavens, the power,
> The thought, the image, and the silent joy. (Bk xii, ll. 270–1)

Thus he found his earlier impression strengthened. It was the man who lived close to Nature who was led to true knowledge. He saw it as part of his poetic task to celebrate this Imaginative Man and he devoted the concluding book of *The Prelude* to an account of him.

It was a certain mountaineering excursion by night that helped him to crystallize his ideas concerning the imagination. He had gone with a friend to see the sunrise from the top of Snowdon. They had come up through thick mist for an hour or so, when quite suddenly they found themselves above it. The moon was shining from a clear sky and surrounding them was a sea of mist through which appeared the peaks of distant hills. The whole scene appeared to group itself round a chasm in the mist through which

> Mounted the roar of waters, torrents, streams
> Innumerable, roaring with one voice.
>
> (Bk xiii, ll. 58–9)

This chasm seemed to Wordsworth to concentrate the meaning of the whole scene. When he reflected on the magnificent panorama that had been before him, he saw in it the image of an imaginative mind—

> Of one that feeds upon infinity,
> That is exalted by an underpresence,
> The sense of God.   (Bk xiii, ll. 70–2)

Just as all the mountains seemed to group themselves about the roaring chasm, which dominated the entire scene, so the imaginative mind, perceiving the world, assembles and regroups the phenomena presented to it into their significant relations. Such an idea clearly raises big questions. For example, is there one absolute significance in any scene, which the imaginative mind grasps, or does that mind simply regroup phenomena into relations significant for its own needs at the time? If there is an absolute significance

in the scene, what is to guarantee that the mind will
perceive it free from distortion? Further, what do we mean
by absolute significance? In other words, what is the
meaning of meaning? Wordsworth never went fully into
the difficulties of this position. In *The Prelude* he restated
what he had already said in *Tintern Abbey*—that the world
is partly perceived, partly created by the mind—

> I felt that the array
> Of outward circumstance and visible form
> Is to the pleasure of the human mind
> What passion[1] makes it, that meanwhile the forms
> Of Nature have a passion[1] in themselves.
>
> (Bk xii, ll. 286–90)

The meaning of this passage will be considered more
fully in the next chapter.

Wordsworth wanted to show the strength and independence of imaginative minds. When such a mind hears,
say, a Beethoven symphony, it hears not merely a succession
of notes, nor even only pleasing tunes, it perceives the real
meaning of the composition:

> Whene'er it [a work of imagination] is
> Created for them, [they] catch it by an instinct.
>
> (Bk xiii, ll. 95–6)

But imaginative minds are not dependent on the
symphonies of others. They can make, not necessarily
symphonies, but at least their own imaginative compositions, can 'build up greatest things from least suggestions'
(Bk xiii, ll. 98–9)—they can themselves impress form
upon formlessness, and thus 'the enduring and the transient
both serve to exalt them' (Bk xiii, ll. 97–8).

[1] The word 'passion' as used by Wordsworth, probably following
Hartley, appears to mean something more like what we mean by 'affection'
or 'feeling'.

> Such minds are truly from the Deity,
> For they are Powers: and hence the highest bliss
> That can be known is theirs...
> ...hence religion, faith,
> And endless occupation for the soul...
> Hence truth in moral judgements and delight
> That fails not in the external universe.
>
> (Bk xiii, ll. 106–19)

The true gradations of men are not of wealth or even of talents but of imaginative power. This power must come from within us,

> Here must thou be, O man!
> Strength to thyself; no Helper hast thou here.
> Here keepest thou thy individual state...
> The prime and vital principle is thine
> In the recesses of thy nature, far
> From any reach of outward fellowship,
> Else is not thine at all.   (Bk xiii, ll. 188–97)

That he had been able to discover this vital principle in himself, and to rise superior to the deadly powers of habit and convention, Wordsworth ascribed to love. The imaginative life is sustained by love, not by human love only, though that has its place, but by intellectual love—

> ...that comes into the heart
> With awe and a diffusive sentiment.
>
> (Bk xiii, ll. 162–3)
>
> ...By love, for here
> Do we begin and end, all grandeur comes,
> All truth and beauty, from pervading love.
>
> (Bk xiii, ll. 149–51)

But we may ask, what has become of that power of Nature which seems to have been the inspiration of all his youth? Has he not virtually admitted in these lines that all the grandeur and beauty of nature, which were such a strong influence on him as a boy, came from love—from a love which informed nature with beauty, and his own mind with the power to perceive it?

Wordsworth would not have denied it. It is possible that if he is more explicit than earlier in *The Prelude*, the reason is to be found in the circumstances in which this last book of the poem was written. In February 1805, his brother John was drowned when his ship sank. Wordsworth felt this loss deeply—it is that 'private grief, keen and enduring' which he speaks of in ll. 416–17. There is reason to believe, as we shall see later, that the event caused him to reflect more deeply than he had ever done before, and to modify some of his views. It was a gain in depth to speak of 'love' rather than 'Nature'. But it was still by no means clear what he meant by love.

He goes on to tell us that the only genuine liberty is the imaginative life, and that this arises from our true self. If we can find 'the prime and vital principle' in ourselves, preserve and enlarge it, and so raise ourselves to the height of intellectual love, i.e. the imaginative life 'for they are each in each and cannot stand dividually' (Bk XIII, l. 187)— we shall inherit all joy in thought and all blessing in life. The great consummation will take place, the wedding of our minds to this goodly universe, each of which is exquisitely matched with the other. We shall constantly perceive, and with 'deep enthusiastic joy' take part in

> The rapture of the Hallelujah sent
> From all that breathes and is. . . .   (Bk XIII, ll. 262–3)

In drawing *The Prelude* to a close, Wordsworth gives thanks to Dorothy, to Coleridge, and to Calvert, for the great blessings he has received from them. In offering his poem to Coleridge, he hopes they will go forward together, as prophets of Nature (again Nature) to be

> United helpers forward of a day
> Of firmer trust, joint-labourers in a work
> > (Bk XIII, ll. 438–9)

for the redemption of mankind.

WORDSWORTH'S VIEW OF NATURE

It is a noble conception. In the dawn of an age which was to see an unprecedented development of intellectual activity, they would hallow at the outset every mental process by teaching men to look with love and with reverence upon the human mind.

One hundred and forty years later, this vision of mankind as a happy company of imaginative freemen seems as far off as ever. It was a promised land which Wordsworth saw from a mountain height. He himself never attained this imaginative freedom. Even before *The Prelude* was finished, there were poems of his in existence which showed that there was either something at fault with his view of life or some larger hindrance to the achievement of it than he suspected. In *The Prelude* itself we hear an ominous note. If this view is consistent throughout *The Prelude*, yet how changed is the light which falls on its later pages! The noontide blaze from Switzerland with its—

> hope that can never die,
> Effort, and expectation, and desire,
> And something evermore about to be
>
> (Bk vi, ll. 540–2)

has given place to a sad evening light—

> I see by glimpses now; when age comes on,
> May scarcely see at all, and I would give,
> While yet we may, as far as words can give,
> A substance and a life to what I feel:
> I would enshrine the spirit of the past
> For future restoration. (Bk xi, ll. 338–43)

Perhaps that promised land was not altogether a vain hope, and we may be able to discover, in a more critical review of his attitude to Nature, some of the false tracks which prevented his reaching his true life.

CHAPTER FOUR

WORDSWORTH'S ATTITUDE TO NATURE REVIEWED

We have already briefly hinted at the solution which Wordsworth thought he had found for his problems. In order to
study his attitude thoroughly, we must return to that point
in 1795 when he began to find his way 'through the weary
labyrinth of thought to open day'. He knew that his difficulties were a challenge to him to formulate his own philosophy. He wrote, in *The Prelude*, of one of the darker
moments in the French Revolution:

> Then was the truth received into my heart,
> That under heaviest sorrow earth can bring,
> Griefs bitterest of ourselves and of our kind,
> If from the affliction somewhere do not grow
> Honour which could not else have been, a faith
> An elevation, and a sanctity,
> If new strength be not given, or old restored
> The blame is ours not Nature's. (Bk x, ll. 423–30)

He knew that his 'business was upon the barren sea', his
'errand to sail to other coasts' (Bk xi, ll. 55–6). The voyage
from the natural behaviour of childhood, through self-consciousness to the establishment or finding of the real centre
from which we live as adults, is an essential journey for every
self-conscious man. As we have shown, Wordsworth's
voyage had come to grief. But at Racedown he was provided
with nearly all the conditions in which he could refit and
make ready to sail once more. He did venture forth again,
but he never made the essential crossing. His whole work
became the exploration of the coasts with which he had
been familiar as a boy.

This is not to say that his work was valueless. Entirely apart from its worth as poetry, it was the work of a mind strong in the power of psychological analysis. His observations on many subjects were, and are, of considerable interest. But he could not shine forth as a light to later generations, from that further shore which he had hoped to reach. I believe that the way he took never wholly satisfied him.

We shall consider first of all his attitude to Nature and its consequences for him, and then pass on to a study of the possible effects of his views for others.

He tried to take his stand within the emotional ground which the love of Dorothy gave him, and to live in the blessing of her simple faith. He saw in his sister one who 'conversed with things in higher style' than he did. In her humility and in her delight in every hour as it came, she seemed to make a perfect response to life and to make it quite spontaneously. In Dorothy he saw the living embodiment of the being he had always believed in—the ground of all his hopes in the French Revolution—the perfectly natural being. He had seen something of this same natural goodness in the country people he had known as a boy. And as he responded to his sister's affection and became attuned to her spirit, it appeared to him that his previous critical habits represented a lack of faith. Those Godwinian questions simply ought not to have arisen. In *Paradise Lost*, those who debated endlessly

> Of Providence, foreknowledge, will, and fate,
> Fix'd fate, free will, foreknowledge absolute,
> And found no end, in wandering mazes lost,
> (*Paradise Lost*, Bk ii, ll. 559–61)

—were of Satan's host.

There was no road to truth along those lines. It seemed to him that Nature, as it appeared in Dorothy, was the ultimate ground of Man's life, and that the intellect must not be employed to unsoul it 'by syllogistic words' or 'charm of logic ever within reach' (*Prel.* Bk xi, l. 83). He was right to see that his sister's faith was a beautiful thing—even though, like her mother's, it was unquestioning and immediate. The deliberate, self-conscious consideration of the relation of the self to the universe was a problem that simply had not arisen for her. She was secure within her trust in God and in her brother. But Wordsworth's life no longer had any immediacy, it was entirely reflective. However much he might admire Dorothy, it was not possible for a self-conscious being such as he had become to live again from an unconscious centre which he had lost. His attempt to do so was wrong in another important respect, that it overlooked entirely the main driving force in man, the will to power. The expression of life in a woman is different from that in a man. Some women appear to lead beautiful lives without any kind of ambition; in others the will to power finds expression in their aspirations for their men folk. But in men, in greater or less degree, according as they are born masters or men, the will to power is the driving force. Dorothy required nothing more than to be and to love. Wordsworth, on the other hand, had large ambitions which could not be satisfied by any simple domestic happiness. But feeling himself to be wrong and Dorothy right, he tried to believe, and teach, that the be-all and end-all of human life was such a simple domestic life of 'pure religion breathing household laws'. We shall see in due course the effects of his trying to force himself into the straitjacket of this belief.

Furthermore, by accepting Dorothy thus without serious thought, he made assumptions about her which had no secure foundation. He thought of her as spontaneous—but one who could speak to her brother 'in a voice of sudden admonition' cannot have been wholly ignorant

of conflict. He thought of her as stable, and he prophesied
for her
> An old age serene and bright
> And lovely as a Lapland night.[1]

—but in later years she suffered the loss of her reason. For
a life which is according to Nature but is not conscious of
its Nature, is at the mercy of strange accidents.

And he thought of her as 'Nature's Inmate'—but that
thought was only safe if he looked in one direction—to the
source of Nature. If he looked, as he did, in the other
direction—to the naturalness of her behaviour—he was in
danger of forgetting that her exquisite qualities sprang from
the best of what was natural in eighteenth-century England,
and that what had come to seem natural then, if it owed
something to Nature, owed something also to Christianity.
Dorothy took all her environment, including Bible and
Church, in equal trust. The standard of conduct which
appears natural in any society is in constant process of
change. Gladiatorial contests, the burning of heretics and
witches had all seemed natural in earlier times. In Wordsworth's time slavery was in process of being branded unnatural. The teaching and suffering of men whose faith had
led them beyond the standards of their time had raised the
quality of what was natural. By the end of the eighteenth
century, respect for liberty and life, and a certain graciousness of behaviour had become generally accepted in England
as natural. In Dorothy, Wordsworth was taking all this,
and probably other and finer elements of inherited discipline, for granted. We can see from the foregoing considerations that that spontaneous 'Nature' which inspired
the *Lyrical Ballads* was not likely to provide safe ground for
a philosophy of life.

But he was right thus far—that Nature could be a vital
restorative power to all who had suffered a breakdown of
their faith, and in making the beauty and the healing power

[1] *To a Young Lady Reproached for Taking Long Walks.* O.W. p. 218.

of Nature felt in his poems, he did a valuable work. He was also right—and in this thought he found the first material for his reawakened desire to write—in seeing that to give the primacy to the intellect in the search for truth, as Godwin had done, was a mistake. It is a pity that *The Borderers* is such poor drama. Had it been even a more readable play it might have had a valuable influence at the present time, when we have seen in propaganda the sinister uses to which the reason may be put. Wordsworth set out to show in this play 'the dangerous use which may be made of reason when a man has committed a great crime'.[1] The power that is set over against reason is Nature, and the view of Nature which he later made fully explicit is already present in this play. Herbert, the old man who is to be treacherously murdered, is attracted by Marmaduke, the leader of the Borderers, because of 'Nature unbetray'd in him'. This unbetrayed Nature in Marmaduke is shown as in constant conflict with his reason which is worked on by the unscrupulous Oswald. It is important to notice that not only has Marmaduke a strong inward feeling that he ought not to do the murder, he also receives confirmation of this feeling from external nature.

> ...his face turned toward me; and I tell thee
> Idonea's filial countenance was there
> To baffle me—it put me to my prayers.
> Upwards I cast my eyes, and, through a crevice,
> Beheld a star twinkling above my head,
> And by the living God, I could not do it.
>
> *(The Borderers*, ll. 985–90)[2]

In other words, Nature never did betray the heart in which she is unbetrayed. She could be relied on to give man intimations of truth and her forms might be regarded as the text of her revelation—as he called them elsewhere, the Bible of the Universe. It was not long after he had

---

[1] Preface to *The Borderers*.

[2] Cf. Socrates in *Phaedrus* 'The men of those days, not being clever like you moderns, were content, in their simplicity, to listen to an oak or a stone, if only it spake the truth.' Plato, *Five Dialogues* (Everyman Edition), p. 282.

reached this position that he met Coleridge—a Coleridge then eloquently certain of the entire wisdom of the philosopher David Hartley. Wordsworth was soon enthusiastically at work welding his own view and a Coleridgean version of Hartley into a philosophical system of his own. But there were dangers here which he did not notice. He could see the application of Hartley's principles to certain aspects of his earlier life, but not having any of Coleridge's intellectual mobility, and not having a sure understanding of his own experience, he did not see until much later, that the essence of his experience was totally at variance with Hartley's philosophy.

In order to make the argument quite clear it will be necessary at this stage to give the main points of this philosophy.

David Hartley, whose *Observations on Man* was first published in 1749 was a scientist and a religious man. Like other notable scientists from Sir Francis Bacon onwards, he strove to co-ordinate his scientific principles and his religious beliefs. Following Newton, he believed that mechanical principles would eventually explain all phenomena, including the workings of the human mind, and he set out to show that all mental events could be explained by the great law of association, which he regarded as the counterpart in psychology of the law of gravity in physics. Hartley had an unshaken belief in the goodness of God, and believed that His purpose was to lead all men to a good and a happy life. The means which the Creator employs to this end is the law of association, and so effective is this law that in a normal human being the attainment of the good life is inevitable. Hartley denies that we have an innate moral sense. In fact all the higher social and spiritual qualities only appear quite late in our development. We begin with simple sensations, and by associating pleasure and pain with different objects we gradually pass through sensation,

ATTITUDE TO NATURE REVIEWED

imagination, ambition, self-interest, until we reach sympathy, and at last theopathy and the moral sense. The in-
accuracy of even the chronological order of these states in
the development of many people will be apparent. Other
defects of the system are hardly less obvious. For instance,
we are told that this beneficent progress is inevitable and
yet that 'he who would obtain the maximum of the sensible
pleasures, even those of Taste, must not give himself up to
them; but restrain them and make them subject to Benevolence, Piety and the Moral sense'. We might reply, 'On
what compulsion must I, tell me that'—if all is already
determined. But more important for our argument is the
fact that Hartley never explains how we know we are making
this happy progression, nor by what faculty we deem one
pleasure 'higher' or of more worth than another.

Just how much of Hartley's outlook and philosophy
Wordsworth absorbed is very difficult to determine. In
Hartley he either found, or found confirmation for, two
closely linked ideas[1]—the idea that our thoughts and

[1] The influence of Hartley—and of other philosophers—upon Wordsworth has been greatly exaggerated. Lines of Wordsworth's poetry which
are clearly the spontaneous utterance of deep mystical experience have been
interpreted as merely deliberate statements of philosophical principles. The
extreme of this kind of perversity and lack of sensibility is Hazlitt's comment
on the lines   'A motion and a spirit that impels
                    All thinking things, all objects of all thought
                    And rolls through all things.'
—'Perhaps the doctrine of what has been called philosophical necessity was
never more fully expressed.'
    Nevertheless, I am not able to follow Mr J. C. Smith (*A Study of Words-
worth*, pp. 89 ff.) in dismissing the influence of Hartley outright. Both the
phraseology and the ideas in the Preface to *Lyrical Ballads* suggest to me
strongly the influence of Hartley's principles. It is of course possible that
Wordsworth only heard these principles from Coleridge, but even so, they
would come from Coleridge with even more force than from the printed
page. And I think it unlikely that Wordsworth would write (to Richard
Sharp, 1808): 'Take, for instance, in Philosophy, Hartley's book upon
Man—how many years did it sleep in almost entire oblivion'—about a
book which he had never opened.

feelings are associated in the mind with the sense experiences which accompany them, and the idea that this process of association is carried on in the mind by 'the grand elementary principle of pleasure'.[1] However, with one or two exceptions—notably the passage of associationist speculation about babyhood (Bk II, ll. 237–80)—Wordsworth accepted these ideas only in as far as they agreed with his own experience. He believed in the freedom of the will and not, with Hartley, that progress toward good is inevitable. He recognized that a child has a conscience which is there ~~the law of association~~ has developed a moral sense. ~~...~~ children are not little animals who by a divinely ordained law of association acting on their sensations develop inevitably through self-interest and ambition into quiet and God-fearing citizens.

But it is by no means clear that he recognized the deep gulf between his own experience and Hartley's sensationalism.

He could see the workings of association in his own development. Nature had given him inspiring and ennobling thoughts while he had been thinking of nothing but enjoying himself—

> ...the beauteous forms
> Of Nature were collaterally attach'd
> To every scheme of holiday delight,
>
> (Bk II, ll. 51–3)

—by the law of association. But the law did not explain why he found them 'beauteous', and unfortunately he did not inquire. Satisfied with the happiness of his experience he was too often willing to leave the explanation of it in doubt—

> ...I mean to speak
> Of that interminable building rear'd
> By observation of affinities

[1] Preface to *Lyrical Ballads*. L.B. p. 23.

ATTITUDE TO NATURE REVIEWED

> In objects where no brotherhood exists
> To common minds. My seventeenth year was come
> And whether from this habit, rooted now
> So deeply in my mind, or from excess
> Of the great social principle of life,
> Coercing all things into sympathy,
> To unorganic natures I transferr'd
> My own enjoyments, or, the power of truth
> Coming in revelation, I convers'd
> With things that really are, I, at this time
> Saw blessings spread around me like a sea.
>
> (Bk ii, 401–14)

But it was vital to him to know whether he was conversing with things that really are. To be 'contented if he might enjoy the things which others understand'[1] was a triumph only so long as the enjoyment lasted, and that proved to be not very long.

Even in 1798, at the end of his west country days, which had abounded in valuable discussions with Coleridge, he was still uncertain whether there was any kind of connection between his mystical experiences and his delight in natural forms, and in *Tintern Abbey* there is an indication of the fateful direction his thought would take—

> ...well pleased to recognize
> In nature *and the language of the sense*
> The anchor of my purest thoughts, the nurse,
> The guide, the guardian of my heart, and soul
> Of all my moral being.[2]

We have already suggested (ch. 1) that it was not unreasonable to expect that if an experience had occurred more than once in a particular setting, it was likely to do so again, but the associationist principle undoubtedly strengthened his attachment to the language of the sense, and it was in this, in the direction it gave to his thinking, rather than in any particular wrong views that Hartley's

[1] *A Poet's Epitaph*. L.B. p. 298.
[2] L.B. p. 174 (my italics).

63

philosophy did harm. The element of matter-of-factness, of 'clinging to the palpable' which Coleridge was later to deplore in Wordsworth, needed no encouragement. When he came to conduct his 'recherche du temps perdu' and to write the story of his own poetic development he became so absorbed in tracing out the law of association and the workings of the great pleasure principle through all mental processes, that the consideration of what it was that gave value to his thoughts and worth to his pleasures, fell into a second place. He admitted that his joy and delight in Nature rested on a predisposition towards good, but he hardly seems to have noticed that his system of Natural education was worth little if he failed to say clearly what were the fount and origin of that predisposition. As we have seen, at the very end of *The Prelude*, he became a little more explicit. The foundation of all good was a spirit of love in the universe. It would not be true to say that he left this term entirely undefined. He meant by it a power whose attributes included those qualities of grandeur, beauty and tenderness, which it developed in human beings. But he was so happy in explaining *how* these blessings given by the spirit worked upon him, that the spirit itself remained in the background as 'eternity', 'infinity', 'wisdom and spirit of the universe', etc.

He saw at moments the clear opposition between the world of spirit and the world of sense. He shrank back

> From every combination that might aid
> The tendency, too potent in itself,
> Of habit to enslave the mind, I mean
> Oppress it by the laws of vulgar sense,
> And substitute a universe of death,
> The falsest of all worlds, in place of that
> Which is divine and true.   (Bk xiii, ll. 137–43)

In view of such a confession, it is surprising that he did not realize clearly that he was most certainly in possession of

the truth when he was '*laid asleep in body*'—in other words
that his mystical experiences were the only starting point
for all true insight 'into the life of things', and that he must
at all costs pin his faith to *them*, and not to the language of
the sense. In those moments, I venture to suggest, he was
in touch with the Creator of man and of nature; he was, in
them, possessed by the God who had given the benignity
of his mother, and the faith of his sister; who had given him
that 'religious dignity of mind', that 'prepossession towards
good' from which came all his delight, and all his knowledge of nature, and his love of Man. Those experiences
were the only possible foundation for the vigorous life of
the imagination which he hoped to lead. In them he was
in possession of the great secret. The tragedy was that he
let it go because he did not value it sufficiently. In so deep
a matter as this it is difficult to judge another man. We do
not know all the circumstances, we cannot put ourselves
back into the climate of thought which surrounded him.
But to me it seems possible that if Wordsworth, instead of
being content with having such experiences and thinking
of the glory of the human mind which was capable of
receiving them, could have thought only of the Giver of
them, he might have come within sight of that destiny to
which in an earlier mystical experience he had been dedicated. He might have been led to consider that if the spirit
interfused through all creation had really created men as
the highest of all earthly beings, that spirit could hardly be
less than personal itself. From this thought of the spirit as
supra-personal rather than simply impersonal, infinite, it
would have been but a short step to the thought of the
possibility of a personal relationship between the spirit and
man. And this thought might have opened the way for him
to a real understanding of Christianity.

Such a development would have helped him in his own
problems. For Wordsworth was a poet tormented by

ethical considerations— he was much too concerned with them for the good of his poetry. It was his very trouble over problems of conduct which led him to try to forget them in the happiness of Nature. But that proved to be no way out of his difficulty. In his high hours of mystical experience he was united to the source of all Beauty—beauty of conduct as well as of nature. That he did eventually come to something like this view *The Excursion* bears witness, but that was only years later, when the vitality and flexibility of youth were gone, and his course of life was set. If he could have come to it in 1798, I believe that his life would have been both happier and more fruitful. In applying himself steadily to the understanding of his mystical experience he would certainly have found

> ...endless occupation for the soul
> Whether discursive or intuitive.
> *(The Prelude*, Bk XIII, 112–13)

I believe he might have had 'visitations more awful' which would have shown him a way of fulfilment for even the strongest will to power. That way would have led to the splendid life of the imagination which he had once seen in prospect.

Unhappily he thought he could live on the revival of his earlier feelings and could trust for their maintenance to the law of association working on sense impressions. But by this reliance on sensible impressions to produce spiritual effects, and by the use of the term 'Nature' which made it too easy to confuse the Creator and the creation, he was unconsciously inviting Nature to guide him to the light of common day and be his guardian there. Let it be admitted that it is not surprising that he did not notice this at Racedown. While the contrast with his previous life was strong, and every day brought some new delight in Nature, his feelings came fresh upon him. Truth was breathed by cheerfulness and wisdom felt in every happy step of health. Life itself was for the time being a lyrical ballad. It was then, when his attitude to Nature was most nearly natural, being the legitimate joy of the convalescent at renewed health, that he wrote his best lyrics.

But when time distanced the first contrasts and surprises, when the joy of

> ...the endless store of things
> Rare or at least so seeming, every day
> Found all about me in one neighbourhood
> > (Bk I, ll. 118–20)

became 'matured into a sober pleasure' he found that his earlier feelings no longer came upon him with the same frequency. For the nourishment of his mind he had more and more to rely on certain

> ...spots of time
> Which with distinct pre-eminence retain
> A vivifying Virtue....
> ...passages of life in which
> We have had deepest feeling that the mind
> Is lord and master, and that outward sense
> Is but the obedient servant of her will.
> > (Bk XI, ll. 258–60, 270–73)

But these moments were for the most part 'hiding places ten years deep'[1] or even further back in childhood, and their power to lift him up when fallen was not unlimited. By settling (at Christmas 1799) at Grasmere amid scenes familiar to him as a boy, he made it easier to recapture such moments, but even by this means he could do no more than delay the end of inspiration derived from earlier times.

It was then that he began to find that nature as the mind's Bible was insufficient to his needs. When he had first gone to Racedown he had been in a state not unlike that of Faust

[1] *The Waggoner.*

after the betrayal of Gretchen. Not that his conduct towards Annette had been as criminal as Faust's, but his sensitiveness painted it in the same colours. He felt that he had bidden 'eternal farewell to unmingled joy and the light dancing of the thoughtless heart'.[1] He longed for the restoration of a clean conscience, but he did not know how to obtain it. He knew that sin was of deep significance, that the frame of things was altered by it. As we have seen, in his renewed happiness at Racedown and Alfoxden he partially got over his trouble. He also found another way of assuaging his pain in the working out of what he conceived as his poetic mission—to show the strength of the primary affections in simple folk. The forsaken Annette appears as Martha Ray in *The Thorn* and as *Ruth* and in *The Complaint of a Forsaken Indian Woman*.

But this was not a wholly satisfactory way of dealing with his problem. He admitted that he enjoyed composing poetry—and this was still true even though the labour of composition often made him ill and tired. He was therefore allowing himself to make pleasure and poetic reputation out of his own wrongdoing. He permitted himself a curious mixture of suffering and self-congratulation. Such a solution played into the hands of his always inordinate desire for self-esteem. It had the further disadvantage that it only eased, not cured the trouble, and when circumstances were less favourable he felt it again. Nature alone could not speak to his condition, and his creed of self-dependence became a burden. It was a sad feature of Wordsworth's later life. Beneath all his solemn concern for human dignity was a man longing for joy, for the happiness of a clear conscience.

In the long years at Grasmere he wandered about under a grey and imponderable cloud. Perplexity concerning his true life and an indefinable sense of guilt continued to

[1] *The Borderers*, ll. 1546–7.

haunt him. In the *Lyrical Ballads* and in *The Prelude*,
which he completed in the spirit which had inspired its
beginning, we feel we are still in the company of men. We
hear in his verse the sounds of human intercourse, whether
cheerful or sad. But after his settlement at Grasmere he
seems to go away from men into isolation—not into the
solitude of the monk—but into 'the silence and the calm
of mute insensate things'.[1] And they do not lead him from
joy to joy. We find him writing:

> We Poets in our youth begin in gladness;
> But thereof come in the end despondency and madness.[2]

It is only now and again that a break in the clouds occurs,
and his heart leaps up when he beholds a rainbow—the
sign of mercy—and he cannot but be gay, for a few minutes,
gazing at the daffodils. But the movement of that poem is
not that of a dance. His attitude to Nature begins to revert
to what it had been in the dark years when he wanted to
become immersed in Nature to ease the pain of life. Then,
he had written:

> The very ocean has its hour of rest,
> I too was calm, though heavily distress'd!
> Oh me, how quiet sky and ocean were!
> My heart was healed within me, I was bless'd
> And looked, and looked along the silent air,
> Until it seemed to bring a joy to my despair.
>> (*The Female Vagrant*, ll. 103–8)

So later he seeks the 'ministry of the groves'

> To interpose the covert of your shades,
> Even as a sleep, betwixt the heart of man
> And the uneasy world, 'twixt man himself,
> Not seldom, and his own unquiet heart.
>> (*The Prelude*, Bk xi, ll. 16–19)

[1] L.B. p. 275.
[2] *Resolution and Independence*. O.W. p. 196.

He has been criticized for saying that he was alone when he saw the daffodils and the leech-gatherer, when in fact he was with Dorothy. But in spirit he was alone. He had discovered by then the impossibility of living as Dorothy lived, a child of Nature.

In the delights of their West-Country days he had not noticed that he and she were moving in a circle, each in the other's love. Dorothy was content to leave the movement of life to others—in short to William. But William, looking back to Dorothy, could see no movement, only delighted contemplation, a reverent love of all things that seemed the perfection of human nature.

> ... Her the birds
> And every flower she met with, could they but
> Have known her, would have lov'd. Methought such charm
> Of sweetness did her presence breathe around
> That all the trees, and all the silent hills
> And everything she look'd on, should have had
> An intimation how she bore herself
> Towards them and to all creatures. God delights
> In such a being; for her common thoughts
> Are piety, her life is blessedness.   (Bk xi, ll. 214–23)

He, too, wanted his days to be bound together by natural piety, and so he also tried to be simple and natural. But what was wholly satisfying to his sister failed to satisfy him because—and here the ambiguity of the word appears—it was not according to Nature, his nature.

It was a mistake for him to try to live the same kind of life as Dorothy. That in the light of her humility he had been cured of his critical restlessness and had found ambitious virtues please him less, was a definite gain. Nevertheless, his own quite legitimate will to power needed some great object to which to attach itself—it needed to be converted into full self-giving to some great cause. But he did not find this, and he really seems to have supposed that he could get rid of the will to power by simply ignoring it and by trying to live in tune with Dorothy's humility. The results were what might have been expected. As he truly said, by that 'knowledge full of peace' to which he was restored he was 'moderated and composed'—he was not made whole. He could not exercise his whole force in any direction. He could only moderate pride by humility. In his life of wandering the public roads and inquiring into the conditions of rural occupations, he found 'healing and repose' to every angry passion. And when the angry passions had reposed they rose up strengthened, and he had to turn again to the unassuming daisies to bring him back to humility.

> If stately passions in me burn,
> And one chance look to Thee should turn,
> I drink out of an humbler urn
> A lowlier pleasure.[1]

There is too much anger in his condemnation of the philosopher, the lawyer and the moralist, in *The Poet's Epitaph*. It is the anger of frustration. He knew that they were wrong, but he also knew that he had found no better way to set against theirs. A man who has found his true imaginative life is too absorbed in it to think very often, as Wordsworth did, about the 'little enmities and low desires' which he has escaped. Wordsworth having no secure hold on life, was uneasily slipping towards the thing he condemned. The moralist is rampant in *The Excursion*.

He had been genuinely grateful after his long wanderings to settle at Grasmere with Dorothy, but he was never quite easy in his mind about doing so. He had at times an uncomfortable feeling that it was not the right life for him. Nature seemed to throw back to him the challenge of his own questions. The trees and icy brooks had appeared to ask—

> ...Whence come ye? To what end?[2]

[1] *To The Daisy.* O.W. p. 158.
[2] *Bleak season was it, turbulent and wild.* O.W. p. 622.

He tried to answer that all was well—

> On Nature's invitation do I come
> By Reason sanctioned.[1]

But the question breaks out again—

> Can the choice mislead,
> That made the calmest, fairest spot on earth,
> With all its unappropriated good,
> My own?[1]

—He was never quite certain.

In these perplexities his joy, if not his faith, in Nature began to wane. It was then that the danger of attachment to the language of the sense became apparent. Only 'reason in her most exalted mood', only 'absolute strength and clearest insight' (Bk XIII, ll. 168–70)—in short the Imagination—contemplating the life of Nature can support a faith that 'all which we behold is full of blessings', and find in her a power that leads us on from joy to joy. The plain observation of Nature is not likely to do so. For the obvious aspect of Nature is that of a system of endless inevitable repetitions. It appears to be fate rather than faith which governs its life. It is true that the countryman feels the steadiness of the life of Nature; he does not 'glance upon the hours in restless pride' but neither does he look upon them in hope. He feels that what has been will be. It is exactly this kind of resignation which we hear in Wordsworth after his long contemplation of the River Duddon. And incidentally, these lines are more certainly pantheistic than anything he wrote in youth, though they were written long after he had attached himself to the Church of England.

> And may thy Poet, cloud-born Stream! be free—
> The sweets of earth contentedly resigned,
> And each tumultuous working left behind

[1] *On Nature's Invitation.* O.W. p. 621.

At seemly distance—to advance like Thee;
Prepared, in peace of heart, in calm of mind
And soul, to mingle with Eternity!

.   .   .   .   .

Still glides the Stream, and shall for ever glide;
The Form remains, the Function never dies;
While we, the brave, the mighty, and the wise,
We Men, who in our morn of youth defied
The elements, must vanish;—be it so!
Enough, if something from our hands have power
To live, and act, and serve the future hour;
And if, as toward the silent tomb we go,
Through love, through hope, and faith's transcendent dower,
We feel that we are greater than we know.

(*The River Duddon.* Sonnet xxxiv. O.W. p. 384)

The words may speak of faith; the voice is the voice of resignation.

Such were, I suggest, some of the consequences of the religion of Nature for Nature's priest. What were the consequences for the laity?

THE PHILOSOPHY OF NATURE

The doctrine of Nature and Man which Wordsworth strove to establish was not so baneful in its effects on others as the foregoing review might lead us to suppose. It was a mixture of truth and error, there being more of truth in his view of Nature, and more of error in his view of Man. We have already gathered from our study his leading ideas on Nature. Briefly restated they are: The universe is inter-fused throughout by an eternal creative spirit. It is a spirit of love which he sometimes speaks of as God, but more frequently as Nature. The physical universe is the pure signature of the Creator—the forms of Nature are 'types and symbols of eternity'.

The mind of man, being animated by this same spirit, is

73

specially fitted to enjoy and to understand these symbols. There is a universal power

> ...And fitness in the latent qualities
> And essences of things, by which the mind
> Is moved by feelings of delight. (Bk ii, ll. 344–7)

The feelings of delight attach themselves to those objects through which the Spirit desires to lead a man to the truth. If a man will be wisely passive in the presence of nature he will find his feelings purified and enlarged, and he will receive knowledge fitted to his needs. Moreover, in this process, he may have rare moments in which he is lifted above his usual existence into a communion with the Spirit, in which he perceives the true life of the universe.

Wordsworth's confidence in man is based on his belief in the peculiar fitness of the mind to perceive truth through external nature. If for any reason a generation, e.g. the Hitler Youth, should become perverted, that need not be cause for undue anxiety, for the ever-living universe, acting in conjunction with certain indestructible dispositions of the human mind, is always tending to bring men back to the truth. But it follows that truth is most likely to be found with those who live closest to nature. The countryman, because his passions 'are incorporated with beautiful and permanent forms of nature' has deeper feelings and truer thoughts than the townsman. All evils—greed, meanness, jealousy, and the greater evils of ambition and pride which disturb the equilibrium of society and create further evils of social and economic injustice—are due to getting away from nature. If a man finds he has gone into wrong ways, he can be set right by returning to nature and to solitude. 'A world of fresh sensations will open upon him as his mind puts off its infirmities...and precious feelings of disinterested, that is, self-disregarding joy and love may be regenerated and restored.'[1] Wordsworth insisted so strongly on the interaction of nature and the human mind, that to do justice to his views, it will be necessary to survey not only his view of Nature, but also of the Imagination and of Man.

I. NATURE

(a) 'TYPES AND SYMBOLS OF ETERNITY'

The view that the entire world of nature is purely and solely a revelation of God has an attraction for the human mind.[2] The advantages of such a view if it could be established are obvious. It would place the criterion of judgement and the inspiration of conduct outside particular events in history, subject as these are to varieties of interpretation which grow in complexity as time distances the events. Nature preceded human speech; nature is available to all men everywhere and at all times.

Wordsworth reflecting on what he had learned as a child and a boy, from the Bible of the universe, was led to the

[1] Reply to letter of Mathetes in *The Friend*, 1809. (*Prose Works of W. Wordsworth*, edited A. B. Grosart, vol. i, p. 320.)

[2] The idea of natural forms as types and symbols of Eternity has been worked out in some detail by Mary Webb in *The Spring of Joy*. A single passage must suffice to show her close kinship in feeling and in thought with Wordsworth:

'Just as a certain air introduced continually in a piece of music expresses the idea of the composer so this perpetual reincarnation of the same cabalistic signs in nature might help us, if we could gather the scattered meanings, to a clearer understanding of the plasmic force behind them, a force patient and vast, vouchsafing no explanation. In this occult script the world might find a new bible of spiritual enlightenment—a writing, not in fire upon tables of stone but in subtle traceries on young leaves and buds. Have not all symbolic artists, children, and priests of new religions some intuition of this? For the thought—so dim and so dear—that all true contours are a direct message from God, is rooted deep in the minds of the simple-hearted, who are the Magi of the world.'

(*The Spring of Joy*, p. 187)

view that 'the forms of Nature have a passion in themselves', which men could discern (*The Prelude*, Bk xii, l. 290). He developed this view in a letter written in 1802, to a correspondent, John Wilson, who had inquired what effect natural environment had upon character. Wordsworth replied that 'there cannot be a doubt that in tracts of country where images of danger, melancholy, and grandeur, or loveliness, softness, and ease prevail, they will make themselves felt powerfully in forming the characters of the people'.[1] The view of nature here expressed implies that natural forms have fixed spiritual meanings—in other words that beauty is objective. We are not here concerned with the truth of this view but with its consequences. Wordsworth's view amounted to this—that a child of Nature or a man in a healthy state of mind[2] will perceive the universe as it really is. The man whose outlook is unhealthy will find the 'array of outward circumstance and visible form what his (unhealthy) passion makes it' (Bk xii, ll. 286–9), but the mind of the pure man will be a clear mirror reflecting the true universe—he will recognize the grandeur and loveliness which the Creator has put into natural forms.

This view of nature, set in an adequate philosophy of Man, might have had a potent effect for good. Stated as it was, however, it may have had some rather curious ethical consequences. The view that beauty is objective was widely held in the nineteenth century. It was applied not only to nature but to the imaginative works of man. Certain productions were great art, great music, great architecture. However, an outer uniformity of judgement was accompanied by an inner nervousness, because no one knew how

---

[1] L.W. *Early Letters*, p. 293.

[2] 'Healthy state of mind' I take to be the equivalent of Wordsworth's phrase in the Preface to the *Lyrical Ballads* 'healthful state of association'. By this Hartleian expression he meant a person whose feelings had been formed by association with the beautiful forms of Nature.

the standards of beauty were being determined. If Wordsworth could have said, concerning a later passage in the
same letter, words to this effect—'In those high mystical
moments in which we see into the life of things, I have
become possessed by a spirit which has shed a light on my
more normal hours, and has revealed to me that gorse is a
beautiful plant, and not unsightly as Cowper thought, that
the nightingale is not a melancholy bird, nor the cry of the
owl necessarily boding'[1]—if he could have said that, he
would have given men some hint of how to discover and to
test beauty for themselves. It would have been consistent
with his request in the Preface to the *Lyrical Ballads*, that
his readers should judge for themselves. He wrote against
the practice of judging a composition according to what
some other class of people might think. But by saying that
natural forms had fixed characters and that these could only
be truly apprehended by 'natural' men—in practice that
meant the small class of dalesmen of his native regions—he
tended to set up the very practice which he condemned.
His own manner of writing encouraged it. It was well for
him to be moved by the beauty of dawn on the Thames, but
to write 'Dull would he be of soul' who did not feel it, was
to set up an orthodoxy of the feelings—to risk making the
living calendar more joyless than the formal one.

It would be absurd to lay at Wordsworth's door the sins
of Mr George Pontifex who at the sight of Mt Blanc[2]
nearly fainted, and then wrote a rhapsody in bad verse,[3]

---

[1] L.W. *Early Letters*, p. 296.
[2] The mention of Mt Blanc serves as a reminder that the young Wordsworth was entirely free from the tyranny of conventional responses—

> '...That day we first
> Beheld the summit of Mount Blanc, and grieved
> To have a soulless image on the eye
> Which had usurp'd upon a living thought
> That never more could be.' (*The Prelude*, Bk vi, ll. 452–6)

[3] Samuel Butler, *The Way of All Flesh*.

but was not Butler satirizing a convention of the Victorians which Wordsworth may unwittingly have helped to create?

It is worth encroaching on our study of the natural man to pursue this matter a little further. Wordsworth's insistence on the virtues of the dalesmen was partly due to a real concern for society. He saw the beginning of a situation which has developed serious proportions since his day, in which the mind was in danger of being blunted and debilitated by 'gross and violent stimulants'.[1] By these he did not mean only 'frantic novels, sickly and stupid German tragedies'.[1] He saw that the hourly communication of news of battles involving thousands of men, and even the accumulation of people in cities itself, meant that the mind became exhausted by constant attempts to adjust itself to new phenomena, and so was likely to be driven into torpor. Furthermore, in cities the individual was apt to become submerged in the mere mass. It was a reverence for the human mind and a concern for the dignity of the individual which led him to condemn city life and to extol the simple life of the dalesman who had a manageable number of people to care for, and was thus able to lead a true emotional life.

By writing of the strength and purity of the affections of simple people as well as by his poems of nature, he hoped to 'rectify men's feelings, . . . to render their feelings more sane, pure, and permanent, in short, more consonant to nature, that is, to eternal nature'.[2] That was, indeed, a worthy purpose and he achieved considerable success in it. Matthew Arnold, John Stuart Mill and William Hale White, to name only three, all paid tribute to Wordsworth's power to recreate and uphold their emotional life. But it is possible that Wordsworth's efforts sometimes had rather different results, and this for two reasons.

[1] Preface to *Lyrical Ballads*. L.B. p. 13.
[2] Letter to Wilson, June 1802. L.W. *Early Letters*, p. 295.

In the first place, he was not showing forth the life of the dalesmen in its entirety, as he might have done by writing novels. He wrote poems in which, as he said, the feeling gave importance to the action and not vice versa. This tended to bring the feelings into unusual prominence. And secondly, Wordsworth did not fully understand the people he was writing about. He was not living their life, nor did he understand it by an imaginative effort. He merely reported it. There is not a single character in Wordsworth's poems whose sufferings we really feel with any intensity. When he tells us that he and the Wanderer were moved at the sufferings of Margaret (*The Excursion*, Bk 1) the effect is to make us feel that they must have been persons of an exquisite degree of sensibility which is beyond our reach. I suggest that this was not infrequently the effect on his contemporaries. When we take into consideration also Wordsworth's frequent references to the hollowness of town life, we see that the resulting effect on the townsman was likely to be a certain nervousness about his own feelings coupled with reverence for the dalesman as a mysterious figure of ideal feelings. The rising intellectual classes, the people who read Wordsworth's poems, wanted to have the right feelings. At the same time they could not be dalesmen. The safest thing seemed to be to let it be known that they had strong feelings. They could not then be far wrong. It is possible that in this way Wordsworth unconsciously contributed to the strange Victorian seriousness about feelings, in particular to their solemnity about death. It would not be well to pursue such a speculation too far. But was it not perhaps an unhappy warrior with a conscience about the happy warrior he 'should wish to be' whom Mr Bernard Shaw had to deflate in the name of common sense, in *Arms and the Man*?

(*b*) 'THE BIBLE OF THE UNIVERSE'

Attractive as is the view that nature can be the mind's Bible, the difficulties of it are obvious, and in fact, it has never commended itself universally to mankind. Altogether apart from the difficulty that we may read back our own moods and thoughts into nature, there is the possibility that the deep cleavage between good and evil which divides human nature may extend through the whole of nature. The popular attitude towards butterflies and flowers on the one hand and to spiders and slugs on the other seems tacitly to support such a view.

In the second place the difficulty of interpreting the text of nature is enormous. In this we might hope to receive some help from the scientists, but unhappily we do not. They have extended our knowledge of the physical world so that the wonder, as well as the burden, of the mystery ever increases, but they do not seem to know what interpretation to put on their discoveries. One who is both a scientist and a theologian, Canon Raven, sees nature as a revelation of the Creator, and he finds that revelation to be of the same quality and meaning as the revelation in the Christian Gospel.[1] Such a view makes it not impossible that Man should find at least some inspiration for right conduct in the contemplation of nature. But another able theologian, Dr Albert Schweitzer, has concluded that no kind of life-view can be built up from a world view—in other words that our view of nature can have no relevance for our conduct.[2]

Nature is a mystery 'vouchsafing no explanation'. That Man should live in any simple harmony with Nature is an illusory hope. The attempt to do so was satirized by Dr Johnson in *Rasselas* and caused Matthew Arnold to

[1] See *The Creator Spirit*, especially ch. IV.
[2] *Civilisation and Ethics*, ch. XVII.

exclaim impatiently against an Independent preacher who proclaimed it:

> 'In Harmony with Nature?' Restless fool
> Who with such heat dost preach what were to thee
> When true, the last impossibility;
> To be like Nature strong, like Nature cool;
> Know, man hath all that Nature hath, but more,
> And in that more lie all his hopes of good.
> Nature is cruel; man is sick of blood;
> Nature is stubborn; man would fain adore:
> Nature is fickle; man hath need of rest;
> Nature forgives no debt, and fears no grave;
> Man would be mild and with safe conscience blest.
> Man must begin, know this, where Nature ends;
> Nature and man can never be fast friends.
> Fool if thou canst not pass her, rest her slave!

But Arnold, too, could on occasion turn to Nature for restoration of feeling and power.

> "Ah! once more," I cried, "Ye Stars, Ye Waters,
> On my heart your mighty charm renew:
> Still, still, let me, as I gaze upon you,
> Feel my soul becoming vast like you."
>
> From the intense, clear, star-sown vault of heaven,
> Over the lit sea's unquiet way,
> In the rustling night air came the answer—
> "Wouldst thou *be* as these are? *Live* as they."[1]

That Arnold could write thus after all that he had said against Nature in the poem previously quoted, seems to show that there is a recurrent longing in the heart of man to be in harmony with Nature. But we have already illustrated from Wordsworth's own history how difficult it is to achieve this harmony. All 'the mighty sum of things for ever speaking' cannot speak all that man needs to hear.

[1] *Self-Dependence.*

Another poet, Francis Thompson, who, like Wordsworth, was 'long time benighted heart and mind'—found this difficulty of reading nature, insuperable.

> In vain my tears were wet on Heaven's grey cheek.
> For ah! we know not what each other says,
> These things and I; in sound *I* speak—
> *Their* sound is but their stir, they speak by silences,[1]

Wordsworth was never able to give an example of a man whom Nature had brought into harmony with herself by her own unaided speech. He seems to have intended Peter Bell for such a person. But the poem of that name was much revised, and in the form in which it was published, Peter's conversion was achieved partly with the aid of human speech. Nature by her ministry of fear, by adroitly presenting things as they were not, certainly prepared his mind and led him to where he could hear the voice of the Methodist preacher, but it was the preacher's message of salvation which really breathed into him 'a second breath more searching than the breath of spring'. As in *The Prelude*, so in the letter to Wilson already quoted, Wordsworth admitted that if the forms of Nature were to produce their good effect on character, 'there must be a peculiar sensibility of *original* organization, combining with moral accidents'[2] —again the admission that the text of nature alone is not sufficient for 'the soul of all (our) moral being'. And in fact we do not notice in the simple natural characters Wordsworth portrayed any special qualities of faith or resilience or adaptability. They are no more and no less at the mercy of calamity than any city-dweller. The grand and beautiful forms of Nature are not so many parts of their armour of faith, they are only shapes of a dreamworld which com-

---

[1] *The Hound of Heaven.*
[2] L.W. *Early Letters*, p. 294 (my italics).

pensates for 'the many shapes of joyless day-light'.[1] Yet Wordsworth thought of the dalesmen as imaginative men, though their lives do not seem to accord with his idea of the imaginative life.

II. IMAGINATION

Wordsworth would probably have accepted Uncle Gottfried in Romain Rolland's *Jean Christophe* as a fair example of the simple Imaginative Man. The occasion on which the little pedlar first goes for a walk with Christopher on the banks of the Rhine at sunset, gives a perfect illustration of the difference between the true and the false imaginative life. After the boy has tired himself out with teasing his uncle he falls silent for a while. The evening is peaceful and the river flowing quietly. Presently, seeming to arise from the stillness of the evening, a clear, pure melody is heard; Christopher looks round in surprise—his uncle is singing; and, still more surprising to Christopher, it is a beautiful song. He asks his uncle to sing another, but Gottfried refuses—the occasion has given its appropriate natural song and he cannot go beyond what is given. He asks Christopher to sing—and the boy gives one of his vain and meretricious compositions, fumes of the dust and vanity of the small-state musical society in which his father moved. He is mortified when Gottfried pronounces it ugly. This is the false imaginative life as Gottfried's is the true one. But would Gottfried have called himself 'his own upholder'? I think it doubtful. Yet there was about his life something more resilient than about Wordsworth's natural men, something which helped him to stand the derision and the

[1] A good example of this is *The Farmer of Tilsbury Vale*:
> 'In the throng of the town like a stranger is he,
> Like one whose own country's far over the sea;
> And Nature, while through the great city he hies,
> Full ten times a day takes his heart by surprise.'

WORDSWORTH'S VIEW OF NATURE

poverty, to see the death of hope and yet to hope again. He would have felt truly at the loss of a relative, but he would not have pined away from the strength of his affection. His attitude was not resignation, it was acceptance.[1]

But such an attitude requires an effort of will. Wordsworth seemed to believe—a typical Romantic failing—that once the imaginative life had been achieved it would continue automatically. But there is an abundance of testimony that there are periods of life, during which the life of the imagination has to be achieved anew each day and is only so renewed by effort.

Wordsworth said that the prime and vital principle of the imaginative life was within us, in the recesses of our nature. This is true inasmuch as it is not possible to borrow the gift, and also true in the sense of William Watson's lines:

> In far retreats of elemental mind
> Obscurely comes and goes
> The imperative breath of song.[2]

But does not the first line of this quotation hint that song comes not from *our* nature but from Nature, as Wordsworth used the word, meaning the Spirit interfused in the universe? If the Spirit is the source of the imaginative life—and Wordsworth perhaps implied this when he said that imagination was inseparable from intellectual love—then the Spirit and not Man, must be the object, and the judge, of that life. Wordsworth wanted to make Man the supreme arbiter of all things, even spiritual things. In his letter of advice to the young he warned the young man against the 'false Gloriana' of worldly success. But he can only offer him as an alternative, 'Intellectual Prowess, with a pale cheek and a serene brow, leading in chains Truth,

[1] At the end of *L'Adolescent* he consoles Christopher: 'On ne fait pas ce qu'on veut. On veut et on vit. Cela fait deux. Il faut se consoler. L'essentiel, vois-tu, c'est de ne pas se laisser de vouloir et de vivre. Le reste ne dépend pas de nous.'

[2] *Lacrimae Musarum.*

her beautiful and modest captive'.[1] We are apt to laugh at such a solemn absurdity, but it represents an attitude which may have unpleasant consequences.

To inspire Man to 'start out of the worm-like state in which he is' and thereafter to live the life of the creative imagination, was so far good, but to do so without setting up any higher judge of that life than Man, was to call into being a race of gods and devils—to produce a situation which held far more dreadful possibilities than were present in a simple community which asked no more than to go on with its own habitual occupations. It is obvious that the imagination may be healthy or diseased. Wordsworth had written of Oswald in *The Borderers*—'his imagination is powerful, being strengthened by the habit of picturing possible forms of society where his crimes would be no longer crimes'[2]—the same might safely be predicated of Hitler. The imagination may recreate the world according to the mind's own desire. To rule the senses by imagination is obviously the first task, but the vital problem is, in whose name is the imagination to be ruled? It was not sufficient simply to leave the imagination undefined, nor to fill it with a vague content of 'intellectual love'. In youth all things grow together, the life of the body and the life of the spirit. But there comes a time when intellectual love and human love part company. Wordsworth had really reached this point though he did not want to recognize it. He wanted to go back to the former position when he had been an undivided being. It was because he found this going back to the natural life so difficult that he insisted so loudly upon it. It was not the way to the true life of the imagination. Moreover, he did not fully understand the people he thought he was representing—the dalesmen.

[1] Reply to Mathetes, 1809. *Prose Works of W. Wordsworth*, edited A. B. Grosart, vol. 1, p. 316.

[2] *Wordsworth's Poetical Works: Early Poems.* Oxford, 1940. Edited E. de Selincourt, p. 346.

III. MAN

'OF ALL VISIBLE NATURES CROWN'

Wordsworth said in the letter to Wilson already quoted that he wanted his poems to please 'human nature as it has been and ever will be'.[1] We were to find the best measure of this

...by stripping our own hearts naked, and by looking out of ourselves toward men who lead the simplest lives, and those most according to nature; men who have never known false refinements, wayward and artificial desires....This latter class is the most to be depended upon, but it is very small in number. People in our rank of life are perpetually falling into one sad mistake, namely, that of supposing that human nature and the persons they associate with are one and the same thing. Whom do we generally associate with? Gentlemen, persons of fortune, professional men, ladies, persons who can afford to buy...(expensive and elegant) books. These persons are, it is true, a part of human nature, but we err lamentably if we suppose them to be fair representatives of the vast mass of human existence.[1]

The small class of professional people and gentry are not fair representatives of mankind, but neither is that even smaller class in whom Wordsworth finds true human nature. But he certainly pinned his faith to a fine type of man. The dalesmen of Cumberland, hardy, independent, strong and generous in feeling, might well seem to him to present human nature as it ought to be. It is a similar class of mountain farmers and shepherds who form the backbone of the very successful Swiss democracy. Wordsworth would have found Schiller's Wilhelm Tell a man after his own heart. In Wordsworth's mind the dalesman was not essentially different—and in this we can see how little the Revolution had really changed his ideas—from that natural man depicted in *Descriptive Sketches*:

> Once a man entirely free, alone and wild,
> Was blest as free—for he was Nature's child.

[1] L.W. *Early Letters*, p. 295.

He, all superior but his God disdain'd,
Walk'd none restraining, and by none restrain'd
Confess'd no law but what his reason taught,
Did all he wish'd and wish'd but what he ought.

(ll. 520-5)

The dalesman was right because he was natural. Wordsworth's whole social and political thinking was governed by the thought that the actions and requirements of the dalesmen are self-evidently right. The business of politics is to provide or to preserve from encroachment, the conditions in which the dalesman can flourish.

Wordsworth said that he heard from the dalesmen 'a song of honour'. Unhappily, he never let us hear it. He was content simply to tell us *that* he heard it. And it is doubtful if he heard all the undertones in the music of that song. For he was not living the life of a dalesman. If, as he claimed (*Prel.* Bk xii, ll. 173–5), he wanted to discover the relation between agricultural labour and virtue, he should have tried to live the question, i.e. to put himself in the position of a man who is in a strict economic relationship with Nature, who must work according to her rhythm or starve. He would then have discovered that the essence of that life is not in its particular conditions—the independent possession of a modest property in land—but in the discipline which Nature imposes. It is the acceptance of that discipline which is the source of the vitality and the sense of independence which characterizes the dalesmen. Wordsworth was right that the beauty of nature in the Lake District gave them a sense of the dignity of their occupations, but these fortunate circumstances were nevertheless the accidents rather than the substance of their life. They knew that Nature was a power to be respected but also to be mastered. The old miner in Galsworthy's play *Strife*, who is for calling off the strike because Nature says it is time to stop, is laughed to scorn by his fellow-workers. They listen

87

with approval to their leader, Roberts, when he says in effect that it is necessary to punch Nature in the face to get results from her. It might be suggested that Wordsworth felt neither the pinch nor the punch of Nature. The life of the dalesmen was not a spontaneous outflow from a pure natural source of energy in them; it was an equilibrium resulting from a conflict of forces. The dignity of that life, like the beauty of a garden, was achieved by Man's working partly with, partly against Nature. Nature alone will reduce any garden to weeds in a short time—not a sight to 'lift the Being into magnanimity'. It would have been inexcusable to mention so obvious a fact had it not been that Wordsworth so frequently overlooked the parallel truth about human character. The burden of humanity's song from the beginning has been that Man's nature is not single but dual, or even multiple, and life a permanent conflict.[1]

Wordsworth, not understanding the essence of the dalesmen's life, supposed that a harmonious society might be achieved if all men might have the same conditions of modest independence that they had. He wrote

> Why is this glorious Creature [Man] to be found
> One only in ten thousand? What one is,
> Why may not many be? What bars are thrown
> By Nature in the way of such a hope?
> Our animal wants and the necessities
> Which they impose, are these the obstacles?
> If not, then others vanish into air.   (Bk xii, ll. 90–6)

---

[1] Wordsworth must have known St Paul's famous expression of this conflict in Romans vii. 18–25 and he may also have known Goethe's lines in *Faust*:

> 'Zwei Seelen wohnen ach! in meiner Brust;
> Die eine will sich von der andern trennen.
> Die eine hält, in derber Liebeslust,
> Sich an die Welt mit klammernden organen;
> Die andre hebt gewaltsam sich vom Dust,
> Zu den Gefilden hoher Ahnen.'

It really is difficult to understand how Wordsworth came to write that last line. For it is clear as day, that though Nature throw no other bars, there is a much stronger force working against goodness than animal wants—one which by no means vanishes into air. It is surprising that the man who had seen during the Revolution the 'reservoir of guilt . . . filled up from age to age' (Bk x, ll. 437–8) and who had analysed the evil in himself with such penetration as he had done in the Preface to *The Borderers*, should have paid such scant attention to the power of evil. We see here one of the worst results of his attempts to forget the years of his trouble, and to live on the tide of present happiness. He is back in the old Romantic position, believing that Man is inherently good and that evil is only an illegitimate extension of a just desire for self-preservation. Nature will flourish if the opposite evils of false refinement and poverty are removed. The husband of Margaret in *The Ruined Cottage* is a good and contented man until poverty sours him. The sailor in *Guilt and Sorrow* is innocent until an injustice done to him sets up in him a passion of vengeance.

This view of Man is the origin of that Utopian liberalism which believes that if Government will secure fair conditions for all, a happy and stable society will automatically result. Not only does this view not understand the nature of evil, it can give no direction to society because it does not understand that human life is dynamic, not static. Furthermore, when individual liberty is made the first of the fair conditions for all, life immediately becomes unfair to some —it is weighted in favour of the strong. The consequences of this view of Man are that the evil forces are always at an advantage, and the good can only imperfectly right things later. Dorothy Wordsworth noticed this effect. In a letter to Catherine Clarkson in 1817, she wrote:

. . . I rejoice that Government seems now to be rouzed to vigilance; but it is our misfortune that we never act till our negligence has made it *necessary* that something should be done...why not have amended the Poor Laws when the poor were suffering less? Why not *then* have established Savings Banks?[1]

She attributed these conditions to negligence, but I suggest that they were also partly due to false philosophy. A society founded on the Natural Man is always in this position. It is only the Imaginative Man who can be beforehand with evil.

It would be foolish to underestimate the amount of evil that can be removed by improving material conditions, but the source of evil, as of good, does not lie in particular conditions. Evil is the unredeemed will to power. In the England of Wordsworth's time the desire for power, taking to itself power production, was beginning to produce economic and social injustice on a scale impossible in a purely agricultural community. Wordsworth wrote:

> True it is, where oppression worse than death
> Salutes the Being at his birth, where grace
> Of culture hath been utterly unknown,
> And labour in excess and poverty
> From day to day pre-occupy the ground
> Of the affections, and to Nature's self
> Oppose a deeper nature, there indeed
> Love cannot be.   (*The Prelude*, Bk xii, ll. 194–201)

But it was just such 'oppression worse than death' which was the lot of thousands of child workers in factories and mines in the new industrial society. They woke every day to 'labour in excess and poverty'. Incidentally, how helpless a thing was the Wordsworthian 'Nature' if oppression could successfully oppose a *deeper* nature to it. Wordsworth, not seeing life in terms of an intense conflict of good and evil, did not appear to understand that it was the task of all who loved England as he did to try to establish in the new society as much of justice and liberty—of Nature in his

[1] L.W. vol. ii, p. 787.

sense—as possible. But it seemed that he could only lament the evils of town-life, and point to the life of the dalesmen as the only beautiful life. He had something of the perfectionism of sensitive spirits[1] and while he sympathized with some kinds of reformers, e.g. the Chartists, he was against the use of force in bringing in reforms. He wanted to wait for 'God's good time'[2] and pointed out that 'even the interests of Eternity become distorted when looked at through impure means'.[2] But such an attitude would never have secured the passing of the Factory Acts.

His political action was ineffective. His political thinking, however, was by no means valueless. He had acute and sometimes prophetic insight.[3] It was partly his love of his native dales that helped to develop his strong patriotism. This patriotism was not insular. He recognized that other peoples were forming into nations, that knowledge was spreading and that these peoples must eventually receive constitutional liberty. He looked forward to the day when Italy and Germany should be strong and united nations. His strong sense of independence showed him that it was to the interest of every freedom-loving country to maintain the freedom of the others, and even the liberty of France he only wished to restrain as far as this principle required.

[1] There was, however, a blind spot in this sensitiveness, in his thought about France. He openly rejoiced in the discomfiture of the French in 1812, and wrote then that 'Carnage was God's daughter'.

[2] Letter to J. K. Miller (17 December 1831) quoted by E. C. Batho, *The Later Wordsworth*, p. 182.

[3] E.g. he saw that the 'manufacturers' (=factory workers) were likely to get too many new ideas by reason of their nomadic life: '...every individual is constantly being brought into contact with new notions and new feelings and being unsettled in his own accordingly.' (Letter to Wrangham, June 1808.) Therefore he is in favour of setting up Public Libraries. They may act as a kind of regulator to the townspeople, steadying their ideas by putting them in touch with 'the great Nature that exists in works of mighty Poets'.

Thus his patriotism and his nationalism followed logically from his view of the requirements of the independent dalesmen. Nationalism was really the counterpart of Nature in the political life of Man. Just as his conception of Nature was permeated with unrecognized Christian elements, so also his nationalism was founded on strong moral principles whose origin was not always acknowledged. One of his great political principles was that a house divided against itself cannot stand. Therefore all institutions, including the Church, must serve the nation. His argument against the equalization of the incomes of the clergy shows a real understanding of the problems involved, but it is inspired throughout by a concern for the nation rather than for the Church.[1]

His tract on the Convention of Cintra is perhaps his best, as it is his longest, piece of political writing. It reveals the strength as well as the dangers of his political ideas and ideals. Britain is to fight for the liberty of Spain as she had fought for Portugal, not for any military necessity in securing ports and harbours, but for 'victory in the empire of reason and for the strongholds of the imagination'. His belief in the essential soundness of the common man makes him 'still of that odious class of men called democrats'. When a central government in Spain became necessary it should have passed from the small juntas—which had only failed because they had not had time to gain experience —not to an oligarchy, but to the Cortes, the government of the whole people.

But his belief in the natural rights of man led him to the view that a nation may be judge in its own cause, and that when a people is strongly moved in a good cause it speaks with the voice of God. It is obvious that such beliefs contain the seeds of fascism and political immorality. But in Wordsworth they were held upright by his strong sense of

[1] *Prose Works of W. Wordsworth*, edited A. B. Grosart, vol. I, pp. 285–94, especially p. 289.

principle. His love of the nation made him distrust the Whigs because they had opposed the government at a time when the life of the nation was endangered. But his respect for principle made him look with disfavour on the Tories because they frequently abandoned principles for momentary advantages. Strong though his patriotism was, he did not make the nation into a sacred myth. Nations were only the aggregate of the individuals who composed them, and were to be governed by the same laws as individuals. At the same time he gave a remarkable example of having his precepts the way he wanted them for the sake of the nation —and this exposes the danger of making the nation the first object of devotion. When a nation is being unjustly attacked by a power of unlimited wickedness, her only true course, according to Wordsworth, is honourably to defend her rights, by such exercise of force as may be required. It may be the right course, but not for the reason he gave, which was that 'The Christian exhortation for the individual is here the precept for Nations—"Be ye therefore perfect; even as your Father which is in Heaven, is perfect"'.[1] This passage (Matt. v. 48, A.V.) concludes the chapter in which we have been bidden not to resist evil, and to love our enemies. Moreover these words were spoken by a Citizen of an occupied country, and nothing that He said can be interpreted as an exhortation to His people to throw off their oppressors.

It has seemed to me necessary to treat this matter at some length because I believe that this view of the nation, and the foundation on which it is based is mistaken. Wordsworth derived this view of national sovereignty from his belief in the essential rightness of the dalesman—the

[1] *Prose Works of W. Wordsworth*, edited A. B. Grosart, vol. I, p. 170. One conclusion of this line of Wordsworth's thinking is wittily given in Mr Shaw's *St Joan*, when De Stogumber says: 'How can what an Englishman believes be heresy?'

natural man. He appealed to the New Testament, but there is no warrant in the New Testament for the belief that the characteristics of the natural man are the salt which can preserve society. If the natural man could have kept society healthy and stable, there had been no need of a Gospel.

The good life is not a mixture of self-assertion and generosity which is natural in the natural man and uneasy in the self-conscious man. It lies in an attitude of complete self-giving to a Reality which is beyond the self. It will be said that that is a counsel of perfection too high for mortality. Undoubtedly that is true, but I believe that our society will be more hopeful if we can acknowledge it as an ideal, and strive in that direction. Fortunately, the idea is gaining ground that something of that national sovereignty, of which Wordsworth was an early prophet, ought to be surrendered for the greater good of humanity. In an hour of national weakness, Wordsworth invoked the spirit of Milton; we, in going forward as we hope to better days for mankind, might do well to look for our inspiration not to Milton, but to his master, Cromwell, who when the modern experiment in democracy was in its infancy, recognized that the representatives of the people do not assemble in the first place to assert the will of the people, but in humility to try to discover what that will ought to be.

CHAPTER FIVE

NATURE IN THE LATER POEMS[1]

I. POEMS 1802—1807

The influential ideas of any writer are apt to be not those of his mature thought but those, usually of his earlier years, which find expression in a telling phrase or paradox. As Mr Cobban has observed, after Rousseau had begun his *Le Contrat Social* with the phrase 'L'homme est né libre et partout il est dans les fers' it mattered little that he spent the rest of his book riveting governmental chains more firmly on the people.[2] Similarly, after Wordsworth had declared his belief that

> One impulse from a vernal wood,
> May teach you more of man,
> Of moral evil and of good,
> Than all the sages can.

—he was hailed as a prophet of Nature. He seemed to give authority to many in later generations who were tired of institutional religion and claimed that they could worship better in the fields than in a church. Not all of those who read his inspired lyrics knew that in later years Nature's priest had found it necessary to admit Duty as well as Nature as a teacher of morality, and few knew that *The Excursion* contained an impeccable statement of orthodox Christianity.

It is after his settlement at Grasmere that a note of uneasiness comes into his poems. It is difficult to know

---

[1] I.e. later than the *Lyrical Ballads*.
[2] A. Cobban, *Edmund Burke*, ch. v, p. 135.

whether the question behind them represents a permanent
state of mind or only a brief mood, but certainly the question
is there in poems like *Resolution and Independence* (1802)
and *Personal Talk* (published 1807). In the former poem
we hear of

>...the fear that kills;
>And hope that is unwilling to be fed;
>Cold, pain, and labour, and all fleshly ills;
>And mighty Poets in their misery dead.[1]

He takes encouragement from the decrepit old man,[2]
but that he should need to, hints that the religion of Nature
has fallen on difficult days.

In the case of *Personal Talk* the question is posed by the
very existence of the poem. If Wordsworth had really
been living a vigorous life of the imagination and 'seeing
into the life of things', would he not have been showing
forth in his poems what he had seen? He would have forgotten all about 'sprightly malice' and 'evil-speaking'.
That he considered such matters at all, meant that they did
'come nigh' him, though he denied it. It is the parable of
the house swept and garnished. He hears the evil voices at
the door because there is no activity in the house. How
could there be, on the view that Man's life is simply to be,
and to contemplate nature—to keep pure not by active love,
but by shrinking from every combination of circumstances

---

[1] O.W. p. 197.

[2] We know from Dorothy's journal that the old man had given up his
trade of leech-gathering, and lived by begging. Nevertheless, his attitude
may well have been one of fortitude. It is more difficult for a man of independent spirit to maintain 'so firm a mind' when compelled to beg, than
merely during hard times in his own trade. Wordsworth did not mention
the leech-gatherer's change of occupation because he could portray the old
man's character truthfully and·more forcefully by leaving it out. The view
of Señor de Madariaga (*Shelley, Calderon and Other Essays*, pp. 163–5)
that Wordsworth invented the resolution and the independence, seems to
me wholly unacceptable.

which might lead to impurity? The poem is really a dialogue of two voices within himself:

> Better than such discourse, doth silence long,
> Long, barren silence, square with my desire;
> To sit without emotion, hope, or aim,
> In the loved presence of my cottage-fire,
> And listen to the flapping of the flame.[1]

Was this the way the prophet of Nature spent his time? Was this a gospel to rouse 'the vacant and the vain to noble raptures'?

> Nor can I not believe but that hereby
> Great gains are mine—[1]

and yet—to spend a lifetime reading Spenser and Shakespeare; was that likely to help forward a better day for mankind?

> And thus from day to day my little boat
> Rocks in its harbour peaceably—

but the water lapped choppily under the gunwales at times, disturbing the mariner with thoughts of the wide sea and the voyage he was not making.

But until the end of 1804 he maintained, at least in his poems, his original faith in Nature. The sonnet *To Toussaint L'Ouverture* shows that events could still inspire him to proclaim, almost as gladly as he had hailed the early triumphs of the revolution, that Nature was a joint agent with man in the struggle for freedom and liberty.

> ...Thou hast left behind
> Powers that will work for thee; air, earth, and skies;
> There's not a breathing or the common wind
> That will forget thee; thou hast great allies,
> Thy friends are exultations, agonies,
> And love, and man's unconquerable mind.[2]

[1] O.W. p. 488.   [2] O.W. p. 305.

The particular belief that the elements are on the side of freedom did not desert him, but after the events of the year 1805, he could no longer look on nature in any simple optimism. It was a critical year in his development. His sorrow at the loss of his brother, in February of that year, has already been mentioned. We know from his letter to Sir George Beaumont at the time, that the event caused him to meditate upon the subject of personal immortality, and on the nature of God. I believe it may also have had the effect of making him a little ashamed of having lived his whole life 'in pleasant thought, as if life's business were a summer mood'.[1] This feeling, as well as a question whether 'all which we behold [of nature] is full of blessings' appear in the elegiac stanzas on Peele Castle.

> I would have planted thee, thou hoary pile,
> Amid a world how different from this!
> Beside a sea that could not cease to smile;
> On tranquil land, beneath a sky of bliss.
>
> .   .   .   .
>
> Such, in the fond illusion of my heart,
> Such picture would I at that time have made;
> *And seen the soul of truth in every part,*
> A steadfast peace that might not be betrayed.
>
> So once it would have been—'tis so no more;
> I have submitted to a new control:
>
> .   .   .   .
>
> Not for a moment could I now behold
> A smiling sea, and be what I have been:
> The feeling of my loss will ne'er be old;
> This, which I know, I speak with mind serene.[2]

These lines also show how easily the mind tends to see in nature the reflection of its own thoughts. Air, earth and skies do not speak now of freedom and joy, but of mystery

---

[1] *Resolution and Independence.*   [2] O.W. p. 578 (my italics).

and grief. When he came to complete the *Immortality Ode* he recognized the change—

> The clouds that gather round the setting sun,
> Do take a sober colouring from an eye
> That hath kept watch o'er man's mortality.

But he was not immediately thinking of philosophy. At least for a time he had submitted to a new ethical control. We see it in the *Ode to Duty*. But here he was in a dilemma. He could not deny that freedom was not working out happily for him—

> Me this unchartered freedom tires;
> I feel the weight of chance desires;
> My hopes no more must change their name,
> I long for a repose that ever is the same.[1]

—but neither could he deny what he had seen—those enigmatic beings who could somehow be happy and natural, and yet do no wrong—

> Glad hearts! without reproach or blot;
> Who do thy work and know it not.

He rightly believed that spontaneity ought to be possible. He wanted good conduct to come, as Keats wanted poetry to come, as naturally as leaves to the tree. He wanted to be rid of the temptations to self-regard which attend on all deliberated acts of virtue. In *The Waggoner* he had spoken of 'the *pride* of self-denial'. In *Tintern Abbey* he recognized that it is the *unremembered* acts of kindness which flow spontaneously from a being possessed by love, which are the best parts of a good man's life. But it seemed that at least for him the blessings of Nature must be postponed:

> Serene will be our days and bright,
> And happy will our nature be,
> When love is an unerring light,
> And joy its own security.

[1] O.W. p. 492.

We see in this poem too, how straightway his changed attitude is reflected on to nature

> The gentle breezes, the fountains that ran on
> Murmuring so sweetly in themselves
>
> *(The Prelude,* Bk ii, ll. 390–1)

—of nothing but the joy of life, when he was a boy, are now seen to move to the command of Duty:

> Flowers laugh before thee on their beds
> And fragrance in thy footing treads;
> Thou dost preserve the stars from wrong.

But Wordsworth did not help himself or others to find the unerring light he was seeking, by stopping at the thought of Duty. The ode is a sincere statement of his feelings and is not without power, but an appeal to Duty can only be really effective if the reader feels that the writer has a clear understanding of what he means by Duty and from what authority it derives. It is difficult to feel that Wordsworth had this understanding. The same difficulty applies to those patriotic sonnets, written during the Napoleonic wars, in which he tried to rouse England to her duty. Some of these sonnets reached a high level of poetic merit, and in some he hits out hard in rebuke of the evils of the time. But over against the evil which he finds, he can only set a vague humanism, an appeal to undefined traditional values. He bade men remember

> The later Sidney, Marvel, Harrington
> Young Vane, and others who called Milton friend.[1]

—as moralists who 'could act and comprehend'[1]—though few can have known what they acted or comprehended. If he really wanted to restore the public life of the country he should have appealed to something more definite than 'a

[1] *Sonnets on National Independence and Liberty*, Part i, no. xv, O.W. p. 307.

few strong instincts and a few plain rules'.[1] There could be little to stir the mind of youth in phrases like 'the homely beauty of the good old cause';[2] and 'pure religion breathing household laws'.[2] As we have learned from experience of a recent generation on the continent, unless the forces of good can make a powerful, *forward*-looking, imaginative appeal, youth will be likely to prefer the more obvious prizes of 'rapine, avarice and expense'.[3] It is not sufficient to say: 'By the soul only shall the nations be great and free.' So also the Herrenvolk believed. It is necessary to say by what kind of soul.

This vagueness seems to me to derive from that original unwillingness to examine 'Nature', the ground of his faith.

Wordsworth might fume against those who would

> Effeminately level down the truth
> To certain general notions for the sake
> Of being understood at once.
>
> (*The Prelude*, Bk xii, ll. 211–13)

—but if those great conceptions which he was always using—'Nature', 'Imagination', 'Duty', 'Soul'—were not to be understood at once, at least there should have been some guarantee that they could be understood at length. Unhappily, there was no such certainty. The Victorians assumed that everyone knew what was meant by 'pure religion' and what were 'household laws'. But in fact no one was quite sure. Roger Fry tells us that as a child he went about in constant fear because he found that the household laws were an inexplicable hidden code of behaviour, so that he never knew when some quite innocent act might bring wrath on his head.[4] So that here also Wordsworth may have contributed to that outer uniformity

---

[1] *Sonnets on National Independence and Liberty*, Part ii, no. xii, O.W. p. 315.
[2] Ibid. Part i, no. xiii, O.W. p. 307.
[3] Ibid.
[4] *Roger Fry*—a Biography by Virginia Woolf, p. 27.

of conduct coupled with inner insecurity which characterized Victorian society.

Wordsworth's last great utterance before *The Excursion*
was the ode on the *Intimations of Immortality from Recollections of Early Childhood.* It is perhaps his best known and
therefore most influential poem. It is of some importance,
then, that the view of Nature in it appears to show a considerable difference from what we have been led to expect
from Wordsworth. At first sight, as Professor Willey has
said, it looks as though Wordsworth, by shifting all the
glory back into pre-existence and super-nature, had degraded earth into a foster-mother and 'Nature into a medium
to which the heaven born visitant is gradually subdued'.[1]
But on closer inspection, I believe that this change of view
may prove to be more apparent than real. It is difficult to
speak with certainty, because it is difficult to be certain of
what Wordsworth intended by the poem. The difficulty
centres in verse five. After the question 'Whither has fled
the visionary gleam?' are we to understand the ensuing
lines as a statement of belief?—'Our birth *is* but a sleep
and a forgetting'—do we actually 'come from God who is
our home'?—or is this only reverie, the poet's dream of a
possible explanation of our origin? Wordsworth, in the
Fenwick note to the poem, expressly disclaimed any attempt
to inculcate a belief in pre-existence, and admitted what has
been urged against him,[1] the introduction of a piece of
mythology for a merely poetic purpose. But the note does
not entirely relieve him of responsibility. He may not have
wished to influence his readers particularly in the matter of
their beliefs, but the poem does suggest that he himself
believed in pre-existence, and there can be few readers who
in ignorance of the Fenwick note, would suppose that he
was only using a piece of mythology. However that may
be, what stands written in the ode is not inconsistent with

[1] Basil Willey, *The Eighteenth-Century Background*, p. 285.

his utterances elsewhere. In *The Prelude*, which is on the whole a reliable account of his views, there are passages which are the matrix of the idea of pre-existence; the idea is really in them in germ, and is not other than that which is fully explicit in the ode:

> A tract of the same isthmus which we cross
> In progress from our native continent
> To earth and human life.   (Bk v, ll. 560–2)

The only difference, surely, is that in the ode he names our native continent. That he does name it, is perhaps significant. The creed of *The Excursion* is already in being.

Professor Willey appears to think that Wordsworth ascribed 'a *supernatural* endowment to childhood' simply to emphasize the contrast between the child's and the adult's consciousness.[1] But if I have understood *The Prelude* rightly it was not an ascription, it was a belief. Wordsworth never denied the supernatural, either the idea or the word. He wrote of the false child, the dwarf man,

> . . . fear itself,
> Natural or supernatural alike,
> Unless it leap upon him in a dream,
> Touches him not.
>   (*The Prelude*, Bk v, ll. 315–18)

As it seems to me *The Prelude* is permeated throughout with the idea of the supernatural.

And Nature, in the ode, is not to be regarded as the enemy of the supernatural. That it perhaps appears so is because Wordsworth is trying to bring out vividly the contrast between the lost moments of supernatural insight and the blessings of the common day. His use of his terms is not inconsistent with his usage elsewhere.

What is happening is that he is seeing quite clearly at

[1] Op. cit. p. 286 (my italics).

last, the difference between the twó kinds of blessings which Nature had brought him, studied in this book under 'Nature as Education' and 'Nature as Religion'.[1] *One* of his central certainties, but not the more important one, is thàt Nature 'fits our new existence to existing things' (*The Prelude*, Bk i, l. 583) by feelings of delight. He never had any hesitation in saying that the appearances of Nature develop in Man the practical qualities he requires in the light of common day—

> ... Attention comes
> And comprehensiveness and memory,
> From early converse with the works of God
> Among all regions; ...   (Bk vii, ll. 716–19)

But the other and more important certainty is that from Nature he has received 'gleams like the flashing of a shield' (Bk i, l. 614), 'fleeting moods of shadowy exultation' (Bk ii, l. 331) 'a dim and undetermined sense of unknown modes of being, in his thoughts . . . a darkness, call it solitude or blank desertion' (Bk i, ll. 419–22)—in the ode 'blank misgivings of a creature moving about in worlds not realized'. To emphasize the difference between these two aspects of Nature he calls the first aspect 'Earth', in the ode. But by Nature he means what he means throughout *The Prelude*—the breath of God. The Child comes from God; the Youth is Nature's Priest. The Child comes in glory; the Youth has still not lost the vision splendid.

In *The Prelude* he had deemed those 'fleeting moods of shadowy exultation' not profitless, and that for two reasons: that they were 'kindred to our purer mind and intellectual life' (Bk ii, l. 333)—and he had laboured hard with the assistance of the associationist principle to show in what way they were kindred—to show that there was an 'universal power and fitness in the latent qualities and essences of things' (Bk ii, l. 344) which moved the mind

---

[1] See especially supra pp. 19–27.

by feelings of delight. But now, in the ode, he recognized that the other reason really showed the greater profit, and that at the time he had not valued it sufficiently—that 'the soul…retains an obscure sense of possible sublimity' (Bk II, l. 336) has intimations of an immortal spirit in the universe. The profit was in the shadows—not in the exultation.

But now that time has gone. He sees that it cannot be recaptured, and the only consolation, apparently, is 'the philosophic mind'. What kind of consolation that was, appears in *The Excursion*.

II. *THE EXCURSION*[1]

The Excursion was intended as the second of the three books of Wordsworth's long projected philosophical poem on Man, Nature and Society, which was to be called *The Recluse*. Some fragments of the first book were prefixed to it as a Prospectus, but the first and third books were never completed. Thus *The Excursion*, as it stands, is that Gothic church, to use Wordsworth's simile, to which *The Prelude* was intended as an ante-chapel, and it represents the only comprehensive statement of his mature view of life.

Wordsworth was rightly disappointed with *The Excursion*. Even more than about *The Prelude* he felt that a dead weight hung about it. He might have reflected that only a poet of superabundant vitality could have introduced so many actual deaths without producing a dead weight. And *The Excursion* bears clear testimony that Wordsworth was no longer in the first flush of his energy.

The poem might well have been called *The Recluse*. For the first thing that strikes us about it is a curious sense of distance from mankind. We seem to be upon some hillside in the far north of Scotland looking towards the bare shapes of mountains. Few people are seen and for hours there is

[1] All references are to the final text of the poem [1849–50].

no sound save the wind over the grasses and no movement except the shadows of clouds dimming the afternoon sunshine. The effect of this sense of distance from human affairs is to weaken the power of what is being said by the speakers, although they are discussing matters of vital importance for humanity. The problems of ethics are much more to the fore than in any other of Wordsworth's poems, but well stated though his views are, we cannot feel that they have the power of his early faith in Nature.

In fact the final ideas of *The Excursion* are not those by which Wordsworth influenced the world, nor did they bring about any radical change in his own life. They are mainly of interest as showing how his views of Nature developed. There is a difficulty in studying them, in that the writing of the poem was spread over a number of years and the poet has not always, even in the final text, brought the ideas of the earlier books into line with his later thought.

At first sight it seems as though his original faith in Nature were not abandoned, but only modified to the extent that he recognized the part played by religion in his development. The education of the Wanderer is substantially the Natural education as we have seen it in *The Prelude*:

> He, many an evening, to his distant home
> In solitude returning, saw the hills
> Grow larger in the darkness; all alone
> Beheld the stars come out above his head,
>
> .   .   .   .
>
> So the foundations of his mind were laid.
> In such communion, not from terror free,
> While yet a child, and long before his time,
> Had he perceived the presence and the power
> Of greatness; and deep feelings had impressed
> So vividly great objects that they lay
> Upon his mind like substances, whose presence
> Perplexed the bodily sense.
>
> (*The Excursion*, Bk I, ll. 126–39)

But now we hear also that—

> The Scottish church, both on himself and those
> With whom from childhood he grew up, had held
> The strong hand of her purity; and still
> Had watched him with an unrelenting eye.
> This he remembered in his riper age
> With gratitude, and reverential thoughts.
>
> (Bk i, ll. 397–402)

And now, as he had never done hitherto, he makes a clear connection between the church's teaching and his faith in Nature. In a magnificent passage, not surpassed even in *The Prelude*, he describes the mystical experience of the Youth in the presence of nature. When his existence was 'in this sort . . . possessed'

> O then how beautiful, how bright, appeared
> The written promise!   (Bk i, ll. 222–3)

But he still prefers the revelation in nature—

> Early had he learned
> To reverence the volume that displays
> The mystery, the life which cannot die.
> But in the mountains did he *feel* his faith;
> All things responsive to the writing, there
> Breathed immortality . . .
> and there his spirit shaped
> Her prospects, nor did he believe—he *saw*.
>
> (Bk i, ll. 223–32)

It is also apparent that he is interpreting nature and Scripture partly in terms of each other. He feels that nature is the creation of a spirit of Love, but on the other hand in Scripture he sees mainly the eternity, the infinity of God. He is still not thinking of the more personal aspects of the Christian faith.

He explains in the character of the Solitary how it was that he had not come to this view earlier. As a young man, he had read the Bible, but the gift of faith had been wanting

(Bk iii, ll. 861–4), and the events of life had brought him to despondency. The Solitary is the personification of the restless intellectual Wordsworth of the Godwinian days and also the lover of Annette. Seeking relief from his remorse he had gone to America in the hope of finding happiness among unspoiled natural men. He did find these originals but they turned out to be not what he had expected. Instead of 'a creature great and good' he found—

> A creature, squalid, vengeful, and impure,
> Remorseless, and submissive to no law
> But superstitious fear, and abject sloth.

(Bk iii, ll. 953–5)

So then at last, it appears, Wordsworth gave up his views of the inherent goodness of Man. He was coming into line with Christian orthodoxy, and he tried to alter his view of Nature accordingly. The Wanderer, summing up in Bk ix, declares again his belief in the ever-living Universe, but now he says that the passions in the forms of Nature are not necessarily of pure good—

> To every Form of being is assigned
> . . . . . .
> An active Principle;—howe'er removed
> From sense and observation, it subsists
> In all things, in all natures...
> . . . . . .
> Whate'er exists hath properties that spread
> Beyond itself, communicating good,
> A simple blessing, or with evil mixed.

(Bk ix, ll. 1–12)

This passage does not read harmoniously. It seems very probable that the words 'with evil mixed' were tacked on in response to his change of view. But taking the words at their face value, we may ask, if this is so, what becomes of the scheme of natural education? If the forms of Nature may be either good or evil or a mixture of both, can they be

NATURE IN THE LATER POEMS

made the set text for Man's education? He does not
seriously tackle this question and he is, on the whole, still
happy about Nature. Nor do we hear whence comes this
evil. But in a later poem he speaks of

> ...some uneasy seat
> In nature's struggling frame
> Some region of impatient life:
> And jealousy, and quivering strife,

as being responsible for the turbulence of the Spring[1]—
which is very far from the thought of the *Lyrical Ballads*:

> Love now an universal birth,
> From heart to heart is stealing,
> From earth to man, from man to earth;
> It is the hour of feeling.

He is not much more explicit about the evil in Man. It
may arise

> Through sinful choice; or dread necessity
> On human nature from above imposed.
>
> (Bk iv, ll. 128–9)

It is not clear whether these factors are complementary
causes, or whether he is undecided as to which one is the
cause.[2] But if evil may arise at all from divinely imposed
necessity, he is suggesting a view of the Creator which
hardly seems in keeping with the faith which the Wanderer
frequently professes.

---

[1] O.W. p. 498.

[2] In a poem called *Afterthought* he appears to think that evil exists in order
that faith and love may be strengthened:

> 'Oh Life! without thy chequered scene
> Of right and wrong, of weal and woe,
> Success and failure, could a ground
> For magnanimity be found;
> For faith, mid ruined hopes, serene?
> Or whence could virtue flow?
>
> (Composed 1832. O.W. p 337)

The Wanderer tries to correct the despondency of the Solitary with what, rightly interpreted, is a statement of Christian faith—

> . . . One adequate support
> For the calamities of mortal life
> Exists—one only; an assured belief
> That the procession of our fate, howe'er
> Sad or disturbed, is ordered by a Being
> Of infinite benevolence and power;
> Whose everlasting purposes embrace
> All accidents, converting them to good.
>
> (Bk IV, ll. 10–17)

Obviously the worth of this statement turns on the meaning of 'good' in the last line. But Wordsworth did not change his view of the good life. When the Solitary inquires where are to be found the genuine seats of power, the Wanderer replies with a description of the typical dalesman's youth as a shepherd:

> . . . Early he perceives
> Within himself, a measure and a rule,
> Which to the sun of truth he can apply,
> That shines for him, and shines for all mankind.
> Experience daily fixing his regards
> On nature's wants, he knows how few they are,
> And where they lie, how answered and appeased.
> This knowledge ample recompense affords
> For manifold privations; he refers
> His notions to this standard; on this rock
> Rests his desires; and hence, in after life,
> Soul-strengthening patience, and sublime content.
>
> (Bk IV, ll. 807–18)

This life is contrasted with the worldling's life of trivial ostentation and superfluous cares. But such a vain life is not the only alternative to the life of his child of Nature. The alternative to the Houynhnhnm is not necessarily the Yahoo nor vice versa. Wordsworth makes no place in his scheme for those, like the woman described by the Pastor, who have

> A mind by nature indisposed to aught
> So placid, so inactive, as content;
> A mind intolerant of lasting peace.   (Bk vi, ll. 730–2)

If the good to which all accidents are converted must always be a simple life of few wants, moving only in contemplation of 'things which lie at rest within the bosom of [the divine] will' (*The Prelude*, Bk x, l. 397) there can never be any real adventure. No man would ever have been inspired to climb Mt Everest, or to explore the Poles, or to conquer the tse-tse fly. There could have been no science, no art, no poetry—no one to write the books which Wordsworth's student ploughman reads (*The Excursion*, Bk vii, ll. 428–53). The explorers, in whatever field, not the traditionalists, are the full-grown imaginative men. But for Wordsworth simplicity and spontaneity are always right; self-consciousness and discontent always wrong. Fundamentally his view has not changed. Even all the effort of will which is so much more prominent in this poem, is only to get back to an original Eden, of which a first condition is a simple agricultural economy. Though he might celebrate the triumphs of applied science, and prophesy imperial conquests, he did not really accept the new industrial society. And he could not see that discontent might have a reputable origin. It may have been the long struggle to throw off a discontent arising from a better source than restless pride which made him so weary. He cannot have been much over forty when the last part of the poem was written, yet it reveals in many places a weariness of spirit amounting almost to exhaustion, an overmastering desire for rest.

It is true that *The Wanderer* ends more cheerfully

> ...The food of hope
> Is meditated action...
> ...We see by the glad light
> And breathe the sweet air of futurity.
>
> (Bk ix, ll. 19–25)

and he has given the Solitary excellent, if stoic, advice for the cure of his trouble—all that he, the Wanderer, has learned in the struggle 'to keep, Heights which the soul is competent to gain' (Bk iv, ll. 138–9)— and bids him go on his way rejoicing. But in what may he rejoice?—'In the sublime attractions of the grave' (Bk iv, l. 238) and the chief attraction by far is ever-lasting rest. The Solitary assumed that it was the desire for rest which caused the men of the Middle Ages to retire to monasteries.

> ...A life of peace,
> Stability without regret or fear.
>
> (Bk iii, ll. 385–6)

> What other yearning was the master tie
> Of the monastic brotherhood...
> ...What but this,
> The universal instinct of repose,
> The longing for confirmed tranquillity,
> Inward and outward; humble, yet sublime:
> The life where hope and memory are as one.
>
> (Bk iii, ll. 392–9)

In the sixth and seventh books, the Pastor makes an itinerary of the graves in his churchyard among the mountains, and reconstructs the lives of the dead, his aim being to provide the Solitary with evidence of the victories of religion. But the only victory of Christianity, apparently, is its power to soften the blows of calamity. And the direction of the pastor's thought is not towards faith—he contemplates the stout tree-feller and observes:

> But, green in age and lusty as he is
> . . . . . .
> His own appointed hour will come at last;
> And, like the haughty Spoilers of the world,
> This keen Destroyer, in his turn, must fall.
>
> (Bk vii, ll. 625–31)

And this by a minister of the God of the living. Can this be 'the faith that looks through death'? There is nothing here of the good news which sent the company of the apostles to the ends of the earth aglow with their faith. Wordsworth had not understood the matter at all. *The Excursion* abounds in statements of religious truth—e.g. 'life is energy of love, divine or human' (Bk v, l. 1012), 'Hope below this consists not with belief in mercy carried infinite degrees beyond the tenderness of human hearts' (Bk iv, l. 191) but they are like water lilies upon a lake of calm resignation.

Contrary to what is often supposed, Wordsworth was ceaselessly active in thought, to the end of his life. The poems written after *The Excursion* show him still seeking better explanations of the burden of the mystery. But he was gravely handicapped by working against certain ideas and habits of thought, which, I suggest, derived from his earlier mistaken attitudes. He continued to look on things from the outside, and therefore he did not reach full understanding of them. He thought the martyrs sustained their pangs by their inflexible will (*Exc.* Bk i, l. 171) but—in as far as that is the right explanation at all—their will was an effect not a cause, the cause being the sense of the presence of their Master. Wordsworth never understood his religion in that personal sense. As the Wanderer he might read in the faces of the clouds unutterable love (Bk i, l. 205) and that thought did breed in him perpetual benediction of a kind, but the love remained as distant as the clouds, it never became intimate and personal.

The eye was the master of the heart, though he said it was not. His only way of reaching what he called the imagination was by gazing upon long stretches of finitude until they suggested infinitude. In his reply to Landor's criticism of *Laodamia* occur these words: '... Except in those passages where things are lost in each other and limits vanish and aspirations are raised, I read with something too like indifference; but all great Poets are in this sense powerful religionists.' But as he himself said in a wise letter on education to Wrangham, 'that which is exclusively considered can never be understood'. Though his gaze was constantly toward boundless prospects which spoke of eternity, he understood eternity mainly in the horizontal sense of infinitely extended time and space. He was not really aware that the gospel which the Wanderer officially[1] professed, meant by eternal life eternity in the vertical sense, of life in a different dimension—the life in which he himself had once seen into the life of things.

[1] I say 'officially'. Crabb Robinson after reading *The Excursion* wrote concerning Wordsworth's religion as follows: 'I believe his religion to be that of the German metaphysicians, a sentimental and metaphysical mysticism in which the language of Christianity is used, which is a sort of analogy to this poetical and philosophical religion.'
(*Books and Their Writers*, vol. i, p. 158.)

CHAPTER SIX

CONCLUSION

Wordsworth said, concerning *The Prelude*, 'it was a thing unprecedented in literary history that a man should talk so much about himself'. It was, and yet for all his self-revelation in *The Prelude* and elsewhere, he remains an enigma. The many and diverse interpretations of his life and poetry, give some justification for venturing the opinion that no student has yet understood him. Several of his critics appear to have become exasperated in the attempt, and to have tried to fit him into a theory. How perverse and ill supported by the evidence are some of these theories, has been pointed out by another student of Wordsworth, Miss E. C. Batho.[1] Wordsworth cannot be explained by any theory; the sense of puzzlement he leaves with us does not arise from the mystery of human nature as such, but from his own baffling personality. If he has proved thus so difficult to understand, it will be obvious that the concluding lines of a short study such as this, cannot add significantly to what is known of him. At most they may hope to present some of the known facts in a different light.

But first, it will be well to draw together the main conclusions of the preceding chapters. I have tried to show that, as I believe, Wordsworth's great positive contribution to thought was his strong belief that the universe is animated in every part by a living spirit. Earth and Man alike partake of it.

> Spirit that knows no insulated spot,
> No chasm, no solitude; from link to link
> It circulates, the Soul of all the worlds.
> *(The Excursion*, Bk IX, ll. 13–15)

[1] E. C. Batho, *The Later Wordsworth*, pp. 339–41.

This spirit, he found, was 'reverenced least, and least respected in the human Mind, its most apparent home' (*Exc.* Bk ix, l. 18). He tried to remedy this state of affairs. It followed almost as a corollary from his belief in the omnipresent spirit that the best educating force for the mind and soul of Man was Nature. This seemed to be confirmed by the life of the dalesmen of his native region. He therefore tried to present in a natural language, the best of Nature both earthly and human, in order that men's feelings might be purified and their thoughts uplifted. He was right to see that Man must ground his life and action in Nature. Intellectual activity can be founded on Nature, but human beings and human society must not be distorted to fit a pre-determined intellectual framework. But he was not right to think that modern man can retain after a certain point, the wholeness which even the most perfect Natural education can give him. Nor is it matter for lament that he cannot do so. There is a way forward through self-consciousness to a new spontaneity, to what Kierkegaard called 'immediacy after reflection'. We were not bidden to remain children, but to *become as* little children.

Wordsworth, was, however, a pioneer in more than his attitude to Nature. By his beliefs and his poetic practice he put an end to the idea that only prose could tell the truth, and that poetry was an optional luxury, a pleasure for the fancy. He claimed that poetry, no less than science, could reveal truth.

The Man of science seeks truth as a remote and unknown benefactor; he cherishes and loves it in his solitude: the Poet, singing a song in which all human beings join with him, rejoices in the presence of truth as our visible friend and hourly companion. Poetry is the breath and finer spirit of all knowledge; it is the impassioned expression which is in the countenance of all Science.[1]

[1] L.B. p. 25.

Poetry from his day forward claimed the whole of life for her province. And not only of life as it was then. The Preface to the *Lyrical Ballads* is a Poets' charter for all time.

If the labours of Men of science should ever create any material revolution, direct or indirect, in our condition, and in the impressions which we habitually receive, the Poet will sleep then no more than at present, but he will be ready to follow the steps of the Man of science, not only in those general indirect effects, but he will be at his side, carrying sensation into the midst of the objects of the Science itself.[1]

It was not until the present century that poets realized their full rights—and duties—under this charter.

As against these contributions to progress I have suggested that Wordsworth made two serious mistakes. First, that he did not sufficiently prize the mystical experiences which he had had; that he chose to depend for the continuance of his imaginative life on the forms of nature rather than on the interfusing spirit in nature. The consequence of this was that he was cut off from the source of his imaginative life—the spring of 'hope and effort and expectation and desire', with the result that his life became static, and he only stoical. Secondly, the mistake mentioned above—he tried to revive the original wholeness of his nature, by trying to come into tune with the life of his sister, who retained her original spontaneity. This was a mistake for three reasons: (*a*) it made him wholly dependent on his feelings; (*b*) he did not understand that 'Nature' of his sister on which he relied, and therefore in certain cardinal matters he could not obtain the help from Her that he needed; and (*c*) it overlooked his own nature, and allowed him to develop a philosophy of Man which ignored the will to power, and conceived of human life as static rather than dynamic. The consequences of this for him were, at first, frustration and hypochondria, and then, as feeling failed,

[1] L.B. p. 26.

117

an increasing reliance on the will. He could not let himself go sufficiently to the changes of feeling which the years inevitably brought; he tended to idealize certain states of feeling as objectively right. The effort to achieve these feelings led to a certain strain, a lack of ease, which took the form of inflexibility in his relations with others. The gospel of spontaneity and freedom ended in a stately rigidity. To some extent, these consequences may have been reflected in the solemn orthodoxy of the feelings which characterized the Victorians. In politics, his love of his native region led to a strong patriotism which later became nationalism. Nationalism is 'Nature' writ large.

About the first mistake mentioned, I am anxious to avoid misunderstanding. I do not suggest for a moment that Wordsworth should have tried to recreate mystical experiences, by yogic practices or by any other means. I mean only that he should have tried to understand his experiences. Like Socrates, Wordsworth had, on occasion, passed from the forms of beauty into the presence of the invisible Beauty. But Socrates, when he had thus seen into the life of things was very certain that it was Beauty's self and not her semblance which had quickened him, and he had no wish to go back to his earlier delight in external forms.[1] I have tried to show in chapter II, that Wordsworth had a truly religious sensitiveness. Because I believe this, I find his apparent lack of curiosity concerning his mystical experience difficult to understand. I think it is possible, even probable, that he may have been at fault himself, but I think part of the blame for his failure here must be laid upon the Church of England of his time. Wordsworth himself said, when asked why he did not go to church, that it was because the ministers were such a poor lot. The Church of England was certainly in a deplorably low state at the time.[2] Candi-

---

[1] *Symposium*: Plato, *Five Dialogues* (Everyman Edition), p. 67.
[2] See E. Halévy, *History of the English People in* 1815, vol. III, ch. I.

dates for Orders were very frequently political nominees, and in any case they were not required to pass more than a ridiculously easy test of theological knowledge. Wordsworth was not likely to have heard from any incumbent of his day, a gospel which would have suggested a connection between Christianity and his religion of Nature. It was a loss for more than himself. For he had really shown in *The Prelude* that he 'worshipped among the depths of things' a Power which was in a living relationship with him, whose influence he felt even in his breathing and the flow of his blood. By no means all Christian churches have understood that this relationship is of more importance than a sound doctrinal position for a vital religious life. It is perhaps a daring speculation but it appears at least possible, that if Wordsworth could have known the importance of his discovery, and could have seen much earlier in his life the importance of connecting the revelation in nature with the revelation in Scripture, he might have started a line of thought which would have done much to break the shock of Darwinism when it came. It might even have prevented science and religion falling apart into hostile camps as they did.

I have suggested that Wordsworth did not find his true destiny. To the large question thus raised I have found, as yet, no satisfying answer. It is possible that much turns upon the happenings of those mysterious days in 1793 when he was wandering alone upon Salisbury Plain. How far his mysterious vision there was a determinant of his mature outlook it is difficult to say without a detailed inquiry too long to be entered upon here. But it is possible to look at the definitely known facts of his life in a way which may suggest new lines of thought concerning him.

The great mystical experience, which came to Wordsworth at Hawkshead during his first summer vacation from Cambridge, is always referred to by Professor de Selincourt as Wordsworth's dedication to poetry. But at this point Wordsworth does not mention poetry. He only says that he knew himself to be a 'dedicated spirit'. His letters to his friend Mathews in 1794 when they were planning a magazine, do not give the impression that poetry is his first interest. He is much more concerned with politics. He himself said that he had given twelve hours thought to politics for everyone given to poetry. But those letters do reveal, for all their haughty tone, a man with a concern for the good of mankind. 'I know that the multitude walk in darkness. I would put into each man's hand a lantern to guide him....'[1]

He wanted to be a poet, and he certainly had poetic gifts. But the suffering of the war years, both what he had witnessed and what he had felt, had brought poetry under suspicion. In the face of such suffering, the kind of poetry held up to admiration in the eighteenth century, the style in which his own youthful poems were written, seemed to him intolerably artificial. Poetry must deal with actuality, or be abandoned. The 'stern mood' the 'underthirst of vigour never utterly asleep' (*The Prelude*, Bk vi, l. 490) were now thoroughly awake, and challenging the poet's soul with his 'thousand tender dreams', to establish his titles in plain day. If the poet could not show that he was 'free from taint of something false and weak' (Bk xi, l. 66) he must be banished. The poet was eventually able to do so, and triumphantly, in the Preface to the *Lyrical Ballads*, which is Wordsworth's *apologia pro vita sua*. He had found a way of harnessing poetry to his desire to serve mankind. He would show forth the beauty of nature, and the strength and humanity of those who lived closest to Nature, and thereby uplift and purify men's feelings. To add to all the other joys of his West Country days came this discovery— that all his major interests and gifts, his love of nature, his interest in psychology, and his poetic gifts, could all be used

[1] Letter to Mathews—June 1794. L.W. *Early Letters*, p. 121.

in the service of mankind. It is this excitement which inspires the *Lyrical Ballads*. But the purpose came before the poetry. 'The principal object, then, which I proposed to myself in these poems was to choose. . . .'[1] There is a more than ordinary deliberateness about that statement. I seem to hear in it already, the disciple of Milton with his 'conscious step of purity and pride' (*The Prelude*, Bk III, l. 293). And later he writes: 'I am at liberty to supply myself with images. . . .'[1] Fortunately, he did not always supply himself, he sometimes allowed himself to be supplied, as when he put down

> Breaking the silence of the seas
> Among the farthest Hebrides.[2]

When the poet and the psychologist have, as it were, had their permits granted by the moral purpose, they are free to go ahead—but which of them in the *Lyrical Ballads* really has the lead? Surely the psychologist. Wordsworth did genuinely want to discover how far the language of simple people was a suitable vehicle for poetic pleasure, but it was not his major interest. He was much more interested in the workings of the human mind than in the workings of language. It is the psychologist who supplies the more important argument for writing in metre:

'I related in metre the Tale of Goody Blake and Harry Gill (because) I wished to draw attention to the truth, that the power of the human imagination is sufficient to produce such changes even in our physical nature as might almost appear miraculous. . . . And I have the satisfaction of knowing that it has been communicated to many hundreds of people who would never have heard of it, had it not been narrated as a Ballad. . . .'[3]

His interest in psychology is foremost. It meets us at every turn in his prose works, and his frequent sorting and re-sorting of his poems into different psychological categories

[1] L.B. p. 8.   [2] *The Solitary Reaper*, O.W. p. 289.
[3] L.B. p. 35.

—'Poems of the Imagination', 'Poems of the Fancy', etc., is a further proof of it.

The poet was not really taking the trouble to be a poet, in the large sense of the word. He never put himself alongside the people he was writing about, and so he did not reach an imaginative understanding of them. That could only have been done by a genuine sympathy. Men were not likely to reveal the 'strength of the primary affections' to one who came to them as a scientific investigator.

And in the narrower sense of the word poet, his gift was held in check by his sense of purpose. He did not practise sufficiently that wise passiveness which he commended. We get several kinds of pleasure from reading Wordsworth, but, as it seems to me, very little specifically *poetic* pleasure. There is a certain quiet and refreshing simplicity, and there is sometimes a noble eloquence, but these are not specifically poetic pleasures. Too often he only tells us *that* there are 'Powers that touch each other to the quick in modes which the gross world no sense hath to perceive'[1]—he does not show forth the powers. There is, it is true, something else in his poetry—especially in *The Prelude*—which is cognate with poetic pleasure, though different from it: I mean a sense of the numinous, a feeling of awe at the sense of a hidden Presence. When he speaks of:

A dim and undetermin'd sense
Of unknown modes of being; in my thoughts
There was a darkness, call it solitude,
Or blank desertion, no familiar shapes
Of hourly objects, images of trees,
Of sea or sky, no colours of green fields;
But huge and mighty Forms that do not live
Like living men mov'd slowly through the mind
By day and were the trouble of my dreams.
                    (*The Prelude*, Bk i, ll. 419–27)

[1] *Address to Kilchurn Castle.* O.W. p. 290.

CONCLUSION

—there is an excitement due to this sense of the numinous (though I should admit that the word 'hourly' is used poetically). But when Byron writes:

> She walks in beauty, like the night
> Of cloudless climes and starry skies;

he sets up an excitement of a different kind, which I should call poetic excitement. Of this kind of excitement or pleasure, I find very little in Wordsworth. It is in the Lucy poems, it is in one of two of the sonnets, notably in the sonnet on Sir Walter Scott's leave-taking from Abbotsford, in certain passages of *The Prelude*, and in odd words and lines here and there. There is, admittedly, a sense in which he was very much a poet, both a poet and a prophet. He had an ear that was very sensitive to the movements of the nation's thought. He frequently caught and recorded these movements. But such a sense is not confined to writers, and it need not interfere with other activities. Of all parts of our mental life it is the most shadowy and least under conscious control.

If then Wordsworth's other interests were so much stronger than his interest in poetry, why did he have to think of himself as committed to poetry for life? Could he not have reached the position that poetry was only one of many means of doing good to mankind, to be taken up or laid aside as the situation required? I have said that 1805 was a critical year in his development. His sorrow at his brother's death had evoked the *Elegiac Stanzas on Peele Castle*, in which he had exclaimed:

> Farewell, farewell the heart that lives alone,
> Housed in a dream, at distance from the Kind!
> Such happiness, wherever it be known,
> Is to be pitied; for 'tis surely blind.

123

In June of that year he had completed *The Prelude*, in which he had extolled the Imaginative Man, the man whose life was not swayed by sensible appearances—the free-man of the universe. His own writings might well have inspired him to make some change in his way of life. And perhaps if Coleridge could have helped him, he might have made it. The light of hope, for Wordsworth, had always seemed to centre on Coleridge, and he had depended on Coleridge for inspiration more than he cared to admit. But, as we know, Coleridge came back from Malta a broken man, and avoided Wordsworth as long as he could. When the meeting eventually came it was painful for both men. Wordsworth was deeply disappointed. And so the ode on the *Intimations of Immortality*, which was lying incomplete, ending with the question 'whither has fled the visionary gleam?' was finished in the only way that seemed possible.

The philosophic mind was to endure forty-four years longer.

I have tried to show that Wordsworth's attitude to Nature was not natural. He was not in a natural relation to physical nature nor to his own nature, nor to that Nature which he extolled in the dalesmen. He was not of society and he was not of their society. That he was not really liked by them, the investigations of Canon Rawnsley have shown. He stood in a no-man's land between town and country. He was the first poet to be consistently class-conscious. He put the dalesmen in inverted commas. He would have been as dismayed as Mr C. E. Montague at finding that an England of 'boundlessly advertised heroes and saints had ousted the England where you would never . . . have been given wrong change on a bus',[1] but essentially his own attitude of proclaiming the virtues of a particular class

[1] C. E. Montague, *Disenchantment*, ch. xv.

marked the beginning—not of the deterioration of character—but of the wide publicity now given to every act
of courage or fortitude.

The lines beginning: 'It is the first mild day of March'
do not herald any gospel of Nature:

> No joyless forms shall regulate
> Our living Calendar:
> We from to-day, my Friend, will date
> The opening of the year.

So exclaims the poet joyfully—but he is mistaken. The
man of purpose has things well in hand. The calendar is
already settled—it is only 'this *one day* we'll give to idle-
ness'. But the poem and its three sister poems[1] are a perfect
invitation to a holiday. And it was in this sense that Wordsworth's nature poems did their good work. [He drew the
attention of an industrial society away from the artificial
pleasures of the town, to the pure delights which were to be
found in the out-of-doors.] He showed that recreation in
the presence of Nature could be in the fullest sense recreation.] Here as elsewhere, he was most successful when
least deliberate. It is not in the loud procession of vocatives
to his native hills in conscious gratitude for their gifts, but
in quieter passages, when 'the winds come to him from the
fields of sleep', and he hears 'the mountain streams to their
own far off murmurs listening', that he is at his best. It is
in lyrics like *The Fountain* and *Three Years She Grew in Sun
and Shower*; in lines here and there in which natural observation and poetic sensibility are perfectly blended, as in

> He is retired as noontide dew,
> Or fountain in a noonday grove.

When he forgot his theory of poetic diction and wrote as
he would, he could really present Nature—as we have seen

---

[1] *Expostulation and Reply*; *The Tables Turned*; *Lines written in Early
Spring*.

in many passages quoted from *The Prelude*, and as Coleridge illustrated by a verse from the poem *Fidelity*—

> There sometimes doth a leaping fish
> Send through the tarn a lonely cheer;
> The crags repeat the raven's croak
> In symphony austere;
> Thither the rainbow comes—the cloud—
> And mists that spread the flying shroud;
> And sunbeams; and the sounding blast
> That, if it could, would hurry past;
> But that enormous barrier holds it fast.

Wordsworth said that he wished to be thought of primarily as a teacher, and he certainly had the teacher's temperament. But if a teacher would teach by poetry, i.e. in darkness, he must become a poet, and let the teaching take care of itself. If he would teach by precept and philosophy, i.e. in the light, he must make all his concepts as clear and definite as possible. Wordsworth tried to combine these methods, and the result was not an entire success. His poetic impulses were denied their full fruition by an intellectually conceived purpose, and the poet's distrust of the intellect kept his philosophy of Nature vague and confusing.

In as far as he found, rather than made, his philosophy of Nature, by 'fetching (his) goodness from times past', and in as far as in so doing he reflected the society of his time, it meant that that society was living on the spiritual capital of the past. It was not satisfactory even in his own day. To-day, when the crisis of civilization has become so much more acute, it has become of the greatest importance and urgency that we do not try to live on 'Nature', but seek again 'the prime and vital principle' of all life.

INDEX

INDEX

128